# PEACE AND WAR:
# A FEW QUOTATIONS

Jon Thormodsson

# PEACE AND WAR: A FEW QUOTATIONS

*Peace and War: A Few Quotations*

Abbreviation of *Peace and War: Niagara of Quotations* (about 1,300 pages)

Jon Thormodsson, Icelandic lawyer
LL.M., Harvard Law School, 1972
E-mail: jon.thormodsson@talnet.is

Quote: Jon Thormodsson, *Peace and War: A Few Quotations* (Reykjavik: Jon Thormodsson, 2017), p. ..., and another source as appropriate

ISBN: 1546923365
ISBN-13: 9781546923367

Available at Amazon.com, www.createspace.com/7198371 and other retailers

# INTRODUCTION

Kennedy liked it, Edward M., that is:

"I was impressed and touched by your project to publish a collection of peace and war quotations. The many eloquent examples you enclosed make clear that the project is both needed and especially timely in today's world.

"I look forward to its publication, and I would hope and expect to see it take its place among the great and most widely used quotations volumes of our time."

Peace is needed. Almost everybody wants it. Almost nobody knows how. The 1945 Constitution of the United Nations Educational, Scientific and Cultural Organization provides a guidance:

[S]ince wars begin in the minds of men, it is in the minds of men that the defences of peace must be constructed;...

This book is for those who want peace, that is, almost everybody. It is a scholarly work, education for peace, abridged and somewhat simplified from the original work, *Peace and War: Niagara of Quotations*. The quotations relate to the benefits of peace, the horrors of war. They contain arguments for peace, for leaders and those led, wisdom and information of the generations for the generations, of the millennia for the millennia.

Old wisdom from old originals or translations. New materials of a public nature or usable in a scholarly work or on the basis of fair use, interesting materials of the United Nations and thoughtful contributions of Nobel Peace Prize recipients thankfully included. Thanks also to Erika Wolfe for improving my English text and to Thorunn Gudmundsdottir for her dove of peace.

There must be a need for this book, based on over thirty years of part-time work. And I hope it will be used. As Pablo Casals said:

For me the life of a single child is worth more than all my music;...

Everybody has to do something, sometime, somehow.

If no one does his duty history may repeat itself in one form or another:

- Germany lost about one third of its national resources, gathered through centuries, in World War I.
- There were about six million orphans after World War I.
- One did not know whether some of the victims after the atomic bombing of Nagasaki, at the end of World War II, were men or women.
- Almost 4,000,000,000 human lives are estimated to have been lost in wars.

Extinction of civilization is even possible, bearing in mind, as Kennedy put it, John F., that is:

Even small wars can be dangerous in a nuclear world.

# TABLE OF CONTENTS

Summary ............................................................................................ 1

Quotations ....................................................................................... 33

Index ............................................................................................... 255

Author ............................................................................................ 283

# SUMMARY

## ACHIEVEMENT
**1** The Greeks regarded the pyramid tomb of Khufu as one of the seven wonders of the world  ▸ Fay-Cooper Cole and Harris Gaylord Warren, on the Great Pyramid, built shortly after 2600 B.C.

**2** He worked on the picture for four years or more ... It is called *Mona Lisa*  ▸ Thomas Craven, on Leonardo da Vinci about 1500

**3** the Taj Mahal ... blue at dawn, white at noon, and the yellow of the sky at sunset  ▸ John D. Hoag, on a seventeenth-century Indian mausoleum of love

**4** Then ... my mother returned ... she said one word: 'Wallenberg.'  ▸ Tommy Lapid, on Raoul Wallenberg's rescue of Jews in Budapest in 1944

## ADVANTAGE
**5** the blessing of a peaceful home is realized when that peace is upset  ▸ Chinese proverb, taken from a seventeenth-century book

## AGGRESSION
**6** National Socialism does not harbour the slightest aggressive intent towards any European nation  ▸ Adolf Hitler, 1935

**7** The Court ... went on to show that, already at the outbreak of the war, resort to aggressive war was an international crime  ▸ Memorandum of the secretary-general of the United Nations on the 1946 judgment of the Nuremberg Tribunal, 1949

## AGITATION
**8** ALSO, CARTHAGE, METHINKS, OUGHT UTTERLY TO BE DESTROYED  ▸ Cato the Elder, before the Third Punic War (149-146 B.C.)

## AGREEMENT
**9** just for a scrap of paper Great Britain was going to make war  ▸ Theobald von Bethmann Hollweg, 1914, according to Edward Goschen

## AIR RAID
**10** Guernica ... was completely destroyed yesterday afternoon  ▸ *Times*, special correspondent's cable of April 27, 1937

**11** the bombing of Hamburg resulted in as many victims as the bombing of Hiroshima ... the civilian population must not be harmed  ▸ The International Committee of the Red Cross, 1963, referring to the air raids on Hamburg in 1943 and the bombing of Hiroshima in 1945

## ALIEN
**12** You shall not wrong or oppress a resident alien  ▸ The Bible, Exodus 22:21 (the Lord to the Israelites)

### ALLIANCE
**13** an armed attack against one or more of them ... shall be considered an attack against them all ▸ North Atlantic Treaty, 1949

### AMUSEMENT
**14** War has always been the chief amusement of mankind ▸ Halldór Laxness, 1968

### ANARCHY
**15** anarchy should have no place in the life of man ▸ Plato (428 or 427-348 or 347 B.C.), supposedly in his later years

### ANIMAL
**16** all war is a symptom of man's failure as a thinking animal ▸ John Steinbeck, 1958

### ARBITRATION
**17** Sooner shall these mountains crumble into dust than Argentines and Chileans break the peace ▸ Part of the inscription on *The Christ of the Andes*, a peace monument unveiled in 1904

### ARMISTICE
**18** an armistice ... shall be arranged ... to permit the removal, exchange and transport of the wounded left on the battlefield ▸ Geneva Convention for the Amelioration of the Condition of the Wounded and Sick in Armed Forces in the Field, 1949

### ARMS
**19** uranium 238 ... is used to make the cores of shells for conventional weapons ▸ Helen Caldicott, 1994

### ARMS RACE
**20** in a spiraling arms race, a nation's security may well be shrinking even as its arms increase ▸ John F. Kennedy, 1961

### ART
**21** art knows no national boundaries ... the artist ... building bridges of experience between peoples ▸ John F. Kennedy, 1962

### ASSASSINATION
**22** History indicates that the assassination of a ruler very seldom changes the prevailing tendencies in the national life ▸ Ezra Hoyt Byington, on the assassination of James A. Garfield, 1881

### ATROCITY
**23** they will be brought back to the scene of their crimes and judged on the spot ▸ Winston S. Churchill, Franklin D. Roosevelt and Joseph Stalin, in their Declaration of German Atrocities, 1943

### ATTACK
**24** commit not the injustice of attacking them first ▶ The Qur'an (Koran), "The Cow," verse 186

**25** It has always been popular to attack the weak ▶ Halldór Laxness, 1968

### ATTITUDE
**26** the concept concerning the urgent need to replace a culture of violence and war by a culture of dialogue and peace ▶ Vladimir Lomeiko, on the concept proposed by Federico Mayor in 1987

### BALLOT
**27** the ballot is stronger than the bullet ▶ Abraham Lincoln, 1856

### BATTLE
**28** No state should believe its fate ... to be dependent upon one battle ▶ Karl von Clausewitz, 1818-1830

### BATTLEFIELD
**29** the road ... from Moscow to the frontier ... looks like one continuous battlefield ▶ Xavier de Maistre, 1812

### BEGINNING
**30** Paris ... went berserk ... there was a wildly festive mood ▶ Pablo Casals, on World War I, 1914

### BENEFIT
**31** There is no instance of a country having been benefited from prolonged warfare ▶ Sun Tzu [Sunzi; Sun Zi], about 500 B.C.

### BIOLOGICAL WARFARE
**32** the Mongols practised biological warfare in the 14th century ... 25 million ... became victims of the 'Black Death' ▶ Erhard Geissler, on the Mongols in the fourteenth century

### BISHOP
**33** The charity of Deogratias, bishop of Carthage, was their only consolation and support ▶ Edward Gibbon, on the help provided by Deogratias to Roman captives after the Vandals' 455 sacking of Rome

### BLAME
**34** He must be blamed who is the cause of war ▶ Buddha (ca. 563-ca. 483 B.C.)

### BLESSING
**35** peace is the first of blessings ▶ Hermocrates, 424 B.C.

### BOOK
**36** *War and Peace*, the epic work on the Napoleonic invasion of 1812 ▶ Richard Freeborn, on Leo Tolstoy's 1863-1869 novel

**37** This story of a tragic love affair is set on the Italian front during World War I
▶ Frank N. Magill, referring to Ernest Hemingway's 1929 novel *A Farewell to Arms*

### BOOK TITLE
**38** *'Who's Living in My House?'*  ▶  Title of an Amnesty International publication,
relating to Bosnia and Herzegovina, 1997

### BRIDGE
**39** The construction of ... the railway of "The Bridge on the River Kwai" ... cost the
lives of tens of thousands of civilians and prisoners of war  ▶  Gerhard L. Weinberg,
on the compulsory building of a bridge in Burma in 1943

### BROTHERHOOD
**40** The Bantu is our brother, the Arab, and the White man too  ▶  National
anthem of Senegal, 1960

### CANAL
**41** The Suez Maritime Canal shall always be free and open ... to every vessel of
commerce or of war  ▶  Convention respecting the Free Navigation of the Suez
Maritime Canal, 1888

### CARE
**42** If some one had cared for me sooner, I should have lived, whereas, this
evening, I will die  ▶  An old sergeant to Jean Henri Dunant after the Battle of
Solferino in 1859

### CAUSE
**43** Who was the cause of a long ten years war, / ... Woman!  ▶  Thomas Otway,
on the Trojan War (ca. 1200 B.C.)
**44** in each country political and military leaders did certain things, which led
to mobilizations and declarations of war, or failed to do certain things which might
have prevented them  ▶  Sidney Bradshaw Fay, on the outbreak of World War I in
1914

### CHANCE
**45** war is full of unpleasant surprises  ▶  Winston S. Churchill, 1940

### CHEMICAL WARFARE
**46** *Determined* for the sake of all mankind, to exclude completely the
possibility of the use of chemical weapons  ▶  Convention on the Prohibition of the
Development, Production, Stockpiling and Use of Chemical Weapons and on Their
Destruction, 1993

### CHILD
**47** Six million children were deprived of their fathers by the Great War ... what
became of them?  ▶  Jay Winter, on World War I orphans

**48** Most of the casualties are children. A million die. Another million are saved by the airlift of food and medicine to Biafra ▸ Back cover of *Airlift to Biafra*, on the Nigerian Civil War (1967-1970)

**49** Count out 60 seconds and 30 of the world's children will have died for lack of food and adequate health care ▸ Norman Myers, 1984

### CHRISTIANITY
**50** the command to love one's enemy is an absolute necessity for our survival ▸ Martin Luther King, 1963

### CITY
**51** a bombardment that destroyed all but ten of the 450 houses ▸ *Historical Dictionary of Luxembourg*, referring to a French attack on the city of Luxembourg in 1684

### CIVILIAN
**52** The civilian population as such, as well as individual civilians, shall not be the object of attack ▸ Protocol Additional to the Geneva Conventions of 12 August 1949, and Relating to the Protection of Victims of International Armed Conflicts (Protocol I), 1977

### CIVIL WAR
**53** civil war ... of all wars the worst ▸ Plato (428 or 427-348 or 347 B.C.), supposedly in his later years

**54** Pantanassa Church and convent at Mistra is the only inhabited building of a city which once numbered 40,000 ▸ Lyn Harrington, on the Greek Civil War (1944-1945 and 1946-1949)

### COLD
**55** no parallel in the history of the sufferings of war ... Hunger, cold, and exhaustion produced greater ravages than the bullets of the Russians ▸ Georg Weber, on the retreat of Napoleon I from Moscow in 1812

### COLONIALISM
**56** Brazil in a network of laws ... a decree forbids the ... distillation of native alcohol ▸ Stefan Zweig, 1941

### COMMANDER
**57** Cœsar's actions ... surpassed them all ... his humanity and clemency to those he overpowered ▸ Plutarch, on Julius Caesar's wars in Gaul from 58 to 51 B.C.

### COMMUNICATION
**58** The correspondence between these two leaders ... was instrumental in avoiding international catastrophe during the Cuban missile crisis ▸ U.S. Department of State, on the Cuban missile crisis of 1962

## COMPARISON
**59** Peace maintains the farmer well ... war but ill  ▸  Menander (ca. 343 or 342-291 or 290 B.C.)

## COMPENSATION
**60** A Party ... which violates the provisions of the Conventions or of this Protocol shall, if the case demands, be liable to pay compensation  ▸  Protocol Additional to the Geneva Conventions of 12 August 1949, and Relating to the Protection of Victims of International Armed Conflicts (Protocol I), 1977

## CONCENTRATION CAMP
**61** the planning and execution of the greatest crime in the history of mankind  ▸ Janusz Gumkowski, on the Oswiecim-Brzezinka (Auschwitz-Birkenau) concentration camp (operated 1940-1945)
**62** there is only one way out—through the chimney  ▸  Karl Fritzsch, German Nazi deputy commandant of Auschwitz (1940-1941)
**63** the Brzezinka gas chambers could exterminate some 60,000 people per twenty-four hours  ▸  Jan Sehn, on the Oswiecim-Brzezinka (Auschwitz-Birkenau) camp (operated 1940-1945)
**64** It is estimated that 11 million civilians were killed in Hitler's gas ovens  ▸  Louis L. Snyder, on the German Nazis in World War II

## CONCILIATION
**65** conciliatory settlements are more desirable than legal judgments in small face-to-face societies  ▸  William Ian Miller, 1990

## CONFERENCE
**66** the Paris Conference may prove one of the historic failures of the world  ▸ Jan Christiaan Smuts, 1919, on the preparations for the Treaty of Versailles

## CONQUEROR
**67** if another conquer himself, he is the greatest of conquerors  ▸  *The Gospel of Buddha*, "The Dharmapada"
**68** A man like me does not count the lives of a million of men  ▸  Napoleon I, 1813
**69** A conqueror is always a lover of peace ... he would like to make his entry into our state unopposed  ▸  Karl von Clausewitz, 1818-1830

## CONSCIENCE
**70** *I will leap laughing to my grave ... I have five million people on my conscience*  ▸  Adolf Eichmann, toward the end of World War II

## CONSTITUTION
**71** the Japanese people forever renounce war as a sovereign right of the nation and the threat or use of force as means of settling international disputes  ▸ Constitution of Japan, as revised in 1947

## COUNTRY
**72** The earth is but one country, and mankind its citizens  ▸  Baha'ullah (1817-1892)

## COURT

**73** The German Government recognises the right of the Allied and Associated Powers to bring before military tribunals persons accused of having committed acts in violation of the laws and customs of war ▸ Treaty of Versailles, 1919

**74** the most serious crimes of concern to the international community as a whole must not go unpunished ▸ Rome Statute of the International Criminal Court, 1998

## CRIME

**75** War is the greatest of all crimes ▸ Voltaire (1694-1778)

**76** To initiate a war of aggression ... is not only an international crime; it is the supreme international crime ▸ Judgment of the Nuremberg Tribunal, 1946

**77** it is necessary ... to affirm ... the principle that there is no period of limitation for war crimes and crimes against humanity ▸ Convention on the Non-Applicability of Statutory Limitations to War Crimes and Crimes against Humanity, 1968

**78** grave breaches of these instruments shall be regarded as war crimes ▸ Protocol Additional to the Geneva Conventions of 12 August 1949, and Relating to the Protection of Victims of International Armed Conflicts (Protocol I), 1977

## CULPABILITY

**79** the sole culpability of the enemy is, as always, a war-time myth ▸ Arthur Ponsonby, 1928

## CULTURAL EXCHANGE

**80** whatever makes for cultural development is working also against war ▸ Sigmund Freud, 1932

## CULTURAL HERITAGE

**81** while the Turks were besieged by the Greeks on the Acropolis, they ran out of lead for their bullets ... we'll send you some ▸ Melina Mercouri, referring to an incident in the Greek War of Independence (1821-1832)

**82** *The General Assembly ... Invites* Member States to take all necessary steps for the return ... of cultural property ▸ United Nations General Assembly resolution, 1979

## CULTURE

**83** it is prohibited to commit any acts of hostility directed against historic monuments, works of art or places of worship ▸ Protocol Additional to the Geneva Conventions of 12 August 1949, and Relating to the Protection of Victims of Non-International Armed Conflicts (Protocol II), 1977

## CUSTOM

**84** We are not impressed by the prestige of war as an ancient institution ... the holding of slaves ... these customs ▸ Henry J. Cadbury, for the American Friends Service Committee (the Quakers), 1947

## DEATH

**85** The fittest place where man can die / Is, where he dies for man! ▸ Michael J. Barry, 1844

**86** the great task remaining before us ... that we here highly resolve that these dead shall not have died in vain  ▸  Abraham Lincoln at Gettysburg, 1863

**87** there's some corner of a foreign field / That is for ever England  ▸  Rupert Brooke, 1914

### DEFEAT
**88** There are some defeats more triumphant than victories  ▸  Michel de Montaigne, on Thermopylae, Greece, in 480 B.C.

**89** The outcome of the struggle has not been decided by the Battle of France  ▸  Charles de Gaulle, 1940

### DEFENSE
**90** Stranger, go tell the Lacedœmonians, that we lie here, obedient to their commands  ▸  Herodotus, on the Battle of Thermopylae, Greece, in 480 B.C.

**91** Our wonderful Great Wall! ... it never kept out the Huns  ▸  Lu Hsun or Lusin [Lu Xun], 1925

### DEFINITION
**92** War is a mere continuation of policy by other means  ▸  Karl von Clausewitz, 1818-1830

### DESTRUCTION
**93** a generation of men who, even though they may have escaped its shells, were destroyed by the war  ▸  Erich Maria Remarque, on World War I

### DEVELOPMENT
**94** conditions of stability and well-being ... necessary for peaceful and friendly relations among nations  ▸  Charter of the United Nations, 1945

### DIARY
**95** All died. Only Tanya remains  ▸  Tanya Savicheva, a twelve-year-old girl in besieged Leningrad, 1942

### DIPLOMACY
**96** shouldn't we spend a billion or two preparing for peace?  ▸  Kofi Annan, 1997

### DISAPPEARANCE
**97** Each State shall take effective ... measures to prevent and terminate acts of enforced disappearance  ▸  United Nations General Assembly resolution, 1992

### DISARMAMENT
**98** more important by far ... is the «disarmament» of the people from within  ▸  Fridtjof Nansen, 1922

**99** their principal aim ... an agreement on general and complete disarmament  ▸  Treaty Banning Nuclear Weapon Tests in the Atmosphere, in Outer Space and under Water (the Nuclear Test Ban Treaty), 1963

## DISASTER
**100** Out of the half-million soldiers ... only 20,000 staggered back ▸ Antony Brett-James, referring to the invasion of Napoleon I into Russia in 1812

## DISPUTE RESOLUTION
**101** Divide the living child in two ▸ The Bible, 1 Kings 3:25 (Solomon, king of Israel (ca. 961-922 B.C.))

**102** both of them claimed that the silk was his own ▸ Chinese tale, written in the second century

**103** negotiation, enquiry, mediation, conciliation, arbitration, judicial settlement, resort to regional agencies or arrangements, or other peaceful means ▸ Charter of the United Nations, 1945

## DIVERSITY
**104** The war we have to wage today has only one goal, and that is to make the world safe for diversity ▸ U Thant, 1964

## DREAM
**105** My dream is a peace bomb ▸ Ögmundur Helgason, about 1964.

## EARTH
**106** on earth peace, good will toward men ▸ The Bible, Luke 2:14

## ECONOMIC SANCTION
**107** The modern world is prepared to exert economic power instantly ▸ Herbert S. Houston, 1918

## EDUCATION
**108** since wars begin in the minds of men, it is in the minds of men that the defences of peace must be constructed ▸ Constitution of the United Nations Educational, Scientific and Cultural Organization, 1945

**109** The preparation of the child ... understanding, peace, tolerance, equality of sexes, and friendship among all peoples ▸ Convention on the Rights of the Child, 1989

## EMPIRE
**110** Rome shall perish ▸ William Cowper, referring to a revolt against Roman rule in England in or about the year 61

## END
**111** You might as well try to sweep back Niagara as stop war when its rumblings are heard ▸ King Vidor, 1925

## ENEMY
**112** so adjust your heart that you long for ... the happiness of your enemies ▸ Buddha (ca. 563-ca. 483 B.C.)

**113** he never ... treated any enemy as irreconcilably opposed to him ▸ Pericles (ca. 490-429 B.C.), according to Plutarch

**ENVIRONMENT**
**114** Care shall be taken in warfare to protect the natural environment against widespread, long-term and severe damage ▶ Protocol Additional to the Geneva Conventions of 12 August 1949, and Relating to the Protection of Victims of International Armed Conflicts (Protocol I), 1977
**115** destruction of the environment, not justified by military necessity and carried out wantonly, is clearly contrary to existing international law ▶ United Nations General Assembly resolution, 1992

**ESPIONAGE**
**116** a spy ... in Tokyo: the precise date of the German attack on the USSR ▶ M. R. D. Foot, on Richard Sorge in 1941

**EVACUATION**
**117** Wars are not won by evacuations ▶ Winston S. Churchill, on Dunkirk, 1940

**EXHORTATION**
**118** From the tops of those Pyramids forty centuries look upon you! ▶ Napoleon Bonaparte, at the beginning of the Battle of the Pyramids, 1798
**119** England expects that every man will do his duty! ▶ Horatio Nelson, at the beginning of the Battle of Trafalgar, off southern Spain, 1805

**EXPANSIONISM**
**120** they who are fain to annex their neighbours' holdings frequently are defeated and fail ▶ Menander (ca. 343 or 342-291 or 290 B.C.)

**FAMILY**
**121** May he careful be, and come back to me ▶ Ancient Chinese poem, composed before 660 B.C.

**FAMINE**
**122** of an army of one hundred and twenty thousand foot ... a fourth part out of India ... so diminished ... most by famine ▶ Plutarch on Alexander the Great's return from India in 325 B.C.

**FIGHT**
**123** An Irishman is never at peace except when he's fighting ▶ Irish proverb
**124** We shall fight on the beaches ... we shall fight in the hills ▶ Winston S. Churchill, 1940

**FILM**
**125** Antiwar, antimilitary themes ... an honored place ... *All Quiet on the Western Front* ... *Paths of Glory* ▶ Lawrence H. Suid, on films released in 1930 and 1957

**FLIGHT**
**126** Look, that is the way to the enemy ▶ Julius Caesar in North Africa, 47-46 B.C.

**FOLLY**
**127** that a man should have the right to kill me ... because his ruler has a quarrel with mine  ▸  Blaise Pascal, 1657-1658

**FORCE**
**128** Keep peace with the Lords of the Jungle—the Tiger, / the Panther, and Bear  ▸  Rudyard Kipling, in one of his laws of the jungle, 1895

**FORGIVENESS**
**129** To forgive is not just to be altruistic. It is the best form of self-interest  ▸  Desmond Tutu, 1999

**FREEDOM**
**130** freedom will never be crushed as long as there are men as brave as the men of D-Day  ▸  Darryl F. Zanuck, 1961

**FUTURE**
**131** there is posterity for the peaceable  ▸  The Bible, Psalms 37:37 (a psalm of David, king of Israel (ca. 1000-ca. 961))

**GENERAL**
**132** a single general's reputation / Is made out of ten thousand corpses  ▸  Ts'ao Sung [Cao Song] (flourished ca. 870-920)

**GENERATION**
**133** We never knew love  ▸  Semyon Petrovich Gudzenko, 1945

**GENOCIDE**
**134** genocide is a crime under international law ... shall be punished ... rulers, public officials or private individuals  ▸  Convention on the Prevention and Punishment of the Crime of Genocide, 1948
**135** You don't have to kill everyone to have genocide  ▸  Simon Wiesenthal, according to Roy Gutman in 1993

**GHETTO**
**136** a German in Warsaw received daily 2,310 calories, a Pole 634 cal. and a Jew 184  ▸  Reuben Ainsztein, referring to occupied Warsaw, including the Warsaw ghetto, in World War II

**GIFT**
**137** Gifts break rocks  ▸  Portuguese proverb

**GLORY**
**138** Yung Ching's policy ... caring nothing for the so-called glory of foreign wars and costly expeditions  ▸  Demetrius Charles Boulger, on Yung-cheng [Yongzheng], emperor of China (1723-1735)

## GOD
**139** The Lord is peace  ▸  The Bible, 6 Judges 24 (the name which Gideon (ca. twelfth century B.C.) gave to the altar at Ophrah)

## GOLD
**140** If another king come that hath better iron than you, he will be master of all this gold  ▸  Solon to Croesus, about 560 B.C.

**141** We Spaniards ... are troubled with a heart disease for which gold is the only cure  ▸  Hernán Cortés, 1519-1520

## GOLDEN RULE
**142** In everything do to others as you would have them do to you  ▸  The Bible, Matthew 7:12 (Jesus to the people, in the Sermon on the Mount)

## GOOD
**143** let us work for the good of all  ▸  The Bible, Galatians 6:10 (The Letter of Paul to the Galatians)

## GOODNESS
**144** Spread goodness in words and deeds everywhere  ▸  Buddha (ca. 563-ca. 483 B.C.)

**145** He who sows good will reap peace  ▸  Moroccan proverb

## GOVERNMENT
**146** Well, fancy giving money to the Government! / ... / Ten to one they'll start another war  ▸  A. P. Herbert, 1930

## GRATITUDE
**147** Never in the field of human conflict was so much owed by so many to so few  ▸  Winston S. Churchill, on British airmen, 1940

## GREATNESS
**148** The great man is he who does not lose his child's heart  ▸  Mencius [Mengzi] (372-289 B.C.)

## HAPPINESS
**149** how can there be any happiness without peace?  ▸  *Bhagavadgita*, part of *Mahabharata*, the Indian epic, completed about 200

## HARVEST
**150** The harvest was never gathered  ▸  Chinese poem, about 124 B.C.

## HATRED
**151** let not hatred towards any induce you to do wrong  ▸  The Qur'an (Koran), "The Table," verse [11]

## HERBICIDE
**152** future employment of herbicides ... a widely held interpretation of the Geneva Protocol of 1925 makes illegal their use in war  ▶  Arthur H. Westing, 1983

**153** Viet Nam has an estimated one million Agent Orange victims, of which 150,000 are children  ▶  Philip Jones Griffiths, 2003

## HERO
**154** our helpers display heroism in their cheerfulness and affection  ▶  Anne Frank, on the Dutch, 1944

## HISTORY
**155** History repeats itself  ▶  English proverb

## HOME
**156** AT fifteen I went with the army, / At fourscore I came home  ▶  Old Chinese poem

**157** His Majesty's Government view with favour the establishment in Palestine of a national home for the Jewish people  ▶  Balfour Declaration, 1917

## HORROR
**158** the marshes and deep rivers were made passable to the Roman foot by the vast quantity of dead bodies  ▶  Plutarch, referring to Julius Caesar crushing the revolt of the Belgae in 57 B.C.

**159** seventy thousand Moslems ... put to the sword ... the harmless Jews ... burnt in their synagogue  ▶  Edward Gibbon, describing the conquest of Jerusalem by the Crusaders in 1099

**160** The hospital of S. Bazile ... all the broken windows and walls were stuffed with feet, legs, arms, hands, trunks, and heads  ▶  Robert Wilson, on Vilnius in 1812

## HOSPITAL
**161** Miss Nightingale arrived at Scutari ... Want, neglect, confusion, misery  ▶  Lytton Strachey, on Florence Nightingale in Turkey in 1854

**162** Civilian hospitals ... may in no circumstances be the object of attack  ▶  Geneva Convention Relative to the Protection of Civilian Persons in Time of War, 1949

## HUMAN BEING
**163** Bring back the fathers! Bring back the mothers!  ▶  Toge Sankichi, on Hiroshima in 1945

## HUMAN RIGHTS
**164** certain unalienable Rights ... Life, Liberty and the pursuit of Happiness  ▶  Declaration of Independence, 1776

**165** Universal Declaration of Human Rights ... a common standard of achievement for all peoples and all nations  ▶  Universal Declaration of Human Rights, 1948

**166** A European Commission of Human Rights ... A European Court of Human Rights  ▸  Convention for the Protection of Human Rights and Fundamental Freedoms [European Convention on Human Rights], 1950

**167** recognition of the inherent dignity and of the equal and inalienable rights of all members of the human family is the foundation of ... peace in the world  ▸ International Covenant on Economic, Social and Cultural Rights, 1966

**168** Any propaganda for war shall be prohibited by law  ▸  International Covenant on Civil and Political Rights, 1966

**169** to them should be added the right which underlies them all: **the right to peace**  ▸  Federico Mayor, 1997

## INDEPENDENCE

**170** his great civil-disobedience movement ... freed his country ... one of the great accomplishments of history  ▸  William L. Shirer, on Mahatma Gandhi (1869-1948)

**171** the most important decision facing Lithuania: Either independence or eternal slavery  ▸  Kazimieras Motieka, 1991

## INHUMANITY

**172** Man's inhumanity to man / Makes countless thousands mourn!  ▸  Robert Burns, 1785

## INITIATIVE

**173** the journey of a thousand lĩ commenced with a single step  ▸  Lao-tzu [Laozi] (from 604 to at least 517 B.C.)

## INTERVENTION

**174** the American continents ... are henceforth not to be considered as subjects for future colonization by any European powers  ▸  James Monroe, 1823

## INVASION

**175** "A lot of men are going to die tonight," he told his wife  ▸  An English coastguardsman on D-day, June 6, 1944

## INVENTION

**176** Accurst be he that first invented war  ▸  Christopher Marlowe, about 1587

## ISSUE

**177** Little issues can be adjudicated ... we might better explore the possibility of turning big issues ... into little ones  ▸  Roger Fisher, 1962

## JEW

**178** No monument stands over Babii Yar  ▸  Yevgeny Yevtushenko, on a mass grave in Ukraine, 1961

## JOURNALIST

**179** Journalists engaged in dangerous professional missions in areas of armed conflict shall be considered as civilians  ▸  Protocol Additional to the Geneva

Conventions of 12 August 1949, and Relating to the Protection of Victims of International Armed Conflicts (Protocol I), 1977

### KILLING
**180** in carrying on your government, why should you use killing at all?  ▸ Confucius [Kongfuzi] (551-479 B.C.)

### LANDMINE
**181** once peace is declared the landmine does not recognize that peace  ▸ Jody Williams, 1997

### LAW
**182** the cave men believed in killing—in the law of the jungle  ▸  Thomas Craven, on cave men living thirty to fifty thousand years ago
**183** In cases not covered ... civilians and combatants remain under the protection ... of the principles of international law derived from established custom, from the principles of humanity and from the dictates of public conscience  ▸  Protocol Additional to the Geneva Conventions of 12 August 1949, and Relating to the Protection of Victims of International Armed Conflicts (Protocol I), 1977

### LEADER
**184** Lead others, not by violence, but by law and equity  ▸  *The Gospel of Buddha*, "The Dharmapada"
**185** first in war, first in peace, and first in the hearts of his countrymen  ▸ Resolutions in Congress, on the death of George Washington, 1799
**186** Never in the field of human conflict was so much owed by so many to one man  ▸  Göran Liljestrand, referring to Winston S. Churchill in World War II

### LIBERTY
**187** we shall pay any price ... to assure the survival and the success of liberty  ▸ John F. Kennedy, 1961

### LIE
**188** In the longest time of peace man does not speak as much nonsense, and tell as many a lie, as in the shortest time of war  ▸  Jean Paul (Johann Paul Friedrich Richter), 1808

### LIFE
**189** In war and peace / We give our lives for thy sake  ▸  National anthem of Egypt, 1979 (lyrics and music by Sayed Darwish (1892-1923))

### LIFESAVING
**190** He ... missed no opportunity ... even from the moving train window ... to issue still a few *more* life-saving documents  ▸  Chiune Sugihara, from 1939 to 1940, according to Hillel Levine
**191** I cannot stay in Sweden ... Every day costs human lives  ▸  Raoul Wallenberg, 1944

**192** Oscar Schindler's Jews miraculously survived  ▶  The Internet, referring to World War II

### LIMITATION
**193** In any armed conflict, the right of the Parties to the conflict to choose methods or means of warfare is not unlimited  ▶  Protocol Additional to the Geneva Conventions of 12 August 1949, and Relating to the Protection of Victims of International Armed Conflicts (Protocol I), 1977

### LOSS
**194** So great was the loss ... that polygamy had to be permitted  ▶  Christie Davies, referring to the Thirty Years' War (1618-1648)
**195** At least thirteen million civilians perished during the conflict  ▶  Fay-Cooper Cole and Harris Gaylord Warren, on some of the effects of World War I
**196** The USSR lost 20,000,000 of its sons and daughters  ▶  M. M. Minasyan, on Soviet losses in World War II

### LOVE
**197** a pilgrim who believed ... that love and understanding and tolerance and compassion and non-violence ... would liberate mankind  ▶  William L. Shirer, on Mahatma Gandhi (1869-1948)
**198** Love is the most durable power in the world  ▶  Martin Luther King, 1963

### MADNESS
**199** whole generations may be swept away by the madness of kings in the space of a single hour  ▶  Edward Gibbon, referring to a remark on the Battle of Châlons in 451

### MANKIND
**200** he who slayeth any one ... shall be as though he had slain all mankind  ▶  The Qur'an (Koran), "The Table," verse 35

### MARCH
**201** The Red Army fears not the trials of a distant march  ▶  Mao Tse-tung [Mao Zedong], 1935

### MARRIAGE
**202** marriage is ... a field of battle, and not a bed of roses  ▶  Robert Louis Stevenson, 1881

### MARTYR
**203** prisoner 16670 had stepped forward and offered himself in the other man's place  ▶  Mary Craig, referring to Maximilian Kolbe in Auschwitz in 1941

### MASSACRE
**204** Four of the Lidice women who were about to give birth were first taken to a maternity hospital in Prague  ▶  William L. Shirer, on Lidice, a village near Prague, in 1942

**MEDICAL UNIT**

**205** Medical units shall be respected and protected at all times and shall not be the object of attack  ▶  Protocol Additional to the Geneva Conventions of 12 August 1949, and Relating to the Protection of Victims of International Armed Conflicts (Protocol I), 1977

**MEMORY**

**206** the rejection of memory ... would doom us to repeat past disasters, past wars  ▶  Elie Wiesel, 1986

**MERCENARY**

**207** States Parties shall not recruit, use, finance or train mercenaries  ▶  International Convention against the Recruitment, Use, Financing and Training of Mercenaries, 1989

**MERCY**

**208** In a war he preaches forbearance and mercy for the sufferings of people  ▶  Buddha (ca. 563-ca. 483 B.C.), according to *The Teaching of Buddha*

**MESSAGE**

**209** My centre is giving way, my right retreats, situation excellent. I am attacking!  ▶  Ferdinand Foch, 1914 (in World War I)

**MIGHT**

**210** right makes might  ▶  Abraham Lincoln, 1860

**MILITARY ESTABLISHMENT**

**211** we must guard against the acquisition of unwarranted influence ... by the military-industrial complex  ▶  Dwight D. Eisenhower, 1961

**MONUMENT**

**212** the Monument to the Missing of the Battle of the Somme ... Total casualties on both sides exceeded 1 million men  ▶  Jay Winter, on World War I

**MOTHER**

**213** the solemn pride that must be yours to have laid so costly a sacrifice upon the altar of freedom  ▶  Abraham Lincoln, to a mother of fallen soldiers, 1864

**MOURNING**

**214** no Athenian, through my means, ever wore mourning  ▶  Pericles, near the end of his life in 429 B.C.

**MURDER**

**215** You shall not murder  ▶  The Bible, Deuteronomy 5:17 (the Fifth Commandment)

**216** The murder of one person is called unrighteous ... attacking states ... they applaud it, calling it righteous  ▶  Mo Ti (Mo-Tzu) [Mozu] (470?-391? B.C.)

## MUSIC
**217** Be embraced, millions all; / This kiss for the world is meant!  ▸  Words from the "Ode to Joy" by Friedrich von Schiller (1785), used in Ludwig van Beethoven's Ninth Symphony (1824)

**218** *Finlandia* ... focused ... unwelcome attention on the plight of the Finns ... in Estonia in 1903 ... it went under the title 'Impromptu for orchestra'  ▸  Robert Layton, on Jean Sibelius in 1903

**219** For me the life of a single child is worth more than all my music  ▸  Pablo Casals, recalling World War I during that war

## NATION
**220** fascism and nazism ... ended by ruining the nations they sought to exalt  ▸  Jawaharlal Nehru, on the downfall of Italian fascism in 1943 and German nazism in 1945

## NATIONALISM
**221** Nationalism ... the greatest obstacle to mutual understanding between peoples  ▸  Albert Schweitzer, 1954

## NATURE
**222** war, in which, instead of sons burying their fathers, fathers bury their sons  ▸  Croesus, in or about 546 B.C.

**223** The [tendency of] man's nature to goodness is like the [tendency of] water to flow downwards  ▸  Mencius [Mengzi] (372-289 B.C.)

## NAVAL BATTLE
**224** *Bismarck* turned keel-up ... more than 2,000 officers and men ... only 110 were rescued  ▸  Barrie Pitt, on events in the Battle of the Atlantic in 1941

## NAVY
**225** The "Invincible Fleet" was destroyed by storms, and the skill and courage of the English  ▸  Georg Weber, on the Spanish Armada in 1588

**226** the greatest fleet that ever sailed  ▸  Douglas Botting, on the fleet heading for Normandy, France, in June 1944

## NEGOTIATION
**227** Let us never negotiate out of fear. But let us never fear to negotiate  ▸  John F. Kennedy, 1961

## NEIGHBOR
**228** a good neighbour is a great blessing  ▸  Hesiod (flourished ca. 800 B.C.)

## NEUTRALITY
**229** there can be no justification for the interests of the belligerents to prevail over the rights of neutrals  ▸  Declaration of Panama, 1939

## NEWS
**230** Miltiades ... ordered him to carry the good news of victory ... to the city fathers of Athens ▸ John Kieran, on the run of Pheidippides from Marathon to Athens in 490 B.C.

**231** Their numerous bodies carried the news of our victory ... all along the banks ▸ Napoleon Bonaparte, referring to the Battle of the Pyramids in 1798

## NOBEL PEACE PRIZE
**232** nationalism, xenophobia and exclusion ... building bridges, friendship and practical links ▸ Asbjørn Eide, referring to the themes of Nobel Peace Prize recipients, 1995

## NONCOOPERATION
**233** there can be no violence simultaneously with non-co-operation ▸ Mahatma Gandhi, 1920

## NONINTERNATIONAL ARMED CONFLICT
**234** It is prohibited to order that there shall be no survivors ▸ Protocol Additional to the Geneva Conventions of 12 August 1949, and Relating to the Protection of Victims of Non-International Armed Conflicts (Protocol II), 1977

## NONPARTICIPATION
**235** If war is evil, then I do not take part in it ... Not fighting but suffering ▸ Henry J. Cadbury, for the American Friends Service Committee (the Quakers), 1947

## NONVIOLENCE
**236** Until we take all Christ's principles to our hearts, war, hatred and violence will continue ▸ Mahatma Gandhi, 1931

## NUCLEAR ACCIDENT
**237** a meltdown ... could contaminate an area the size of Pennsylvania for hundreds to thousands of years making it uninhabitable ▸ Helen Caldicott, on the partial nuclear meltdown in Harrisburg, Pennsylvania, in 1979

## NUCLEAR AGE
**238** Even little wars are dangerous in a nuclear world ▸ John F. Kennedy, 1963

## NUCLEAR WEAPON
**239** We had had the one hundred thousand people killed in Tokyo in one night of [conventional] bombs, and it had had seemingly no effect whatsoever ▸ George C. Marshall, at the end of World War II, according to Richard Rhodes

**240** I am surprised that very worthy people ... should adopt the position that rather than throw this bomb, we should have sacrificed a million American and a quarter of a million British lives ▸ Winston S. Churchill, 1945

**241** dropping the bomb was completely unnecessary ... no longer mandatory as a measure to save American lives ▸ Dwight D. Eisenhower to Henry L. Stimson in 1945

**242** It was impossible to know whether some of them were men or women ▸ Kakuji Miyazaki, referring to Nagasaki in 1945

**243** Only forty of the former nearly two thousand pupils appeared the first day ▸ Masaki Morimoto, on the reopening of his school in Nagasaki in October 1945

**244** the 1954 superbomb ... energy released ... greater than that of all the explosives used in all of the wars ▸ Linus Pauling, on the 1954 hydrogen bomb

**245** The explosion of perhaps less than two dozen C-bombs might be sufficient to destroy all life on the earth's surface ▸ Fay-Cooper Cole and Harris Gaylord Warren, on cobalt bombs, 1955

**246** I knew that the only defense against atom bombs was peace ▸ Pablo Casals, in or about 1960

**247** Any State using nuclear and thermo-nuclear weapons is to be considered ... as committing a crime against mankind and civilization ▸ Declaration on the Prohibition of the Use of Nuclear and Thermo-Nuclear Weapons, 1961

**248** An objective of a no-first-use proposal is to make less likely the introduction of nuclear weapons into armed conflict between states ▸ Richard A. Falk, 1968

**249** Today's nuclear arsenals contain the combined potential firepower of over one million Hiroshimas ▸ Norman Myers, 1984

### NUMBER
**250** Mankind has fought over 14,000 large and small wars ▸ Yuri Kashlev, 1976

### NURSE
**251** "lady with a lamp" ... they kissed her shadow as it passed ▸ Lytton Strachey, on Florence Nightingale in the Crimean War (1854-1856)

### OFFER
**252** I have nothing to offer but blood, toil, tears and sweat ▸ Winston S. Churchill, on having become prime minister, 1940

### OLYMPIC GAMES
**253** hostilities were suspended during ... the sacred month during which athletes and spectators were allowed to journey to and from the games with safety ▸ John Kieran, on the Olympic Games in ancient times (776-394 B.C.)

### OPINION
**254** They could never understand that he, too, had a heart and that he was not evil ▸ Rudolf Höss, former commandant of Auschwitz, of himself, 1947

### OPPONENT
**255** I tell you Wellington is a bad general, the English are bad soldiers; we will settle the matter by lunch time ▸ Napoleon I, on the battlefield of Waterloo, Belgium, in 1815

### ORACLE
**256** if Crœsus should make war on the Persians, he would destroy a mighty empire ▸ The oracles at Delphi, Greece, about 546 B.C.

### ORDER
**257** The *Führer* has ordered that the Jewish question be solved once and for all ▸ Heinrich Himmler, 1941, according to Rudolf Höss, the commandant of Auschwitz

**258** Paris ... the German commander ... dared to disobey an order to burn it down ▸ M. R. D. Foot, on Dietrich von Choltitz in 1944

### ORGANIZATION
**259** Each catastrophe apparently teaches mankind to set up institutions that might have prevented it ▸ Kenneth E. Boulding, 1967

### PAINTING
**260** *Guernica* is generally considered to be a painting of war ... *Guernica* is not a painting of war—in the traditional sense ▸ Eugenio F. Granell, evaluating Pablo Picasso's painting of 1937

**261** I am too weak for that sort of thing ... but I am still strong enough to wage war ▸ Winston S. Churchill, on whether he was painting, 1944

### PATRIOTISM
**262** I only regret that I have but one life to lose for my country ▸ Nathan Hale, during the American Revolution, 1776

### PEACEFUL STRUGGLE
**263** the Christian doctrine of love, operating through the Gandhian method of nonviolence ▸ Martin Luther King, 1963

### PEACEMAKER
**264** possession ... embankment ... Buddha ... stake that which is priceless against that which has no intrinsic value whatever? ▸ Buddha (ca. 563-ca. 483 B.C.)

**265** there are ... records of his journeying to distant states to prevent the outbreak of a war when he had heard of such a possibility ▸ Mo Ti (Mo-Tzu) [Mozu] (470?-391? B.C.), according to *Encyclopædia Britannica*

**266** Blessed are the peacemakers ▸ The Bible, Matthew 5:9 (Jesus, in the Sermon on the Mount)

**267** we have some faith in the good which exists even in our opponents ▸ Fridtjof Nansen, 1922

**268** Peace is a daily, a weekly, a monthly process ▸ John F. Kennedy, 1963

### PEOPLE
**269** People throughout the world may look different ... but they are all the same ▸ Mother Teresa, 1996

### PEOPLE'S WAR
**270** a people's war, it should ... never condense into a solid body ▸ Karl von Clausewitz, 1818-1830

## PHOTOGRAPHY
**271** the photos of the Iwo Jima flag raising are still an inspiration to millions of Americans of all ages ▸ Tedd Thomey, referring to the Japanese island of Iwo Jima on February 23, 1945

## PILOT
**272** Hitler ... was denied victory by the resolute pilots of Hurricanes and Spitfires ▸ Douglas Pike, on the Battle of Britain (1940-1941)
**273** They had the mission to come to the battlefield like mechanized angels ▸ Otto F. Apel, Jr., and Pat Apel, on the pilots of helicopters for medical evacuation in the Korean War (1950-1953)

## PLAN
**274** The Führer estimates that the operation will take four months ▸ Josef Goebbels, referring, in 1941, to Germany's World War II plan to invade the Soviet Union
**275** This vast operation is undoubtedly the most complicated and difficult that has ever occurred ▸ Winston S. Churchill, on the invasion of Normandy, France, in 1944

## POVERTY
**276** continuing poverty and distress are a ... cause of international tensions, of the conditions that can produce war ▸ Lester B. Pearson, 1957

## POWER
**277** exalted / Above the heavens—the man with boundless power / Who yet forbears to use it indiscreetly ▸ *Mahabharata*, the Indian epic, completed about 200
**278** Power tends to corrupt and absolute power corrupts absolutely ▸ Lord Acton, 1887

## PREFERENCE
**279** *there never was a good War, or a bad Peace* ▸ Benjamin Franklin, 1783

## PREVENTION
**280** over three hundred years ... we have mostly learned that war could have been prevented ▸ Henry J. Cadbury, for the American Friends Service Committee (the Quakers), 1947
**281** Conflict prevention must be made the cornerstone of collective security in the twenty-first century ▸ Kofi Annan, 2000

## PRINCE
**282** his name shall be called ... The Prince of Peace ▸ The Bible, Isaiah 9:6 (ca. 738-701 B.C.)

## PRISONER
**283** a liberation of all political prisoners, of all prisoners of conscience ▸ Andrei Sakharov, 1975

## PRISONER OF WAR

**284** the deputy commander of Auschwitz ... took ... Soviet POWs ... and experimented on them with ZYKLON B pesticide ▶ *Encyclopedia of the Holocaust*, on German Nazi experiments in 1941

**285** Prisoners of war must at all times be humanely treated ▶ Geneva Convention Relative to the Treatment of Prisoners of War, 1949

## PROFIT

**286** a city ... the best means of fortifying it ... brick ... timber ... leather ▶ Aesop (ca. 620-ca. 564 B.C.)

## PROTECTION

**287** the only foreign diplomat to stay behind in Pest ... 100,000 or more people owed their lives to him ▶ Per Anger, on Raoul Wallenberg in Budapest from July 1944 to January 1945

## PROVOCATION

**288** Wound not another, though by him provoked ▶ Code of Manu (the Hindu Noah), about fifth century B.C.

## PURCHASE

**289** The First Consul of the French Republic desiring to give ... a strong proof of his friendship, doth hereby cede ... the said territory ▶ Treaty for the Cession of Louisiana, 1803

## PURGE

**290** the Purge cost the country 54 per cent of the Red Army's generals and 80 per cent of its colonels ▶ Nicholas Bethell, on Joseph Stalin's purge of the commanders of the Red Army of the Soviet Union in the 1930s

## QUARANTINE

**291** a strict quarantine on all offensive military equipment under shipment to Cuba is being initiated ▶ John F. Kennedy, 1962

## QUEEN

**292** As long as a single foot of free Belgian soil remains ... I will be on it ▶ Elisabeth, queen of the Belgians, in World War I

## RACE

**293** The noble-hearted / Regard the human race as all akin ▶ *Panchatantra* (a collection of Indian fables), about 200 B.C.

## RADIO

**294** international radio broadcasts ... why not try to use them in order to promote the ideals of the United Nations, of Unesco and of world peace? ▶ Séan MacBride, 1981

## RAPE
**295** Women shall be especially protected agains any attack on their honour, in particular against rape　▸　Geneva Convention Relative to the Protection of Civilian Persons in Time of War, 1949

**296** rape in the conduct of armed conflict constitutes a war crime and under certain circumstances ... a crime against humanity and an act of genocide　▸　Beijing Platform for Action, 1995

## RECONSTRUCTION
**297** With malice toward none, with charity for all ... let us strive on to finish the work we are in, to bind up the nation's wounds　▸　Abraham Lincoln, 1865

## RECRUITMENT
**298** Daddy, what did you do in the Great War?　▸　English recruiting poster, World War I

## REFUGEE
**299** meet the fugitive with bread　▸　The Bible, Isaiah 21:14 (ca. 738-701 B.C.)

## REGIONAL ORGANIZATION
**300** Member States pledge to settle all disputes among themselves by peaceful means　▸　Charter of the Organization of African Unity, 1963

## RELATIONS
**301** No territorial acquisition resulting from the threat or use of force shall be recognized as legal　▸　Declaration on Principles of International Law concerning Friendly Relations and Co-operation among States in accordance with the Charter of the United Nations, 1970

## RELIGION
**302** those who do good ... These shall be the inmates of Paradise　▸　The Qur'an (Koran), "Jonah, Peace Be on Him!", verse 27

**303** Requite evil with good, and he who is your enemy will become your dearest friend　▸　The Qur'an (Koran), "Revelations Well Expounded," verse 19

**304** A chief commandment of the Koran was, to diffuse Islam by every means, and to compel the nations to receive it by fire and sword　▸　Georg Weber, on the Qur'an (Koran)

**305** the Thirty Years' War, waged ... under the pretext of religion ... nobody knew for what or for whom he had been fighting　▸　Élie Ducommun, on the Thirty Years' War (1618-1648)

**306** The founders of all religions have affirmed that they appeared for the benefit of all beings　▸　Buddhadasa Bhikkhu, 1988

## RELOCATION
**307** 1,523 factories ... were shifted to and restarted in the Urals, Siberia, the Volga area and Kazakhstan　▸　M. M. Minasyan, on the Soviet Union between July and November 1941

## REPARATION
**308** Germany must pay in kind for the losses caused by her to the Allied nations ▸ Protocol of the Proceedings of the Crimea Conference, signed at Yalta in 1945

## REPATRIATION
**309** Parties to the conflict are bound to send back to their own country ... seriously wounded and seriously sick prisoners of war ▸ Geneva Convention Relative to the Treatment of Prisoners of War, 1949

## RESISTANCE
**310** even the most complex situations can be solved by a dialogue and not by force ▸ Lech Walesa, on Poland, 1983

## RESPONSIBILITY
**311** individuals performing acts of State are criminally responsible under international law ▸ Memorandum of the secretary-general of the United Nations on the 1946 judgment of the Nuremberg Tribunal, 1949

## RESTRICTION
**312** the use in war of ... gases ... has been justly condemned by the general opinion of the civilised world ▸ Protocol for the Prohibition of the Use in War of Asphyxiating, Poisonous or Other Gases, and of Bacteriological Methods of Warfare, 1925

## RETALIATION
**313** Then we ought not to retaliate or render evil for evil to any one ▸ Socrates, 399 B.C., according to Plato

## RETURN
**314** I shall return ▸ Douglas MacArthur, on his arrival in Australia from the Philippines, 1942

## REVOLUTION
**315** Sire, it is not a Revolt, it is a Revolution ▸ François Alexandre Frédéric, duke of Liancourt, to Louis XVI, 1789
**316** a revolution is not a dinner party ▸ Mao Tse-tung [Mao Zedong], 1927

## RIDICULE
**317** they came in sight of thirty or forty windmills ... look there ... thirty or more monstrous giants ▸ Miguel de Cervantes Saavedra, 1605 (Don Quixote, in the Battle of the Windmills)

## RIGHT
**318** the peoples of our planet have a sacred right to peace ▸ Declaration on the Right of Peoples to Peace, 1984

## RISK
**319** The victory in war is always doubtful ▸ Hitopades'a, a medieval collection of Indian tales

**320** millions of men ... who have taken part in war ... a risk against world peace ▸ Henry J. Cadbury, for the American Friends Service Committee (the Quakers), 1947

## SACRIFICE
**321** In the winter of 1612-1613 ... Susanin deliberately led the Poles astray in a dense, swampy forest, an act for which he was later tortured to death ▸ *Great Soviet Encyclopedia*, on Ivan Susanin

## SATIRE
**322** The 1920s ... Jaroslav Hašek's *The Good Soldier Švejk*, one of the funniest satires on militarism in general ▸ Christie Davies, 1990

## SCULPTURE
**323** No. I Pit is a military formation ... 3,210 terracotta foot soldiers ▸ Arthur Cotterell, on the tomb of Shih-huang-ti [Shi Huangdi], the first emperor of China (221-210 B.C.)

## SELF-DEFENSE
**324** the inherent right of individual or collective self-defense ... until the Security Council has taken the measures necessary to maintain international peace and security ▸ Charter of the United Nations, 1945

## SELF-DETERMINATION
**325** All peoples have the right of self-determination ▸ Vienna Declaration and Programme of Action, 1993

## SETTLEMENT
**326** Benevolence subdues its opposite just as water subdues fire ▸ Mencius [Mengzi] (372-289 B.C.)
**327** the Koran teaches that if the enemy inclines toward peace, do thou also incline toward peace ▸ Bill Clinton, on the occasion of the Israeli-Palestinian declaration of principles, 1993

## SIEGE
**328** 641,803 people died of hunger during the blockade ▸ M. M. Minasyan, on the Siege of Leningrad from 1941 to 1944

## SLAVERY
**329** on the first day of January ... all persons held as slaves ... shall be then, thenceforward, and forever free ▸ The Emancipation Proclamation, issued by Abraham Lincoln, 1863
**330** it is not a trade, but a system of consecutive murders ▸ David Livingstone, on slave trade in Africa in the late 1860s

## SOLDIER
**331** not one battle famous in history / Sent all its fighters back again ▸ Li Po [Li Bo] (701-762)

**332** Old soldiers never die; they just fade away ▸ Old barracks ballad, referred to by Douglas MacArthur in 1951

## SOLIDARITY
**333** All free men, wherever they may live, are citizens of Berlin ▸ John F. Kennedy, 1963

## SOLUTION
**334** the Final Solution was deliberately designed and personally willed and ordered by Hitler ▸ Front flap of Gerald Fleming's book, 1985
**335** Our problems are manmade—therefore, they can be solved by man ▸ John F. Kennedy, 1963

## SONG
**336** All we are saying / Is give peace a chance ▸ John Lennon, 1969

## SPACE
**337** The moon shall be used by all States Parties exclusively for peaceful purposes ▸ Agreement Governing the Activities of States on the Moon and Other Celestial Bodies, 1979

## SPOILS
**338** The former rights of Russia violated by the treacherous attack of Japan in 1904 shall be restored ▸ Agreement Regarding Japan, signed at the Crimea (Yalta) Conference in 1945

## SPORT
**339** O Sport, you are Peace! ▸ Pierre de Coubertin, 1912

## STARVATION
**340** Starvation of civilians as a method of combat is prohibited ▸ Protocol Additional to the Geneva Conventions of 12 August 1949, and Relating to the Protection of Victims of Non-International Armed Conflicts (Protocol II), 1977

## STATE
**341** An hour may lay it in the dust ▸ George Gordon Byron, Lord Byron, 1810

## STATESMAN
**342** no one can be a true statesman ... who looks only, or first of all, to external warfare ▸ Plato (428 or 427-348 or 347 B.C.), supposedly in his later years

## STEP
**343** small steps are better than no steps at all ... passes to visit their relatives over Christmas ▸ Willy Brandt, referring to Berlin, 1971

## STRENGTH
**344** The great fish eats the little one ▸ Greek proverb

## SUPERIORITY
**345** attacked the army of Persians, of ten times their number ... and gave them a complete overthrow ▸ Georg Weber, on the Greeks in the Battle of Marathon in 490 B.C.

## SUPERPOWER
**346** the two strongest powers are the two in the most danger of devastation ▸ John F. Kennedy, on the Soviet Union and the United States, 1963

## SURPRISE ATTACK
**347** YESTERDAY, December 7, 1941—a date which will live in infamy ▸ Franklin D. Roosevelt, on the Japanese surprise attack on Pearl Harbor, 1941

## TANK
**348** Soviet forces smashed almost 30 enemy divisions, including seven panzer divisions, and destroyed over 3,500 aircraft ▸ M. M. Minasyan, on the Battle of Kursk in 1943

## TELEGRAM
**349** In a million American homes, mothers, fathers, wives ... read telegrams from Washington that broke their hearts ▸ Tedd Thomey, on World War II

## TELEVISION
**350** it really was the television cameras and not NATO, let alone the United Nations, that saved Sarajevo ▸ David Rieff, on Sarajevo in 1994

## TEMPER
**351** better ... one whose temper is controlled than one who captures a city ▸ The Bible, Proverbs 16:32 (the proverbs of Solomon, king of Israel (ca. 961-922 B.C.))

## TERRITORY
**352** Civilians shall not be compelled to leave their own territory for reasons connected with the conflict ▸ Protocol Additional to the Geneva Conventions of 12 August 1949, and Relating to the Protection of Victims of Non-International Armed Conflicts (Protocol II), 1977

## TERRORISM
**353** all States shall ... [t]ake the necessary steps to prevent the commission of terrorist acts ▸ United Nations Security Council resolution, 2001
**354** The 11 September attacks were assaults on humanity, and humanity must respond to them as one ▸ Kofi Annan, 2001

## THOUGHT
**355** no great improvements in the lot of mankind are possible, until a great change takes place in ... their modes of thought ▸ John Stuart Mill (1806-1873)

**TIME**
**356** Human beings have existed ... for at least 300 000 years ... wars seem to have existed for only the last 9000 years ▶ Birgit Brock-Utne, 1988

**TORTURE**
**357** An order from a superior officer ... may not be invoked as a justification of torture ▶ Convention against Torture and Other Cruel, Inhuman or Degrading Treatment or Punishment, 1984

**TRICK**
**358** The wooden horse ... Sinon's story was a clever lie devised to deceive the Trojans ▶ Susan Woodford, on the fall of Troy (ca. 1200 B.C.)

**TRUCE**
**359** the Truce of God was instituted by the Church ... only a small fraction of the year in which to quarrel ▶ Fay-Cooper Cole and Harris Gaylord Warren, on peace efforts of the Roman Church in feudal times
**360** *The General Assembly ... Calls upon Member States to reaffirm the observance of an Olympic Truce during the ... Centennial Games ... at Atlanta, United States ... 1996, and also ... in advance of each Summer and Winter Olympic Games* ▶ United Nations General Assembly resolution, 1995

**TRUTH**
**361** in war truth is the first casualty ▶ Dictum

**TYPE**
**362** two kinds of war ... the overthrow of our adversary ... some conquests on the frontier ▶ Karl von Clausewitz, 1827

**TYRANT**
**363** he is always stirring up some war or other, in order that the people may require a leader ▶ Socrates (ca. 470-399 B.C.), according to Plato

**UNION**
**364** "United we stand—divided we fall!" ▶ George Pope Morris, referring to the Americans, 1851

**UNITED NATIONS**
**365** WE THE PEOPLES OF THE UNITED NATIONS ... armed force shall not be used, save in the common interest ▶ Charter of the United Nations, 1945
**366** All Members shall refrain in their international relations from the threat or use of force ▶ Charter of the United Nations, 1945
**367** in the development of this organization rests the only true alternative to war ▶ John F. Kennedy, 1961
**368** malaria ... over 55 per cent of the population living in the world's original malarious areas had been freed ▶ United Nations, on the World Health Organization's campaign against malaria by the end of 1965

**369** The entire UN system could run for nearly two centuries on only one year's world military spending  ▶  Norman Myers, 1984

**370** *The Security Council ... Authorizes* Member States co-operating with the Government of Kuwait ... to restore international peace and security in the area  ▶  United Nations Security Council resolution, on Iraq's invasion of Kuwait and the Persian Gulf War, 1990

**371** The United Nations has ... played an important role in preventing another global conflict  ▶  Declaration on the Occasion of the Fiftieth Anniversary of the United Nations, 1995

## VALUE

**372** Work for the sake of the children is better than pilgrimage and the holy war  ▶  Moroccan wisdom

## VICTIM

**373** nuclear war ... the end of civilisation, it would also prejudice the existence of life ... 2,000 million victims  ▶  Yevgeny Chazov, on behalf of International Physicians for the Prevention of Nuclear War, 1985

**374** War leaves no victors, only victims  ▶  Elie Wiesel, 1986

## VICTORY

**375** The superior man ... victory (by force of arms) is to him undesirable  ▶  Lao-tzu [Laozi] (from 604 to at least 517 B.C.)

**376** one other such would utterly undo him ... lost a great part of the forces ... almost all his particular friends and principal commanders  ▶  Pyrrhus, 279 B.C., according to Plutarch

**377** I came, saw, and conquered  ▶  Julius Caesar, after a victory in Asia Minor in 47 B.C.

**378** He knows to win that knows how to prevent  ▶  English proverb

**379** Peace hath her victories / No less renowned than War  ▶  John Milton, 1652

**380** All hearts resolved on victory or death  ▶  French national anthem adopted in 1795 (lyrics and music from 1792)

**381** Then conquer we must, for our cause it is just  ▶  National anthem of the United States, 1931 (lyrics from 1814)

**382** No victory can make good their loss  ▶  Harry S. Truman, on the death of American men and women in World War II, 1945

**383** 70 percent ... of the wars were won by the wealthier party  ▶  Steven Rosen, referring to international wars from 1815 to 1945

## VIKING

**384** the most lasting ... achievement of the Viking Age: the military conquest and permanent occupation of a major European nation  ▶  Magnus Magnusson, on the Battle of Hastings in 1066

## VIOLENCE

**385** the concept of warfare, the concept of violence is out of date  ▶  Tenzin Gyatso, the Fourteenth Dalai Lama of Tibet, 2000

**VIRTUE**
**386** The virtuous are honoured wherever they go, but a king is great only in his country  ▸  Tibetan wisdom

**WALK**
**387** We met no one on the walk who didn't want peace, but no one seemed to know how to achieve it  ▸  Satish Kumar, on his eight-thousand-mile peace-pilgrimage from 1962 to 1964

**WALL**
**388** The Great Wall winds in and out, over mountain and stream, for about 1,500 miles  ▸  Fay-Cooper Cole and Harris Gaylord Warren, on the Great Wall of China, mostly completed about 214 B.C.

**WARRIOR**
**389** nobody is more pacific than I am  ▸  Napoleon I, 1813

**WEAPON**
**390** the sword is fine-looking / but the sword is bad-mannered  ▸  *Kalevala*, the Finnish epic (on Ilmarinen, the craftsman)

**WIDOW**
**391** I'm the husband, I'm the cow. / I'm the wife and I'm the plow  ▸  From a song which was sung by soldiers' widows in Russian villages in World War II

**WIFE**
**392** oh, will there never be an end to war?  ▸  From an anonymous Chinese poem, probably written some time between the ninth and the seventh centuries B.C.

**WILL**
**393** God knows that I wanted peace  ▸  Adolf Hitler, 1941

**WOMAN**
**394** a beautiful woman is as good a reason for having a war as any other  ▸ A. P. Herbert, referring to Agamemnon's words on Helen of Troy and the Trojan War (ca. 1200 B.C.)
**395** The Amazons ... appeared with the left breast bare ... the right breast was destroyed  ▸  Oliver Goldsmith, 1762
**396** O ladies! sisters! If we really mean / To make the men make Peace, there's but one way  ▸  Aristophanes, 412 B.C. (Lysistrata in *Lysistrata*)
**397** the MAID OF ORLEANS ... aroused the sinking courage of Charles and his soldiers  ▸  Georg Weber, on Joan of Arc in 1429
**398** the full and complete development of a country, the welfare of the world and the cause of peace require the maximum participation of women ▸  Convention on the Elimination of All Forms of Discrimination against Women, 1979
**399** Women's rights are human rights  ▸  Beijing Declaration, 1995

## WORLD
**400** Socrates ... said ... he was not an Athenian or a Greek, but a citizen of the world  ▸  Plutarch, on Socrates (ca. 470-399 B.C.)

**401** A world that does not offer a fair chance to all ... will be neither prosperous nor peaceful  ▸  Kofi Annan, 2003

## WORLD WAR I
**402** it is highly probable that the war of 1914 would not have occurred if the international system had possessed a more objective ... information system  ▸  Kenneth E. Boulding, 1967

## WORLD WAR II
**403** The total for the globe as a whole probably reached 60 million  ▸  Gerhard L. Weinberg, on World War II deaths, 1994

## WORLD WAR III
**404** not to understand how murderous and hideous war is ... danger ... global blood bath  ▸  Isao Nozaki, 1978

## WORLD WAR IV
**405** what weapons ... I can tell you what they'll use in the fourth—rocks!  ▸  Albert Einstein, 1949

## WOUND
**406** I knew that I was hit and leaned over and put my hand on my knee. My knee wasn't there  ▸  Ernest Hemingway, 1929

## WRONG
**407** I would rather suffer wrong than do wrong  ▸  Socrates (ca. 470-399 B.C.), according to Plato

## YOUTH
**408** war likes to hunt down men who are young  ▸  Sophocles (ca. 496-406 B.C.) (*The Men of Scyros*)

# QUOTATIONS

## 1 ACHIEVEMENT

The Greeks regarded the pyramid tomb of Khufu as one of the seven wonders of the world, and it still remains an object for deep consideration by both the historically and mystically minded.

The Great Pyramid was a tomb built for Khufu, second king of the Fourth Dynasty, who reigned around 2650 B.C. and was one of the most powerful men who ever lived. He had at his command all the resources of the country, and it seems clear that the principal event of his time was the building of the pyramid. It was to be a structure which could be penetrated by no human being, and which would house forever the remains of the king. Herodotus, who lived in the fifth century B.C., related the Egyptian tradition that a hundred thousand men were engaged in its construction for twenty years, and we can well believe that such was the case.

Fay-Cooper Cole (1881-1961), American anthropologist, and Harris Gaylord Warren (1906-1988), American historian, on the Great Pyramid, built during the reign of the Egyptian pharaoh Khufu (Greek, Cheops) ca. 2590-2567 B.C.

*Source:* Fay-Cooper Cole and Harris Gaylord Warren, *An Illustrated Outline History of Mankind*, vol. I (Chicago: Spencer Press, 1955), p. 21.

*Explanation: Herodotus* (ca. 484-ca. 425 B.C.): Greek historian, known as "the Father of History," whose *History*, on the Greco-Persian Wars waged intermittently from about 546 to about 448 B.C., is believed to have been published before 425 B.C.

## 2 ACHIEVEMENT

Leonardo.... He had consented to paint the portrait of the wife, the third wife, of a man named Francesco del Giocondo;... He worked on the picture for four years or more, when he was in the mood, and the finished product now hangs in the Louvre, a picture as widely celebrated as *The Last Supper*. It is called *Mona Lisa*, a contraction of Madonna Lisa, that is to say, Madam Lisa; and it is called *La Gioconda* in the museum catalogue, the feminine form of the husband's name.

    ....

Romancers have it that he was in love with Mona Lisa, but there is no record that he loved this smiling sitter or any other woman. He found in Mona Lisa the type of face he loved to paint, but he prized the painting more than the subject, and would not deliver it to the husband who had ordered it. He made the excuse that it was unfinished, and when he left Florence on his second visit to Milan, he took the portrait with him and kept it with him till he died.

Thomas Craven (1889-1969), American writer, critic and lecturer on art, reflecting, in his 1943 book *The Story of Painting, from Cave Pictures to Modern Art*, on the painting of the *Mona Lisa* (from 1503 to 1506?) by Italian artist and scientist Leonardo da Vinci (1452-1519).

*Source:* Thomas Craven, *The Story of Painting, from Cave Pictures to Modern Art* (New York: Simon and Schuster, 1943), pp. 45-46.

*Explanation: Lisa:* Mona Lisa (Lisa Gherardini Gioconda, La Gioconda, Lisa del Giocondo) (1474 or 1479-1542 or ca. 1551), "a beautiful woman of Florence," Italy.

*Note:* The *Mona Lisa* is in the Louvre, Paris.

*Remark:* Why did the man who painted the *Mona Lisa* invent the machine gun?

### 3 ACHIEVEMENT

Shihab al-Din Shah Jehan (1628-58), born Prince Khuram in 1592 at Lahore, seems to have been a more conventional Muslim than his grandfather or his father, though never so fanatical as his son Aurangzeb was to become. Despite a well-earned reputation for ruthlessness and cruelty, his redeeming feature was his great love for his wife, Arjuman Banu Begum, later given the title Mumtaz Mahal or Light of the Palace. On her death in 1631, he began his greatest work and one of the most famous buildings of all time in her honor—the Taj Mahal.

....

.... As generations of visitors attest, the Taj is blue at dawn, white at noon, and the yellow of the sky at sunset.

John D. Hoag (b. 1919), [American] author, describing, in his 1977 book *Islamic Architecture*, the seventeenth-century marble tomb Taj Mahal, "the mausoleum of Indian love," situated outside the city of Agra in Uttar Pradesh, northwestern India.

*Source:* John D. Hoag, *Islamic Architecture* (New York: Harry N. Abrams, 1977), pp. 378, 380.

*Explanations:*  ▶  *Begum:* Arjumand Banu Baygam, empress of India (1628-1631), married in 1612, mother of fourteen children.  ▶  *Lahore:* earlier a city in India (now in Pakistan).  ▶  *Shah Jehan:* Shah Jahan (1592-1666), Mogul (Mughal) emperor of India (1628-1658).

*Notes:*  ▶  The building of Taj Majal was begun in 1632 and the complex took 22 years to complete, over 20,000 workmen being employed at a given time. *Encyclopædia Britannica* (1964), under "Taj Mahal."  ▶  Taj Mahal is on the World Heritage List.

*Remark:* A Muslim remembered for a building, perhaps the most beautiful building in the world.

### 4 ACHIEVEMENT

One morning, a group of these Hungarian Fascists came into the house and said all the able-bodied women must go with them. We knew what this meant. My mother kissed me and I cried and she cried. We knew we were parting for ever and she left me there, an orphan to all intents and purposes. Then, two or three hours later, to my amazement, my mother returned with the other women. It seemed like a mirage, a miracle. My mother was there—she was alive and she was hugging me and kissing me, and she said one word: 'Wallenberg.'

Tommy Lapid (Joseph Tommy Lapid, originally Tomislav Lampel) (1931-2008), Israeli journalist, author, playwright and lecturer, born in Yugoslavia, director-general of the Israeli Broadcasting Authority in Jerusalem (1979-1984), referring to the 1944 rescue (when he was thirteen), of his mother and other Jews in Budapest by the Swedish businessman and diplomat Raoul Wallenberg (Raoul Gustav Wallenberg) (1912-1947?).

*Source:* John Bierman, *Righteous Gentile: The Story of Raoul Wallenberg, Missing Hero of the Holocaust* (New York: Viking Press, 1981), p. 89.

*Notes:* ▸ Lapid's mother, Katarina-Edna Nachumi (née Bierman) (1907-1973), was one of the hundred thousand or more Jews Wallenberg saved in Hungary from July 1944 to January 1945.

▸ Lapid's father, Doctor of Law Bela Lampel (1898-1944), Yugoslav lawyer and journalist, was killed in the German Nazi concentration camp at Mauthausen, built in August 1938 east of Linz, Austria, a camp which has been described as follows:

The food was completely inadequate, and housing and sanitary conditions were as bad as can be imagined. Many people died of hunger and exhaustion. Numerous prisoners were shot, hanged, or fatally abused....

Prisoners who were ill or incapable of work were separated from the others.... They were then "euthanized" in special killing facilities, either gassed in the camp's own gas chambers or in a gas van...; or they were killed by poison injections in the camp infirmary. In a special place near the crematorium, prisoners were shot in the nape of the neck after being told that they were to have a medical examination. HUMAN EXPERIMENTS (such as surgery performed on healthy prisoners and experiments with tuberculosis serum) claimed more victims.

(*The Encyclopedia of the Third Reich* (1997), under "Mauthausen")

▸ From 2003 to 2004 Lapid served as minister of justice of Israel.

*See* Protection.

*Remark:* She said one word, and what a word!

### 5 ADVANTAGE

The blessing of health is realized on the sickbed; the blessing of a peaceful home is realized when that peace is upset.

Chinese proverb, taken from the book "*A Night's Talk*," apparently written in the seventeenth century by an anonymous author calling himself "Mr. Tut-Tut!" and revised by "Mr. Pfui-Pfui!".

*Source:* Lin Yutang, ed., *The Wisdom of China and India* (New York: Random House, 1942), pp. 1091, 1094 (proverb no. 21, translator Lin Yutang).

*Remark:* The world is our home.

### 6 AGGRESSION

National Socialism does not harbour the slightest aggressive intent towards any European nation.

Adolf Hitler (1889-1945), chancellor of the Third Reich of Nazi Germany (1933-1945), at a National Socialist German Workers' Party congress in 1935.

*Source:* Adolf Hitler, *Adolf Hitler: From Speeches 1933-1938*, Terramare Publications, no. 8-10, ed. Richard Mönnig (Berlin: Terramare Office, 1938), p. 16.

*Remark:* Was it self-defense after all?

## 7 AGGRESSION

The Court did not, however, content itself with this affirmation of the justice of punishing the individuals responsible for the German aggressions. It went on to show that, already at the outbreak of the war, resort to aggressive war was an international crime. In its demonstration the Court relied in the first place on the Kellogg-Briand Pact, binding, in 1939, 63 nations, among them Germany, Italy and Japan. It cited the first two articles wherein the Parties solemnly declare that they condemn recourse to war for the solution of international controversies and renounce it as an instrument of national policy between themselves, and wherein they further agree that the settlement of disputes of every kind, which may arise among them, shall never be sought except by pacific means. The Court thereafter expounded the legal effect of the pact in the following way: "The nations who signed the pact or adhered to it unconditionally condemned recourse to war for the future as an instrument of policy, and expressly renounced it. After the signing of the pact, any nation resorting to war as an instrument of national policy breaks the pact. In the opinion of the Tribunal, the solemn renunciation of war as an instrument of national policy necessarily involves the proposition that such a war is illegal in international law; and that those who plan and wage such a war, with its inevitable and terrible consequences, are committing a crime in so doing. War for the solution of international controversies undertaken as an instrument of national policy certainly includes a war of aggression, and such a war is therefore outlawed by the pact."

From the memorandum on the September 30 and October 1, 1946 judgment of former German Nazi leaders by the International Military Tribunal in Nuremberg, Germany (the Nuremberg Tribunal), submitted in 1949 by Trygve Lie (Trygve Halvdan Lie) (1896-1968), Norwegian lawyer and statesman, secretary-general of the United Nations (1946-1953).

*Source:* United Nations, Secretary-General, *The Charter and Judgment of the Nürnberg Tribunal: History and Analysis* (Lake Success, New York: United Nations, General Assembly, International Law Commission, 1949), pp. 43-44.

*Explanations:* ▸ *Aristide Briand* (1862-1932): French minister of foreign affairs (for the last time from 1926 to 1932), recipient of the 1926 Nobel Peace Prize, who, on June 20, 1927, had suggested a bilateral treaty on renunciation of war, between France and the United States, to which Frank Billings Kellogg (1856-1937), American secretary of state (1925-1929), reacted by suggesting a multilateral treaty. ▸ *Kellogg-Briand Pact* (Kellogg Pact, Briand-Kellogg Pact, Pact of Paris): General Treaty for Renunciation of War as an Instrument of National Policy, which was signed at Paris on August 27, 1928, and entered into force on July 24, 1929.

*Note:* Briand was awarded the 1926 Nobel Peace Prize along with another negotiator of the 1925 Locarno Treaty (Pact of Locarno), Gustav Stresemann (1878-1929), German minister of foreign affairs from 1923 to 1929 (chancellor in 1923).

## 8 AGITATION

[R]eturning quickly to Rome, he acquainted the senate that the former defeats and blows given to the Carthaginians had not so much diminished their strength, as it had abated their imprudence and folly; that they were not become weaker, but more experienced in war, and did only skirmish with the Numidians to exercise themselves the better to cope with the Romans: that the peace and league they had made was but a kind of suspension of war which awaited a fairer opportunity to break out again.

Moreover, they say that, shaking his gown, he took occasion to let drop some African figs before the senate. And on their admiring the size and beauty of them, he presently added, that the place that bore them was but three days' sail from Rome. Nay, he never after this gave his opinion, but at the end he would be sure to come out with this sentence, "ALSO, CARTHAGE, METHINKS, OUGHT UTTERLY TO BE DESTROYED." But Publius Scipio Nasica would always declare his opinion to the contrary, in these words, "It seems requisite to me that Carthage should still stand." For seeing his countrymen to be grown wanton and insolent, and the people made, by their prosperity, obstinate and disobedient to the senate, and drawing the whole city, whither they would, after them, he would have had the fear of Carthage to serve as a bit to hold the contumacy of the multitude; and he looked upon the Carthaginians as too weak to overcome the Romans, and too great to be despised by them. On the other side, it seemed a perilous thing to Cato that a city which had been always great, and was now grown sober and wise, by reason of its former calamities, should still lie, as it were, in wait for the follies and dangerous excesses of the over-powerful Roman people; so that he thought it the wisest course to have all outward dangers removed, when they had so many inward ones among themselves.

Thus Cato, they say, stirred up the third and last war against the Carthaginians....

Plutarch (ca. 46-120), Greek biographer, describing, in his later years' work *Parallel Lives* (the biography of Marcus Cato), the warmongering of the Roman politician Marcus Porcius Cato, called Cato the Censor, later Cato the Elder (234-149 B.C.), which led to the Third Punic War (149-146 B.C.) between the cities of Rome and Carthage (now a suburb of the city of Tunis). More particularly, the agitation followed Cato's embassy to Carthage, probably in 153 B.C.

*Source:* Plutarch, *Plutarch's Lives: The "Dryden Plutarch,"* rev. Arthur Hugh Clough, Everyman's Library, vol. I (1910; reprint, London: J. M. Dent & Sons; New York: E. P. Dutton & Co., 1914), pp. 516, 540-541.

*Notes:* ▸ By the end of the war, Carthage was utterly destroyed and almost its entire population of about 500,000 perished. The mere 50,000 survivors were sold into slavery. ▸ The archaeological site of Carthage is on the World Heritage List.

*Remark:* Cato did not live to see almost 500,000 corpses, 50,000 slaves.

### 9 AGREEMENT

I then said that I should like to go and see the Chancellor, as it might be, perhaps, the last time I should have an opportunity of seeing him. He begged me to do so. I found the Chancellor very agitated. His Excellency at once began a harangue, which lasted for about twenty minutes. He said that the step taken by His Majesty's Government was terrible to a degree; just for a word—"neutrality," a word which in war time had so often been disregarded—just for a scrap of paper Great Britain was going to make war on a kindred nation who desired nothing better than to be friends with her. All his efforts in that direction had been rendered useless by this last terrible step, and the policy to which, as I knew, he had devoted himself since his accession to office had tumbled down like a house of cards. What we had done was unthinkable; it was like striking a man from behind while he was fighting for his life against two assailants. He held Great Britain responsible for all the terrible events that might happen. I protested strongly against that statement, and said that, in the same way as he and Herr von Jagow wished me to understand that for strategical reasons it was a matter of life and death to Germany to advance through Belgium and violate the latter's neutrality, so I would wish him to understand that it was, so to speak, a matter of "life and death" for the honour of Great Britain that she should keep her solemn engagement to do her utmost to defend Belgium's neutrality if attacked. That solemn compact simply had to be kept, or what confidence could anyone have in engagements given by Great Britain in the future?

Sir Edward Goschen (1847-1924), British ambassador to Germany, in a letter dated August 8, 1914, to Sir Edward Grey (1862-1933), British foreign secretary (1905-1916), on the ambassador's August 4, 1914 meeting with Theobald von Bethmann Hollweg (1856-1921), German imperial chancellor (1909-1917).

*Source:* Great Britain, Foreign Office, *British and Foreign State Papers*, 1914 (part II), vol. CVIII [108] (London: His Majesty's Stationery Office, 1918), pp. 693, 784, 785.

*Explanation: Von Jagow:* Gottlieb von Jagow (1863-1935), German diplomat, minister of foreign affairs of Germany (1913-1916).

*Remark:* Not just "a scrap of paper" but "a solemn engagement."

### 10 AIR RAID

Spain was in the ninth month of the Civil War when something extraordinary happened in the ancient Basque village:

On April 26, 1937, a Monday (and therefore, like all Mondays at Guernica, a market day) the small farmers from nearby were bringing into the main square the fruits of the week's toil.... At half-past four in the afternoon, a single peal of church bells announced an air raid.... At twenty minutes to five, Heinkel 111s began to appear....

....

The newspapers reported the event. The cable of the *Times* read as follows:

Guernica, the most ancient town of the Basques and the center of their cultural tradition, was completely destroyed yesterday afternoon by insurgent air-raiders. The bombardment of the open town far behind the lines occupied precisely three hours and a quarter, during which a powerful fleet of aeroplanes consisting of three German types, Junkers and Heinkel bombers and Heinkel fighters, did not cease unloading on the town bombs weighing from 1,000 lbs. downwards.... The fighters meanwhile flew low from above the centre of town, machine-gunning those of the civilians who had taken refuge in the fields. The whole of Guernica was soon in flames except the historic Casa de Juntas.

....

The event produced a radical division in world opinion. People were divided according to their attitudes regarding the destruction of Guernica. In this manner Guernica came to surpass the limited meaning of its original name. The name became the herald of what would be, in a possible future, the range and power of aerial expeditions of punishment as conceived by the modern techniques of war.

....

.... It goes without saying that the bombardment of Guernica remains one of the most significant events of the Civil war, if not the most universal of all, along with the defense of Madrid, first by the militia and subsequently by the Popular Republican Army.

Eugenio F. Granell (Eugenio Fernandez Granell) (1912-2001), Spanish writer, professor of Spanish literature and painter, writing on the destruction, by German airplanes flying for General Francisco Franco, of the Basque village Guernica in the province of Biscay, northern Spain, on April 26, 1937, during the Spanish Civil War of 1936-1939. Later in 1937, the Spanish painter Pablo Picasso (Pablo Ruiz y Picasso) (1881-1973) protested the air raid in his famous mural painting *Guernica*, which is now kept in the Prado Museum in Madrid.

*Source:* E. F. Granell, *Picasso's Guernica: The End of a Spanish Era* (Ann Arbor, Michigan: UMI Research Press, 1981), pp. 3, 4, 9 (first paragraph indented; footnote reference omitted; revision of a doctoral thesis from 1967).

*Explanation: Francisco Franco* (Francisco Paulino Hermenegildo Teódulo Franco Bahamonde) (1892-1975), Spanish general, leader of the Nationalist forces, head of state after the Spanish Civil War until his death, or from 1939 to 1975.

*Note: Times* of London reported:

In the form of its execution and the scale of the destruction it wrought, no less than in the selection of its objective, the raid on Guernica is unparalleled in military history. Guernica was not a military objective. A factory producing war material lay outside the town and was untouched. So were two barracks some distance from the town. The town lay far behind the lines. The object of the bombardment was seemingly the demoralization of the civil population and the destruction of the cradle of the Basque race....

....

.... The whole town of 7,000 inhabitants, plus 3,000 refugees, was slowly and systematically pounded to pieces...

.... In the hospital of Josefinas, which was one of the first places bombed, all the 42 wounded militiamen it sheltered were killed outright. In a street leading downhill from the Casa de Juntas I saw a place where 50 people, nearly all women and children, are said to have been trapped in an air raid refuge under a mass of burning wreckage. Many were killed in the fields, and altogether the deaths may run into hundreds. An elderly priest named Aronategui was killed by a bomb while rescuing children from a burning house.

(*Times*, April 28, 1937, p. 17; cable of April 27, 1937)

## 11 AIR RAID

The International Committee had ... the duty to do something. It proceeded from the fact that the wholesale bombing of towns during the Second World War did not «pay» from a purely military point of view. Indeed, in the bombed industrial regions, factories never ceased work and even increased production. If governments, therefore, do not admit that total, indiscriminate war is criminal, they will, perhaps, heed the argument that it is not good tactics.

The International Committee has had an idea which may perhaps provide the key to the problem: It should not concentrate its effort against any particular weapon, such as the atom bomb, as this would go unheeded by governments and would, in any case, be insufficient. What must be done is to oppose a particular form of war.

In fact, the bombing of Hamburg resulted in as many victims as the bombing of Hiroshima.

Once a weapon is prohibited, an even more frightful one will be invented to take its place. In the French village of Oradour, where the entire population was burnt alive in the church, the weapon was a mere box of matches!

The principle to be established is, therefore, that whatever weapons are employed, the civilian population must not be harmed or at least not exposed to risks out of all proportion to the military objectives.

Léopold Boissier (1893-1968), Swiss jurist, professor, diplomat and president of the International Committee of the Red Cross (1955-1964), in a Nobel lecture, "Some Aspects of the Mission of the International Committee of the Red Cross," given in Oslo on behalf of the committee on December 11, 1963.

*Source:* Frederick W. Haberman, ed., *Nobel Lectures Including Presentation Speeches and Laureates' Biographies: Peace*, vol. 3, *1951-1970* (Amsterdam: Elsevier Publishing Company, for the Nobel Foundation, 1972), pp. 293, 301, 307.

*Explanations:* ▸ *Hamburg:* the city of Hamburg, northern Germany, heavily bombed in July and August 1943. ▸ *Hiroshima:* a Japanese city upon which the first atomic bomb was dropped at the end of World War II, on August 6, 1945 (local time). ▸ *Oradour:* Oradour-sur-Glane, a French village near Limoges, a city of south central France (*see* Massacre (June 10, 1944)).

### 12 ALIEN
You shall not wrong or oppress a resident alien, for you were aliens in the land of Egypt.

The Bible, Exodus 22:21 (the Lord speaking to the Israelites through Moses).
*Source: The Holy Bible Containing the Old and New Testaments*, New Revised Standard Version (New York: Oxford University Press, 1989).
*Explanation: Moses:* Jewish lawgiver and prophet (thirteenth century B.C.).

### 13 ALLIANCE
The Parties to this Treaty reaffirm their faith in the purposes and principles of the Charter of the United Nations and their desire to live in peace with all peoples and all governments.

They are determined to safeguard the freedom, common heritage and civilization of their peoples, founded on the principles of democracy, individual liberty and the rule of law.

They seek to promote stability and well-being in the North Atlantic area.

They are resolved to unite their efforts for collective defense and for the preservation of peace and security.

They therefore agree to this North Atlantic Treaty:

....

*Article 5*

The Parties agree that an armed attack against one or more of them in Europe or North America shall be considered an attack against them all; and consequently they agree that, if such an armed attack occurs, each of them, in exercise of the right of individual or collective self-defense recognized by Article 51 of the Charter of the United Nations, will assist the Party or Parties so attacked by taking forthwith, individually and in concert with the other Parties, such action as it deems necessary, including the use of armed force, to restore and maintain the security of the North Atlantic area.

Any such armed attack and all measures taken as a result thereof shall immediately be reported to the Security Council. Such measures shall be terminated when the Security Council has taken the measures necessary to restore and maintain international peace and security.

....

*Article 9*

The Parties hereby establish a council, on which each of them shall be represented, to consider matters concerning the implementation of this Treaty. The council shall be so organized as to be able to meet promptly at any time. The council shall set up such subsidiary bodies as may be necessary; in particular it shall establish immediately a defense committee which shall recommend measures for the implementation of Articles 3 and 5.

The preamble to and Articles 5 and 9 of the North Atlantic Treaty, which was signed at Washington on April 4, 1949, and entered into force on August 24, 1949. The treaty became the foundation for the North Atlantic Treaty Organization (NATO), a military defense organization.

*Source:* United Nations, *Treaty Series*, vol. 34, pp. 243, 244, 246.

*Note:* Article 3 deals with "individual and collective capacity to resist armed attack."

## 14 AMUSEMENT

War has always been the chief amusement of mankind. Other amusements are a surrogate for war. What are the Olympic Games? Bullshit.

Halldór Laxness (Halldór Gudjónsson, known for some time as Halldór Kiljan Laxness) (1902-1998), Icelandic writer, recipient of the 1955 Nobel Prize in Literature, in his novel *Christianity at Glacier* (Icelandic, *Kristnihald undir Jökli*), published in Icelandic in 1968 (chapter 23).

*Source:* Halldór Laxness, *Christianity at Glacier*, trans. Magnus Magnusson (Reykjavík: Helgafell, 1972), p. 122 (Saknussemm II speaking to Embi).

*Note:* Laxness received the 1955 Nobel Prize in Literature "for his vivid epic power, which has renewed the great narrative art of Iceland." Horst Frenz, ed., *Nobel Lectures Including Presentation Speeches and Laureates' Biographies: Literature, 1901-1967* (Amsterdam: Elsevier Publishing Company, for the Nobel Foundation, 1969), p. 504.

## 15 ANARCHY

[F]rom youth upwards we ought to practise this habit of commanding others, and of being commanded by others; anarchy should have no place in the life of man or of the beasts who are subject to man.

Plato (428 or 427-348 or 347 B.C.), Greek philosopher, in his dialogue *Laws*, supposedly composed in his later years (book XII, section 942; an Athenian stranger speaking to Cleinias, a Cretan, and Megillus, a Lacedaemonian (Spartan)).

*Source:* Plato, *The Dialogues of Plato,* trans. B. Jowett, 2nd ed. rev., vol. V (Oxford: Clarendon Press, 1875), pp. 1, 193, 513.

### 16 ANIMAL
[A]ll war is a symptom of man's failure as a thinking animal,...

John Steinbeck (John Ernst Steinbeck) (1902-1968), American novelist, in an introduction to his 1958 book *Once There Was a War.*
*Source:* John Steinbeck, *Once There Was a War* (New York: Viking Press, 1958), p. xx.
*Notes:*  ▶ The contents of the book, Steinbeck's war correspondent's dispatches on World War II, were previously serialized by the *New York Herald Tribune* Syndicate in 1943.
  ▶ Steinbeck received the 1962 Nobel Prize in Literature "for his realistic as well as imaginative writings, distinguished by a sympathetic humour and a keen social perception." Horst Frenz, ed., *Nobel Lectures Including Presentation Speeches and Laureates' Biographies: Literature, 1901-1967* (Amsterdam: Elsevier Publishing Company, for the Nobel Foundation, 1969), p. 571.
*Remark:* Sometimes just an animal.

### 17 ARBITRATION
The first anniversary, March 13, 1905, of the placing of the colossal statue of Christ on the Andean border between Chile and the Argentine Republic, 14,000 feet above the sea, has recalled the unique and impressive events which led to the erection of this remarkable peace monument. The story of this series of events is substantially as follows:
Five years ago these two prosperous and high-spirited republics of South America were on the verge of war. They were increasing their armaments to the utmost of their ability. They had each two gigantic warships of the latest pattern building in the shipyards of Europe. They were spending incredible sums of money upon these preparations for war....
What brought them so near to conflict was the revival of an old dispute which had caused much trouble and expense in the past, about the boundary between them on the Andes, a controversy involving the question of the title to about eighty thousand square miles of territory....
The British Ministers residing at Buenos Ayres and Santiago used their good offices with the two governments to prevent the calamity of war and to secure a peaceful settlement of the dispute. This effort to prevent hostilities was powerfully supported by Dr. Marcolino Benavente, Bishop of San Juan de Cuyo, Argentina, and Dr. Ramon Angel Jara, Bishop of San Carlos de Ancud, Chile. On Easter Sunday, 1900, during the festival of the Catholic Church at Buenos Ayres, Bishop Benavente made a fervent appeal in behalf of peace, and proposed that some day a statue of Christ should be placed on the Andean border between the two countries, where it might be seen by all comers and goers, and prevent, if possible, any recurrence of animosity and strife between the two republics....
The result was that a treaty was entered into by the two governments, submitting the controversy to the arbitration of the King of England. He entrusted the case to eminent jurists and expert geographers, who examined it carefully, and in due

time submitted their decision, awarding a part of the disputed territory to one of the republics and a part to the other. The decision was cheerfully accepted by both.

Much gratified with the outcome of the arbitration, and urged forward by a powerful popular movement, the two governments then went further, and in June, 1903, concluded a treaty by the terms of which they pledged themselves for a period of five years to submit all controversies arising between them to arbitration, the first general arbitration treaty ever concluded. In a further treaty they agreed to reduce their armies to the proportions of police forces, to stop the building of the great battleships then under construction, and to diminish the naval armaments which they already possessed.

....

The results of this disarmament—for it is a real disarmament—have been most remarkable....

But more significant than any of these material results has been the change in the attitude of the Argentines and Chileans toward each other. All the old bitterness and distrust have passed away, and the most cordial good feeling and confidence have taken their place.

The suggestion of Bishop Benavente as to the erection of a statue of Christ on the boundary at Puente del Inca was quickly carried into execution.... The work was entrusted to the young Argentine sculptor, Mateo Alonso. When his design was completed and accepted, the statue was cast at the arsenal of Buenos Ayres from old cannon taken from the ancient fortress outside of the city.

....

It was not till in February, 1904, that the final steps were taken for its erection.... The Argentines ranged themselves on the soil of Chile and the Chileans on the Argentine side. There was music and the booming of guns, whose echoes resounded through the mountains. The moment of unveiling, after the parts had been placed in position, was one of solemn silence. The statue was then dedicated to the whole world as a practical lesson of peace and goodwill. The ceremonies of the day, March 13, 1904, were closed, as the sun went down, with a prayer that love and kindness might penetrate the hearts of men everywhere.

.... The figure of Christ above, in bronze, is twenty-six feet in height.... On the granite base are two bronze tablets,... on the other are inscribed the words:

"Sooner shall these mountains crumble into dust than Argentines and Chileans break the peace to which they have pledged themselves at the feet of Christ the Redeemer."

It is not easy to compare events and say which is the greatest. But taking it all in all, the long quarrel of seventy years which it closed, the arbitration of the boundary dispute, the general treaty of arbitration and the practical disarmament which preceded it, the remarkable transformation of public opinion expressed in its consummation, and the sublime prophecy of peace for the future which it gives not only for Chile and Argentina but for the whole world, the erection of the Christ of the Andes stands without parallel among the events of recent years.

From the American Peace Society's story of the peace monument *The Christ of the Andes*, unveiled in 1904, after the 1902 arbitral award of an old territorial dispute between Argentina and Chile, on the basis of a specific arbitration treaty, as well as the 1903 general arbitration treaty and a disarmament treaty between the countries.

*Source:* The American Peace Society, *The Christ of the Andes: The Story of the Erection of the Great Peace Monument on the Andean Boundary between Chile and Argentina* (Boston: The American Peace Society, 1905), pp. 2-7.

*Explanations:*  ▸  *Mateo Alonso* (1878-1955): Argentine sculptor.  ▸  *Andes:* a mountain range along the western part of South America.  ▸ *Marcolino Benavente:* Marcolino del Carmelo Benavente (1845-1910), Argentine bishop (bishop of San Juan de Cuyo, 1899-1910).  ▸  *Ramon Angel Jara:* Ramón Angel Jara Ruz (1852-1917), Chilean bishop (bishop of San Carlos de Ancud, 1898-1909).  ▸  *King of England:* Edward VII (1841-1910), king of Great Britain and Ireland (1901-1910), who in 1902 pronounced an arbitral award on the Argentine-Chilean boundary.

*Remark:* Diamond solution, "a practical lesson of peace and goodwill."

### 18 ARMISTICE

Whenever circumstances permit, an armistice or a suspension of fire shall be arranged, or local arrangements made, to permit the removal, exchange and transport of the wounded left on the battlefield.

Article 15, paragraph 2, of the Geneva Convention for the Amelioration of the Condition of the Wounded and Sick in Armed Forces in the Field of August 12, 1949, which was signed at Geneva on August 12, 1949, and entered into force on October 21, 1950.

*Source:* United Nations, *Treaty Series*, vol. 75, pp. 31, 40.

*Note:* In Articles 56 and 59 of the convention there are references to the Geneva Conventions of 1864, 1906 and 1929 for the Relief of the Wounded and Sick in Armies in the Field, all of which are replaced by the 1949 convention in relation to the high contracting parties. *Same source*, p. 66.

### 19 ARMS

Because uranium 238 is an extremely dense material, it is used to make the cores of shells for conventional weapons, giving the weapons the capability of penetrating the armor plating of a tank. It is provided free to weapons manufacturers by the government-sponsored nuclear industry.

During the six-week land war against Iraq in 1991, at least 10,000 uranium 238 shells were used and at least 40 tons of this material was dispersed in Iraq and Kuwait. Children now play with empty shells; thus, they are exposed to external doses of gamma radiation, as well as inhaling and ingesting uranium particles, which can cause kidney disease, lung cancer, bone cancer, and leukemia. The death rate of children under five has doubled; in the first eight months after the war 50,000 children died of various causes; their diseases included cancer and stomach ailments. The United Kingdom Atomic Energy Authority reports that this 40 tons of uranium could cause tens of thousands of deaths and contaminate soil and drinking water in Iraq and Kuwait forever.

Helen Caldicott (Helen Mary Broinowski Caldicott) (b. 1938), Australian physician (pediatrician), antinuclear activist and environmentalist, referring specifically to the Persian Gulf War or the Gulf War (1990-1991), in her 1994 book *Nuclear Madness*.

*Source:* Helen Caldicott, *Nuclear Madness: What You Can Do*, rev. ed. (New York: W. W. Norton & Company, 1994), p. 56.

*Note:* In his *New York Times* article, "Making the Desert Glow," Eric Hoskins (Eric William Hoskins) (b. 1960), Canadian physician, public health specialist and humanitarian, suggests that the United Nations "consider recommending that depleted uranium penetrators be banned in accordance with international treaties on chemical and radioactive weapons." *New York Times*, January 21, 1993, p. A25.

*Remark:* Once upon a time it was decided that the generals should not be allowed to use poison gas. There should be limits.

### 20 ARMS RACE

[M]en may no longer pretend that the quest for disarmament is a sign of weakness—for in a spiraling arms race, a nation's security may well be shrinking even as its arms increase.

John F. Kennedy (John Fitzgerald Kennedy) (1917-1963), president of the United States (1961-1963), in his September 25, 1961 address before the General Assembly of the United Nations.

*Source:* John F. Kennedy, *Public Papers of the Presidents of the United States: John F. Kennedy ... 1961* (Washington: United States Government Printing Office, 1962), pp. 618, 620.

### 21 ART

Thus today, as always, art knows no national boundaries.

Genius can speak at any time, and the entire world will hear it and listen. Behind the storm of daily conflict and crisis, the dramatic confrontations, the tumult of political struggle, the poet, the artist, the musician, continues the quiet work of centuries, building bridges of experience between peoples, reminding man of the universality of his feelings and desires and despairs, and reminding him that the forces that unite are deeper than those that divide.

John F. Kennedy (John Fitzgerald Kennedy) (1917-1963), president of the United States (1961-1963), speaking, on November 29, 1962, at a closed-circuit television broadcast on behalf of the National Cultural Center in Washington.

*Source:* John F. Kennedy, *Public Papers of the Presidents of the United States: John F. Kennedy ... 1962* (Washington: United States Government Printing Office, 1963), p. 846, 846.

*Remark:* Let us build bridges, all types of bridges.

### 22 ASSASSINATION

History indicates that the assassination of a ruler very seldom changes the prevailing tendencies in the national life. Caesar was stricken down in the name of freedom, but the dagger of Brutus did not restore the liberties of Rome. William the Silent was the victim of the Jesuits, but his assassination nerved his countrymen to new struggles for the Protestant religion, and the independence of Holland; and his son was enabled to carry to a successful issue the policy for which his father had given his life. And our own Lincoln was slain by the very last shot fired in the defence of slavery, but his death gave no strength to the lost cause. The death of President Garfield makes it simply impossible to return to the system which regards the great number of positions in the service of the government as prizes to be distributed among the most subservient followers of the party in power.... We have been startled to learn recently that, for years, threats of assassination have been made by men who have failed to secure from the President the favors they desired, and now that the threat has been executed upon one who had been hardly four months in office, we have the strongest proof that it is unsafe for the Republic to continue this system of appointments to the public service, which has grown out of the assumption that the offices are the spoils, due to the victors in a political election.

Ezra Hoyt Byington (1828-1901), American clergyman, in a September 26, 1881 memorial address delivered in Monson, Massachusetts, on the day of the funeral of James A. Garfield (James Abram Garfield) (1831-1881), president of the United States (1881).

*Source:* E. H. Byington, *Memorial Address, Delivered in Monson, Mass., Sept. 26, 1881, the Day of the Funeral of President Garfield* (Worcester, Massachusetts: Press of Blanchard & Wilson, [1881]), pp. 18-19 (misspelling in the word "slavery" corrected).

*Explanations:* ▸ *Brutus:* Marcus Junius Brutus (also Quintus Caepio Brutus) (85-42 B.C.), Roman politician and conspirator, one of Caesar's assassins. ▸ *Caesar:* Julius Caesar (Gaius Julius Caesar) (100-44 B.C.), Roman general and statesman, by 44 B.C. dictator of Rome. ▸ *Jesuits:* members of the Society of Jesus, a Catholic religious order, founded in 1540. ▸ *Lincoln:* Abraham Lincoln (1809-1865), president of the United States (1861-1865). ▸ *William the Silent* (1533-1584): count of Nassau and prince of Orange, Dutch political leader, born in Germany, leader of the Dutch struggle for independence from Spain.

*Remark:* The last bullet for slavery, the last death for freedom.

### 23 ATROCITY

The United Kingdom, the United States and the Soviet Union have received from many quarters evidence of atrocities, massacres and cold-blooded mass executions which are being perpetrated by the Hitlerite forces in the many countries they have overrun and from which they are now being steadily expelled. The brutalities of Hitlerite domination are no new thing and all the peoples or territories in their grip have suffered from the worst form of government by terror. What is new is that many of these territories are now being redeemed by the advancing armies of the liberating Powers and that in their desperation, the recoiling Hitlerite Huns are redoubling their ruthless cruelties. This is now evidenced with particular clearness by monstrous crimes of the Hitlerites on the territory of the Soviet Union which is being liberated from the Hitlerites, and on French and Italian territory.

Accordingly, the aforesaid three allied Powers, speaking in the interests of the thirty-two [*thirty-three*] United Nations, hereby solemnly declare and give full warning of their declaration as follows:

At the time of the granting of any armistice to any government which may be set up in Germany, those German officers and men and members of the Nazi party who have been responsible for, or have taken a consenting part in the above atrocities, massacres and executions, will be sent back to the countries in which their abominable deeds were done in order that they may be judged and punished according to the laws of these liberated countries and of the free governments which will be created therein. Lists will be compiled in all possible detail from all these countries having regard especially to the invaded parts of the Soviet Union, to Poland and Czechoslovakia, to Yugoslavia and Greece, including Crete and other islands, to Norway, Denmark, the Netherlands, Belgium, Luxemburg, France and Italy.

Thus, the Germans who take part in wholesale shootings of Italian officers or in the execution of French, Dutch, Belgian or Norwegian hostages or of Cretan peasants, or who have shared in the slaughters inflicted on the people of Poland or in territories of the Soviet Union which are now being swept clear of the enemy, will know that they will be brought back to the scene of their crimes and judged on the spot by the peoples whom they have outraged. Let those who have hitherto not imbrued their hands with innocent blood beware lest they join the ranks of the guilty, for most assuredly the three allied Powers will pursue them to the uttermost ends of the earth and will deliver them to their accusers in order that justice may be done.

The above declaration is without prejudice to the case of the major criminals, whose offences have no particular geographical localisation and who will be punished by the joint decision of the Governments of the Allies.

Declaration of German Atrocities, of October 30, 1943, signed by Winston S. Churchill (Winston Leonard Spencer Churchill) (1874-1965), prime minister of the United Kingdom (1940-1945, 1951-1955), Franklin D. Roosevelt (Franklin Delano Roosevelt) (1882-1945), president of the United States (1933-1945), and Joseph Stalin (Joseph Vissarionovich Dzhugashvili) (1879-1953), premier of the Soviet Union (1941-1953) and general secretary of the Central Committee of the Communist Party (1922-1953). The declaration was released to the press on November 1, 1943, after the Moscow Conference (Tripartite Conference of Foreign Ministers), which took place from October 19 to 30, 1943.

*Source:* United States, Department of State, *Department of State Bulletin*, vol. IX, no. 228, publication 2021 (November 6, 1943), pp. 310, 310-311.

*Explanation: Huns:* a nomadic people invading southeastern Europe about 370, powerful there and in central Europe until about 450.

## 24 ATTACK

[F]ight for the cause of God against those who fight against you: but commit not the injustice of attacking them first: God loveth not such injustice.

The Qur'an (Koran), chapter (sura) II, "The Cow," verse 186.
*Source: The Koran,* trans. J. M. Rodwell, Everyman's Library (1909; reprint, London: J. M. Dent & Sons, 1918), pp. 338, 358 (colon replaced by period at the end of the verse).

*Explanations:* ▶ *God:* Allah (Arabic). ▶ *The Qur'an* (Arabic, "recitation, reading"): the sacred book of Islam, the Muslim religion (Arabic, "submission to the will of God"), founded by the Arab prophet Mohammed (Muhammad, meaning "praised" or "praiseworthy") (ca. 570-632).

## 25 ATTACK

It has always been popular to attack the weak. A great temptation to take them on—no matter whether they are white, black, or red. A bitter disappointment when it turned out they could defend themselves; tragic; it's like pricking oneself on a rose.

Halldór Laxness (Halldór Gudjónsson, known for some time as Halldór Kiljan Laxness) (1902-1998), Icelandic writer, recipient of the 1955 Nobel Prize in Literature, in his novel *Christianity at Glacier* (Icelandic, *Kristnihald undir Jökli*), published in Icelandic in 1968 (chapter 23).

*Source:* Halldór Laxness, *Christianity at Glacier*, trans. Magnus Magnusson (Reykjavík: Helgafell, 1972), p. 122 (Saknussemm II speaking to Embi).

*Note:* Laxness received the 1955 Nobel Prize in Literature "for his vivid epic power, which has renewed the great narrative art of Iceland." Horst Frenz, ed., *Nobel Lectures Including Presentation Speeches and Laureates' Biographies: Literature, 1901-1967* (Amsterdam: Elsevier Publishing Company, for the Nobel Foundation, 1969), p. 504.

*See* Power (Lord Acton).

## 26 ATTITUDE

The industrialization of war leading to the creation of more sophisticated and expensive arms absorbs an increasingly bigger share of the intellectual potential and material resources of humankind. Thus the solutions for global problems, such as the enormous gap between rich and poor, and a dangerous ecological situation on our planet are hampered. The world community for the first time in its history could approach a point of no return and the logic of survival of humankind demands that the course and values be revised.

Among possible scenarios for finding a way out of a deadlock, the concept concerning the urgent need to replace a culture of violence and war by a culture of dialogue and peace acquires great importance. This concept was proposed by the biologist, philosopher and poet Federico Mayor who, since 1987, is the Director-General of UNESCO.

Vladimir Lomeiko (Vladimir Borisovich Lomeiko) (1935-2009), Russian diplomat, special adviser to the director-general of the United Nations Educational, Scientific and Cultural Organization (UNESCO), in an address to the International Symposium on Culture of Peace held in Baden-Baden, Germany, from August 18 to 23, 1997, as part of the 9th International Conference on Systems Research, Informatics and Cybernetics.

*Source:* Vladimir Lomeiko, "How to Replace a Culture of Violence and War by a Culture of Dialogue and Peace," *A Design for Peace: Advances in Systems Research of Peace: How to Replace Culture of War by Culture of Peace*, ed. George E. Lasker and Vladimir Lomeiko (Windsor, Ontario: International Institute for Advanced Studies in Systems Research and Cybernetics, 1997), p. 20, 20 (paragraphs indented).

*Explanation: Federico Mayor:* Federico Mayor Zaragoza (b. 1934), Spanish biologist and poet, director-general of UNESCO (1987-1999) who proposed the concept of the culture of peace shortly after he became director-general of UNESCO.

*Note:* The publication contains the proceedings of the symposium.
*Remark:* "Violence and war" or "dialogue and peace."

## 27 BALLOT
I will not say that we may not sooner or later be compelled to meet force by force; but the time has not yet come, and, if we are true to ourselves, may never come. Do not mistake that the ballot is stronger than the bullet. Therefore let the legions of slavery use bullets; but let us wait patiently till November and fire ballots at them in return; and by that peaceful policy I believe we shall ultimately win.

Abraham Lincoln (1809-1865), American statesman, later president of the United States (1861-1865), in a speech delivered on May 29, 1856 before the first Republican State Convention of Illinois held at Bloomington, Illinois.
*Source:* Abraham Lincoln, *The Writings of Abraham Lincoln*, ed. Arthur Brooks Lapsley, vol. 2, *1843-1858*, Works of Abraham Lincoln, Federal Edition (New York: G. P. Putnam's Sons, 1905), pp. 247, 269.
*Remark:* Ballots instead of bullets.

## 28 BATTLE
No State should believe its fate, that is, its entire existence, to be dependent upon one battle, let it be even the most decisive.

Karl von Clausewitz (Karl Marie von Clausewitz) (1780-1831), Prussian general and military strategist, in his work *On War* (German, *Vom Kriege*), written from 1818 to 1830 and published posthumously in German in 1832 (book VI, chapter XXVI).
*Source:* Carl von Clausewitz, *On War*, trans. J. J. Graham, three volumes in one, vol. II (London: N. Trübner & Co., 1873), p. 177.

## 29 BATTLEFIELD
I can give you no idea of the route I have covered. The corpses of Frenchmen obstruct the road which, from Moscow to the frontier (about eight hundred versts), looks like one continuous battlefield.

Xavier de Maistre (Xavier, comte de [count of] Maistre) (1763-1852), French novelist, painter and soldier who was serving in the Russian army when Napoleon I (Napoleon Bonaparte) (1769-1821), emperor of France (1804-1814, 1815), invaded Russia in 1812, writing a letter dated December 21, 1812, from Vilna, to his brother, Joseph de Maistre (Joseph Marie, comte de [count of] Maistre) (1753-1821), French political philosopher and diplomat, ambassador of Victor Emmanuel I (1759-1824), king of Sardinia (1802-1821), to St. Petersburg (1803-1817).
*Source:* Antony Brett-James, comp., ed. and trans., *1812: Eyewitness Accounts of Napoleon's Defeat in Russia* (London: Macmillan and Company, 1966), p. 281.
*Explanations:* ▶ *About eight hundred versts:* about 530 miles (850 kilometers).
▶ *Vilna:* a city, in 1812 ruled by the Russians (now Vilnius in Lithuania).

## 30 BEGINNING
I was in Paris when the war broke out. The city went berserk. One would have thought there might be some awareness of the terrible calamity that had

overtaken the country, but no, on the contrary, there was a wildly festive mood. Bands playing martial music, flags flying from every window, bombastic speeches about glory and patriotism! What a macabre masquerade! Who knows how many of those young men who paraded smiling through the streets of Paris died in muddy trenches, or came home crippled for life? And in how many other cities and countries were similar parades taking place?

Pablo Casals (Pau Carlos Salvador Defilló de Casals) (1876-1973), Spanish cellist and conductor, opponent of fascism and crusader for peace, eye-witnessing the reaction to the beginning of World War I in Paris in 1914.
*Source:* Pablo Casals, *Joys and Sorrows: Reflections by Pablo Casals, as Told to Albert E. Kahn* (London: Macdonald and Co. (Publishers), 1970), p. 146.
*See* Amusement.

### 31 BENEFIT
There is no instance of a country having been benefited from prolonged warfare.

Sun Tzu (Sun-tzu) (personal name Sun Wu) [Sunzi; Sun Zi] (flourished ca. 500 B.C.), Chinese military writer, in his book *The Art of War* (Chinese, *Ping-fa* [*Bingfa*]), the oldest military treatise in the world, written about 500 B.C. (chapter 2 (Waging War)).
*Source:* Sun Tzu Wu, *The Art of War*, trans. Lionel Giles (Harrisburg, Pennsylvania: Military Service Publishing Company, 1944), p. 45.

### 32 BIOLOGICAL WARFARE
As reported by de Mussis ... the Mongols practised biological warfare in the 14th century. In 1346 after a three-year unsuccessful siege they hurled plague-infected cadavers over the walls of the essentially impregnable Crimean seaport Caffa (the present-day Feodosija) which had been constructed by the Genoese. De Mussis, an eyewitness, reports: 'The Tatars, fatigued by such a plague and pestiferous disease, stupefied and amazed, observing themselves dying without hope of health, ordered cadavers placed on their hurling machines and thrown into the city of Caffa, so that by means of these intolerable passengers the defenders died widely. Thus there were projected mountains of dead, nor could the Christians hide or flee, or be freed from such disaster'.... Finally the Genoese gave up the city and fled by water. De Mussis then reports of the further dissemination of plague by those who fled from Caffa. His ship had plague victims aboard of whom scarcely 10 of 1000 survived. His ship and undoubtedly many others carrying refugees from Caffa brought the disease to a number of islands, including Sicily, Sardinia, Corsica, and finally to Genoa.... From there it spread throughout Italy and over Europe, destroying large parts of the population. In addition, it induced large-scale massacres of Jews who were accused of being responsible for the 'Black Death'. Every second inhabitant of a plague-stricken city died. Altogether an estimated 25 million, that is about 30 per cent of the European population, became victims of the 'Black Death'....

Erhard Geissler (b. 1930), German molecular biologist, on biological warfare in the fourteenth century, in his introduction to the 1986 book *Biological and Toxin Weapons Today*.

*Source:* Erhard Geissler, ed., *Biological and Toxin Weapons Today* (New York: Oxford University Press, 1986), p. 7.

*Explanations:* ▸ *Black Death:* a plague which ravaged Europe from 1347 to 1351. ▸ *Caffa:* a town, Kaffa, under Genoese control, on the south coast of Crimea (now Feodosiya in Ukraine). ▸ *De Mussis:* Gabriele de Mussis (ca. 1280-ca. 1356), Italian lawyer (of Piacenza) who wrote his account in 1348 or 1349.

## 33 BISHOP

On the third day after the tumult, Genseric boldly advanced from the port of Ostia to the gates of the defenceless city. Instead of a sally of the Roman youth, there issued from the gates an unarmed and venerable procession of the bishop at the head of his clergy. The fearless spirit of Leo, his authority and eloquence, *again* mitigated the fierceness of a barbarian conqueror: the king of the Vandals promised to spare the unresisting multitude, to protect the buildings from fire, and to exempt the captives from torture; and although such orders were neither seriously given, nor strictly obeyed, the mediation of Leo was glorious to himself, and in some degree beneficial to his country.... Many thousand Romans of both sexes, chosen for some useful or agreeable qualifications, reluctantly embarked on board the fleet of Genseric; and their distress was aggravated by the unfeeling barbarians, who, in the division of the booty, separated the wives from their husbands, and the children from their parents. The charity of Deogratias, bishop of Carthage, was their only consolation and support. He generously sold the gold and silver plate of the church to purchase the freedom of some, to alleviate the slavery of others, and to assist the wants and infirmities of a captive multitude, whose health was impaired by the hardships which they had suffered in the passage from Italy to Africa. By his order, two spacious churches were converted into hospitals: the sick were distributed in convenient beds, and liberally supplied with food and medicines; and the aged prelate repeated his visits both in the day and night, with an assiduity that surpassed his strength, and a tender sympathy which enhanced the value of his services.

Edward Gibbon (1737-1794), English historian, referring, in his work *The History of the Decline and Fall of the Roman Empire*, published from 1776 to1788 (chapter XXXVI), to the Vandals' sacking of Rome (June 15-29, 455), and its aftermath.

*Source:* Edward Gibbon, *The History of the Decline and Fall of the Roman Empire*, ed. William Smith, vol. IV (London: John Murray, 1862), pp. 256, 258 (reference to footnotes omitted).

*Explanations:* ▸ *Carthage:* an ancient city on the north coast of Africa (now a suburb of the city of Tunis). ▸ *Deogratias:* Deogratias (St. Deogratias) (d. 457), bishop of Carthage for the final three years of his life, who, after the Vandals' 455 sacking of Rome, helped the Roman captives in Carthage until his death. ▸ *Genseric:* Gaiseric (ca. 390-477), king of the Vandals (428-477), a Teutonic people of East Germanic stock who waged wars in Gaul, Spain, North Africa and Italy in the fourth and fifth centuries. ▸ *Leo* (fourth century-461): Leo I (St. Leo I) (ca. 400-461), Italian pope (440-461). ▸ *Ostia:* an ancient town and port southwest of Rome.

*Remark:* Rome and Carthage, courage and charity.

## 34 BLAME

The Tathâgata teaches that all warfare in which man tries to slay his brother is lamentable, but he does not teach that those who go to war in a righteous cause after having exhausted all means to preserve the peace are blameworthy. He must be blamed who is the cause of war.

Buddha (the Enlightened One), Gautama Buddha (Siddhartha Gautama) (ca. 563-ca. 483 B.C.), Indian prince, born in the district Nepal, founder of Buddhism, answering General Simha's question concerning annihilation.

*Source:* Paul Carus, *The Gospel of Buddha according to Old Records*, 12th ed. (Chicago: Open Court Publishing Co., 1909), pp. 124, 127 (chapter LI [51], "Simha's Question concerning Annihilation," verse 17).

*Explanation: Tathâgata* (Tathagata): the Perfect One (Buddha); *same source*, pp. 17, 34.

*Remark:* When has one "exhausted all means to preserve the peace"?

## 35 BLESSING

[I]n the face of the universal consent that peace is the first of blessings, how can we refuse to make it amongst ourselves; or do you not think that the good which you have, and the ills that you complain of, would be better preserved and cured by quiet than by war; that peace has its honours and splendours of a less perilous kind, not to mention the numerous other blessings that one might dilate on, with the not less numerous miseries of war? These considerations should teach you not to disregard my words, but rather to look in them every one for his own safety. If there be any here who feels certain either by right or might to effect his object, let not this surprise be to him too severe a disappointment. Let him remember that many before now have tried to chastise a wrongdoer, and failing to punish their enemy have not even saved themselves; while many who have trusted in force to gain an advantage, instead of gaining anything more, have been doomed to lose what they had. Vengeance is not necessarily successful because wrong has been done, or strength sure because it is confident; but the incalculable element in the future exercises the widest influence, and is the most treacherous, and yet in fact the most useful of all things, as it frightens us all equally, and thus makes us consider before attacking each other.

Hermocrates (ca. 460-ca. 407 B.C.), political leader in the city of Syracuse, Sicily, addressing an assembly of Sicilians in the town Gela in 424 B.C., according to Thucydides (ca. 460-ca. 400 B.C.), Greek historian, in his work *The History of the Peloponnesian War* (book IV, chapter XIII, section 62).

*Source:* Thucydides, *History of the Peloponnesian War*, trans. Richard Crawley, Everyman's Library (1910; reprint, London: J. M. Dent & Sons; New York: E. P. Dutton & Co., 1929), p. 285.

*Explanation: The Peloponnesian War:* a war mainly between Athens and Sparta (Lacedaemon), fought intermittently from 431 to 404 B.C., with Syracuse and other Sicilian cities being involved, and in which the Spartans (Lacedaemonians) finally defeated the Athenians. The war is named after Peloponnese or Peloponnesus, a peninsula in southern Greece.

## 36 BOOK

Certain features of Tolstoy's realism were ... well developed long before he began writing *War and Peace*, the epic work on the Napoleonic invasion of 1812 which occupied the next seven years and brought him lasting international fame....

....

The novel grew like Topsy, and did not even receive its present title until 1865. It exists now in four volumes with two epilogues. The first volume covers approximately the six months from June to late November 1805; the second volume as many years, from 1806 to 1811. The final two volumes deal with the climactic events of 1812, culminating in the battle of Borodino, the burning of Moscow and the French retreat. The first epilogue carries the story forward to approximately 1820 and ties certain knots; the second epilogue develops Tolstoy's theory of history, based largely on the preceding fiction....

....

The greatness of *War and Peace* lies in the very multiplicity of its many locales, characters and viewpoints, in its boldness as a fiction that makes experience of the past more realistic than any historical record, and in its power totally to absorb the reader in a range of emotions and ideas without parallel in earlier historical novels. The true merit of its achievement is that it has become a benchmark of greatness for historical fiction in any language since its time.

Description by Richard Freeborn (Richard Harry Freeborn) (b. 1926), Welsh-born British professor emeritus of Russian literature, writer and translator, of *War and Peace*, the masterpiece of the Russian novelist and moral philosopher Leo Tolstoy (Lev (Lyev) Nikolayevich Tolstoy), Count Tolstoy (1828-1910), a novel written between 1863 and 1869 according to the *Great Soviet Encyclopedia*.

*Source:* Richard Freeborn, "The Nineteenth Century: The Age of Realism, 1855-80," in *The Cambridge History of Russian Literature*, Charles A. Moser, ed. (Cambridge: Cambridge University Press, 1989), pp. 248, 299-300, 303.

*Explanations:* ▶ *Borodino:* a Russian village, 70 miles (113 kilometers) west-southwest of Moscow, the site of the Battle of Borodino on September 7, 1812, wherein the French and the Russians both claimed victory. ▶ *Napoleonic invasion:* the invasion of Russia in 1812 by Napoleon I (Napoleon Bonaparte) (1769-1821), emperor of France (1804-1814, 1815), an invasion ending in defeat.

*See* Battlefield (the 1812 road from Moscow to the frontier).

*Remark:* Is history more unbelievable than fiction can ever be?

## 37 BOOK

This story of a tragic love affair is set on the Italian front during World War I. Hemingway tells his tale with an abundance of realistic detail. Rather than a celebration of the "Triumph of victory and the agony of defeat," the author's vision is uncompromisingly disillusioned. Not only is war useless, but efforts to maintain any meaningful relationship with individuals in the modern world are equally doomed.

Frank N. Magill (Frank Northen Magill) (1907-1997), American educator, editor and writer, referring, in 1989, to the 1929 novel *A Farewell to Arms* by the American novelist and short-story writer Ernest Hemingway (Ernest Miller Hemingway) (1899-1961), recipient of the 1954 Nobel Prize in Literature.

*Source:* Frank N. Magill, ed., *Masterpieces of World Literature* (New York: HarperCollins Publishers, 1989), p. 295, 295 (italics omitted).

*Notes:* ▸ "His fame as a novelist was consolidated by *A Farewell to Arms* (1929) which incarnated his sense of war's immorality through the tragic story of a U.S. officer and a British nurse in wartime Italy and neutral Switzerland."

(*Encyclopœdia Britannica* (1964), under "Hemingway, Ernest Miller")

▸ Hemingway received the 1954 Nobel Prize in Literature "for his powerful mastery of the art of storytelling, most recently displayed in *The Old Man and the Sea*, and for his influence on contemporary style." Horst Frenz, ed., *Nobel Lectures Including Presentation Speeches and Laureates' Biographies: Literature, 1901-1967* (Amsterdam: Elsevier Publishing Company, for the Nobel Foundation, 1969), p. 496 (typeface changed).

*Remark:* Is war useless? Is war hell? Why do some people want to go to hell?

## 38 BOOK TITLE
*'Who's Living in My House?'*

Title of a 1997 publication of Amnesty International, recipient of the 1977 Nobel Peace Prize, relating to the aftermath of the war in Bosnia and Herzegovina (1992-1995) where, at the end of 1994, more than two million people, or over half of the inhabitants, had been driven from their homes, partly as a result of "ethnic cleansing."

*Source:* Amnesty International, *'Who's Living in My House?': Obstacles to the Safe Return of Refugees and Internally Displaced People* (New York: Amnesty International USA, 1997).

*See* Blessing ("Peace is the first of blessings.") and Civil war (Lyn Harrington, on the Greek Civil War).

## 39 BRIDGE
The Japanese never took anti-submarine warfare as seriously as the Allies, a fact which served to increase their vulnerability, which was in any case enormous because they could draw on the resources of the great empire they had conquered practically only by sea transport. Similarly, they could supply and reinforce their now far-flung garrisons only by using the sea routes, a point already mentioned in connection with their employment of submarines for this purpose. It is true that they attempted to reduce their vulnerability by drastic measures. The construction of the notorious railway from Thailand to Burma—the railway of "The Bridge on the River Kwai"—which cost the lives of tens of thousands of civilians and prisoners of war, was a part of the effort to create alternative methods of transportation.

Gerhard L. Weinberg (Gerhard Ludwig Weinberg) (b. 1928), German-born American professor of history, spotlighting, in his 1994 work *A World at Arms*, the forced-labor construction of a railway between Burma (now Myanmar) and Thailand in World War II (a bridge over the River Kwai being built mostly in the latter half of 1943 and destroyed in June 1945).

*Source:* Gerhard L. Weinberg, *A World at Arms: A Global History of World War II* (1994; reprint, Cambridge: Cambridge University Press, 1994), p. 391.

*Notes:*  ▸  To be more exact, "16,000 out of 46,000 prisoners of war and 60,000 out of 150,000 Asian forced laborers died"; *same source*, p. 1080 (footnote no. 119).

▸  Pierre Boulle (Pierre François Marie-Louis Boulle) (1912-1994), French novelist and screenwriter, wrote a book on the building of the bridge, *Le pont de la rivière Kwaï*, published in French in 1952, and in English in 1954, as *The Bridge on the River Kwai*. In 1957 an award-winning film, *The Bridge on the River Kwai*, directed by the English director and screenwriter David Lean (1908-1991), was released.

*Remark:* One little footnote, so many tragedies.


### 40 BROTHERHOOD

Senegal, like thee, like all our heroes,
We will be stern without hatred, and with open arms.
The sword we will put peacefully in its sheath,
For work and words will be our weapon.
The Bantu is our brother, the Arab, and the
White man too.


From the national anthem of Senegal adopted in 1960 on the occasion of the country's independence that year, lyrics by Léopold Sédar Senghor (1906-2001), Senegalese poet, philosopher, scholar and statesman, president of Senegal (1960-1980).

*Source:* W. L. Reed and M. J. Bristow, eds., *National Anthems of the World*, 6th ed. (1985; reprint, Poole, Dorset, England: Blandford Press, 1986), pp. 383, 386 (translator of the anthem: Elizabeth P. Coleman).

*Explanation: Bantu:* Black Africans speaking the Bantu language, the tribes of which are found in eastern, central and southern Africa.


### 41 CANAL

The Suez Maritime Canal shall always be free and open, in time of war as in time of peace, to every vessel of commerce or of war, without distinction of flag.

Consequently, the High Contracting Parties agree not in any way to interfere with the free use of the Canal, in time of war as in time of peace.

The Canal shall never be subjected to the exercise of the right of blockade.


Article I of the Convention between Great Britain, Germany, Austria-Hungary, Spain, France, Italy, the Netherlands, Russia, and Turkey, respecting the Free Navigation of the Suez Maritime Canal, which was signed at Constantinople on October 29, 1888, and entered into force on December 22, 1888.

*Source: Parliamentary Papers*, C. 5623 (1889), p. 5 (translation).

*Explanation: The Suez Maritime Canal:* an about 100-mile (160-kilometer) long artificial waterway traversing Egypt, connecting the Mediterranean Sea and the Red Sea.

*Note:* The following explanation can be found in D. A. Farnie, *East and West of Suez: The Suez Canal in History, 1854-1956* (Oxford: Clarendon Press, 1969), p. 337:

The Convention of Constantinople was signed on 29 October 1888 to regulate the passage through the Canal of warships and not of merchant vessels. In its first and primary article it proclaimed absolute freedom of transit through the Canal.

## 42 CARE

The sun on the twenty-fifth of June, 1859, shines above one of the most frightful sights imaginable. The battlefield is everywhere covered with corpses of men and horses. They appear as if sown along the roads, in the hollows, the thickets and the fields, above all, near the village of Solferino.

....

Those who cross this vast field of yesterday's battle meet at every step, in the midst of a confusion without parallel, inexpressible despair and suffering of every kind.

....

.... Unfortunately, it is possible that, because of the unavoidable rapidity in this labor, and because of the carelessness and inattention of the paid workmen, more than one living man is buried with the dead.

....

Then, melancholy scenes occur. There is water; there is food; and nevertheless the wounded are dying of hunger and thirst....

....

"Ah, sir, how I suffer!" say to me some of these poor fellows. "We are abandoned, left to die miserably, and yet we fought bravely!"...

....

An old sergeant, decorated with many chevrons, repeated with profound melancholy and an air of conviction full of bitterness; "If some one had cared for me sooner, I should have lived, whereas, this evening I will die." That evening he died.

....

.... Recognizing me, they stopped to express their gratitude because I had nursed them in Castiglione. "We called you 'the gentleman in white,'" said one, in his picturesqe language, "for you were always dressed entirely in white...."

....

The women of Castiglione, seeing that I make no distinction in nationality, imitate my example, showing the same kindness to all these men of such different origin and who are to them all equally strangers....

....

The battle of Solferino is the only one during our century to be compared by the magnitude of its losses with the battles of Moscow, Leipzig and Waterloo.

As a consequence of the twenty-fourth of June, 1859, it has been calculated that there were in killed and wounded, in the Austrian and Franco-Sardinian Armies, three field-marshals, nine generals, fifteen hundred and sixty-six officers of all grades, of whom six hundred and thirty were Austrians and nine hundred and thirty-six allies, and about forty thousand soldiers and non-commissioned officers.

....

If one does not consider the military point of view, the battle of Solferino was then, from the point of humanity a European catastrophe.

....

Would it not be possible to establish in every country of Europe, Aid Societies, whose aim would be to provide, during war, volunteer nurses for the wounded, without distinction of nationality?

Jean Henri Dunant (1828-1910), Swiss humanitarian, writing, in his 1862 book *Un Souvenir de Solferino* (English, *A Memory of Solferino*), on the Battle of Solferino, northern Italy, on June 24, 1859. Approximately 300,000 men total fought there, on the one hand, the army of Austria, commanded by Francis Joseph I (1830-1916), emperor of Austria (1848-1916), and, on the other hand, the victorious Franco-Sardinian armies, under Napoleon III (Charles Louis Napoleon Bonaparte) (1808-1873), emperor of France (1852-1870), and Victor Emmanuel II (1820-1878), king of Sardinia (1849-1861; king of Italy 1861-1878). The casualties were nearly 40,000 men.

*Source:* Henri Dunant, *The Origin of the Red Cross: "Un Souvenir de Solferino,"* trans. Mrs. David H. Wright [Anna B. Heylin Wright] (Philadelphia: John C. Winston Co., 1911), pp. 15, 17, 21, 26-27, 30, 36, 38, 40, 69-70, 71, 78.

*Notes:* ▸ "The allied army is in possession of the conquered field." *Same source*, p. 13.

▸ Dunant promoted the founding of the International Committee for the Relief of the Wounded in 1863 (now the International Committee of the Red Cross) and received the first Nobel Peace Prize in 1901 along with Frédéric Passy (1822-1912), French economist, founder and president of the first French peace society.

▸ "Henri Dunant has decreased the abomination of war; Frederick Passy fought to make it impossible." *Same source*, p. x (preface), quoting Signor Ruyssin in the review *Peace by Right*.

*Remark:* "Victorious armies?" It was Dunant's and mankind's victory.

## 43 CAUSE

Who was the cause of a long ten years war,
And laid at last old Troy in ashes? Woman!

Thomas Otway (1652-1685), English dramatist, referring to the Trojan War (ca. 1200 B.C.) in his tragic masterpiece *The Orphan, or The Unhappy Marriage*, produced in 1680 (act III, scene I; Castalio speaking to Ernesto).

*Source: The British Drama; Comprehending the Best Plays in the English Language*, vol. I, part I, *Tragedies* (London: William Miller, 1804), pp. 217, 232.

*Explanation: Troy:* a city in northwestern Asia Minor (now Turkey) where the Trojan War was fought about 1200 B.C.

*Note:* Who was this woman, Helen? "She was a daughter of Tyndareus, King of Sparta, who once, while sacrificing to the gods, entirely forgot Aphrodite. To punish him the angry goddess decreed that his daughters should be repeatedly unfaithful to their husbands, and should bring disaster and sudden death upon any other men who loved them." John Erskine, *The Private Life of Helen of Troy* (Indianapolis, New York: Bobbs-Merrill Company, 1947) (preface).

*Additional explanation: Aphrodite:* Greek goddess of love, beauty and fertility.

## 44 CAUSE

[A] European War broke out. Why? Because in each country political and military leaders did certain things, which led to mobilizations and declarations of war, or failed to do certain things which might have prevented them. In this sense, all the European countries, in a greater or less degree, were responsible. One must abandon the dictum of the Versailles Treaty that Germany and her allies were solely responsible. It was a dictum exacted by victors from vanquished, under the influence of the blindness, ignorance, hatred, and the propagandist misconceptions to which war had given rise. It was based on evidence which was incomplete and not always sound. It is generally recognized by the best historical scholars in all countries to be no longer tenable or defensible. They are agreed that the responsibility for the War is a divided responsibility. But they still disagree very much as to the relative part of this responsibility that falls on each country and on each individual political or military leader.

Sidney Bradshaw Fay (1876-1967), American educator, professor of modern European history, writing, in his 1928 book, on the origins of World War I which broke out in 1914.

*Source:* Sidney Bradshaw Fay, *The Origins of the World War*, vol. II, *After Sarajevo: Immediate Causes of the War* (New York: Macmillan Company, 1928), pp. 548-549 (reference to footnote omitted).

*Explanation: Versailles Treaty:* Treaty of Versailles, a treaty of peace after World War I, between the Allied and Associated Powers and Germany, which was signed at Versailles, a town near Paris, on June 28, 1919, and entered into force on January 10, 1920. The United States signed but did not become a party to the treaty.

*Remark:* Complicated causes (a book of 1,100 pages on the origins of one war in history).

## 45 CHANCE

[W]ar is full of unpleasant surprises.

Winston S. Churchill (Winston Leonard Spencer Churchill) (1874-1965), British statesman, orator and author, prime minister of the United Kingdom (1940-1945 and 1951-1955), in his speech on the situation early in World War II, given to the House of Commons on October 8, 1940.

*Source: Parliamentary Debates*, Commons, 5th series, vol. 365, pp. 289, 290.

## 46 CHEMICAL WARFARE

The States Parties to this Convention,

....

*Recalling* that the General Assembly of the United Nations has repeatedly condemned all actions contrary to the principles and objectives of the Protocol for the Prohibition of the Use in War of Asphyxiating, Poisonous or Other Gases, and of Bacteriological Methods of Warfare, signed at Geneva on 17 June 1925 (the Geneva Protocol of 1925),

*Recognizing* that this Convention reaffirms principles and objectives of and obligations assumed under the Geneva Protocol of 1925, and the Convention on the Prohibition of the Development, Production and Stockpiling of Bacteriological (Biological) and Toxin Weapons and on their Destruction signed at London, Moscow and Washington on 10 April 1972,

....

*Determined* for the sake of all mankind, to exclude completely the possibility of the use of chemical weapons, through the implementation of the provisions of this Convention, thereby complementing the obligations assumed under the Geneva Protocol of 1925,

*Recognizing* the prohibition, embodied in the pertinent agreements and relevant principles of international law, of the use of herbicides as a method of warfare,

*Considering* that achievements in the field of chemistry should be used exclusively for the benefit of mankind,

....

*Have agreed* as follows:

ARTICLE I
GENERAL OBLIGATIONS

1. Each State Party to this Convention undertakes never under any circumstances:

....

(b) To use chemical weapons.

From the preamble to and Article I of the Convention on the Prohibition of the Development, Production, Stockpiling and Use of Chemical Weapons and on Their Destruction (the Chemical Weapons Convention), which was opened for signature at Paris on January 13, 1993, and entered into force on April 29, 1997.

*Source:* United Nations, *Treaty Series*, vol. 1974, pp. 45, 317-319 (underlining replaced by italics; reference to footnotes omitted; semicolon replaced by period at the end).

*Note:* Among the parties to the Chemical Weapons Convention are China, France, the Russian Federation, the United Kingdom and the United States.

### 47 CHILD

Perhaps 3 million of the 9 million men killed in the war left widows behind. If British figures are an indication of the approximate size of their young families, each widow had two small children to look after. Six million children were deprived of their fathers by the Great War. How did they mourn and what became of them?

Jay Winter (Jay Murray Winter) (b. 1945), American lecturer of history, writing on World War I orphans in his 1995 book *Sites of Memory, Sites of Mourning*.

*Source:* Jay Winter, *Sites of Memory, Sites of Mourning: The Great War in European Cultural History*, Studies in the Social and Cultural History of Modern Warfare (Cambridge: Cambridge University Press, 1995), p. 46 (reference to footnote omitted).

### 48 CHILD

Most of the casualties are children. A million die. Another million are saved by the airlift of food and medicine to Biafra. Politicians and officialdom are enraged as ordinary people support this bunch of 'meddling missionaries' and 'do-gooders'.

Biafra was the first TV war. Ordinary people were horrified at what they saw. They dug deep into their pockets to support the airlift to alleviate the suffering of the children whose starving faces they had seen in their own sitting-rooms. Relief organisations like Concern were formed and continue to do great work today. The Nigerians responded in generosity later, welcoming the defeated Biafrans back. There was no genocide, no war-crimes trials, no revenge.

From the back cover of *Airlift to Biafra*, on the Nigerian Civil War (1967-1970).

*Source:* Tony Byrne, *Airlift to Biafra: Breaching the Blockade* (Dublin: Columba Press, 1997), back cover (paragraphs indented).

*Explanation: Concern:* an international relief organization, with headquarters in Dublin, originating from famine relief in the Nigerian Civil War.

*Notes:* ▶ The following description is given of the last relief flight to Biafra, on January 11, 1970, at the end of the civil war:

Later that day, Fr Tom Cunningham flew with Captain Johnsonn and an Icelandic crew in a spirited attempt to use an airstrip at Ugah to get in further medical supplies. The facilities were poor and they had just unloaded their cargo when the Nigerian forces began to overrun the airstrip. In the ensuing panic, soldiers and civilians scrambled on board the JCA aircraft. Johnsonn had to take off in a hurry, with the cargo door still open, as the plane was hit repeatedly by machine-gun fire. The door sheared off in mid-flight, adding to the fear in the crowded plane. They were lucky to get back to São Tomé, at all.

That was the last JCA flight.

(*Same source*, p. 191 (epilogue))

▶ Michael Crowder (1934-1988), British historian, educator, editor and author, born in England, has written:

A number of factors account for the length of the resistance by the secessionist forces. In the first place they firmly believed the propaganda so effectively disseminated by the Biafra government, and spread by overseas sympathizers, that the Federal troops were intent on genocide. They had, of course, the bitter experience of the massacres in the North to give conviction to them, so that they fought to the last ditch and with people starving for want of food supplies rather than come under Federal control.

(Michael Crowder, *The Story of Nigeria*, 4th ed. rev. (London: Faber and Faber, 1978), pp. 273, 276)

*Additional explanations:* ▶ *Fr Tom Cunningham:* Father Thomas Cunningham, Irish missionary priest (b. 1929). ▶ *JCA:* Joint Church Aid, a title used for the cooperation of, among others, the mainly Protestant World Council of Churches and the Catholic Caritas Internationalis. ▶ *Johnsonn:* Thorsteinn Elton Jónsson (1921-2001), Icelandic pilot, volunteer fighter pilot for the Royal Air Force in the United Kingdom in World War II (he was one of three to survive out of a class of thirty-one, which reminds one of the novel *All Quiet on the Western Front*). ▶ *São Tomé:* a Portuguese colony in central Africa which became independent in 1975 (Democratic Republic of São Tomé and Príncipe).

*See* Achievement (Tommy Lapid, on Raoul Wallenberg's rescue of Jews in Budapest in 1944).

*Remark:* Great work.

## 49 CHILD

Count out 60 seconds and 30 of the world's children will have died for lack of food and adequate health care. Count out another 60 seconds: in this short space of time, the world will have spent $1.4 million on its military.

Norman Myers (b. 1934), English environmental scientist, conservationist, writer and photographer, writing about the cost of militarism in the 1984 book *Gaia*.

*Source:* Norman Myers, Uma Ram Nath and Melvin Westlake, *Gaia: An Atlas of Planet Management*, Norman Myers, gen. ed. (Garden City, New York: Anchor Press/Doubleday and Company, 1984), p. 246.

*Remark:* A question of priorities.

### 50 CHRISTIANITY

Far from being the pious injunction of a Utopian dreamer, the command to love one's enemy is an absolute necessity for our survival. Love even for enemies is the key to the solution of the problems of our world. Jesus is not an impractical idealist; he is the practical realist.

Martin Luther King (1929-1968), American clergyman and civil rights leader, in his sermon "Loving Your Enemies," written while jailed in Georgia, United States, rewritten "for the eye" and published in 1963.

*Source:* Martin Luther King, Jr., *Strength to Love* (New York: Harper & Row, Publishers, 1963), p. 34, 34, cf. pp. ix-x.

*Note:* King received the 1964 Nobel Peace Prize.

### 51 CITY

**CHIMAY, COUNT OF.** Governor of Luxembourg who surrendered Luxembourg to the French in 1684 after the city had sustained a bombardment that destroyed all but ten of the 450 houses in the city.

*Historical Dictionary of Luxembourg*, referring to a French attack on the city of Luxembourg in 1684.

*Source:* Harry C. Barteau, *Historical Dictionary of Luxembourg*, European Historical Dictionaries (Lanham, Maryland: Scarecrow Press, 1996), p. 61 (beginning indented).

*Explanation: Chimay:* a town in southern Belgium.

*Note:* The old quarters and fortifications of the city of Luxembourg are on the World Heritage List.

*Remark:* A tale of one city.

### 52 CIVILIAN

*Article 50.* Definition of civilians and civilian population....

....

3. The presence within the civilian population of individuals who do not come within the definition of civilians does not deprive the population of its civilian character.

*Article 51.* Protection of the civilian population....

2. The civilian population as such, as well as individual civilians, shall not be the object of attack. Acts or threats of violence the primary purpose of which is to spread terror among the civilian population are prohibited.

....

4. Indiscriminate attacks are prohibited. Indiscriminate attacks are:

(a) Those which are not directed at a specific military objective;

....

6. Attacks against the civilian population or civilians by way of reprisals are prohibited.

7. The presence or movements of the civilian population or individual civilians shall not be used to render certain points or areas immune from military operations, in particular in attempts to shield military objectives from attacks or to shield, favour or impede military operations. The Parties to the conflict shall not direct the movement of the civilian population or individual civilians in order to attempt to shield military objectives from attacks or to shield military operations.

....

*Article 52.* GENERAL PROTECTION OF CIVILIAN OBJECTS. 1. Civilian objects shall not be the object of attack or of reprisals....

....

*Article 54.* PROTECTION OF OBJECTS INDISPENSABLE TO THE SURVIVAL OF THE CIVILIAN POPULATION. 1. Starvation of civilians as a method of warfare is prohibited.

....

*Article 57.* PRECAUTIONS IN ATTACK. 1. In the conduct of military operations, constant care shall be taken to spare the civilian population, civilians and civilian objects.

From certain articles of the Protocol Additional to the Geneva Conventions of 12 August 1949, and Relating to the Protection of Victims of International Armed Conflicts (Protocol I), which was adopted at Geneva on June 8, 1977, and entered into force on December 7, 1978.

*Source:* United Nations, *Treaty Series*, vol. 1125, pp. 3, 26-27, 29.

*Remark:* To be civilized, to spare civilians.

## 53 CIVIL WAR

[T]here are two kinds of war,—one which is universally called civil war, and is, as we were just now saying, of all wars the worst; the other, as we should all admit, in which we fall out with other nations who are of a different race, is a far milder form of warfare.

Plato (428 or 427-348 or 347 B.C.), Greek philosopher, in his dialogue *Laws*, supposedly composed in his later years (book I, section 629; an Athenian stranger speaking to Cleinias, a Cretan, and to Megillus, a Lacedaemonian (Spartan)).

*Source:* Plato, *The Dialogues of Plato*, trans. B. Jowett, 2nd ed. rev., vol. V (Oxford: Clarendon Press, 1875), pp. 1, 193, 198.

*See* Civil war (Lyn Harrington, on Greece) and Book title (*Who's Living in My House?*, on Bosnia and Herzegovina).

## 54 CIVIL WAR

Before the civil war ended, 700,000 Greeks—a tenth of the population—were homeless....

....

*Pantanassa Church and convent at Mistra is the only inhabited building of a city which once numbered 40,000. The ruins sheltered the homeless during the civil war*

Lyn Harrington (Evelyn Davis Harrington) (b. 1911), Canadian freelance writer and librarian, writing, in her book, *Greece & the Greeks*, originally published in 1962, on the Greek Civil War (December 1944-January 1945 and 1946-1949).
*Source:* Lyn Harrington, *Greece & the Greeks*, rev. ed. (Camden, New Jersey: Thomas Nelson & Sons, 1968), p. 143.
*Explanation: Mistra (Misithra):* a city on the outskirts of Sparta, on the Peloponnesian peninsula of southern Greece.

## 55 COLD

From all this it was apparent that the Russians were waging a war of extermination; and yet Napoleon, from some unaccountable delusion, suffered himself to be decoyed, by the artfully sustained hopes of a peace, into remaining thirty-four days in Moscow without perceiving that Kutusoff was seeking to detain him till the commencement of winter, that during the retreat the cold might destroy the half-clad soldiers, who were suffering from want of the necessaries of life. At length, late in October, was commenced that fatal retreat of the grand army, which has no parallel in the history of the sufferings of war.... Who can describe all the sufferings, battles, and fatigues, by which the grand army was gradually destroyed in the midst of the stern winter? Hunger, cold, and exhaustion produced greater ravages than the bullets of the Russians or the lances of the Cossacks. It was a horrible sight to see thousands of starved or frozen soldiers lying in the public roads, or on the desolate steppes covered with snow and ice, intermingled with fallen horses, abandoned arms, and rich articles of plunder.... After the passage of the Beresina, Napoleon had still 8,000 soldiers fit for service. Ney was the last man of the rearguard. According to the official account, 243,600 enemies' bodies were buried in Russia. Half of Europe had cause to mourn. On the 3d of December, Napoleon published the celebrated 29th bulletin, which informed the expectant people, who had been without intelligence for months, that the emperor was safe and the grand army destroyed.

Georg Weber (1808-1888), German historian and educator, writing, in his book *Outlines of Universal History*, first published in German in 1851 (*Weltgeschichte in übersichtlicher Darstellung*), on the 1812 retreat from Moscow of Napoleon I (Napoleon Bonaparte) (1769-1821), emperor of France (1804-1814, 1815).
*Source:* George Weber, *Outlines of Universal History, from the Creation of the World to the Present Time*, trans. M. Behr, rev. Francis Bowen, 6th ed. (Boston: Hickling, Swan and Brown, 1856), pp. 458-459.
*Explanations:* ▸ *Beresina:* Berezina, a Belorussian (now Belarusian) river, tributary of the Dnieper River. ▸ *Kutusoff:* Mikhail Illarionovich Kutuzov (Mikhail Illarionovich Golenishchev-Kutuzov) (1745-1813), Russian field-marshal. ▸ *Ney:* Michel Ney (1769-1815), French commander.

## 56 COLONIALISM

With the object of getting as much as possible out of its colony, the Portuguese Crown involves Brazil in a network of laws which strangle the young country's powerful arteries of world trade. For instance, just in this land where cotton grows naturally and in abundance, the government prohibits the manufacture of textile goods, so as to force Brazil to order its finished products from Lisbon. Such prohibitions grow increasingly stupid and unreasonable. In 1775, in fact, a decree forbids the production of soap and the distillation of native alcohol, to force the consumers to drink more Portuguese wine. The governor denies entrance to his palace to anyone wearing clothes not made of Portuguese material. The country, which has already a population of two and a half million inhabitants, is being forbidden to plant rice. In the century of philosophy and enlightenment, the cities are denied the right to print newspapers and books. No Brazilian is allowed to buy a foreign ship. No foreigner may live in Rio, and hardly a soul is allowed to land there. Brazil is being closed off like the King of Portugal's private gardens. Even in the nineteenth century, when Humboldt wants to enter the country in order to write his famous account, which really discovers Brazil for the world, the officials receive secret orders to make all possible difficulties on the arrival of "a certain Baron Humboldt."

Stefan Zweig (1881-1942), Austrian writer who became British citizen, describing Portuguese colonialism in his book on Brazil, published in German in 1941 and in English the following year.

*Source:* Stefan Zweig, *Brazil: Land of the Future*, trans. Andrew St. James [pseudonym for James Andrew Stern] (London: Cassell and Company, 1942), p. 62.

*Explanation: Humboldt:* Alexander, Baron von [baron of] Humboldt (Friedrich Heinrich Alexander, Baron von Humboldt) (1769-1859), German explorer and scientist who explored Central and South America from 1799 to 1804.

*Remark:* Imaginative colonialists.

### 57 COMMANDER

Thus far have we followed Cæsar's actions before the wars of Gaul. After this, he seems to begin his course afresh, and to enter upon a new life and scene of action. And the period of those wars which he now fought, and those many expeditions in which he subdued Gaul, showed him to be a soldier and general not in the least inferior to any of the greatest and most admired commanders who had ever appeared at the head of armies. For if we compare him with the Fabii, the Metelli, the Scipios, and with those who were his contemporaries, or not long before him, Sylla, Marius, the two Luculli, or even Pompey himself, whose glory, it may be said, went up at that time to heaven for every excellence in war, we shall find Cæsar's actions to have surpassed them all. One he may be held to have outdone in consideration of the difficulty of the country in which he fought, another in the extent of territory which he conquered; some, in the number and strength of the enemy whom he defeated; one man, because of the wildness and perfidiousness of the tribes whose good-will he conciliated, another in his humanity and clemency to those he overpowered; others, again, in his gifts and kindnesses to his soldiers; all alike in the number of the battles which he fought and the enemies whom he killed. For he had not pursued the wars in Gaul full ten years when he had taken by storm above eight hundred towns, subdued three hundred states, and of the three millions of men, who made up the gross sum of those with whom at several times he engaged, he had killed one million and taken captive a second.

Plutarch (ca. 46-120), Greek biographer, referring, in his work *Parallel Lives* (the biography of Caesar), to the wars waged in Gaul (mainly present-day France and

Belgium) from 58 to 51 B.C. by the Roman general and statesman Julius Caesar (Gaius Julius Caesar) (100-44 B.C.), proconsul (governor) of Gaul from 58 to 49 B.C.

*Source:* Plutarch, *Plutarch's Lives: The "Dryden Plutarch,"* rev. Arthur Hugh Clough, Everyman's Library, vol. II (1910; reprint, London: J. M. Dent & Sons; New York: E. P. Dutton & Co., 1914), pp. 530, 541.

*Explanation: Pompey* (Gnaeus Pompeius Magnus) (106-48 B.C.): Roman general and statesman who, in 60 B.C., formed the First Triumvirate with Caesar and the Roman soldier and statesman Marcus Licinius Crassus (Marcus Licinius Crassus Dives) (ca. 115-53 B.C.), but was defeated by Caesar at Pharsalus (modern Phersala), Greece, in 48 B.C.

*See,* as for Caesar's capture of eight hundred towns, Temper (Solomon).

*Remark:* Some humanity!

### 58 COMMUNICATION

The correspondence between these two leaders was unique in a number of ways. It gave rise to the first informal written exchange between Cold War leaders. Its existence as a reliable, direct, and quick channel of communications was instrumental in avoiding international catastrophe during the Cuban missile crisis.

The United States Department of State, referring, in 1996, to the correspondence between John F. Kennedy (John Fitzgerald Kennedy) (1917-1963), president of the United States (1961-1963), and Nikita Khrushchev (Nikita Sergeyevich Khrushchev) (1894-1971), premier of the Soviet Union (1958-1964), during the October 1962 Cuban missile crisis.

*Source:* United States, Department of State, *Foreign Relations of the United States, 1961-1963,* vol. VI, *Kennedy-Khrushchev Exchanges* (Washington: United States Government Printing Office, 1996), p. x.

*Note:* Nikita Khrushchev, the Soviet political leader, who was born in Ukraine, within the Russian Empire, was first secretary of the Communist Party of the Soviet Union from 1953 to 1964.

*Remark:* Informal communication—one of the roads to peace.

### 59 COMPARISON

Peace maintains the farmer well, even on stony ground; war but ill, even upon the plain.

Menander (ca. 343 or 342-291 or 290 B.C.), Greek playwright.
*Source:* Menander, *Menander: The Principal Fragments,* trans. Francis G. Allinson [Francis Greenleaf Allinson] (1921; reprint, rev., London: William Heinemann; New York: G. P. Putnam's Sons, 1930), p. 527 (fragment no. 719 K).

### 60 COMPENSATION

A Party to the conflict which violates the provisions of the Conventions or of this Protocol shall, if the case demands, be liable to pay compensation. It shall be responsible for all acts committed by persons forming part of its armed forces.

Article 91 of the Protocol Additional to the Geneva Conventions of 12 August 1949, and Relating to the Protection of Victims of International Armed Conflicts

(Protocol I), which was adopted at Geneva on June 8, 1977, and entered into force on December 7, 1978.

*Source:* United Nations, *Treaty Series*, vol. 1125, pp. 3, 45.

*Remark:* Violator pays.

### 61 CONCENTRATION CAMP

Rudolf Höss's deposition and written reports contributed fresh information from a most authentic source.... His writings have made it possible to supplement the results of the inquiry, and to complete the picture of the planning and execution of the greatest crime in the history of mankind—a crime committed on Polish soil.

....

Of the 400,000 or so inmates registered at Oswiecim, only one-third survived. Millions of innocent people, never recorded in the camp files, arrived in drafts and perished at once in the Brzezinka gas chambers and crematoria. Altogether, some four million human beings met their death at Oswiecim.

The martyrdom and death of millions of victims in Nazi concentration camps constitute a warning to the whole of mankind against the danger of any ideology based on violence and war; they should stimulate every one of us to fight for a future wherein hatred and wars have no place, wherein friendship and peace shall reign among the nations.

Janusz Gumkowski (Janusz Stanislaw Gumkowski) (1905-1984), Russian-born Polish lawyer, director of The Chief Commission for the Investigation of Nazi Crimes in Poland, in a foreword to the 1957 book *Concentration Camp Oswiecim-Brzezinka (Auschwitz-Birkenau)*.

*Source:* Jan Sehn, *Concentration Camp Oswiecim-Brzezinka (Auschwitz-Birkenau)*, trans. Klemens Keplicz, The Chief Commission for the Investigation of Nazi Crimes in Poland (Warsaw: Wydawnictwo Prawnicze, 1957), pp. 5, 9 (Sehn's earlier writings on the subject in 1946 and 1955; *same source*, p. 5).

*Explanations:*  ▸ *Rudolf Höss:* Rudolf Höss (Rudolf Franz Ferdinand Höss) (1900-1947), German commandant (from May 1, 1940, to November 1943) of the Auschwitz (Auschwitz-Birkenau) concentration camp, operated by the German Nazis in the province of Cracow in southern Poland from 1940 to 1945. ▸ *Oswiecim:* Auschwitz (Auschwitz-Birkenau), the site of said concentration camp, now the site of a state museum.

*Notes:*  ▸ Höss was sentenced to death by the Supreme National Tribunal in Warsaw on April 2, 1947 (*same source*, p. 157), and hanged later that month, on April 16, in Auschwitz. ▸ Auschwitz-Birkenau is on the World Heritage List.

*Remark:* Four million human beings—at Auschwitz alone.

### 62 CONCENTRATION CAMP

*Lagerführer* M. Fritzsch used to greet the newcomers thus: "You have come to a concentration camp, not to a sanatorium, and there is only one way out—through the chimney. Any one who does not like it can try hanging himself on the wires. If there are Jews in this draft they have no right to live longer than a fortnight; if there are priests, their period is one month—the rest, three months".

Jan Sehn (1909-1965), Polish judge, writing, in his 1957 book *Concentration Camp Oswiecim-Brzezinka (Auschwitz-Birkenau)*, about the Auschwitz (Auschwitz-

Birkenau) concentration camp operated by the German Nazis in the province of Cracow in southern Poland from 1940 to 1945.

*Source:* Jan Sehn, *Concentration Camp Oswiecim-Brzezinka (Auschwitz-Birkenau)*, trans. Klemens Keplicz, The Chief Commission for the Investigation of Nazi Crimes in Poland (Warsaw: Wydawnictwo Prawnicze, 1957), p. 58 (Sehn's earlier writings on the subject in 1946 and 1955; *same source*, p. 5).

*Explanation: Karl Fritzsch* (1903-1945): German Nazi deputy commandant of Auschwitz (1940-1941); came from the Dachau camp, near Munich, Germany.

### 63 CONCENTRATION CAMP

The vast documentary evidence accumulated by the Soviet State Extraordinary Commission, and by the Chief Commission for the Investigation of Nazi Crimes in Poland, reveals that the Brzezinka gas chambers could exterminate some 60,000 people per twenty-four hours. The chambers were built especially for poisoning with cyclon B. Although they could easily be adapted to poisoning with other technical gases, this proved unnecessary because the simplest, strongest and quickest in effect was hydrogen cyanide, in its technical form called cyclon B.

Jan Sehn (1909-1965), Polish judge, writing, in his 1957 book *Concentration Camp Oswiecim-Brzezinka (Auschwitz-Birkenau)*, about the Auschwitz (Auschwitz-Birkenau) concentration camp operated by the German Nazis in the province of Cracow in southern Poland from 1940 to 1945.

*Source:* Jan Sehn, *Concentration Camp Oswiecim-Brzezinka (Auschwitz-Birkenau)*, trans. Klemens Keplicz, The Chief Commission for the Investigation of Nazi Crimes in Poland (Warsaw: Wydawnictwo Prawnicze, 1957), p. 125 (Sehn's earlier writings on the subject in 1946 and 1955; *same source*, p. 5).

*See* Prisoner of war (*Encyclopedia of the Holocaust:* "The method was thus found that would kill millions of people with minimal effort.").

*Remark:* Science or ethics, or both?

### 64 CONCENTRATION CAMP

It is estimated that 11 million civilians were killed in Hitler's gas ovens. By far the largest proportion consisted of 6 million Jews from all parts of Europe, but the ovens also claimed Poles, Russians, Gypsies, and others. Nothing in history can be compared to this gigantic effort to purge Europe of "inferior races." It remained for a Polish scholar, Raphael Lemkin, to invent the word "genocide" to describe it....

....

.... Hitler's opposition to Jews turned to fanatical hatred after his invasion of the Soviet Union in June 1941. In his mind the Jews were responsible not only for the ills of capitalism but also for communism. At the Wannsee Conference held on January 20, 1942, the course of action was completed. The meeting was attended by 15 leading Nazi bureaucrats, headed by Reinhard Heydrich ... who declared that he was the plenipotentiary "for the final solution of the Jewish question." While no documentary evidence implicates Hitler personally in the work of this conference, it is clear that nothing of its importance could have taken place in the Third Reich without his knowledge and support. The Wannsee Protocol stated: "In the course of the execution of the Final Solution, Europe will be combed from west to east."

....

The macabre procedure was used in countries occupied by Germans. Nearly 3 million Jews disappeared in conquered Poland. At least 2 million Jews from Austria, Hungary, Belgium, Holland, Czechoslovakia, Yugoslavia, France, and Greece were put to death in German extermination camps. A million more from occupied Russia and the Baltic states are believed to have suffered the same fate.

....

.... Although estimates vary, it is probable that at least 6 million Jews were annihilated in this Final Solution. The extermination campaign was unprecedented in history. European Jews found it difficult to escape from the planned industrialized murder. No identification with Nazism, no change of domicile inside Nazi Europe, seemed to help. Those who were sentenced to death without trial had committed the crime of having had Jewish grandparents. There had been violence against Jews for centuries, but nothing to compare with the Final Solution in magnitude and total configuration.

Louis L. Snyder (Louis Leo Snyder) (1907-1993), American historian, writing, in his 1982 book *Historical Guide to World War II*, on extermination camps and "the final solution of the Jewish question."

*Source:* Louis L. Snyder, *Louis L. Snyder's Historical Guide to World War II* (Westport, Connecticut: Greenwood Press, 1982), pp. 228, 236-237 (single quotation marks corrected to double ones after the word "genocide" in paragraph 1).

*Explanations:* ▶ *Final solution:* "Nazi plan to destroy the Jews of Europe"; *same source*, p. 235. ▶ *Genocide:* certain "acts committed with intent to destroy, in whole or in part, a national, ethnical, racial or religious group, as such." The definition in full is in Article II of the Convention on the Prevention and Punishment of the Crime of Genocide, which was annexed to resolution 260 (III) (Prevention and Punishment of the Crime of Genocide), adopted on December 9, 1948, by the General Assembly of the United Nations, and entered into force on January 12, 1951. For the text of the resolution and convention, see United Nations, *Resolutions, 21 September-12 December 1948* (General Assembly, Official Records: Third Session, Part I (A/810)), p. 174, 174. For the text of the convention, *see also* United Nations, *Treaty Series*, vol. 78, p. 277. *See also* Genocide (the full text of the definition). ▶ *Heydrich:* Reinhard Heydrich (Reinhard Tristan Eugen Heydrich) (1904-1942), German Nazi, deputy chief of the Secret State Police (Geheime Staatspolizei (Gestapo)), assassinated as Reich protector (governor) of Bohemia-Moravia (occupied Czechoslovakia) (assassination attempt on May 27, death on June 4, 1942). ▶ *Hitler:* Adolf Hitler (1889-1945), chancellor of the Third Reich of Nazi Germany (1933-1945). ▶ *Raphael Lemkin* (1900-1959): Polish-American lawyer and scholar, prosecutor in the trials of former German Nazi leaders before the International Military Tribunal in Nuremberg, Germany, 1945-1946. ▶ *Wannsee Conference:* a January 20, 1942 meeting of Nazi officials in a Berlin suburb, dealing with the final solution of the Jewish question.

*Remark:* "Jewish grandparents."

## 65 CONCILIATION

Orthodox dispute-processing scholarship postulates that conciliatory settlements are more desirable than legal judgments in small face-to-face societies....

William Ian Miller (b. 1946), American professor of law, in his 1990 book *Bloodtaking and Peacemaking*.

*Source:* William Ian Miller, *Bloodtaking and Peacemaking: Feud, Law, and Society in Saga Iceland* (Chicago: University of Chicago Press, 1990), p. 275.

*Remark:* Different situations, different solutions.

## 66 CONFERENCE

I am seriously afraid that the peace to which we are working is an impossible peace, conceived on a wrong basis; that it will not be accepted by Germany, and, even if accepted, that it will prove utterly unstable, and only serve to promote the anarchy which is rapidly overtaking Europe....

To my mind certain points seem quite clear and elementary:

1. We cannot destroy Germany without destroying Europe;

2. We cannot save Europe without the co-operation of Germany.

Yet we are now preparing a peace which must destroy Germany, and yet we think we shall save Europe by so doing! The fact is, the Germans are, have been, and will continue to be, the *dominant factor* on the Continent of Europe, and no permanent peace is possible which is not based on that fact. The statesmen of the Vienna Congress were wiser in their generation; they looked upon France as necessary to Europe. And yet we presume to look down upon them and their work! My fear is that the Paris Conference may prove one of the historic failures of the world;...

Jan Christiaan Smuts (1870-1950), South African soldier and statesman, minister of defense (1910-1920), later prime minister (1919-1924, 1939-1948), reflecting on the Treaty of Versailles, then under preparation after World War I, in a March 26, 1919 letter addressed to David Lloyd George (1863-1945), British statesman, prime minister from 1916 to 1922.

*Source:* [Jan Christiaan Smuts], *Selections from the Smuts Papers*, ed. W. K. Hancock and Jean van der Poel, vol. IV, *November 1918-August 1919* (Cambridge: Cambridge University Press, 1966), pp. 83, 83-84.

*Explanations:* ▶ *Treaty of Versailles*: a treaty of peace after World War I, between the Allied and Associated Powers and Germany, which was signed at Versailles, a town near Paris, on June 28, 1919, and entered into force on January 10, 1920. The United States signed but did not become a party to the treaty. ▶ *Vienna Congress*: the Congress of Vienna of 1814-1815 held at the end of the Napoleonic Wars (1800-1815). The wars followed the French Revolutionary Wars (1792-1799) and were waged mainly during the rule of Napoleon I (Napoleon Bonaparte) (1769-1821), emperor of France (1804-1814, 1815).

## 67 CONQUEROR

If one man conquers in battle a thousand times a thousand men, and if another conquer himself, he is the greatest of conquerors.

From *The Gospel of Buddha according to Old Records*, first published in 1894, chapter XLVIII [48], "The Dharmapada," verse 8.

*Source:* Paul Carus, *The Gospel of Buddha according to Old Records*, 12th ed. (Chicago: Open Court Publishing Co., 1909), p. 111, 111.

*Explanations:* ‣ *Buddha* (the Enlightened One): Gautama Buddha (Siddhartha Gautama) (ca. 563-ca. 483 B.C.), Indian prince, born in the district Nepal, founder of Buddhism. ‣ *The Dharmapada:* "the path of religion pursued by those who are Buddha's followers" ; *same place* (verse 1).
*See* Temper (Solomon).

### 68 CONQUEROR
A man like me does not count the lives of a million of men.

Napoleon I (Napoleon Bonaparte) (1769-1821), emperor of France (1804-1814, 1815), speaking to Austrian statesman and diplomat Clemens Wenzel Lothar, Prince Metternich-Winneburg (1773-1859), Austria's chancellor and foreign minister (1809-1848), at a June 26, 1813 meeting in Dresden, Germany.
*Source:* Napoleon, *The Corsican: A Diary of Napoleon's Life in His Own Words,* comp. R. M. Johnston [Robert Matteson Johnston] (London: Macmillan and Co., 1910), p. 389.
*Note:* Metternich advocated "balance of power" in Europe.
*See* Concentration camp (Louis L. Snyder, on the eleven million civilians killed in Hitler's gas ovens).
*Explanation: Hitler:* Adolf Hitler (1889-1945), chancellor of the Third Reich of Nazi Germany (1933-1945).

### 69 CONQUEROR
A conqueror is always a lover of peace (as Buonaparte always asserted of himself); he would like to make his entry into our state unopposed;...

Karl von Clausewitz (Karl Marie von Clausewitz) (1780-1831), Prussian general and military strategist, in his work *On War* (German, *Vom Kriege*), written from 1818 to 1830 and published posthumously in German in 1832 (book VI, chapter V).
*Source:* Carl von Clausewitz, *On War,* trans. J. J. Graham, three volumes in one, vol. II (London: N. Trübner & Co., 1873), p. 78.
*Explanation: Buonaparte:* Napoleon I (Napoleon Bonaparte) (1769-1821), emperor of France (1804-1814, 1815).
*Remark:* Some lovers of peace!

### 70 CONSCIENCE
*I will leap laughing to my grave, because the feeling that I have five million people on my conscience is for me a source of extraordinary satisfaction.*
    ....
Eichmann was satisfied with his own work. He had no sense of contrition. On one occasion, talking with a subordinate, he uttered words that accurately described his own character: "I'll die happily with the certainty of having killed almost six million Jews." At heart he preferred dead Jews to live ones.
    ....
.... The Eichmann hunter (*der Eichmann Jäger*) was not a trained gumshoe detective wise in the thousand ways a criminal could avoid capture, but a gifted amateur. Simon Wiesenthal, born in Polish Galicia, was of Jewish background and well-versed in the nature of the Nazi regime—he had spent four years in a series

of concentration camps. After the war he decided to devote his life to the task of retribution. He would search out the many Nazi criminals who had been successful in avoiding Allied attention and bring them to justice.

....

The trial took place from April 11 to August 14, 1961. Eichmann was charged with crimes against the Jewish people, crimes against humanity, and war crimes. The spectacle of the little man sitting in a glass cage for his own protection aroused worldwide attention. This was something unique in the history of jurisprudence.

....

Shortly after midnight on May 31, 1962, Adolf Eichmann mounted the gallows at Ramle....

....

Eichmann's body was cremated. The ashes were scattered in the Mediterranean—outside Israeli waters.

Louis L. Snyder (Louis Leo Snyder) (1907-1993), American historian, writing, in his 1989 book *Hitler's Elite*, on Adolf Eichmann (Karl Adolf Eichmann) (1906-1962), German Nazi official, head of section for the extermination of Jews in World War II, and specifically referring to Eichmann's words toward the end of the war.
*Source*: Louis L. Snyder, *Hitler's Elite: Biographical Sketches of Nazis Who Shaped the Third Reich* (New York: Hippocrene Books, 1989), pp. 217, 227, 228, 231, 232, 232, respectively (chapter 13: "Killer Adolf Eichmann").
*Explanations*: ▶ *Ramle* (Ramleh): a town, east of Jerusalem. ▶ *Simon Wiesenthal* (1908-2005): Jewish architect, born in Buczacz, Austria-Hungary (now Buchach, Ukraine), prisoner in Nazi concentration camps (1941-1943, 1944-1945), later Nazi hunter, founder and director of the Jewish Documentation Centre in Vienna.
*Notes*: ▶ In another source one may read of Eichmann's remark to a friend:
I will jump into my grave laughing because the fact that I have the deaths of five million Jews on my conscience gives me extraordinary satisfaction.
(John Bierman, *Righteous Gentile: The Story of Raoul Wallenberg, Missing Hero of the Holocaust* (New York: Viking Press, 1981), pp. 14-15)
▶ Kidnapped in Argentina, tried in Israel, found guilty of crimes against the Jewish people, crimes against humanity and war crimes, executed, died unrepentant.
*Remark*: Died unrepentant, unlike Judas.

## 71 CONSTITUTION
We, the Japanese people, acting through our duly elected representatives in the National Diet, determined that we shall secure for ourselves and our posterity the fruits of peaceful cooperation with all nations and the blessings of liberty throughout this land, and resolved that never again shall we be visited with the horrors of war through the action of government, do proclaim that sovereign power resides with the people and do firmly establish this Constitution....

We, the Japanese people, desire peace for all time and are deeply conscious of the high ideals controlling human relationship, and we have determined to preserve our security and existence, trusting in the justice and faith of the peace-loving peoples of the world. We desire to occupy an honoured place in an international society striving for the preservation of peace, and the banishment of tyranny and slavery, oppression and intolerance for all time from the earth. We recognize that all peoples of the world have the right to live in peace, free from fear and want.

We believe that no nation is responsible to itself alone, but that laws of political morality are universal; and that obedience to such laws is incumbent upon all nations who would sustain their own sovereignty and justify their sovereign relationship with other nations.

We, the Japanese people, pledge our national honour to accomplish these high ideals and purposes with all our resources.

....

### CHAPTER II. RENUNCIATION OF WAR

**ARTICLE 9.** Aspiring sincerely to an international peace based on justice and order, the Japanese people forever renounce war as a sovereign right of the nation and the threat or use of force as means of settling international disputes.

In order to accomplish the aim of the preceding paragraph, land, sea, and air forces, as well as other war potential, will never be maintained. The right of belligerency of the state will not be recognized.

The preamble to and Article 9 of the 1889 constitution of Japan, as revised after World War II, in effect from 1947.

*Source:* Albert P. Blaustein and Gisbert H. Flanz, eds., *Constitutions of the Countries of the World: Japan*, comps. [Japan] T. S. Y. Lee and Osamu Nishi (Dobbs Ferry, New York: Oceana Publications, 1990), pp. 15, 15-16.

*Explanation: The National Diet:* the Japanese parliament.

*Note:* In his Nobel lecture, "The Pursuit of Peace and Japan in the Nuclear Age," given in Oslo on December 11, 1974, Eisaku Sato (1901-1975), Japanese statesman, former prime minister (1964-1972), recipient of the 1974 Nobel Peace Prize along with the Irish statesman and campaigner for peace Séan MacBride (1904-1988), president of the International Peace Bureau, commented on Article 9, as follows:

Such a declaration renouncing the use of force in the settlement of international disputes, incorporating the philosophy of the Kellogg-Briand pact, has been made by peoples other than the Japanese. It is noteworthy, however, that a major power like Japan should have persevered in this direction by national consensus and be determined to retain this attitude in the future.

(Tore Frängsmyr, ed.-in-charge, Irwin Adams, ed., *Nobel Lectures Including Presentation and Acceptance Speeches and Laureates' Biographies: Peace, 1971-1980* (Singapore: World Scientific Publishing Co., for the Nobel Foundation, 1997), pp. 57, 74, 75 (reference to footnote omitted))

*Additional explanation: Kellogg-Briand Pact* (Kellogg Pact, Briand-Kellogg Pact, Pact of Paris): General Treaty for Renunciation of War as an Instrument of National Policy, which was signed at Paris on August 27, 1928, and entered into force on July 24, 1929.

*Remark:* "We desire to occupy an honoured place in an international society striving for the preservation of peace."

### 72 COUNTRY

It is not for him to pride himself who loveth his own country, but rather for him who loveth the whole world. The earth is but one country, and mankind its citizens.

Baha'ullah (Mirza Husain 'Ali Nuri) (1817-1892), Persian founder of the Baha'i Faith, in one of his reflections.

*Source:* Bahá'u'lláh, *Gleanings from the Writings of Bahá'u'lláh*, trans. Shoghi Effendi (New York: Bahá'í Publishing Committee, 1935), p. 250 (no. CXVII [117]).

*See* World (Plutarch, on Socrates).

## 73 COURT

### ARTICLE 227

The Allied and Associated Powers publicly arraign William II of Hohenzollern, formerly German Emperor, for a supreme offence against international morality and the sanctity of treaties.

A special tribunal will be constituted to try the accused, thereby assuring him the guarantees essential to the right of defence. It will be composed of five judges, one appointed by each of the following Powers: namely, the United States of America, Great Britain, France, Italy and Japan.

....

### ARTICLE 228

The German Government recognises the right of the Allied and Associated Powers to bring before military tribunals persons accused of having committed acts in violation of the laws and customs of war. Such persons shall, if found guilty, be sentenced to punishments laid down by law. This provision will apply notwithstanding any proceedings or prosecution before a tribunal in Germany or in the territory of her allies.

The German Government shall hand over to the Allied and Associated Powers, or to such one of them as shall so request, all persons accused of having committed an act in violation of the laws and customs of war, who are specified either by name or by the rank, office or employment which they held under the German authorities.

Article 227, paragraphs 1-2, and Article 228 of the Treaty of Peace with Germany (the Treaty of Versailles, between the Allied and Associated Powers and Germany), which was signed at Versailles, a town near Paris, on June 28, 1919, and entered into force on January 10, 1920.

*Source:* United States, Department of State, *Treaties and Other International Agreements of the United States of America, 1776-1949*, comp. Charles I. Bevans, vol. 2, *Multilateral, 1918-1930*, publication 8441 (May 1969), pp. 43, 136-137 (the United States was not a party).

*Explanation: William:* William II (Friedrich Wilhelm Victor Albrecht) (1859-1941), German emperor (1888-1918) who escaped to the Netherlands at the end of World War I and was never tried.

*Note:* The United States signed but did not become a party to the Treaty of Versailles.

*Remark:* A special tribunal and military tribunals already in those times and days.

## 74 COURT

[T]he most serious crimes of concern to the international community as a whole must not go unpunished and ... their effective prosecution must be ensured by taking measures at the national level and by enhancing international cooperation,

....

1. The jurisdiction of the Court shall be limited to the most serious crimes of concern to the international community as a whole. The Court has jurisdiction in accordance with this Statute with respect to the following crimes:
(a) The crime of genocide;
(b) Crimes against humanity;
(c) War crimes;
(d) The crime of aggression.

From the preamble to, and Article 5, paragraph 1, of, the Rome Statute of the International Criminal Court adopted in Rome on July 17, 1998, by the United Nations Diplomatic Conference of Plenipotentiaries on the Establishment of an International Criminal Court.

*Source:* United Nations, United Nations Diplomatic Conference of Plenipotentiaries on the Establishment of an International Criminal Court, *Rome Statute of the International Criminal Court*, United Nations document A/CONF.183/13 (vol. I), pp. 1, 3-4.

*Explanation: Genocide:* certain "acts committed with intent to destroy, in whole or in part, a national, ethnical, racial or religious group, as such." The definition in full is in Article II of the Convention on the Prevention and Punishment of the Crime of Genocide, which was annexed to resolution 260 (III) (Prevention and Punishment of the Crime of Genocide), adopted on December 9, 1948, by the General Assembly of the United Nations, and entered into force on January 12, 1951. For the text of the resolution and convention, *see* United Nations, *Resolutions, 21 September-12 December 1948* (General Assembly, Official Records: Third Session, Part I (A/810)), p. 174, 174. For the text of the convention, *see also* United Nations, *Treaty Series*, vol. 78, p. 277. *See also* Genocide (the full text of the definition).

*Note:* The American Society of International Law publishes important new documents, such as the above, without undue delay in *International Legal Materials*.

*Remark:* A bleak future for the criminals.

## 75 CRIME

With what great insight did Voltaire, hating war enormously, declare: «War is the greatest of all crimes; and yet there is no aggressor who does not color his crime with the pretext of justice.»

Ralph J. Bunche (Ralph Johnson Bunche) (1904-1971), American political scientist, United Nations official, who acted as mediator in the Palestine conflict from 1948 to 1949, and recipient of the 1950 Nobel Peace Prize, in his Nobel lecture, "Some Reflections on Peace in Our Time," given in Oslo on December 11, 1950.

*Source:* Frederick W. Haberman, ed., *Nobel Lectures Including Presentation Speeches and Laureates' Biographies: Peace*, vol. 2, *1926-1950* (Amsterdam: Elsevier Publishing Company, for the Nobel Foundation, 1972), pp. 433, 443, 443.

*Explanation: Voltaire:* pseudonym of François Marie Arouet (1694-1778), French philosopher and writer.

## 76 CRIME

To initiate a war of aggression, therefore, is not only an international crime; it is the supreme international crime differing only from other war crimes in that it contains within itself the accumulated evil of the whole.

From the September 30 and October 1, 1946 judgment of former German Nazi leaders by the International Military Tribunal in Nuremberg, Germany.

*Source:* Office of United States Chief of Counsel for Prosecution of Axis Criminality, *Nazi Conspiracy and Aggression: Opinion and Judgment* (Washington: United States Government Printing Office, 1947), p. 16.

*Notes:* ▸ Article 6, paragraph 2 (b), of the Charter of the International Military Tribunal defines war crimes in these words:

*War crimes:* namely, violations of the laws or customs of war. Such violations shall include, but not be limited to, murder, ill-treatment or deportation to slave labour or for any other purpose of civilian population of or in occupied territory, murder or ill-treatment of prisoners of war or persons on the seas, killing of hostages, plunder of public or private property, wanton destruction of cities, towns or villages, or devastation not justified by military necessity.

(United Nations, *Treaty Series*, vol. 82, pp. 279, 280, 284, 288; beginning indented; semicolon replaced by period at the end)

▸ The charter was annexed to, and formed integral part of, the Agreement for the Prosecution and Punishment of the Major War Criminals of the European Axis, which was signed at London on August 8, 1945, and entered into force the same day. The European Axis refers to Germany and Italy as well as Bulgaria, Hungary and Romania.

▸ In his memorandum on the judgment, submitted in 1949, Trygve Lie (Trygve Halvdan Lie) (1896-1968), Norwegian lawyer and statesman, secretary-general of the United Nations (1946-1953), further explains the definition as follows:

The Tribunal did not, however, content itself with the statement that it was bound by the definition of war crimes given in article 6 (b). It furthermore declared, in explicit words, that this definition was in conformity with existing international law.

(United Nations, Secretary-General, *The Charter and Judgment of the Nürnberg Tribunal: History and Analysis* (Lake Success, New York: United Nations, General Assembly, International Law Commission, 1949), p. 61)

### 77 CRIME
[W]ar crimes and crimes against humanity are among the gravest crimes in international law,

... the effective punishment of war crimes and crimes against humanity is an important element in the prevention of such crimes, the protection of human rights and fundamental freedoms, the encouragement of confidence, the furtherance of co-operation among peoples and the promotion of international peace and security,

... the application to war crimes and crimes against humanity of the rules of municipal law relating to the period of limitation for ordinary crimes is a matter of serious concern to world public opinion, since it prevents the prosecution and punishment of persons responsible for those crimes,

... it is necessary and timely to affirm in international law, through this Convention, the principle that there is no period of limitation for war crimes and crimes against humanity, and to secure its universal application.

....

ARTICLE III

The States Parties to the present Convention undertake to adopt all necessary domestic measures, legislative or otherwise, with a view to making possible the extradition, in accordance with international law, of the persons referred to in article II of this Convention.

From the preamble to and Article III of the Convention on the Non-Applicability of Statutory Limitations to War Crimes and Crimes against Humanity contained in an annex to resolution 2391 (XXIII) adopted by the General Assembly of the United Nations on November 26, 1968 (Convention on the Non-Applicability of Statutory Limitations to War Crimes and Crimes against Humanity). The convention entered into force on November 11, 1970. On December 31, 2003, the parties thereto were only 48, not including such states as China, France, the United Kingdom, the United States, Germany and Japan.

*Source:* United Nations, *Resolutions Adopted by the General Assembly during Its Twenty-third Session* (General Assembly, Official Records: Twenty-third Session, Supplement No. 18 (A/7218)), pp. 40, 40-41 (comma replaced by period at the end of the preambular paragraph).

*Note:* For the text of the convention, *see also* United Nations, *Treaty Series*, vol. 754, pp. 73, 75-76.

*Remark:* Prevention, no period of limitation, extradition.

## 78 CRIME

3. In addition to the grave breaches defined in Article 11, the following acts shall be regarded as grave breaches of this Protocol, when committed wilfully, in violation of the relevant provisions of this Protocol, and causing death or serious injury to body or health:

   (a) Making the civilian population or individual civilians the object of attack;
   (b) Launching an indiscriminate attack affecting the civilian population or civilian objects in the knowledge that such attack will cause excessive loss of life, injury to civilians or damage to civilian objects, as defined in Article 57, paragraph 2 (a) (iii);
   (c) Launching an attack against works or installations containing dangerous forces in the knowledge that such attack will cause excessive loss of life, injury to civilians or damage to civilian objects, as defined in Article 57, paragraph 2 (a) (iii);
   (d) Making non-defended localities and demilitarized zones the object of attack;
   (e) Making a person the object of attack in the knowledge that he is *hors de combat*;
   (f) The perfidious use, in violation of Article 37, of the distinctive emblem of the red cross, red crescent or red lion and sun or of other protective signs recognized by the Conventions or this Protocol.
   ....

5. Without prejudice to the application of the Conventions and of this Protocol, grave breaches of these instruments shall be regarded as war crimes.

Article 85, paragraphs 3 and 5, of the Protocol Additional to the Geneva Conventions of 12 August 1949, and Relating to the Protection of Victims of International Armed Conflicts (Protocol I), which was adopted at Geneva on June 8, 1977, and entered into force on December 7, 1978.

*Source:* United Nations, *Treaty Series*, vol. 1125, pp. 3, 42 (parentheses in italics).

*Note:* Furthermore, from Article 75, paragraph 7 (*same source*, p. 38; parentheses in italics):

7. In order to avoid any doubt concerning the prosecution and trial of persons accused of war crimes or crimes against humanity, the following principles shall apply:

(a) Persons who are accused of such crimes should be submitted for the purpose of prosecution and trial in accordance with the applicable rules of international law;...

*Remark:* "Lead me from Hate to Love."

## 79 CULPABILITY

[T]he sole culpability of the enemy is, as always, a war-time myth. The great success of the propaganda, however, leaves the impression fixed for a long time on the minds of those who want to justify to themselves their action in supporting the war and of those who have not taken the trouble to follow the subsequent withdrawals and denials. Moreover, the myth is allowed to remain, so far as possible, in the public mind in the shape of fear of "unprovoked aggression," and becomes the chief, and indeed the sole, justification for preparations for another war.

Arthur Ponsonby (Arthur Augustus William Harry Ponsonby) (1871-1946), British author and politician, born in England, member of Parliament, in his 1928 book *Falsehood in War-Time* (chapter IV, "Germany's Sole Responsibility for the War").

*Source:* Arthur Ponsonby, *Falsehood in War-Time, Containing an Assortment of Lies Circulated throughout the Nations during the Great War* (London: George Allen & Unwin, 1928), pp. 57, 62.

## 80 CULTURAL EXCHANGE

[W]hatever makes for cultural development is working also against war.

Sigmund Freud (1856-1939), Austrian psychiatrist, pioneer of psychoanalysis, born in Moravia (after 1918 a part of Czechoslovakia; since 1993 in the Czech Republic), in his September 1932 letter to German-born Swiss physicist Albert Einstein (1879-1955), later American citizen, recipient of the 1921 Nobel Prize in Physics.

*Source:* Albert Einstein and Sigmund Freud, *Why War?*, trans. Stuart Gilbert, International Series of Open Letters ([Paris]: International Institute of Intellectual Co-operation, League of Nations, 1933), pp. 21, 23, 57.

## 81 CULTURAL HERITAGE

I would like to tell you a short story as we near the end of this journey through Athens. A hundred and sixty years ago, while the Turks were besieged by the Greeks on the Acropolis, they ran out of lead for their bullets, and so began destroying the ancient columns of the Parthenon in order to take out the metal that runs through the centre of them. The Greeks saw what was happening, and sent a message to the Turks to stop destroying the columns. "If you need lead, we'll send you some." [voice-over]

....

And they did. That is how much our ancestors loved this city and its treasures. [on-camera]

Melina Mercouri (Maria Amalia Mercouris) (1925-1994), Greek film actress and politician, born in Athens, referring to an incident in the Greek War of Independence (1821-1832) in the 1979 Canadian television program *Cities*, more particularly *Cities: Melina Mercouri's Athens*.

*Source:* Niels-Ferns International, *Cities: Melina Mercouri's Athens* (Toronto: Nielsen-Ferns International, [1979]), p. 14 (TV-script).

*Explanation: Acropolis:* a citadel in Athens, in its present form from the second half of the fifth century B.C., with ancient temples and other buildings including the Parthenon, the chief temple of Athena, the ancient Greek protectress of cities, goddess of war, handicraft and wisdom.

*Notes:* ▸ Mercouri was minister of culture from 1981 to 1989 and from 1993 to 1994. ▸ Acropolis is on the World Heritage List.

## 82 CULTURAL HERITAGE
*The General Assembly,*

....

*Aware* of the importance attached by the countries of origin to the return of cultural property which is of fundamental spiritual and cultural value to them, so that they may constitute collections representative of their cultural heritage,

*Reaffirming* that the return or restitution to a country of its *objets d'art*, monuments, museum pieces, manuscripts, documents and any other cultural or artistic treasures constitutes a step forward in the strengthening of international co-operation and the preservation and further development of cultural values,

*Supporting* the solemn appeal launched on 7 June 1978 by the Director-General of the United Nations Educational, Scientific and Cultural Organization for the return to those who created it of an irreplaceable cultural heritage,

....

3. *Invites* Member States to take all necessary steps for the return or restitution of cultural property through, *inter alia*, bilateral arrangements.

From the preamble to and operative paragraph 3 of United Nations General Assembly resolution 34/64 of November 29, 1979 (Return or Restitution of Cultural Property to the Countries of Origin).

*Source:* United Nations, *Resolutions and Decisions Adopted by the General Assembly during Its Thirty-fourth Session* (General Assembly, Official Records: Thirty-fourth Session, Supplement No. 46 (A/34/46)), p. 18, 18 (reference to footnote omitted; semicolon replaced by period at the end of paragraph 3).

*Note:* The following has been stated in an appeal to governments and world public opinion, on June 7, 1978, by Amadou-Mahtar M'Bow (b. 1921), Senegalese educationist, director-general of the United Nations Educational, Scientific and Cultural Organization (UNESCO) (1974-1987):

In A.M. M'Bow's opinion, countries which have been stripped of their irreplaceable masterpieces have the right to demand their return.... These nations demand the return of their art treasures, those which are most representative of their culture, those works to which they attach the most importance and whose absence, for psychological reasons, is unbearable to them.

(Edmund Jan Osman´czyk, *The Encyclopedia of the United Nations and International Relations*, 2nd ed. (Bristol, Pennsylvania; London: Taylor & Francis, 1990), p. 206, 206 (under "Cultural property return or reconstruction"))

*Remark:* "A step forward," to make friends, a lot of friends.

### 83 CULTURE

[I]t is prohibited:

(a) To commit any acts of hostility directed against the historic monuments, works of art or places of worship which constitute the cultural or spiritual heritage of peoples;

(b) To use such objects in support of the military effort;

(c) To make such objects the object of reprisals.

From Article 53 of the Protocol Additional to the Geneva Conventions of 12 August 1949, and Relating to the Protection of Victims of International Armed Conflicts (Protocol I), which was adopted at Geneva on June 8, 1977, and entered into force on December 7, 1978.

*Source:* United Nations, *Treaty Series*, vol. 1125, pp. 3, 27.

### 84 CUSTOM

We are not impressed by the prestige of war as an ancient institution any more than we were impressed by the holding of slaves. Both these customs date back before the dawn of history, but within a few generations we found it possible to lead to complete success the struggle for the elimination of slavery in the lands where Friends lived.

Henry J. Cadbury (Henry Joel Cadbury) (1883-1974), American biblical scholar, professor of divinity at Harvard University, founder of the American Friends Service Committee (the Quakers) in 1917 and chairman thereof, commenting on slavery and war in a Nobel lecture, "Quakers and Peace," given in Oslo on December 12, 1947, on behalf of the committee that shared the 1947 Nobel Peace Prize with the Friends Service Council, London.

*Source:* Frederick W. Haberman, ed., *Nobel Lectures Including Presentation Speeches and Laureates' Biographies: Peace*, vol. 2, 1926-1950 (Amsterdam: Elsevier Publishing Company, for the Nobel Foundation, 1972), pp. 371, 391, 392.

*Remark:* Ancient institutions. Good if they are good. Bad if they are bad.

### 85 DEATH

But whether on the scaffold high
    Or in the battle's van,
The fittest place where man can die
    Is, where he dies for man!

Michael J. Barry (Michael Joseph Barry) (1817-1889), Irish poet, in his poem "The Place Where Man Should Die," published in the Dublin newspaper *Nation* on September 28, 1844.

*Source:* [Thomas Osborne Davis, ed.], *The Spirit of the Nation: Ballads and Songs by the Writers of "The Nation," with Original and Ancient Music, Arranged for the Voice and Piano-forte* (Dublin: James Duffy, 1845), pp. 223, 224.

*Remark:* "The fittest place," once in Auschwitz, Poland, where Father Kolbe died for man. "The fittest place," once in Calcutta, India, where Mother Teresa lived for man.

## 86 DEATH
Four score and seven years ago our fathers brought forth on this continent, a new nation, conceived in Liberty, and dedicated to the proposition that all men are created equal.

Now we are engaged in a great civil war, testing whether that nation or any nation so conceived and so dedicated, can long endure. We are met on a great battle-field of that war. We have come to dedicate a portion of that field, as a final resting place for those who here gave their lives that that nation might live. It is altogether fitting and proper that we should do this.

But, in a larger sense, we can not dedicate—we can not consecrate—we can not hallow—this ground. The brave men, living and dead, who struggled here, have consecrated it, far above our poor power to add or detract. The world will little note, nor long remember what we say here, but it can never forget what they did here. It is for us the living, rather, to be dedicated here to the unfinished work which they who fought here have thus far so nobly advanced[.] It is rather for us to be here dedicated to the great task remaining before us—that from these honored dead we take increased devotion to that cause for which they gave the last full measure of devotion—that we here highly resolve that these dead shall not have died in vain—that this nation, under God, shall have a new birth of freedom—and that government of the people, by the people, for the people, shall not perish from the earth.

Abraham Lincoln (1809-1865), president of the United States (1861-1865), in his address at Gettysburg, Pennsylvania, on November 19, 1863, on dedicating a portion of the Gettysburg battlefield as a cemetery for those who died in the battle fought there from July 1 to 3, 1863.

*Source:* Abraham Lincoln, *The Writings of Abraham Lincoln*, ed. Arthur Brooks Lapsley, vol. 7, *1863-1865*, Works of Abraham Lincoln, Federal Edition (New York: G. P. Putnam's Sons, 1906), p. 20, 20.

*Note:* Out of over 160,000 soldiers engaged the losses were over 40,000, about half from each side.

*See* Number.

*Remark:* "After 14,000 wars" in the world, how many of the "nearly 4,000,000,000" died in vain? Shall we prepare for peace?

## 87 DEATH
If I should die, think only this of me:
    That there's some corner of a foreign field
That is for ever England.

Rupert Brooke (Rupert Chawner Brooke) (1887-1915), English poet, in his World War I sonnets *1914*, composed late in 1914 and published posthumously in 1915 (sonnet V, *The Soldier*, composed at the end of 1914, after Christmas).

*Source:* Rupert Brooke, *1914 & Other Poems* (London: Sidgwick & Jackson, 1915), pp. 11, 15 (comma after the word "me" in handwritten manuscript; Rupert

Brooke, *The Complete Poems of Rupert Brooke* (London: Sidgwick & Jackson, 1932), p. ix).

*Note:* Brooke, who served in the Royal Navy, died of blood poisoning and was buried "in an olive grove" on the Greek island of Scyros (Greek, Skíros), in the Aegean Sea.

### 88 DEFEAT

There are some defeats more triumphant than victories. Those four sister-victories, the fairest the sun ever beheld, of Salamis, Platea, Mycale, and Sicily, never opposed all their united glories to the single glory of the discomfiture of King Leonidas and his heroes at the Pass of Thermopylœ.

Michel de Montaigne (Michel Eyquem de Montaigne) (1533-1592), French essayist, referring to the defeat at Thermopylae, Greece, in 480 B.C. in his work *Essays*, more particularly the essay *Of Cannibals*, finished in 1580 and considered to be "a fine example of open-mindedness and tolerance."

*Source:* Michael de Montaigne, *The Complete Works of Michael de Montaigne*, ed. William Hazlitt (London: John Templeman, 1842), pp. 1, 87, 92 (book I, chapter XXX; translator of the essay: Charles Cotton).

*Explanations:* ▶ *Leonidas:* Leonidas I (d. 480 B.C.), king of the Greek city of Sparta (Lacedaemon) (ca. 489 or 488-480 B.C.), leader of the Greeks in the Battle of Thermopylae, Greece, fought between the Greeks and the Persians in 480 B.C. ▶ *Mycale:* a channel between the island of Samos in the Aegean Sea and Asia Minor where Greek and Persian fleets waged a naval battle, the Battle of Mycale, in 479 B.C. ▶ *Platea:* Plataea, an ancient Greek city whose inhabitants, the Plataeans, in 479 B.C. fought, under a Spartan (Lacedaemonian) general, against the Persians (the Battle of Plataea). ▶ *Salamis:* a Greek island, not far from Athens, where the Battle of Salamis, fought between the Greeks and the Persians, took place in 480 B.C. ▶ *Sicily:* the reference is to the victory over the Carthaginians in the Battle of Himera, Sicily, in 480 B.C.

### 89 DEFEAT

This war is not limited to our unfortunate country. The outcome of the struggle has not been decided by the Battle of France. This is a world war. Mistakes have been made, there have been delays and untold suffering, but the fact remains that there still exists in the world everything we need to crush our enemies some day. To-day we are crushed by the sheer weight of mechanised force hurled against us, but we can still look to a future in which even greater mechanised force will bring us victory. The destiny of the world is at stake.

Charles de Gaulle (Charles André Joseph Marie de Gaulle) (1890-1970), French general and statesman, appealing for the first time to the French people in a radio broadcast from London on June 18, 1940, after the Battle of France in World War II was lost.

*Source:* Charles de Gaulle, *War Memoirs*, vol. 1, *The Call to Honour, 1940-1942*, trans. Jonathan Griffin (London: Collins, 1955), pp. 11, 11-12.

*Explanation: The Battle of France:* a battle waged from May to June 1940 between the French and invading Germans.

*Note:* De Gaulle later served as president of France (1959–1969).
*Remark:* A country, not its allies.

### 90 DEFENSE

201. King Xerxes, then, encamped in the Trachinian territory of Malis, and the Greeks in the pass. This spot is called by most of the Greeks, Thermopylæ, but by the inhabitants and neighbours, Pylæ....

202. The following were the Greeks who awaited the Persian in this position. Of Spartans three hundred heavy-armed men;... 204. These nations had separate generals for their several cities; but the one most admired, and who commanded the whole army, was a Lacedæmonian, Leonidas, son of Anaxandrides ... son of Hercules; who had unexpectedly succeeded to the throne of Sparta....

....

.... 220. It is said that Leonidas himself sent them away, being anxious that they should not perish; but that he and the Spartans who were there could not honourably desert the post which they originally came to defend. For my own part, I am rather inclined to think, that Leonidas, when he perceived that the allies were averse and unwilling to share the danger with him, bade them withdraw, but that he considered it dishonourable for himself to depart: on the other hand, by remaining there, great renown would be left for him, and the prosperity of Sparta would not be obliterated. For it had been announced to the Spartans, by the Pythian, when they consulted the oracle concerning this war, as soon as it commenced, "that either Lacedæmon must be overthrown by the barbarians, or their king perish."...

....

226. Though the Lacedæmonians and Thespians behaved in this manner, yet Dieneces, a Spartan, is said to have been the bravest man. They relate that he made the following remark, before they engaged with the Medes, having heard a Trachinian say, that when the barbarians let fly their arrows, they would obscure the sun by the multitude of their shafts, so great were their numbers: but he, not at all alarmed at this, said, holding in contempt the numbers of the Medes, that "their Trachinian friend told them every thing to their advantage, since if the Medes obscure the sun, they would then have to fight in the shade, and not in the sun." This, and other sayings of the same kind, they relate that Dieneces, the Lacedæmonian, left as memorials.... 228. In honour of the slain, who were buried on the spot where they fell, and of those who died before they who were dismissed by Leonidas went away, the following inscription has been engraved over them: "Four thousand from Peloponnesus once fought on this spot with three hundred myriads." This inscription was made for all; and for the Spartans in particular: "Stranger, go tell the Lacedæmonians, that we lie here, obedient to their commands."

Herodotus (ca. 484-ca. 425 B.C.), Greek historian, known as "the Father of History," writing on the Battle of Thermopylae in 480 B.C. in his *History*, believed to have been published before 425 B.C. (book VII, entitled "Polymnia," chapters 201, 202, 204, 220, 226, 228). The battle was fought in the Pass of Thermopylae in the Thessaly District of northern Greece, where the Greeks under Leonidas I (d. 480 B.C.), king of Sparta (Lacedaemon) (ca. 489 or 488-480 B.C.), were on the defensive against the vastly superior force of the Persians under Xerxes I (ca. 519-465 B.C.), king of Persia (486-465 B.C.). The last-man stand of Leonidas and his three hundred Spartans (Lacedaemonians), along with seven hundred Thespians, has been noted ever since.

*Source:* Herodotus, *Herodotus,* trans. Henry Cary, Bohn's Classical Library (London: Henry G. Bohn, 1848), pp. 479, 480, 480, 486, 488, 488-489 (the page numbers refer to the quoted chapter materials, respectively).

*Explanations:* ▸ *Hercules* (Greek, Herakles): Greek legendary hero. ▸ *History:* Herodotus's work on the Greco-Persian Wars waged intermittently from about 546 to about 448 B.C. ▸ *Medes:* a nation of Media, ancient name of northwestern Iran, which was under Persian rule. ▸ *The oracle:* the oracle at Delphi, Greece. ▸ *The Pythian:* the oracle at Delphi (earlier Pytho). ▸ *Sparta:* Lacedaemon, a city and state in the Peloponnesian peninsula of southern Greece. ▸ *Thespians:* citizens of the ancient Greek city of Thespiae, located in the district of Boeotia not far from Thermopylae.

*Remark:* A case of self-defense.

## 91 DEFENSE

Our wonderful Great Wall!

....

Actually, all it has ever done is work many conscripts to death—it never kept out the Huns.

Lu Hsun (Lu Hsün) or Lusin (Chou Shu-jen) [Lu Xun] (1881-1936), Chinese writer and poet, called the father of modern Chinese literature, in his essay "The Great Wall," dated May 11, 1925.

*Source:* Lu Hsun, *Selected Works of Lu Hsun,* vol. 2, trans. Yang Hsien-yi and Gladys Yang (Peking [Beijing]: Foreign Languages Press, 1957), p. 151.

*Explanation: Great Wall:* the Great Wall of China, mostly completed about 214 B.C. by Shih-huang-ti [Shi Huangdi] ("First Sovereign Emperor") (259-210 B.C.), the first emperor of China (221-210 B.C.), previously King Cheng of the state Ch'in in northwestern China (246-221 B.C.).

*See* Wall.

## 92 DEFINITON

War is a mere continuation of policy by other means.

Karl von Clausewitz (Karl Marie von Clausewitz) (1780-1831), Prussian general and military strategist, in his work *On War* (German, *Vom Kriege*), written from 1818 to 1830 and published posthumously in German in 1832 (book I, chapter I, section 24).

*Source:* Karl von Clausewitz, *On War,* trans. O. J. Matthijs Jolles, Modern Library (New York: Random House, 1943), p. 16 (capitalization omitted; period added at the end).

*Notes:* ▸ German text: Der Krieg ist eine bloße Fortsetzung der Politik mit andern Mitteln.

▸ In a note on his work, dated July 10, 1827, the author uses the words "[W]ar is regarded as *nothing but the continuation of state policy with other means.*" *Same source*, p. xxix. German text: *nichts ... als die fortgesetzte Staatspolitik mit andern Mitteln.*

▸ The German text above is taken from: General von Clausewitz, *Vom Kriege* (Berlin: V. Vehr's Verlag (Friedrich Feddersen), 1918), p. 19 (the sentence) and p. xxviii (the note).

### 93 DESTRUCTION

THIS book is to be neither an accusation nor a confession, and least of all an adventure, for death is not an adventure to those who stand face to face with it. It will try simply to tell of a generation of men who, even though they may have escaped its shells, were destroyed by the war.

Erich Maria Remarque (1898-1970), German novelist, who fought in World War I, in an introduction to his 1929 antiwar novel on the war, *All Quiet on the Western Front* (German, *Im Westen nichts Neues*).
*Source:* Erich Maria Remarque, *All Quiet on the Western Front*, trans. A. W. Wheen [Arthur Wesley Wheen] (1929; Boston: reprint, Little, Brown, and Company, 1929), no page.
*Remark:* No monument to the destroyed soldier.

### 94 DEVELOPMENT

With a view to the creation of conditions of stability and well-being which are necessary for peaceful and friendly relations among nations based on respect for the principle of equal rights and self-determination of peoples, the United Nations shall promote:

a. higher standards of living, full employment, and conditions of economic and social progress and development;

b. solutions of international economic, social, health, and related problems; and international cultural and educational cooperation; and

c. universal respect for, and observance of, human rights and fundamental freedoms for all without distinction as to race, sex, language, or religion.

Article 55 of the Charter of the United Nations, which was signed at San Francisco, United States, on June 26, 1945, and entered into force on October 24, 1945.
*Source:* United States, Department of State, *Treaty Series*, vol. 993, *Charter of the United Nations and Statute of the International Court of Justice*, pp. 3, 15-16 (a photocopy of a certified copy).
*Remark:* Note the words "well-being ... necessary for peaceful and friendly relations among nations."

### 95 DIARY

The poignant story of one family's tragic experience during the two-and-a-half-year siege of Leningrad is carefully recorded in the school notebook of Tanya Savicheva, an 11-year-old who lived with her family in an apartment in the heart of the city. As food supplies dwindled and German shelling intensified, death overtook members of Tanya's family one by one. "Zhenya died 28 December, 12:30 in the morning, 1941. Babushka died 25 January, 3 o'clock, 1942. Leka died 17 March, 5 o'clock in the morning, 1942. Dedya Vasya died 13 April, 2 o'clock at night, 1942. Dedya Lesha, 10 May, 4 o'clock in the afternoon, 1942. Mama, 13 May, 7:30 a.m., 1942. All died. Only Tanya remains."

Tanya Savicheva herself was presumed for years to have perished after making the last entry in her notebook. But later it was discovered that, like many other Leningraders, she was evacuated from the city in mid-1942. Sent to a children's home, she died in the summer of 1943 as the result of chronic dysentery that she had contracted during the siege.

Nicholas Bethell (Nicholas William Bethell) (1938-2007), British writer and politician, born in England, member of the House of Lords (1967-1999), referring, in his 1977 book *Russia Besieged*, to the 1941-1942 diary entries of eleven- and twelve-year-old Soviet girl Tanya Savicheva (January 25, 1930-July 1, 1944), in besieged Leningrad, the Soviet Union.

*Source:* Nicholas Bethell, *Russia Besieged*, ed. the editors of Time-Life Books, World War II (Alexandria, Virginia: Time-Life Books, 1977), p. 108.

*Explanations:* ▸ *Babushka:* Russian for grandmother. ▸ *Dedya:* uncle. ▸ *Leningrad:* Saint Petersburg (St. Petersburg) since 1991.

*Notes:* ▸ Soon after twelve-year-old Tanya Savicheva stopped keeping her diary in besieged Leningrad in May 1942, thirteen-year-old Anne Frank started in Amsterdam (she kept her diary while in hiding from July 9, 1942, to August 4, 1944). ▸ "The diary of Tanya Savicheva is now displayed at the St. Petersburg Museum of History and a copy is displayed at the Piskarevsky Memorial Cemetery." The Internet (2005), under "Tanya Savicheva" (Wikipedia, the web-based user-contributed encyclopedia).

*See Siege* (M. M. Minasyan, on the Siege of Leningrad).

*Remark:* All died—Tanya included.

### 96 DIPLOMACY

If war is the failure of diplomacy, then ... diplomacy, both bilateral and multilateral, is our first line of defence. The world today spends billions preparing for war; shouldn't we spend a billion or two preparing for peace?

Kofi Annan (Kofi Atta Annan) (b. 1938), Ghanaian economist and international civil servant, secretary-general of the United Nations (1997-2006), in an address to the National Press Club in Washington on January 24, 1997.

*Source:* Kofi Annan, *The Quotable Kofi Annan: Selections from Speeches and Statements by the Secretary-General* (New York: United Nations, Department of Public Information, 1998), p. 9.

*Note:* Annan shared the 2001 Nobel Peace Prize with the United Nations.

*Remark:* Or three or four billions? Wouldn't we save a lot?

### 97 DISAPPEARANCE

*The General Assembly,*

....

*Deeply concerned* that in many countries, often in a persistent manner, enforced disappearances occur, in the sense that persons are arrested, detained or abducted against their will or otherwise deprived of their liberty by officials of different branches or levels of Government, or by organized groups or private individuals acting on behalf of, or with the support, direct or indirect, consent or acquiescence of the Government, followed by a refusal to disclose the fate or whereabouts of the persons concerned or a refusal to acknowledge the deprivation of their liberty, which places such persons outside the protection of the law,

*Considering* that enforced disappearance undermines the deepest values of any society committed to respect for the rule of law, human rights and fundamental freedoms, and that the systematic practice of such acts is of the nature of a crime against humanity,

....

*Proclaims* the present Declaration of the Protection of All Persons from Enforced Disappearance as a body of principles for all States and urges that all efforts be made so that the Declaration becomes generally known and respected:

### Article 1

1. Any act of enforced disappearance is an offence to human dignity. It is condemned as a denial of the purposes of the Charter of the United Nations and as a grave and flagrant violation of the human rights and fundamental freedoms proclaimed in the Universal Declaration of Human Rights and reaffirmed and developed in international instruments in this field.

....

### Article 3

Each State shall take effective legislative, administrative, judicial or other measures to prevent and terminate acts of enforced disappearance in any territory under its jurisdiction.

....

### Article 7

No circumstances whatsoever, whether a threat of war, a state of war, internal political instability or any other public emergency, may be invoked to justify enforced disappearances.

....

### Article 16

1. Persons alleged to have committed any of the acts referred to in article 4, paragraph 1, above, shall be suspended from any official duties during the investigation referred to in article 13 above.

2. They shall be tried only by the competent ordinary courts in each State, and not by any other special tribunal, in particular military courts.

From the preamble to and certain articles of United Nations General Assembly resolution 47/133 of December 18, 1992 (Declaration on the Protection of All Persons from Enforced Disappearance) (Articles 3 and 7 in full).

*Source:* United Nations, *Resolutions and Decisions Adopted by the General Assembly during Its Forty-seventh Session, vol. I, 15 September-23 December 1992* (General Assembly, Official Records: Forty-seventh Session, Supplement No. 49 (A/47/49)), pp. 207, 207-209 (reference to footnote omitted).

*Notes:* ▸ In the introduction to a United Nations publication from 1997 it is stated that the Working Group on Enforced or Involuntary Disappearances, established by the United Nations Commission on Human Rights in 1980, had, since its creation, dealt with more than 50,000 cases from more than 70 countries. United Nations, *Declaration on the Protection of All Persons from Enforced Disappearance* ([New York]: United Nations, Department of Public Information, 1997).

▸ At Wikipedia, the web-based user-contributed encyclopedia, one may read:

Adolfo Scilingo is serving 640 years (maximum 40) in a Spanish jail after being convicted on April 19, 2005 for crimes committed between 1976 and 1983 during military government Proceso de Reorganizacion Nacional in Argentina. The case is unusual as for the first time it makes use of a new Spanish law whereby people can be prosecuted for crimes committed outside Spain.

(The Internet (2005), under "Adolfo Scilingo"; his name in bold letters in source)

▸ In *Time* further details had been given by Adolfo Scilingo (Adolfo Francisco Scilingo (b. 1946), former Argentine navy captain:

THEY WERE UNCONSCIOUS. WE stripped them, and when the flight commander gave the order, we opened the door and threw them out, naked, one by one. That is the story, and nobody can deny it." With these words, former Argentine navy Captain Adolfo Francisco Scilingo, 48, spilled one of the dirtiest secrets of the "dirty war" that raged in his country from the mid-1970s through the early '80s....

.... As a 28-year old lieutenant, he was stationed in Buenos Aires at the Naval School of Mechanics in 1977; Scilingo says his post, already a notorious detention center for those rounded up on charges of disloyalty, soon became a way station to death.

For the next two years, he remembers, some 15 to 20 prisoners were trucked every Wednesday to the Buenos Aires airport, put on a military plane, and then dropped, drugged but alive, from a height of about 13,000 ft. into the Atlantic Ocean.

(*Time*, March 27, 1995, p. 47)

*Remark:* Too many cases, too many countries. Isn't a decision on sending people to war in a way a decision on enforced disappearance?

## 98 DISARMAMENT

[M]ore important by far than any partial disarmament of armies and fleets, is the «disarmament» of the people from within, the generation, in fact, of sympathy in the souls of men. Here too, in the great and important work that has been carried on, the League of Nations has taken an active part.

....

.... The relief in thousands of homes in seeing the return of their menfolk, the help received by them in their distress; the gratitude this inspires, the confidence in people and in the future, the prospect of sounder working conditions—all this is, I believe, of greater importance for the cause of peace than many ambitious political moves that now seldom reach far beyond a limited circle of politicians and diplomats.

Fridtjof Nansen (1861-1930), Norwegian explorer, scientist (zoologist, oceanographer), artist, statesman and humanitarian, recipient of the 1922 Nobel Peace Prize, in his Nobel lecture, "The Suffering People of Europe," given in Christiania (Oslo) on December 19, 1922.

*Source:* Frederick W. Haberman, ed., *Nobel Lectures Including Presentation Speeches and Laureates' Biographies: Peace,* vol. 1, *1901-1925* (Amsterdam: Elsevier Publishing Company, for the Nobel Foundation, 1972), pp. 351, 361, 369-370.

*Explanation: League of Nations:* an international organization, formally in existence from January 10, 1920, to April 19, 1946, the forerunner of the United Nations set up on October 24, 1945.

*See* Education (the 1945 Constitution of the United Nations Educational, Scientific and Cultural Organization (UNESCO) stating that "it is in the minds of men that the defences of peace must be constructed").

*Remark:* Nansen's disarmament "from within."

## 99 DISARMAMENT

The Governments of the United States of America, the United Kingdom of Great Britain and Northern Ireland, and the Union of Soviet Socialist Republics, hereinafter referred to as the "Original Parties",

Proclaiming as their principal aim the speediest possible achievement of an agreement on general and complete disarmament under strict international control in accordance with the objectives of the United Nations which would put an end to the armaments race and eliminate the incentive to the production and testing of all kinds of weapons, including nuclear weapons,

Seeking to achieve the discontinuance of all test explosions of nuclear weapons for all time, determined to continue negotiations to this end, and desiring to put an end to the contamination of man's environment by radioactive substances,

Have agreed as follows:

*Article I*

1. Each of the Parties to this Treaty undertakes to prohibit, to prevent, and not to carry out any nuclear weapon test explosion, or any other nuclear explosion, at any place under its jurisdiction or control:

(a) in the atmosphere; beyond its limits, including outer space; or under water, including territorial waters or high seas; or

(b) in any other environment if such explosion causes radioactive debris to be present outside the territorial limits of the State under whose jurisdiction or control such explosion is conducted. It is understood in this connection that the provisions of this subparagraph are without prejudice to the conclusion of a treaty resulting in the permanent banning of all nuclear test explosions, including all such explosions underground, the conclusion of which, as the Parties have stated in the Preamble to this Treaty, they seek to achieve.

2. Each of the Parties to this Treaty undertakes furthermore to refrain from causing, encouraging, or in any way participating in, the carrying out of any nuclear weapon test explosion, or any other nuclear explosion, anywhere which would take place in any of the environments described, or have the effect referred to, in paragraph 1 of this Article.

The preamble to and Article I of the Treaty Banning Nuclear Weapon Tests in the Atmosphere, in Outer Space and under Water (the Nuclear Test Ban Treaty, the Partial Test Ban Treaty), which was signed at Moscow on August 5, 1963, by the foreign ministers of the Soviet Union, the United Kingdom and the United States, and entered into force on October 10, 1963.

*Source:* United Nations, *Treaty Series,* vol. 480, p. 43.

*Note:* The Comprehensive Nuclear Test Ban Treaty, adopted by United Nations General Assembly resolution 50/425 of September 10, 1996, had not entered into force on December 31, 2003.

*Remark:* Three big powers "desiring to put an end to the contamination of man's environment by radioactive substances."

### 100 DISASTER

Out of the half-million soldiers who had fought in Russia, only 20,000 staggered back across the Niemen.... Russian losses are reckoned at something over 200,000 men.

Antony Brett-James (Eliot Antony Brett-James) (1920-1984), British senior lecturer in military history, summing up the losses suffered by the army of Napoleon I (Napoleon Bonaparte) (1769-1821), emperor of France (1804-1814, 1815), and the Russians, during the invasion of Russia in 1812.

*Source:* Antony Brett-James, comp., ed. and trans., *1812: Eyewitness Accounts of Napoleon's Defeat in Russia* (New York: St. Martin's Press, 1966), p. 264.

*Explanation: Niemen:* a river, now in Belarus and Lithuania.

*Note:* The English poet John Milton (1608-1674) wrote in his blank verse epic *Paradise Lost*, published in 1667:

Of triumph, to be styl'd great conquerors,

Patrons of mankind, gods, and sons of gods;

Destroyers rightlier call'd, and plagues of men.

(John Milton, *English Poems*, ed. R. C. Browne, Clarendon Press, rev. ed., vol. II (Oxford: Clarendon Press, 1885), p. 120)

*Remark:* Not the only disaster but will we learn?

### 101 DISPUTE RESOLUTION

Then the king said, "The one says, 'This is my son that is alive, and your son is dead'; and the other says, 'No; but your son is dead, and my son is the living one.'" And the king said, "Bring me a sword." So a sword was brought before the king. And the king said, "Divide the living child in two, and give half to the one, and half to the other." Then the woman whose son was alive said to the king, because her heart yearned for her son, "Oh, my lord, give her the living child, and by no means slay it." But the other said, "It shall be neither mine nor yours; divide it." Then the king answered and said, "Give the living child to the first woman, and by no means slay it; she is its mother." And all Israel heard of the judgment which the king had rendered; and they stood in awe of the king, because they perceived that the wisdom of God was in him, to render justice.

The Bible, 1 Kings 3:23-28 (Solomon, king of Israel (ruled ca. 961-922 B.C.)).

*Source: The New Oxford Annotated Bible with the Apocryphal/Deuterocanonical Books,* ed. Bruce M. Metzger and Roland E. Murphy, New Revised Standard Version (New York: Oxford University Press, 1991) (verse reference omitted).

*Remark:* The wisdom of God, justice.

### 102 DISPUTE RESOLUTION

At Linhuai, a silk merchant was carrying a piece of waterproof silk to the city for sale. There came a rain and he spread it over his head for shelter, and soon another man came to stand under it. When the rain had stopped, both of them claimed that the silk was his own. The Chief Minister Hsüeh Hsüan said, "This piece of waterproof silk is only worth several hundred cash. Why fight over it?" Thereupon he cut it in two and gave each one half. As he continued to watch them, he saw the owner was protesting that he had been wronged, while the other man seemed well satisfied. And so he knew to which one the silk rightfully belonged, and the other man was found guilty and punished.

Chinese tale, "The Judgment on a Dispute," told in the work *Fengshut'ung*, written in the second century by Ying Shao (178-197).
*Source:* Lin Yutang, ed., *The Wisdom of China and India* (New York: Random House, 1942), pp. 939, 940 (translator of the tale: Lin Yutang).
*Explanation: Linhuai:* a city in eastern China.
*Remark:* Chinese silk.

## 103 DISPUTE RESOLUTION
### Article 33
1. The parties to any dispute, the continuance of which is likely to endanger the maintenance of international peace and security, shall, first of all, seek a solution by negotiation, enquiry, mediation, conciliation, arbitration, judicial settlement, resort to regional agencies or arrangements, or other peaceful means of their own choice.
2. The Security Council shall, when it deems necessary, call upon the parties to settle their dispute by such means.
   ....

### Article 41
The Security Council may decide what measures not involving the use of armed force are to be employed to give effect to its decisions, and it may call upon the Members of the United Nations to apply such measures. These may include complete or partial interruption of economic relations and of rail, sea, air, postal, telegraphic, radio, and other means of communication, and the severance of diplomatic relations.

### Article 42
Should the Security Council consider that measures provided for in Article 41 would be inadequate or have proved to be inadequate, it may take such action by air, sea, or land forces as may be necessary to maintain or restore international peace and security. Such action may include demonstrations, blockade, and other operations by air, sea, or land forces of Members of the United Nations.

Articles 33, 41 and 42 of the Charter of the United Nations, which was signed at San Francisco, United States, on June 26, 1945, and entered into force on October 24, 1945.
*Source:* United States, Department of State, *Treaty Series*, vol. 993, *Charter of the United Nations and Statute of the International Court of Justice*, pp. 3, 12-13 (a photocopy of a certified copy).
*Remark:* Peaceful means of their own choice, nonmilitary action and military action, in that order.

## 104 DIVERSITY

Two world wars were fought to make the world safe for democracy. Today we have to wage a third war on all fronts. This war has to be waged in peacetime, but it has to be waged as energetically and with as much concentration of total national effort as in times of war. The war we have to wage today has only one goal, and that is to make the world safe for diversity.

.... We are thrown together on this planet and we have to live together. That is why the Charter imposes the imperative on all human beings to practice tolerance and to live together in peace with one another as good neighbors. To my mind this is the simplest definition of peaceful coexistence.

Looking ahead, I hope that in the coming years we may all be imbued with this spirit of tolerance. If all human beings and all nations large and small were to be moved by this spirit we could indeed make the world safe for diversity, and for posterity.

U Thant (1909-1974), educator and civil servant from Burma (now Myanmar), secretary-general of the United Nations (1962-1971), in his Dag Hammarskjöld memorial lecture, "Looking Ahead," given at Columbia University, New York, on January 7, 1964.
*Source:* Andrew W. Cordier and Wilder Foote, eds., *The Quest for Peace: The Dag Hammarskjöld Memorial Lectures* (New York: Columbia University Press, 1965), pp. 39, 48-49 (inbued corrected to imbued).
*Explanation: Hammarskjöld:* Dag Hammarskjöld (Dag Hjalmar Agne Carl Hammarskjöld) (1905-1961), Swedish economist and statesman, secretary-general of the United Nations (1953-1961), who was posthumously awarded the 1961 Nobel Peace Prize.
*Remark:* A spirit of tolerance, to make the world "safe for diversity, and for posterity."

## 105 DREAM

My dream is a peace bomb
Powerful enough
To eradicate division in the world.

I stand with it in my hands
Ready to throw it in the opposing formations of the nations
And the fuse sparks.

But my friends in East and West
Prove to me
That the dream bomb cannot explode.

Ögmundur Helgason (1944-2006), Icelandic linguistics student, in his poem "Daydream," composed about 1964.
*Source:* Ögmundur Helgason, *Fardagar* (Reykjavík: Helgafell, 1970), p. 50 (the whole poem; translation mine).
*Remark:* "A man cannot be too careful in the choice of his" friends.

## 106 EARTH

Glory to God in the highest, and on earth peace, good will toward men.

The Bible, Luke 2:14 (Birth of Jesus; the angels talking to the shepherds).
*Source: The Holy Bible Containing the Old and New Testaments*, The Authorized (King James) Version ([Nashville, Tennessee]: Gideons International, [1979]).

## 107 ECONOMIC SANCTION

The modern world is prepared to exert economic power instantly....

This marked advantage, which economic power possesses over military power, has never been appraised at its full value....

.... There is strong reason to believe, however, that in many cases the use of economic pressure as a preliminary power would be sufficient to bring a recalcitrant nation to a world court for a settlement of its differences, thus avoiding the use of military power altogether.

....

ONE apparently strong and valid argument to be brought against the use of economic pressure is that it would bring great loss to a nation applying it. And that is true. But it is equally true that this loss would be far less than the loss brought by war.... At the beginning of 1918 it was estimated, after careful computations, that the cost of the war to Germany represented one-third of the total wealth which the German Empire had built up through centuries. And the cost to the other nations is relatively as great. In comparison to the staggering sums involved, the loss to commerce from the application of economic pressure would be extremely small. This would be true even if the entire export and import trade of all the belligerent nations should be sacrificed.

....

The trial balance that is being considered is of commerce alone and no account is being taken of the destruction of life and the other great human losses that come with war. But this strict commercial accounting shows a heavy debit against war.

Herbert S. Houston (Herbert Sherman Houston) (1866-1955), American peace writer, member of a committee of the Chamber of Commerce of the United States, on the economic impact of World War I, in his 1918 book *Blocking New Wars*.
*Source:* Herbert S. Houston, *Blocking New Wars* (Garden City, New York: Doubleday, Page & Company, 1918), pp. 61-62, 64-65, 69-70, 73 (from chapters VIII (Fighting Foreign Wars at Home) and IX (War Prevention versus War Cost)).
*Remark:* Economic power or military power?

## 108 EDUCATION

The Governments of the States parties to this Constitution on behalf of their peoples declare, that since wars begin in the minds of men, it is in the minds of men that the defences of peace must be constructed;

that ignorance of each other's ways and lives has been a common cause, throughout the history of mankind, of that suspicion and mistrust between the peoples of the world through which their differences have all too often broken into war;

that the great and terrible war which has now ended was a war made possible by the denial of the democratic principles of the dignity, equality and mutual respect of men, and by the propagation, in their place, through ignorance and prejudice, of the doctrine of the inequality of men and races;

that the wide diffusion of culture, and the education of humanity for justice and liberty and peace are indispensable to the dignity of man and constitute a sacred duty which all the nations must fulfil in a spirit of mutual assistance and concern;

that a peace based exclusively upon the political and economic arrangements of governments would not be a peace which could secure the unanimous, lasting and sincere support of the peoples of the world, and that the peace must therefore be founded, if it is not to fail, upon the intellectual and moral solidarity of mankind.

The beginning of the preamble to the Constitution of the United Nations Educational, Scientific and Cultural Organization (UNESCO), which was signed at London on November 16, 1945, and entered into force on November 4, 1946.
*Source:* United Nations, *Treaty Series*, vol. 4, pp. 275, 276.
*Remark:* Education of humanity for peace, "a sacred duty" of all nations.

### 109 EDUCATION
*Article 29*
1. States Parties agree that the education of the child shall be directed to:
....
(d) The preparation of the child for responsible life in a free society, in the spirit of understanding, peace, tolerance, equality of sexes, and friendship among all peoples, ethnic, national and religious groups and persons of indigenous origin.

Article 29, paragraph 1 (d), of the Convention on the Rights of the Child contained in an annex to United Nations General Assembly resolution 44/25 of November 20, 1989 (Convention on the Rights of the Child). The convention entered into force on September 2, 1990. On December 31, 2003, the parties thereto were 192.
*Source:* United Nations, *Resolutions and Decisions Adopted by the General Assembly during Its Forty-fourth Session*, vol. I (General Assembly, Official Records: Forty-fourth Session, Supplement No. 49 (A/44/49)), pp. 166, 170 (semicolon replaced by period at the end).
*Note:* For the text of the convention, *see also* United Nations, *Treaty Series*, vol. 1577, pp. 3, 44.

### 110 EMPIRE
Rome shall perish,—write that word
   In the blood that she has spilt;
Perish hopeless and abhorr'd,
   Deep in ruin as in guilt.

William Cowper (1731-1800), English poet, in his ode "Boadicea," published in 1782 (stanza 4).
*Source:* William Cowper, *The Works of William Cowper, Esq., Comprising His Poems, Correspondence, and Translations*, ed. Robert Southey, vol. VIII (London: Baldwin and Cradock, 1836), pp. 343, 344.

*Note:* The poet lets a Druid (Celtic priest) speak the words quoted here to Boadicea or Boudicca, British queen of the Iceni tribe in East Anglia who in or about the year 61 led an unsuccessful revolt against Roman rule ending in her death.
*Remark:* The fall of an empire.

### 111 END
You might as well try to sweep back Niagara as stop war when its rumblings are heard.

King Vidor (King Wallis Vidor) (1894-1982), American motion-picture director and producer, in an interview on the occasion of his first musical sound motion picture, *The Big Parade*, released in 1925, dealing with World War I.
*Source: New York Times*, November 8, 1925, section 8, p. 5.
*Explanation: Niagara:* a river on the boundary between Canada and the United States, famous for the Niagara Falls.

### 112 ENEMY
The first meditation is the meditation of love in which you must so adjust your heart that you long for the weal and welfare of all beings, including the happiness of your enemies.

Buddha (the Enlightened One), Gautama Buddha (Siddhartha Gautama) (ca. 563-ca. 483 B.C.), Indian prince, born in the district Nepal, founder of Buddhism, speaking to a disciple.
*Source:* Paul Carus, *The Gospel of Buddha according to Old Records*, 12th ed. (Chicago: Open Court Publishing Co., 1909), pp. 150, 153 (chapter LX [60], "Amitâbha," verse 20).
*Explanation: Amitâbha* (the Buddha Amitabha): the Unbounded Light.

### 113 ENEMY
He was indeed a character deserving our high admiration not only for his equitable and mild temper, which all along in the many affairs of his life, and the great animosities which he incurred, he constantly maintained; but also for the high spirit and feeling which made him regard it the noblest of all his honours that, in the exercise of such immense power, he never had gratified his envy or his passion, nor ever had treated any enemy as irreconcilably opposed to him.

Plutarch (ca. 46-120), Greek biographer, describing, in his work *Parallel Lives* (the biography of Pericles), the character and attitude of the Athenian statesman and general Pericles (ca. 490-429 B.C.).
*Source:* Plutarch, *Plutarch's Lives: The "Dryden Plutarch,"* rev. Arthur Hugh Clough, Everyman's Library, vol. I (1910; reprint, London: J. M. Dent & Sons; New York: E. P. Dutton & Co., 1914), pp. 226, 262-263.
*Remark:* Enemies are not forever.

### 114 ENVIRONMENT
Care shall be taken in warfare to protect the natural environment against widespread, long-term and severe damage.

From Article 55, paragraph 1, of the Protocol Additional to the Geneva Conventions of 12 August 1949, and Relating to the Protection of Victims of International Armed Conflicts (Protocol I), which was adopted at Geneva on June 8, 1977, and entered into force on December 7, 1978.

*Source:* United Nations, *Treaty Series*, vol. 1125, pp. 3, 28.

*See* Herbicide (Arthur H. Westing).

### 115 ENVIRONMENT

*The General Assembly,*

....

*Expressing its deep concern* about environmental damage and depletion of natural resources, including the destruction of hundreds of oil-well heads and the release and waste of crude oil into the sea, during recent conflicts,

*Noting* that existing provisions of international law prohibit such acts,

*Stressing* that destruction of the environment, not justified by military necessity and carried out wantonly, is clearly contrary to existing international law,

*Concerned* that the provisions of international law prohibiting such acts may not be widely disseminated and applied,

....

1. *Urges* States to take all measures to ensure compliance with the existing international law applicable to the protection of the environment in times of armed conflict.

From the preamble to and operative paragraph 1 of United Nations General Assembly resolution 47/37 of November 25, 1992 (Protection of the Environment in Times of Armed Conflict).

*Source:* United Nations, *Resolutions and Decisions Adopted by the General Assembly during Its Forty-seventh Session*, vol. I, *15 September-23 December 1992* (General Assembly, Official Records: Forty-seventh Session, Supplement No. 49 (A/47/49)), p. 290, 290 (semicolon replaced by period at the end).

*Remark:* Not just words but binding law, environmental law.

### 116 ESPIONAGE

Two vital pieces of strategic information were supplied for Stalin by a spy with access to the German embassy in Tokyo: the precise date of the German attack on the USSR, and the certainty that the Japanese would not take part in it.

M. R. D. Foot (Michael Richard Daniell Foot) (b. 1919), English historian, commenting, at a 1973 symposium at the University of Salford, on the 1941 intelligence reports of the German journalist Richard Sorge (1895-1944), a spy for the Soviet Union in Japan before and during World War II.

*Source:* M. R. D. Foot, "What Good Did Resistance Do?", in *Resistance in Europe, 1939-1945,* ed. Stephen Hawes and Ralph White, Pelican Books (Harmondsworth, England: Penguin Books, 1976), pp. 204, 206.

*Explanation: Stalin:* Joseph Stalin (Joseph Vissarionovich Dzhugashvili) (1879-1953), Soviet political leader, born in Georgia, premier of the Soviet Union (1941-1953) and general secretary of the Central Committee of the Communist Party (1922-1953).

*Note:* The following additional information may be found in the 1966 book *The Case of Richard Sorge:*

These advance reports from Sorge warning of the German attack on the Soviet Union constitute one of the most dramatic achievements of the ring. In addition to the material assembled by the Japanese during the ultimate trials, recent articles in the Soviet and East German press reveal some further details. On March 5, 1941, for instance, Sorge is said to have transmitted to Moscow a microfilm containing telegrams from Ribbentrop to Ott which gave the date of the German attack as the middle of June; and on May 15 Sorge radioed the exact day—June 22.

....

.... When war really broke out, Richard was furious. He asked in a puzzled way, 'Why has Stalin not reacted?'

....

It has been suggested that the advance warning sent by Sorge to Moscow, after the Imperial Conference of July 2, 1941, of Japan's intention to strike south into the Pacific and remain neutral on the Siberian border, enabled Stalin to move divisions from the Soviet Far Eastern Army to the Western Front. Thanks to Sorge's intelligence these reinforcements saved Moscow from the Germans.

....

The official Soviet historians, on the other hand, tend to ignore these measures or to minimize their historical significance.

(F. W. Deakin and G. R. Storry, *The Case of Richard Sorge* (London: Chatto & Windus, 1966), pp. 230-231, 233)

*Additional explanations:* ▶ *Ott:* Eugen Ott (b. 1889), German diplomat, ambassador to Japan (1938-1943). ▶ *Ribbentrop:* Joachim von Ribbentrop (1893-1946), German Nazi politician, foreign minister of Germany (1938-1945), later sentenced to hanging by the International Military Tribunal in Nuremberg, Germany, in 1946, and hanged there on October 16, 1946.

### 117 EVACUATION

The Royal Air Force engaged the main strength of the German Air Force, and inflicted upon them losses of at least four to one; and the Navy, using nearly 1,000 ships of all kinds, carried over 335,000 men, French and British, out of the jaws of death and shame, to their native land and to the tasks which lie immediately ahead. We must be very careful not to assign to this deliverance the attributes of a victory. Wars are not won by evacuations.

Winston S. Churchill (Winston Leonard Spencer Churchill) (1874-1965), British statesman, orator and author, prime minister of the United Kingdom (1940-1945 and 1951-1955), in a speech given on June 4, 1940, to the House of Commons on the situation early in World War II, more particularly the evacuation of British and some other Allied troops from Dunkirk (French, Dunkerque), France, from May 26 to June 3, 1940.

*Source: Parliamentary Debates,* Commons, 5th series, vol. 361, pp. 787, 791.

### 118 EXHORTATION

From the tops of those Pyramids forty centuries look upon you!

Napoleon Bonaparte (1769-1821), French military leader, addressing his soldiers in Egypt on July 21, 1798, at the beginning of the Battle of the Pyramids where a French army defeated an army of the Mamelukes, the ruling race in Egypt.

*Source:* Napoleon, *Memoirs of the History of France during the Reign of Napoleon, Dictated by the Emperor at Saint Helena to the Generals Who Shared His Captivity; and Published from the Original Manuscripts Corrected by Himself,* vol. II (London: Henry Colburn and Co. and Martin Bossange and Co., 1823), pp. 236, 246 (italics omitted).

*Notes:* ▸ Napoleon arrived in Egypt on July 1, 1798, and left the country in August 1799.

▸ Of course, Napoleon who later became emperor of France, Napoleon I (1804-1814, 1815), spoke in French: "Soldats, songez que, du haut de ces pyramides, quarante siècles vous contemplent." *The Oxford Dictionary of Quotations* (2nd ed. rev., 1954).

*Remark:* Egypt for the Egyptians?

### 119 EXHORTATION
England expects that every man will do his duty!

Horatio Nelson (1758-1805), English admiral, in a signal to his men at the beginning of the Battle of Trafalgar, off the south coast of Spain, to the northwest of the Strait of Gibraltar, on October 21, 1805, where the British fleet defeated the combined fleets of the French and the Spanish but Nelson fell aboard his ship *Victory.*

*Source:* Robert Southey, *The Life of Nelson* (London: Collins Clear-Type Press, [1813]), p. 357 (chapter IX; capitalization of text omitted).

*Note:* Another version: England expects every man to do his duty.

### 120 EXPANSIONISM
In the front rank of man's woes is grasping greed. For they who are fain to annex their neighbours' holdings frequently are defeated and fail, and to their neighbours' possessions contribute their own in addition.

Menander (ca. 343 or 342-291 or 290 B.C.), Greek playwright.

*Source:* Menander, *Menander: The Principal Fragments,* trans. Francis G. Allinson [Francis Greenleaf Allinson] (1921; reprint, rev., London: William Heinemann; New York: G. P. Putnam's Sons, 1930), p. 495 (fragment on antiexpansion).

*Remark:* Is the playwright right?

### 121 FAMILY
"Alas for my son on service abroad!
    He rests not from morning till eve.
May he careful be, and come back to me!
    While he is away, how I grieve!"


....
"Alas for my child on service abroad!
    He never in sleep shuts an eye.

May he careful be, and come back to me!
　　In the wild may his body not lie!"


....
"Alas! my young brother, serving abroad,
　　All day with his comrades must roam.
May he careful be, and come back to me,
　　And die not away from his home!"

From an ancient Chinese poem, "A Soldier's Thought of Home" according to one translation, the latter halves of the three verses thereof (a Chinese soldier imagines that he hears his father, mother and brother speaking). The poem is from the *Odes of Wei* (ode IV), Wei being a small state which was annexed in or about 660 B.C. (now Shansi province of northern China).
　　*Source:* James Legge, *The Chinese Classics: Translated into English, with Preliminary Essays and Explanatory Notes*, vol. III, *The She King; or, The Book of Poetry* (London: Trübner & Co., 1876), pp. 140, 142, 142-143.
　　*Explanation:* The *Odes of Wei* form part (part I, book IX) of the *Book of Poetry* edited by Chinese philosopher and political theorist Confucius (K'ung Fu-tzu ("Master K'ung"), [Kongfuzi]) (551-479 B.C.).
　　*See* Telegram (Tedd Thomey, on telegrams from Washington in World War II).
　　*Remark:* Strain on families.

## 122 FAMINE
[O]f an army of one hundred and twenty thousand foot and fifteen thousand horse, he scarcely brought back above a fourth part out of India, they were so diminished by disease, ill diet, and the scorching heats, but most by famine. For their march was through an uncultivated country whose inhabitants fared hardly, possessing only a few sheep, and those of a wretched kind, whose flesh was rank and unsavoury, by their continual feeding upon sea-fish.

Plutarch (ca. 46-120), Greek biographer, describing, in his work *Parallel Lives* (the biography of Alexander), the beginning of the return from India, in 325 B.C., of Alexander III or Alexander the Great (356-323 B.C.), king of Macedonia (336-323 B.C.).
　　*Source:* Plutarch, *Plutarch's Lives: The "Dryden Plutarch,"* rev. Arthur Hugh Clough, Everyman's Library, vol. II (1910; reprint, London: J. M. Dent & Sons; New York: E. P. Dutton & Co., 1914), pp. 463, 522.

## 123 FIGHTING
An Irishman is never at peace except when he's fighting.

Irish proverb.
　　*Source:* Sean Gaffney and Seamus Cashman, eds., *Proverbs & Sayings of Ireland* (Portmarnock, Ireland: Wolfhound Press, 1978), p. 59 (period added at the end).

## 124 FIGHTING
Even though large tracts of Europe and many old and famous States have fallen or may fall into the grip of the Gestapo and all the odious apparatus of Nazi

rule, we shall not flag or fail. We shall go on to the end. We shall fight in France, we shall fight on the seas and oceans, we shall fight with growing confidence and growing strength in the air, we shall defend our island, whatever the cost may be. We shall fight on the beaches, we shall fight on the landing grounds, we shall fight in the fields and in the streets, we shall fight in the hills; we shall never surrender, and even if, which I do not for a moment believe, this island or a large part of it were subjugated and starving, then our Empire beyond the seas, armed and guarded by the British Fleet, would carry on the struggle, until, in God's good time, the new world, with all its power and might, steps forth to the rescue and the liberation of the old.

Winston S. Churchill (Winston Leonard Spencer Churchill) (1874-1965), British statesman, orator and author, prime minister of the United Kingdom (1940-1945 and 1951-1955), in a speech given on June 4, 1940, to the House of Commons on the situation early in World War II, more particularly just after the evacuation of British and some other Allied troops from Dunkirk (French, Dunkerque), France, from May 26 to June 3, 1940.
*Source: Parliamentary Debates*, Commons, 5th series, vol. 361, pp. 787, 795.
*Explanation: Gestapo:* an abbreviation of Geheime Staatspolizei (Secret State Police), the political police of Nazi Germany.
*Remark:* Fighting overseas, on the seas, in the air, from beach to hill, even with help from overseas.

### 125 FILM
Antiwar, antimilitary themes have always had an honored place within the war film genre. Lewis Milestone's 1930 classic *All Quiet on the Western Front* and Stanley Kubricks's 1957 *Paths of Glory* both expressed strong antiwar themes, and both were critically acclaimed. However, neither movie portrayed the American military and both dealt with World War I.

Lawrence H. Suid (Lawrence Howard Suid) (b. 1938), American freelance writer and film historian, in his 1978 book on great American war films, here concentrating on two films, from 1930 and 1957.
*Source:* Lawrence H. Suid, *Guts & Glory: Great American War Movies* (Reading, Massachusetts: Addison-Wesley Publishing Company, 1978), p. 175.
*Explanations:* ▸ *Stanley Kubrick* (1928-1999): American screenwriter, film producer and director. ▸ *Lewis Milestone* (1895-1980): American film director, born in Russia, who received the Academy Award for best director for *All Quiet on the Western Front*, the first major antiwar sound film, which won the 1930 Academy Award for best picture.
*Notes:* ▸ The film *All Quiet on the Western Front* was adapted from a 1929 antiwar novel on World War I, *All Quiet on the Western Front* (German, *Im Westen nichts Neues*), by the German novelist Erich Maria Remarque (1898-1970) who fought in the war.
▸ Suid, on p. 179, describes the end of the film *All Quiet on the Western Front* as follows:
At the film's close, the hero reaches for a butterfly, a symbol of hope and beauty, and is shot by a sniper as the armistice is about to begin.

▶ The film *Paths of Glory* has been described as follows:

"Paths of Glory," released in 1957, concerns the court martial and execution of three privates in the French army.... According to Jonathan Baumbach in *Film Culture*, the work "shows war in its naked ugliness, stripped of glory, heroics, and high-sounding causes."

(*Contemporary Authors*, New Revision Series, vol. 33, p. 249)

▶ *Paths of Glory* was adapted from a 1935 antiwar novel, *Paths of Glory*, by the American novelist Humphrey Cobb (1899-1944). Like *All Quiet on the Western Front* the book became a bestseller.

▶ The same year, 1935, the American book reviewer John Chamberlain (John Rensselaer Chamberlain) (1903-1995) wrote on *Paths of Glory*:

If any one ever enlists voluntarily "for the duration" of any war after reading this novel, it will be a matter of surprise to me. For an ironic combination of an onslaught against militarism on the one hand, and against Red Tape on the other, this novel would be hard to match.

(*Current History*, July 1935, pp. iv, vi, vii)

*Remark:* Antiwar novels, antiwar films.

## 126 FLIGHT

In another engagement, also, the enemy had again the better, when Cæsar, it is said, seized a standard-bearer, who was running away, by the neck, and forcing him to face about, said, "Look, that is the way to the enemy."

Julius Caesar (Gaius Julius Caesar) (100-44 B.C.), Roman general and statesman, during his fighting against senatorial forces in the North African period (47-46 B.C.) of the Second Roman Civil War of 49-45 B.C., according to the Greek biographer Plutarch (ca. 46-120) in his work *Parallel Lives* (the biography of Caesar).

*Source:* Plutarch, *Plutarch's Lives: The "Dryden Plutarch,"* rev. Arthur Hugh Clough, Everyman's Library, vol. II (1910; reprint, London: J. M. Dent & Sons; New York: E. P. Dutton & Co., 1914), pp. 530, 568.

## 127 FOLLY

Can anything be more ridiculous than that a man should have the right to kill me because he lives on the other side of the water, and because his ruler has a quarrel with mine, though I have none with him?

Blaise Pascal (1623-1662), French scientist and philosopher, in his work *Pensées* (*Pensées sur la réligion*) [Thoughts (Thoughts on Religion)], mostly put together from 1657 to 1658 and published posthumously in 1669 (section V, "Justice and the Reason of Effects," no. 294).

*Source:* Pascal, *Pascal's Pensées*, trans. W. F. Trotter [William Finlayson Trotter], text prepared by Léon Brunschvicg, Everyman's Library (London, Toronto: J. M. Dent & Sons; New York: E. P. Dutton & Co., 1931), pp. 83, 84.

*See* Human rights (International Covenant on Civil and Political Rights, Article 6, on the right to life).

## 128 FORCE

Keep peace with the Lords of the Jungle—the Tiger,
   the Panther, and Bear.

Rudyard Kipling (Joseph Rudyard Kipling) (1865-1936), English author, in "The Law of the Jungle," part of *The Second Jungle Book*, published in 1895.

*Source:* Rudyard Kipling, *The Second Jungle Book* (New York: Century Co., 1895), p. 30 (semicolon replaced by period at the end).

*Note:* Kipling received the 1907 Nobel Prize in Literature "in consideration of the power of observation, originality of imagination, virility of ideas, and remarkable talent for narration which characterize the creations of this world-famous author." Horst Frenz, ed., *Nobel Lectures Including Presentation Speeches and Laureates' Biographies: Literature, 1901-1967* (Amsterdam: Elsevier Publishing Company, for the Nobel Foundation, 1969), p. 57.

*Remark:* The big powers, the stronger party.

### 129 FORGIVENESS

Our country's negotiators rejected the two extremes and opted for a "third way," a compromise between the extreme of Nuremberg trials and blanket amnesty or national amnesia. And that third way was granting amnesty to individuals in exchange for a full disclosure relating to the crime for which amnesty was being sought. It was the carrot of possible freedom in exchange for truth and the stick was, for those already in jail, the prospect of lengthy prison sentences and, for those still free, the probability of arrest and prosecution and imprisonment.

....

Let us conclude ... by pointing out that ultimately this third way of amnesty was consistent with a central feature of the African *Weltanschauung*....

....

.... To forgive is not just to be altruistic. It is the best form of self-interest.

Desmond Tutu (Desmond Mpilo Tutu) (b. 1931), South African Anglican cleric, recipient of the 1984 Nobel Peace Prize, in his 1999 book *No Future without Forgiveness* (chapter 2; "Nuremberg or National Amnesia? A Third Way").

*Source:* Desmond Mpilo Tutu, *No Future without Forgiveness* (New York: Doubleday, 1999), pp. 30-31.

*Explanations:* ▶ *Nuremberg:* the town of Nürnberg, Germany, where, in 1946, German war criminals, former Nazi leaders, were sentenced by the International Military Tribunal (the Nuremberg Tribunal) set up by the Allies. ▶ *Weltanschauung:* a world view.

*See* Child (*Airlift to Biafra*, on the aftermath of the Nigerian Civil War).

### 130 FREEDOM

I believe that freedom will never be crushed as long as there are men as brave as the men of D-Day. That's what's implied—though not directly stated—in "The Longest Day" and that's why I'm making it and making it now.

Darryl F. Zanuck (Darryl Francis Zanuck) (1902-1979), American motion-picture producer, commenting, in 1961, with regard to his 1962 film *The Longest Day*, which he codirected, on the June 6, 1944 Allied invasion (D-day) at Normandy, northwestern France, then occupied by Germany.

*Source: Variety*, September 20, 1961, p. 7.

*See also* Lawrence H. Suid, *Guts & Glory: Great American War Movies* (Reading, Massachusetts: Addison-Wesley Publishing Company, 1978), p. 156.

*Remark:* "We shall fight in France," Churchill had predicted in 1940. And bravery it was, on the beaches, on the landing grounds, in the fields and in the streets, in the hills.

## 131 FUTURE
Mark the blameless, and behold
    the upright,
for there is posterity for the
    peaceable.

The Bible, Psalms 37:37 (a psalm of David, king of Israel (ruled ca. 1000-ca. 961 B.C.)).
*Source: The Holy Bible Containing the Old and New Testaments,* New Revised Standard Version (New York: Oxford University Press, 1989).
*Remark:* Peace is future.

## 132 GENERAL
Do not let me hear you talking together
    About titles and promotions;
For a single general's reputation
    Is made out of ten thousand corpses.

Ts'ao Sung [Cao Song] (flourished ca. 870-920), Chinese poet, in his poem "A Protest in the Sixth Year of Ch'ien Fu" (879).
*Source:* Arthur Waley, trans., *A Hundred and Seventy Chinese Poems* (London: Constable and Company, 1918), pp. 97, 98.
*Note:* The last part has also been translated as follows:
[A] general's fame
stands on a pile of dry bones
of what were once the people.
(Rewi Alley, trans., *Peace through the Ages: Translations from the Poets of China* (Peking [Beijing]: Rewi Alley, 1954), p. 109, 109 (the poem is there entitled "War"))

## 133 GENERATION
Our mothers are weeping, our girlfriends are silent
                  and sad.
We never knew love, nor the pleasures of workshops
                  and classes.
The back-breaking war-toil of soldiers is all that we had.

Semyon Petrovich Gudzenko (1922-1953), Soviet poet and journalist, born in Kiev (now in Ukraine), and war veteran due to wounds he received, in his poem "My Generation," appearing in 1945.
*Source: Immortality: Verse by Soviet Poets Who Laid Down Their Lives in the Great Patriotic War of 1941-1945* (Moscow: Progress Publishers, 1978), p. 709, 709 (translator of the poem: Dorian Rottenberg).
*Note:* Not only toil but wounds and death—or a short life as in this case, the poet writing soon after World War II (p. 697):

We die not from advancing age—
From our old wounds we die.

*See also* Destruction (Erich Maria Remarque's words on World War I, or "a generation of men who, even though they may have escaped its shells, were destroyed by the war").

## 134 GENOCIDE

*The Contracting Parties,*

*Having considered* the declaration made by the General Assembly of the United Nations in its resolution 96 (I) dated 11 December 1946 that genocide is a crime under international law, contrary to the spirit and aims of the United Nations and condemned by the civilized world;

*Recognizing* that at all periods of history genocide has inflicted great losses on humanity; and

*Being convinced* that, in order to liberate mankind from such an odious scourge, international co-operation is required;

*Hereby agree as hereinafter provided.*

ARTICLE I

The Contracting Parties confirm that genocide, whether committed in time of peace or in time of war, is a crime under international law which they undertake to prevent and to punish.

ARTICLE II

In the present Convention, genocide means any of the following acts committed with intent to destroy, in whole or in part, a national, ethnical, racial or religious group, as such:

(*a*) Killing members of the group;

(*b*) Causing serious bodily or mental harm to members of the group;

(*c*) Deliberately inflicting on the group conditions of life calculated to bring about its physical destruction in whole or in part;

(*d*) Imposing measures intended to prevent births within the group;

(*e*) Forcibly transferring children of the group to another group.

ARTICLE III

The following acts shall be punishable:

(*a*) Genocide;

(*b*) Conspiracy to commit genocide;

(*c*) Direct and public incitement to commit genocide;

(*d*) Attempt to commit genocide;

(*e*) Complicity in genocide.

ARTICLE IV

Persons committing genocide or any of the other acts enumerated in article III shall be punished, whether they are constitutionally responsible rulers, public officials or private individuals.

The preamble to and Articles I-IV of the Convention on the Prevention and Punishment of the Crime of Genocide, of December 9, 1948, which was annexed to resolution 260 (III) (Prevention and Punishment of the Crime of Genocide), adopted on December 9, 1948, by the General Assembly of the United Nations, and entered into force on January 12, 1951.

*Source:* United Nations, *Resolutions, 21 September-12 December 1948* (General Assembly, Official Records: Third Session, Part I (A/810)), pp. 174, 174-175.

*Notes:* ▸ For the text of the convention, *see also* United Nations, *Treaty Series*, vol. 78, p. 277.

▸ On the Internet (2005) one could read:

Academics and lawmakers ... are demanding that the Turkish government abandon what they call a policy of denial that the 1915-23 diaspora of Turkey's Armenian minority even occurred.

"The Armenian genocide is the model, the prototype, for the genocides of the 20th century," said Roger Smith, a college professor who heads the Association of Genocide Scholars, a group committed to preventing genocide.

Some 2,000 people rallied in Times Square on Sunday to remember the deaths and displacement of an estimated 1.5 million Armenians by the Ottoman Turks—80 years before Yugoslavia added the term "ethnic cleansing" to the world's lexicon of misery."

(Associated Press, State & Local Wire, April 26, 1999, Monday)

*Explanation: Roger Smith:* Roger W. Smith (Roger Winston Smith) (b. 1936), American professor.

*Remark:* Note the sad words "at all periods of history genocide has inflicted great losses on humanity" as well as the clear obligation "to prevent and to punish" this crime under international law.

### 135 GENOCIDE

"Please try to come here. There is a lot of killing. They are shipping Muslim people through Luka in cattle cars. Last night there were 25 train wagons for cattle crowded with women, old people and children. They were so frightened. You could see their hands through the openings. We were not allowed to come close. Can you imagine that? It's like Jews being sent to Auschwitz. In the name of humanity, please come."

The voice at the other end of the telephone was a Muslim political leader in Banja Luka, the second largest city in Bosnia-Herzegovina. It was July 9, 1992.

....

The war that began in April 1992 was predictable. What no one could have imagined were the atrocities against Muslim and Croat civilians for which the Serbs invented the euphemism "ethnic cleansing."...

....

.... Police Chief Stojan Zupljanin had a casual explanation for the reversion to Third Reich practices: "None of the refugees asked for first-class carriages."

.... Muslim and Croat politicians had been collecting reports about detention camps set up by the Serbs around northern Bosnia, the most notorious of them at Omarska, an open-pit iron mine north of Banja Luka. "I will tell you about the living conditions in the camps," said a Muslim official. "All the grass has been eaten by the people. Every day in Omarska between 12 and 16 people die. In the first six days they don't receive any food. There is no possibility of any visit. No possibility of packages. No medical help. Two-thirds of them are living under the open skies. It is like an open pit. When it rains, many of them are up to their knees in mud."...

....

.... My thought was that if Omarska was a death camp, this needed to be put in print to alert others....

....

"This story will make a difference," I said to him. "We know that something terrible is going on in the camps. We must find out just what it is. Find me witnesses."...

....

.... Omarska was a death factory. Not everybody who went there died, but if it had not been closed down, the thousands there at the end of July would have been dead in a few weeks. U.S. government interviewers concluded that Serb guards killed as many as 5,000 men at Omarska of the 13,000 or so who were processed there.

....

In Sarajevo, several hundred thousand residents huddled in basement shelters to escape the Serb artillery. In northern Bosnia, Serb artillery and aircraft were attacking Muslim and Croat towns in their drive to open a military corridor from Belgrade to Banja Luka. Everywhere else, Serb "ethnic cleansing," the euphemism for murder, rape, and torture, was continuing against Muslims and Roman Catholic Croats. The Serb onslaught had displaced two million civilians and left tens of thousands dead. It was the most vicious conflict seen in Europe or nearly anywhere else since World War II....

....

The *Newsday* series in this book catalogues only some of the forms of the savagery: random slaughter, organized deportations, death camps, systematic rape and castration, and assaults on refugees fleeing for their lives. The total killed is not known but could amount to 200,000 to 250,000 through June 1993, well over 10 percent of the Muslim population. In aim and method "ethnic cleansing" amounts to genocide, as defined in the International Genocide Convention. This bans killing or harming members of a national, ethnic, racial or religious group with intent to destroy it in whole or in part or imposing measures that would prevent reproduction of the group. "Genocide has many forms," Simon Wiesenthal told this author. "You don't have to kill everyone to have genocide. This is genocide, absolutely."

.... It has since become clear that top Karadzic aides had set up and run death camps and rape camps alike.

Roy Gutman (Roy William Gutman) (b. 1944), American foreign affairs reporter who received the 1993 Pulitzer Prize for international reporting, describing, in his 1993 book *A Witness to Genocide*, the ethnic cleansing in Bosnia and Herzegovina from 1992 to 1993, during the war in Bosnia and Herzegovina (1992-1995).

*Source:* Roy Gutman, *A Witness to Genocide: The First Inside Account of the Horrors of 'Ethnic Cleansing' in Bosnia* (Shaftesbury, Dorset, England: Element Books, 1993), pp. vii, ix, xii, xiv (author's note), xvii, xxxi-xxxii (introduction).

*Explanations:* ▶ *Auschwitz* (Auschwitz-Birkenau): the site of a concentration camp operated by the German Nazis in the province of Cracow in southern Poland from 1940 to 1945, now the site of a state museum. ▶ *Banja Luka* (Banjaluka): a city in northeastern Bosnia and Herzegovina. ▶ *Genocide:* certain "acts committed with intent to destroy, in whole or in part, a national, ethnical, racial or religious group, as such." The definition in full is in Article II of the Convention on the Prevention and Punishment of the Crime of Genocide, which was annexed to resolution 260 (III) (Prevention and Punishment of the Crime of Genocide), adopted on December 9, 1948, by the General Assembly of the United Nations, and entered into force on January 12, 1951. For the text of the resolution and convention, see United Nations, *Resolutions, 21 September-12 December 1948* (General Assembly, Official Records: Third Session, Part I (A/810)), p. 174, 174. For the text of the convention, *see also* United Nations, *Treaty Series*, vol. 78, p. 277. *See also* Genocide (the full text of the definition). ▸ *Karadzic:* Radovan Karadzic (b. 1945), Bosnian-Serb psychiatrist and political leader who stepped down as such in July 1996, having been formally charged with genocide and crimes against humanity by the prosecutor of the Hague-based United Nations International Tribunal for the Former Yugoslavia (the war crimes tribunal) in 1995. ▸ *Sarajevo:* the capital of Bosnia and Herzegovina. ▸ *Third Reich:* the Third Reich of Nazi Germany (1933-1945). ▸ *Wiesenthal:* Simon Wiesenthal (1908-2005), Jewish architect, born in Buczacz, Austria-Hungary (now Buchach, Ukraine), prisoner in Nazi concentration camps (1941-1943, 1944-1945), later Nazi hunter, founder and director of the Jewish Documentation Centre in Vienna. ▸ *Zupljanin:* Stojan Zupljanin (b. 1951), Bosnian-Serb nationalist, commander of Bosnian-Serb security forces in the autonomous region of Krajina, Bosnia and Herzegovina (during the 1992-1995 war in that country), who in 1999 was indicted for genocide, crimes against humanity, violations of the laws or customs of war and grave breaches of the 1949 Geneva conventions, by the prosecutor of the Hague-based United Nations International Criminal Tribunal for the Former Yugoslavia (the war crimes tribunal) (see the Internet (2003), under "Zupljanin case").

*Note:* "Eighty-nine members of his and his wife's Jewish families were annihilated by the Nazis, but, after liberation in 1945, he and his wife, who had managed to pass as a Pole for much of the war, were reunited." *Encyclopædia Britannica Online* (2001), under "Wiesenthal, Simon."

*Remark:* It must be repeated: "In aim and method "ethnic cleansing" amounts to genocide, as defined in the International Genocide Convention."

### 136 GHETTO

The Warsaw ghetto was officially created on October 2, 1940 by a decree issued by Dr. Ludwig Fischer, Governor of the Warsaw Distrikt. Surrounded by a wall sixteen kilometers long and three meters high, which was topped by broken glass and barbed wire, the ghetto became a concentration camp for Jews and also for several thousand Poles of Jewish origin, that is, for people who had cut off their connections with the Jewish people by becoming Christians or whose only link with Jews was a single Jewish grandparent....

.... Calculated in calories, a German in Warsaw received daily 2,310 calories, a Pole 634 cal. and a Jew 184....

On June 30, 1941, when according to some ghetto statisticians the population had reached its peak of 550,000, the gainfully employed, who could count on two bowls of soup a day, numbered 27,000. According to a Jewish chronicler, on May 30, 1941 50 percent of the ghetto dwellers were literally starving to death, 30 per cent were starving "normally," 15 per cent did not have enough to eat, and 10,000 lived well, some of them even better than before the war....

.... However, hunger and disease did not work fast enough to satisfy the Germans, especially as the Jewish doctors helped by the man in the street succeeded in controlling the epidemics....

The chief purpose of the Nazi policy of starvation was, of course, the annihilation of the Jews imprisoned in the Warsaw ghetto. Ludwig Fischer, the Warsaw District Governor, stated it in no unmistakable terms: "The Jews will die from hunger and destitution, and a cemetery will remain of the Jewish question."...

....

That the Germans would exterminate millions of defenseless civilians by mass shootings and gas-chambers was something that no sane Jew in the Warsaw ghetto could envisage, let alone foresee, in 1940 and even in 1941....

....

THE GREAT Liquidation ended officially on September 12, 1942 with the deportation of 310,322 Jews to Treblinka and the murder of 5,961 Jews inside the ghetto....

....

Among the survivors there were hardly any children or old people, for in the final selection carried out on September 7 by SS officers and German industrialists, children had been the first to be sent to Treblinka. The Pole Antoni Szymanowski described the selection in his *Liquidation of the Warsaw Ghetto*:

I saw the most harrowing sights: children being separated from their parents. One father of two children, a six-year-old girl and a baby of a few months whose mother had already been deported, was offered the chance of life, but without his children. He left them in the middle of the street and walked through the gate. The little girl's cry of "Daddy!" had to be heard to be believed....

....

.... In a letter addressed to SS Obergruppenführer Oswald Pohl, the head of the SS Chief Economic Administration, SS Obergruppenführer Friedrich Krueger, SS Gruppenführer (Lieutenant-General) Odilo Globocnik, the man in charge of the extermination program in Poland, and General Eduard Wagner, the Quartermaster-General of the Land Forces on the Russian front, Himmler had explained at the time that although he agreed to leaving some Jewish skilled workers for the needs of the armaments industries, "One day even these Jews must disappear, in accordance with the Führer's wish."

....

When the uprising broke out on August 1, 1944 there were in Warsaw over 900,000 Poles and at the most 7,000 people who according to Nazi criteria were Jews.

Reuben Ainsztein (1917-1981), Jewish journalist and historian, born in Wilno, Poland (now Vilnius, Lithuania), referring, in his 1979 book *The Warsaw Ghetto Revolt*, to occupied Warsaw in World War II, and especially the Warsaw Ghetto Revolt (the Warsaw Ghetto Uprising) of April 19-May 16, 1943.

*Source*: Reuben Ainsztein, *The Warsaw Ghetto Revolt* (New York: Holocaust Library, 1979), pp. 1-3, 16, 55-56, 73-74, 178 (reference to footnotes omitted).

*Explanations*:  ▸ *Fischer*: Ludwig Fischer (1905-1947), German Nazi governor of the Warsaw District in occupied Poland (October 1939-January 1945). ▸ *Führer*: in English "leader," a reference to Adolf Hitler (1889-1945), chancellor of the Third Reich of Nazi Germany (1933-1945).  ▸ *Himmler:* Heinrich Himmler (1900-1945), German Nazi leader, head of the Nazi Party corps SS, responsible for the enforcement of extermination policies.  ▸ *SS:* an abbreviation of the German word Schutzstaffel (Protective Echelon), a Nazi Party corps responsible for, among other things, the administration of concentration (extermination) camps in World War II, declared a criminal organization by the International Military Tribunal in Nuremberg, Germany, in 1946.  ▸ *Szymanowski:* Antoni Szymanowski ("Borowski," "Brun," "Brzeski") (1914-1985), Polish historian and resistance fighter.  ▸ *Treblinka:* after Auschwitz (Auschwitz-Birkenau) in southern Poland, the most notorious German Nazi concentration and extermination camp, a place where 750,000 or more individuals met their fate (situated about 50 miles (80 kilometers) northeast of Warsaw).

*Notes:*  ▸ Ludwig Fischer was extradited to Poland from West Germany in 1946, tried, sentenced, hanged.  ▸ The Warsaw Ghetto Revolt (the Warsaw Ghetto Uprising) of April 19-May 16, 1943, is not to be confused with the Warsaw Rising (the Warsaw Uprising) of August 1-October 2, 1944.  ▸ An interesting book title can be mentioned here: Robert Serebrenik, *The Warsaw Ghetto Revolt: Climax of Jewish Heroism and Resistance in the Last 1800 Years* (New York: World Jewish Congress, 1956).

*See* Recruitment (English recruiting poster in World War I).

*Remark:* "Daddy, what did you do in the world war? Starve Jews, shoot Jews, deport Jews, gas Jews?"

### 137 GIFT
Gifts break rocks.

Portuguese proverb.
Source: Henry G. Bohn, comp., *A Polyglot of Foreign Proverbs Comprising French, Italian, German, Dutch, Spanish, Portuguese, and Danish, with English Translations* (London: Henry G. Bohn, 1857), p. 273 (italics omitted).

### 138 GLORY
Yung Ching's policy disappointed these natural expectations. He was essentially a man of peace, caring nothing for the so-called glory of foreign wars and costly expeditions, and declaring that his proper province was to attend solely to the wants of his own people. Instead, therefore, of despatching fresh armies into Central Asia he withdrew those that were there, leaving the turbulent tribes of that region to fight out their own quarrels and to indulge their petty ambitions as they might feel disposed. The policy in this matter which Yung Ching began with the first day of his reign was continued until the hour of his death.

Demetrius Charles Boulger (Demetrius Charles von Kavanagh (de Kevenagh) Boulger) (1853-1928), British historian and author, born in England, describing, in his book *The History of China*, first published from 1881 to 1884, the policy of Yung-chen [Yongzheng], emperor of China (1723-1735).
*Source:* Demetrius Charles Boulger, *The History of China*, rev. ed., vol. I (London: W. Thacker & Co., 1898), pp. 658-659 (reference mark omitted).
*Remark:* Only eighteenth-century wisdom?

### 139 GOD
The Lord is peace.

The Bible, Judges 6:24 (the sentence forms the name which Gideon (ca. twelfth century B.C.), warrior-judge of Israel, gave to the altar at Ophrah).
*Source: The Holy Bible Containing the Old and New Testaments*, New Revised Standard Version (New York: Oxford University Press, 1989).

### 140 GOLD
When Crœsus, for his glory, showed Solon his great treasures of gold, Solon said to him, "If another king come that hath better iron than you, he will be master of all this gold."

Solon (ca. 638-ca. 558 B.C.), Athenian statesman and poet, one of the Seven Sages, speaking, in about 560 B.C., to Croesus (d. 525 B.C. or later), last king of Lydia and other countries in Asia Minor (ca. 560-ca. 546 B.C.).
*Source:* Lord Bacon [Francis Bacon], *The Moral and Historical Works of Lord Bacon, Including his Essays, Apophthegms, Wisdom of the Ancients, New Atlantis, and Life of Henry the Seventh* (London: George Bell & Sons, 1874), pp. 164, 180.

### 141 GOLD
"We Spaniards," said Cortes, "are troubled with a heart disease for which gold is the only cure."

Hernán Cortés or Hernando Cortés (1485-1547), Spanish conqueror of Mexico (1519-1521), on being asked by an Aztec chieftain in Mexico why he was so hungry for the wealth of Montezuma II (1466-1520), the last Aztec emperor of Mexico (1502-1520).
*Source:* Henry Thomas and Dana Lee Thomas, *The Living Biographies of Famous Rulers* (Garden City, New York: Garden City Publishing Co., 1940), pp. 137, 142.
*See* Education (the 1945 Constitution of the United Nations Educational, Scientific and Cultural Organization (UNESCO) stating that "it is in the minds of men that the defences of peace must be constructed").

### 142 GOLDEN RULE
In everything do to others as you would have them do to you; for this is the law and the prophets.

The Bible, Matthew 7:12 (Jesus to the people in the Sermon on the Mount; the Golden Rule).
*Source: The Holy Bible Containing the Old and New Testaments*, New Revised Standard Version (New York: Oxford University Press, 1989).
*See also same source*, Luke 6:31: Do to others as you would have them do to you.

### 143 GOOD
So let us not grow weary in doing what is right, for we will reap at harvest-time, if we do not give up. So then, whenever we have an opportunity, let us work for the good of all, and especially for those of the family of faith.

The Bible, Galatians 6:9-10 (The Letter of Paul to the Galatians).
*Source: The Holy Bible Containing the Old and New Testaments*, New Revised Standard Version (New York: Oxford University Press, 1989) (verse numbering omitted).
*Explanations:* ▸ *Galatians:* inhabitants of Galatia, an ancient region in Asia Minor. ▸ *Paul* (ca. 3-ca. 64): Saint Paul, the Christian apostle, "Apostle to the Gentiles," a Jew, born in Tarsus, Asia Minor (now in Turkey).
*Note:* The letter was probably written about 55-57.
*Remark:* "Whenever we have an opportunity"....

### 144 GOODNESS
Spread goodness in words and deeds everywhere. In a spirit of universal kindness be ready to serve others with help and instruction; live happily, then, among the ailing; among men who are greedy, remain free from greed; among men who hate, dwell free from hatred;...

Buddha (the Enlightened One), Gautama Buddha (Siddhartha Gautama) (ca. 563-ca. 483 B.C.), Indian prince, born in the district Nepal, founder of Buddhism.
*Source:* Paul Carus, *Nirvâna: A Story of Buddhist Philosophy* (Chicago: Open Court Publishing Co., 1896), p. 45.

### 145 GOODNESS
He who sows good will reap peace.

Moroccan proverb.
*Source:* Edward Westermarck and Shereef 'Abd-es-Salam el-Baqqali, *Wit and Wisdom in Morocco: A Study of Native Proverbs* (1930; reprint, London: George Routledge & Sons, 1980), p. 228.

### 146 GOVERNMENT
Well, fancy giving money to the Government!
    Might as well have put it down the drain
Fancy giving money to the Government!
    Nobody will see the stuff again.
        Well, they've no idea what money's for—
        Ten to one they'll start another war.
        I've heard a lot of silly things, but, Lor'!
Fancy giving money to the Government!

A. P. Herbert (Alan Patrick Herbert) (1890-1971), English novelist, poet and politician, in his poem "Too Much!", published in 1930.
*Source:* A. P. Herbert, *Ballads for Broadbrows* (London: Ernest Benn, 1930), p. 98, 98 (italics omitted).
*Remark:* Too often true?

### 147 GRATITUDE
The gratitude of every home in our Island, in our Empire, and indeed throughout the world, except in the abodes of the guilty, goes out to the British airmen who, undaunted by odds, unwearied in their constant challenge and mortal danger,

are turning the tide of world war by their prowess and by their devotion. Never in the field of human conflict was so much owed by so many to so few.

Winston S. Churchill (Winston Leonard Spencer Churchill) (1874-1965), British statesman, orator and author, prime minister of the United Kingdom (1940-1945 and 1951-1955), in a speech given on August 20, 1940, to the House of Commons on the situation early in World War II, during the Battle of Britain, a series of air battles between British and German planes during German bombing raids on the United Kingdom, mainly waged in August and September 1940 but lasting until the early summer of 1941.
*Source:* Parliamentary Debates, Commons, 5th series, vol. 364, pp. 1159, 1166-1167.
*Remark:* Fighter pilots shielding freedom.

### 148 GREATNESS
The great man is he who does not lose his child's heart.

Mencius or Meng-tzu ("Master Meng") [Mengzi] (372-289 B.C.), Chinese philosopher, according to the *Book of Mencius*, published by his disciples (book IV, part II, chapter XII).
*Source:* James Legge, trans., *The Chinese Classics*, vol. II, *The Life and Works of Mencius* (London: Trübner & Co., 1875), p. 257.

### 149 HAPPINESS
One who is not connected with the Supreme ... can have neither transcendental intelligence nor a steady mind, without which there is no possibility of peace. And how can there be any happiness without peace?

*Bhagavadgita* (*The Divine Song* or *The Song of the Adorable One*), a religious classic forming part of the Indian epic *Mahabharata* (The great poem of the Bharatas), probably the longest epic poem in the world, compiled gradually for centuries in India and probably completed about 200 (chapter (lecture) 2, verse 66).
*Source: Bhagavad-Gita As It Is*, trans. A. C. Bhaktivedanta Swami Prabhupada, rev. and enl. ed. (Los Angeles: Bhaktivedanta Book Trust, 1983), p. 155 (text in bold letters in source).

### 150 HARVEST
THEY fought south of the Castle,
They died north of the wall.
They died in the moors and were not buried.
....
The harvest was never gathered.
....
You served your Prince faithfully,
Though all in vain.

Chinese poem, "Fighting South of the Castle," composed about 124 B.C. by an anonymous poet.

*Source:* Arthur Waley, trans., *A Hundred and Seventy Chinese Poems* (London: Constable and Company, 1918), p. 33, 33.

### 151 HATRED

O true believers, observe justice when ye appear as witnesses before GOD, and let not hatred towards any induce you to do wrong: *but* act justly; this will approach nearer unto piety; and fear GOD, for GOD is fully acquainted with what ye do. GOD hath promised unto those who believe, and do that which is right, that they shall receive pardon and a great reward. But they who believe not, and accuse our signs of falsehood, they shall be the companions of hell.

The Qur'an (Koran), chapter (sura) V, "The Table," verses [11-13].
*Source: The Koran: Commonly Called the Alkoran of Mohammed*, trans. George Sale (London: Frederick Warne and Co., 1891), pp. 73, 74.
*Explanation: The Qur'an* (Arabic, "recitation, reading"): the sacred book of Islam, the Muslim religion (Arabic, "submission to the will of God"), founded by the Arab prophet Mohammed (Muhammad, meaning "praised" or "praiseworthy") (ca. 570-632).

### 152 HERBICIDE

The Second Indochina War of 1961-1975 is noted for the widespread and severe environmental damage inflicted upon its theatre of operations, especially in the former South Viet Nam....

....
Faced during the Second Indochina War with a dispersed and elusive enemy in South Viet Nam, the USA sought to deny this foe sanctuary, freedom of movement, and a local civilian economy from which to derive its sustenance. This strategy was pursued, *inter alia*, through an unprecedentedly massive and sustained expenditure of herbicidal chemical warfare agents against the fields and forests of South Viet Nam. The use of these agents resulted in large-scale devastation of crops, in widespread immediate damage to the inland and coastal forest ecosystems, and in a variety of health problems among exposed humans.
.... The impact on the human population has included long-lasting neuro-intoxications as well as the possibility of increased incidences of hepatitis, liver cancer, chromosomal damage, and adverse outcomes of pregnancy from exposed fathers (especially spontaneous abortions and congenital malformations).
....
Finally the question arises regarding future employment of herbicides as anti-plant chemical warfare agents and of the potentially ecocidal outcome of their use.... Military evaluations have been favourable as regards a diversity of potential operational theatres.... On the other hand, a widely held interpretation of the Geneva Protocol of 1925 makes illegal their use in war. Moreover, their impact—especially as demonstrated by the Second Indochina War—makes it illegal to use them in the light of the Environmental Modification Convention of 1977.

Arthur H. Westing (Arthur Herbert Westing) (b. 1928), American forester, senior research fellow at the Stockholm International Peace Research Institute (SIPRI), in a paper presented to the International Symposium on Herbicides and Defoliants in War, held in Ho Chi Minh City from January 13 to 20, 1983.

*Source:* Arthur H. Westing, "Herbicides in War: Past and Present," Arthur H. Westing, ed., *Herbicides in War: The Long-term Ecological and Human Consequences* (London: Taylor & Francis, 1984), pp. 1, 3, 22-23 (first paragraph indented; reference to footnote omitted).

*Explanations:* ▶ *Environmental Modification Convention of 1977:* Convention on the Prohibition of Military or Any Other Hostile Use of Environmental Modification Techniques, which was adopted by United Nations General Assembly resolution 31/72 of December 10, 1976 (Convention on the Prohibition of Military or Any Other Hostile Use of Environmental Modification Techniques), opened for signature on May 18, 1977, and entered into force on October 5, 1978. For the text of the convention, *see* United Nations, *Resolutions and Decisions Adopted by the General Assembly during Its Thirty-first Session,* vol. I, 21 *September-22 December 1976* (General Assembly, Official Records: Thirty-first Session, Supplement No. 39 (A/31/39)), p. 36, and United Nations, *Treaty Series,* vol. 1108, p. 151. ▶ *Geneva Protocol of 1925:* Protocol for the Prohibition of the Use in War of Asphyxiating, Poisonous or Other Gases, and of Bacteriological Methods of Warfare (Geneva Protocol of 1925), which was signed at Geneva on June 17, 1925, and entered into force on February 8, 1928; for the text of the protocol, *see* League of Nations, *Treaty Series,* vol. XCIV [94], p. 65.

*Remark:* Illegal use of herbicides in warfare may lead to ecocide and genocide.

### 153 HERBICIDE

Dioxin pervades the land of South Viet Nam and an astounding 6% of school children randomly sampled have congenital malformations. This number refers only to the survivors. Of every hundred pregnancies nearly four experience a condition known as a hydatidiform mole in which the foetus degenerates into a formless blood-soaked sponge-like mass. A larger percentage abort spontaneously. And many more are stillborn, while a large number of those that make it alive into this world die within 24 hours.

....

Viet Nam has an estimated one million Agent Orange victims, of which 150,000 are children....

....

The major piece of international humanitarian law prohibiting environmental war was drafted in reaction to what took place in Viet Nam, and is contained in two articles of the 1977 Additional Protocol I to the Geneva Conventions. Article 35 states that "it is prohibited to employ methods or means of warfare which are intended, or may be expected, to cause widespread, long-term and severe damage to the environment." This prohibition is spelled out in detail in two sections of Article 55.

....

.... Scientists in the Chemical and Biological Weapons Department.... What they didn't realise, or possibly chose to ignore, was that 2,4,5-T contained a most toxic substance, dioxin, an unintentional by-product of herbicide production.

....

.... But the end of the spraying was not the end of the story—33 years later Agent Orange is still present in the ecosystem, and the very land of Viet Nam continues to poison its people.

....

In the 1960s, U.S. military policy was to downplay long-term health concerns about chemicals used in Viet Nam in order to assist their war effort. Today, an analogous spin is underwritten by a chemical industry worried about lost profits due to a possible future ban on chlorine-based production. In both instances, the policy is identical: "act now, apologise later." The circumstantial evidence, as this book shows, is overwhelming and the scientific proof is not far behind.

Philip Jones Griffiths (1936-2008), British photographer, born in Wales, writing, in his 2003 book *Agent Orange: "Collateral Damage" in Viet Nam*, on the effects of environmental warfare late in the Vietnam War (1955-1975).
*Source*: Philip Jones Griffiths, *Agent Orange: "Collateral Damage" in Viet Nam* (London: Trolley, 2003), pp. 38, 54, 152, 164, 169, 174.
*Remark*: Care now instead of care later?

## 154 HERO
They all come upstairs every day, talk to the men about business and politics, to the women about food and wartime difficulties, and about newspapers and books with the children. They put on the brightest possible faces, bring flowers and presents for birthdays and bank holidays, are always ready to help and do all they can. That is something we must never forget; although others may show heroism in the war or against the Germans, our helpers display heroism in their cheerfulness and affection.

Anne Frank (Annelies Marie Frank) (1929-1945), German-born Dutch Jew, later a Holocaust victim, in her diary, on January 28, 1944, while hiding from the German Nazis in occupied Amsterdam.
*Source*: Anne Frank, *Anne Frank: The Diary of a Young Girl*, trans. B. M. Mooyaart-Doubleday, Modern Library (New York: Random House, 1952), pp. 158, 159.
*Notes*: ▸ Anne Frank kept her diary while in hiding from July 9, 1942, to August 4, 1944, at which time she was deported to the Auschwitz (Auschwitz-Birkenau) concentration camp operated by the German Nazis in the province of Cracow in southern Poland from 1940 to 1945. She died of typhoid fever and malnutrition in the Bergen-Belsen camp northwest of Celle (near Hanover), Germany, in March 1945, only about one month before the liberation of the camp and about two months before the end of World War II in Europe.
▸ One of the heroes referred to was Mrs. Miep Gies (Hermine Santrouschitz) (1909-2010), Austrian-born Dutch secretary and resistance worker who in a prologue to her 1987 book *Anne Frank Remembered* wrote as follows:
I am not a hero. I stand at the end of the long, long line of good Dutch people who did what I did or more—much more—during those dark and terrible times years ago, but always like yesterday in the hearts of those of us who bear witness. Never a day goes by that I do not think of what happened then.
More than twenty thousand Dutch people helped to hide Jews and others in need of hiding during those years. I willingly did what I could to help. My husband did as well. It was not enough.

(Miep Gies with Alison Leslie Gold, *Anne Frank Remembered: The story of the Woman Who Helped to Hide the Frank Family* (New York: Simon and Schuster, 1987), p. 11 (first paragraph indented)
*Remark:* Heroes, through "cheerfulness and affection," as well as courage.

## 155 HISTORY
History repeats itself.

English proverb.
*Source:* V. H. Collins, *A Book of English Proverbs, with Origins and Explanations* (London: Longmans, Green and Co., 1959), p. 63 (text in bold letters in source).
*Note:* Thucydides (ca. 460-ca. 400 B.C.), Greek historian, expressed the thought as follows in his work *The History of the Peloponnesian War* (book I, chapter I, section 22):
The absence of romance in my history will, I fear, detract somewhat from its interest; but if it be judged useful by those inquirers who desire an exact knowledge of the past as an aid to the interpretation of the future, which in the course of human things must resemble if it does not reflect it, I shall be content.
(Thucydides, *The History of the Peloponnesian War*, trans. Richard Crawley, Everyman's Library (1910; reprint, London: J. M. Dent & Sons; New York: E. P. Dutton & Co., 1936), p. 15)
*Explanation: The Peloponnesian War:* a war mainly between Athens and Sparta (Lacedaemon), fought intermittently from 431 to 404 B.C., and in which the Spartans (Lacedaemonians) finally defeated the Athenians. The war is named after Peloponnese or Peloponnesus, a peninsula in southern Greece.
*Remark:* Let us repeat the good in history.

## 156 HOME
AT fifteen I went with the army,
At fourscore I came home.

Old Chinese poem, called "Old Poem" or "The Old Soldier's Return," composed by an unknown poet.
*Source:* Arthur Waley, trans., *A Hundred and Seventy Chinese Poems* (London: Constable and Company, 1918), p. 32, 32 ("Old Poem").
*Remark:* Alone, at the end of the poem, "tears fell."

## 157 HOME
Foreign Office,
November 2nd, 1917.
Dear Lord Rothschild,
I have much pleasure in conveying to you, on behalf of His Majesty's Government, the following declaration of sympathy with Jewish Zionist aspirations which has been submitted to, and approved by, the Cabinet.
"His Majesty's Government view with favour the establishment in Palestine of a national home for the Jewish people, and will use their best endeavours to facilitate the achievement of this object, it being clearly understood that nothing shall be done which may prejudice the civil and religious rights of existing non-

Jewish communities in Palestine, or the rights and political status enjoyed by Jews in any other country".

I should be grateful if you would bring this declaration to the knowledge of the Zionist Federation.

> Y. sin.
> Arthur James Balfour

The Balfour Declaration, signed on November 2, 1917, on behalf of the British government by the British statesman Arthur James Balfour (1848-1930), former prime minister (1902-1905), in his capacity as foreign secretary (1916-1919), more particularly contained in a letter addressed to Lionel Walter Rothschild (Baron Rothschild (of Tring)) (1868-1937), English collector, taxonomist and patron.

*Source: Encyclopaedia Judaica* (1971), under "Balfour Declaration."

*Note:* Rothschild replied on November 4, 1917, as follows:

> 4 Nov. 1917

Dear Mr. Balfour,

I write to thank you most sincerely for your letter and also for the great interest you have shown in the wishes of the large mass of the Jewish people and also for the efforts and trouble you have taken on their behalf. I can assure you that the gratitude of ten millions of people will be yours, for the British Government has opened up, by their message, a prospect of safety and comfort to large masses of people who are much in need of it. I dare say you have been informed that already in many parts of Russia renewed persecution has broken out.

With renewed thanks to you and His Majesty's government,

> I remain
> yours sincerely
> Rothschild

(*Same place*)


## 158 HORROR

[W]hen he heard that the Belgœ, who were the most powerful of all the Gauls, and inhabited a third part of the country, were revolted, and had got together a great many thousand men in arms, he immediately set out and took his way hither with great expedition, and falling upon the enemy as they were ravaging the Gauls, his allies, he soon defeated and put to flight the largest and least scattered division of them. For though their numbers were great, yet they made but a slender defence, and the marshes and deep rivers were made passable to the Roman foot by the vast quantity of dead bodies.

Plutarch (ca. 46-120), Greek biographer, describing, in his work *Parallel Lives* (the biography of Caesar), the circumstances when the Roman general and statesman Julius Caesar (Gaius Julius Caesar) (100-44 B.C.), proconsul (governor) of Gaul (mainly the present France and Belgium), crushed the revolt of the Belgae in 57 B.C.

*Source:* Plutarch, *Plutarch's Lives: The "Dryden Plutarch,"* rev. Arthur Hugh Clough, Everyman's Library, vol. II (1910; reprint, London: J. M. Dent & Sons; New York: E. P. Dutton & Co., 1914), pp. 530, 545.

**159 HORROR**

[R]esistance might provoke, but neither age nor sex could mollify, their implacable rage; they indulged themselves three days in a promiscuous massacre; and the infection of the dead bodies produced an epidemical disease. After seventy thousand Moslems had been put to the sword, and the harmless Jews had been burnt in their synagogue, they could still reserve a multitude of captives whom interest or lassitude persuaded them to spare.

Edward Gibbon (1737-1794), English historian, describing the conquest of Jerusalem by the crusaders in 1099, in his work *The History of the Decline and Fall of the Roman Empire*, published from 1776 to 1788 (chapter LVIII [58]).
*Source*: Edward Gibbon, *The History of the Decline and Fall of the Roman Empire*, ed. William Smith, vol. VII (London: John Murray, 1862), p. 227 (reference marks omitted).
*Note*: The First Crusade took place from 1096 to 1099.
*Remark*: Muslims and Jews in the same boat.

**160 HORROR**

The hospital of S. Bazile presented the most awful and hideous sight:—seven thousand five hundred bodies were piled like pigs of lead over one another in the corridors; carcases were strewed about in every part; and all the broken windows and walls were stuffed with feet, legs, arms, hands, trunks, and heads to fit the apertures, and keep out the air from the yet living.

Robert Wilson (Robert Thomas Wilson) (1777-1849), English general, commissioner at the headquarters of the Russian army, on the retreat of the French army under Napoleon I (Napoleon Bonaparte) (1769-1821), emperor of France (1804-1814, 1815) from Russia in 1812, referring more particularly to a scene in a hospital in the city of Vilnius, then in Russia (now the capital of Lithuania), late in December 1812.
*Source*: Robert Wilson, *Narrative of Events during the Invasion of Russia by Napoleon Bonaparte, and the Retreat of the French Army. 1812.*, ed. Herbert Randolph, 2nd ed. (London: John Murray, 1860), p. 354.
*Remark*: The glory of war?

**161 HOSPITAL**

Miss Nightingale arrived at Scutari—a suburb of Constantinople, on the Asiatic side of the Bosphorus—on November 4th, 1854; it was ten days after the battle of Balaclava, and the day before the battle of Inkerman....

.... Want, neglect, confusion, misery—in every shape and in every degree of intensity—filled the endless corridors and the vast apartments of the gigantic barrack-house, which, without forethought or preparation, had been hurriedly set aside as the chief shelter for the victims of the war....

....

In these surroundings, those who had been long inured to scenes of human suffering—surgeons with a world-wide knowledge of agonies, soldiers familiar with fields of carnage, missionaries with remembrances of famine and of plague—yet found a depth of horror which they had never known before. There were moments, there were places, in the Barrack Hospital at Scutari, where the strongest hand was struck with trembling, and the boldest eye would turn away its gaze.

Miss Nightingale came, and she, at any rate, in that Inferno, did not abandon hope....

....

.... She stood firm; she was a rock in the angry ocean; with her alone was safety, comfort, life. And so it was that hope dawned at Scutari. The reign of chaos and old night began to dwindle; order came upon the scene, and common sense, and forethought, and decision, radiating out from the little room off the great gallery in the Barrack Hospital where, day and night, the Lady Superintendent was at her task. Progress might be slow, but it was sure.

Lytton Strachey (Giles Lytton Strachey) (1880-1932), English biographer, writing, in his 1918 book *Eminent Victorians*, on the English nurse Florence Nightingale (1820-1910), "founder of modern nursing," more particularly on her arrival to Turkey in 1854, during the Crimean War (1854-1856).
*Source:* Lytton Strachey, *Eminent Victorians: Cardinal Manning, Florence Nightingale, Dr. Arnold, General Gordon* (London: Chatto & Windus, 1918), pp. 116, 127, 129, 130, 132.
*Explanations:* ▸ *Balaclava:* Balaklava, a supply port of British, French and Turkish forces on the Black Sea, near the town of Sevastopol (Sebastopol), Crimea, in the neighborhood of which the doomed charge of a British light brigade took place on October 25, 1854. ▸ *Inkerman:* the site of a November 5, 1854 battle near Sevastopol where British and French forces fought against the Russians.
*Remark:* War for the wounded.

### 162 HOSPITAL
Civilian hospitals organized to give care to the wounded and sick, the infirm and maternity cases, may in no circumstances be the object of attack, but shall at all times be respected and protected by the Parties to the conflict.

Article 18, paragraph 1, of the Geneva Convention Relative to the Protection of Civilian Persons in Time of War of August 12, 1949, which was signed at Geneva on August 12, 1949, and entered into force on October 21, 1950.
*Source:* United Nations, *Treaty Series*, vol. 75, pp. 287, 300.

### 163 HUMAN BEING
Bring back the fathers! Bring back the mothers!
Bring back the old people!
Bring back the children!

Toge Sankichi (Toge Mitsuyoshi) (1917-1953), Japanese A-bomb poet of Hiroshima, on Hiroshima in 1945, in his work *Poems of the Atomic Bomb*, written from 1950 to 1951, more particularly in the first poem thereof, "Prelude."
*Source:* Richard H. Minear, ed. and trans., *Hiroshima: Three Witnesses* (Princeton, New Jersey: Princeton University Press, 1990), p. 305, 305.
*Remark:* "No victory can make good their loss."

## 164 HUMAN RIGHTS

We hold these truths to be self-evident, that all men are created equal, that they are endowed by their Creator with certain unalienable Rights, that among these are Life, Liberty and the pursuit of Happiness.

From the Declaration of Independence of July 4, 1776 ("The unanimous Declaration of the thirteen united States of America").
*Source:* Francis Newton Thorpe, comp. and ed., *The Federal and State Constitutions, Colonial Charters, and Other Organic Laws of the States, Territories, and Colonies Now or Heretofore Forming the United States of America,* vol. I, *United States—Alabama—District of Columbia* (Washington: Government Printing Office, 1909), p. 3, 3.
*Remark:* The right to life.

## 165 HUMAN RIGHTS

PREAMBLE

*Whereas* recognition of the inherent dignity and of the equal and inalienable rights of all members of the human family is the foundation of freedom, justice and peace in the world,

....

*Whereas* the peoples of the United Nations have in the Charter reaffirmed their faith in fundamental human rights, in the dignity and worth of the human person and in the equal rights of men and women and have determined to promote social progress and better standards of life in larger freedom,

....

*Now, therefore,*
*The General Assembly*
*Proclaims* this Universal Declaration of Human Rights as a common standard of achievement for all peoples and all nations, to the end that every individual and every organ of society, keeping this Declaration constantly in mind, shall strive by teaching and education to promote respect for these rights and freedoms and by progressive measures, national and international, to secure their universal and effective recognition and observance, both among the peoples of Member States themselves and among the peoples of territories under their jurisdiction.

ARTICLE 1

All human beings are born free and equal in dignity and rights. They are endowed with reason and conscience and should act towards one another in a spirit of brotherhood.

....

ARTICLE 18

Everyone has the right to freedom of thought, conscience and religion; this right includes freedom to change his religion or belief, and freedom, either alone or in community with others and in public or private, to manifest his religion or belief in teaching, practice, worship and observance.

ARTICLE 19

Everyone has the right to freedom of opinion and expression; this right includes freedom to hold opinions without interference and to seek, receive and impart information and ideas through any media and regardless of frontiers.

....

ARTICLE 24

Everyone has the right to rest and leisure, including reasonable limitation of working hours and periodic holidays with pay.

ARTICLE 25

1. Everyone has the right to a standard of living adequate for the health and well-being of himself and of his family, including food, clothing, housing and medical care and necessary social services, and the right to security in the event of unemployment, sickness, disability, widowhood, old age or other lack of livelihood in circumstances beyond his control.

....

ARTICLE 26

1. Everyone has the right to education. Education shall be free, at least in the elementary and fundamental stages. Elementary education shall be compulsory. Technical and professional education shall be made generally available and higher education shall be equally accessible to all on the basis of merit.

....

ARTICLE 30

Nothing in this Declaration may be interpreted as implying for any State, group or person any right to engage in any activity or to perform any act aimed at the destruction of any of the rights and freedoms set forth herein.

From the preamble to and certain articles of the Universal Declaration of Human Rights adopted and proclaimed by United Nations General Assembly resolution 217 (III) of December 10, 1948 (International Bill of Human Rights; part A, Universal Declaration of Human Rights).

*Source:* United Nations, *Resolutions, 21 September-12 December 1948* (General Assembly, Official Records: Third Session, part I (A/810)), pp. 71, 71-72, 74-77.

*Remark:* Human rights for the human family.

### 166 HUMAN RIGHTS

The Governments signatory hereto, being Members of the Council of Europe,

....

Considering that the aim of the Council of Europe is the achievement of greater unity between its Members and that one of the methods by which that aim is to be pursued is the maintenance and further realisation of Human Rights and Fundamental Freedoms;

Reaffirming their profound belief in those Fundamental Freedoms which are the foundation of justice and peace in the world and are best maintained on the one hand by an effective political democracy and on the other by a common understanding and observance of the Human Rights upon which they depend;

....

Have agreed as follows:

....

*Article 19*

To ensure the observance of the engagements undertaken by the High Contracting Parties in the present Convention, there shall be set up:

(1) A European Commission of Human Rights hereinafter referred to as "the Commission";

(2) A European Court of Human Rights, hereinafter referred to as "the Court".

From the preamble to and Article 19 of the Convention for the Protection of Human Rights and Fundamental Freedoms [the European Convention on Human Rights], which was signed at Rome on November 4, 1950, and entered into force on September 3, 1953.

*Source:* United Nations, *Treaty Series*, vol. 213, pp. 221, 222, 224, 234.

*Explanation: Council of Europe:* an organization of European states, headquartered in Strasbourg, France, which has since 1949 worked for democracy, human rights and unity in Europe through cooperation on legal, cultural and social issues, not in the least treatymaking.

*Remark:* Human rights, "the foundation of justice and peace in the world."

## 167 HUMAN RIGHTS

*The States Parties to the present Covenant,*

*Considering* that, in accordance with the principles proclaimed in the Charter of the United Nations, recognition of the inherent dignity and of the equal and inalienable rights of all members of the human family is the foundation of freedom, justice and peace in the world,

....

*Recognizing* that, in accordance with the Universal Declaration of Human Rights, the ideal of free human beings enjoying freedom from fear and want can only be achieved if conditions are created whereby everyone may enjoy his economic, social and cultural rights, as well as his civil and political rights,

....

*Realizing* that the individual, having duties to other individuals and to the community to which he belongs, is under a responsibility to strive for the promotion and observance of the rights recognized in the present Covenant,

*Agree* upon the following articles:

....

### Article 2

1. Each State Party to the present Covenant undertakes to take steps, individually and through international assistance and co-operation, especially economic and technical, to the maximum of its available resources, with a view to achieving progressively the full realization of the rights recognized in the present Covenant by all appropriate means, including particularly the adoption of legislative measures.

....

### Article 11

1. The States Parties to the present Covenant recognize the right of everyone to an adequate standard of living for himself and his family, including adequate food, clothing and housing, and to the continuous improvement of living conditions. The States Parties will take appropriate steps to ensure the realization of this right, recognizing to this effect the essential importance of international co-operation based on free consent.

....

### Article 13

1. The States Parties to the present Covenant recognize the right of everyone to education. They agree that education shall be directed to the full development of the human personality and the sense of its dignity, and shall strengthen the respect for human rights and fundamental freedoms. They further agree that education shall enable all persons to participate effectively in a free society,

promote understanding, tolerance and friendship among all nations and all racial, ethnic or religious groups, and further the activities of the United Nations for the maintenance of peace.

From the preamble to, and Article 2, paragraph 1, Article 11, paragraph 1, and Article 13, paragraph 1, of, the International Covenant on Economic, Social and Cultural Rights contained in an annex to United Nations General Assembly resolution 2200 (XXI) of December 16, 1966 (International Covenant on Economic, Social and Cultural Rights, International Covenant on Civil and Political Rights and Optional Protocol to the International Covenant on Civil and Political Rights). The covenant entered into force on January 3, 1976.

*Source:* United Nations, *Resolutions Adopted by the General Assembly during Its Twenty-first Session, 20 September-20 December 1966* (General Assembly, Official Records: Twenty-first Session, Supplement No. 16 (A/6316)), pp. 49, 49-51. For the text of the covenant, *see also* United Nations, *Treaty Series*, vol. 993, p. 3.

*Explanations:* ▸ *Charter of the United Nations:* Charter of the United Nations, which was signed at San Francisco, United States, on June 26, 1945, and entered into force on October 24, 1945. ▸ *Universal Declaration of Human Rights:* Universal Declaration of Human Rights adopted and proclaimed by United Nations General Assembly resolution 217 (III) of December 10, 1948 (International Bill of Human Rights; part A, Universal Declaration of Human Rights).

*Remark:* Is the education in your country promoting friendship among all nations or teaching people to earn money?

## 168 HUMAN RIGHTS
*The States Parties to the present Covenant,*

....

*Agree* upon the following articles:

....

### Article 2

....

2. Where not already provided for by existing legislative or other measures, each State Party to the present Covenant undertakes to take the necessary steps, in accordance with its constitutional processes and with the provisions of the present Covenant, to adopt such legislative or other measures as may be necessary to give effect to the rights recognized in the present Covenant.

....

### Article 4

1. In time of public emergency which threatens the life of the nation and the existence of which is officially proclaimed, the States Parties to the present Covenant may take measures derogating from their obligations under the present Covenant to the extent strictly required by the exigencies of the situation, provided that such measures are not inconsistent with their other obligations under international law and do not involve discrimination solely on the ground of race, colour, sex, language, religion or social origin.

2. No derogation from articles 6, 7, 8 (paragraphs 1 and 2), 11, 15, 16 and 18 may be made under this provision.

....

## Article 6

1. Every human being has the inherent right to life. This right shall be protected by law. No one shall be arbitrarily deprived of his life.

....

## Article 9

1. Everyone has the right to liberty and security of person....

....

## Article 12

....

2. Everyone shall be free to leave any country, including his own.

....

4. No one shall be arbitrarily deprived of the right to enter his own country.

....

## Article 18

1. Everyone shall have the right to freedom of thought, conscience and religion....

....

## Article 19

....

2. Everyone shall have the right to freedom of expression; this right shall include freedom to seek, receive and impart information and ideas of all kinds, regardless of frontiers, either orally, in writing or in print, in the form of art, or through any other media of his choice.

....

## Article 20

1. Any propaganda for war shall be prohibited by law.

....

## Article 27

In those States in which ethnic, religious or linguistic minorities exist, persons belonging to such minorities shall not be denied the right, in community with the other members of their group, to enjoy their own culture, to profess and practice their own religion, or to use their own language.

....

## Article 28

1. There shall be established a Human Rights Committee....

....

## Article 41

1. A State Party to the present Covenant may at any time declare under this article that it recognizes the competence of the Committee to receive and consider communications to the effect that a State Party claims that another State Party is not fulfilling its obligations under the present Covenant....

....

## Article 42

1. (a) If a matter referred to the Committee in accordance with article 41 is not resolved to the satisfaction of the States Parties concerned, the Committee may, with the prior consent of the States Parties concerned, appoint an *ad hoc* Conciliation Commission.... The good offices of the Commission shall be made available to the States Parties concerned with a view to an amicable solution of the matter on the basis of respect for the present Covenant;

....

### Optional Protocol to the International Covenant on Civil and Political Rights

*The States Parties to the present Protocol,*

*Considering* that in order further to achieve the purposes of the Covenant on Civil and Political Rights ... and the implementation of its provisions it would be appropriate to enable the Human Rights Committee ... to receive and consider ... communications from individuals claiming to be victims of violations of any of the rights set forth in the Covenant,

*Have agreed* as follows....

From the International Covenant on Civil and Political Rights and the Optional Protocol to the International Covenant on Civil and Political Rights contained in an annex to United Nations General Assembly resolution 2200 (XXI) of December 16, 1966 (International Covenant on Economic, Social and Cultural Rights, International Covenant on Civil and Political Rights and Optional Protocol to the International Covenant on Civil and Political Rights). The covenant, with the exception of Article 41, entered into force on March 23, 1976.

*Source:* United Nations, *Resolutions Adopted by the General Assembly during Its Twenty-first Session, 20 September-20 December 1966* (General Assembly, Official Records: Twenty-first Session, Supplement No. 16 (A/6316)), pp. 49, 52-57, 59 (Partes corrected to Parties in the beginning of Article 42). For the texts of the covenant and protocol, *see also* United Nations, *Treaty Series*, vol. 999, p. 171.

*Remark:* "Any propaganda for war shall be prohibited by law."

### 169 HUMAN RIGHTS

In 1995, the fiftieth anniversary of the United Nations and UNESCO and the United Nations Year for Tolerance, we stressed that it was only through a daily effort to know others better—I am the 'other'—and respect them that we would be able to tackle at source the problems of marginalization, indifference, resentment and hatred. This is the only way to break the vicious circle that leads from insults to confrontation and the use of force.

....

A universal renunciation of violence requires the commitment of the **whole** of society.... Ministries of war and defence must gradually be turned into ministries of peace.

....

It is clear that we cannot simultaneously pay the price of war and the price of peace.... What is needed, then, is to reduce the investment in arms and destruction in order to increase investment in the construction of peace.

....

.... To invest in education is not only to respect a fundamental right but also to build peace and progress for the world's peoples....

....

.... Present generations have the almost impossible, biblical task of 'beating their swords into ploughshares' and making the transition from an instinct for war—developed since time immemorial—to a feeling for peace. To achieve this would be the best and most noble act that the 'global village' could accomplish, and the best legacy to our descendants. With what satisfaction and relief should we be able to look into the eyes of our children! It would be also the best way to celebrate the fiftieth anniversary of the Universal Declaration of Human Rights, in 1998.

Other 'rights' have been added since 1948. These should all be taken into account, and to them should be added the right which underlies them all: **the right to peace**—the right to live in peace! The right to our own 'personal sovereignty', to respect for life and dignity.

Federico Mayor (Federico Mayor Zaragoza) (b. 1934), Spanish biologist and poet, director-general of the United Nations Educational, Scientific and Cultural Organization (UNESCO) (1987-1999), in his January 1997 declaration "The Human Right to Peace: Declaration by the Director-General of UNESCO."

*Source:* International Symposium on Culture of Peace, *A Design for Peace: Advances in Systems Research of Peace: How to Replace a Culture of War by the Culture of Peace*, ed. George E. Lasker and Vladimir Lomeiko (Windsor, Ontario: International Institute for Advanced Studies in Systems Research and Cybernetics, 1997), pp. 1, 1-2, 4-5 (reference to footnotes omitted).

*Note:* The publication contains the proceedings of the International Symposium on Culture of Peace held from August 18 to 23, 1997, in Baden-Baden, Germany.

*See* Human Rights (Declaration of Independence).

*Remark:* "To invest in education is not only to respect a fundamental right but also to build peace and progress for the world's peoples."

### 170 INDEPENDENCE

I watched this man, a saintly, Christlike figure, walk upon this earth, in flesh and blood, at a moment when he had launched his great civil-disobedience movement that began to undermine the British hold on India and that, in the end, freed his country from two and a half centuries of British rule. It was one of the great accomplishments of history and for him a personal triumph such as our world has seldom seen.

....

In a harsh, cynical, violent and materialist world he taught and showed that love and truth and non-violence, ideas and ideals, could be of tremendous force—greater sometimes than guns and bombs and bayonets—in achieving a little justice, decency, peace and freedom for the vast masses of suffering, downtrodden men and women who eke out an existence on this inhospitable planet.

William L. Shirer (William Lawrence Shirer) (1904-1993), American writer and journalist-historian, writing on Mahatma Gandhi (Mohandas Karamchand Gandhi) (1869-1948), Indian political and religious leader and "architect of India's freedom through a nonviolent revolution," in an introduction to his 1979 book *Gandhi: A Memoir*.

*Source:* William L. Shirer, *Gandhi: A Memoir* (New York: Simon and Schuster, 1979), pp. 11-12.

*Explanation: Mahatma:* "great soul."

*Remark:* A great soul using soul force against an empire.

## 171 INDEPENDENCE

Gorbachev's telegram arrived in Vilnius at 2:30 P.M., and at 3:00 P.M. Kazimieras Motieka, deputy chairman of the Supreme Council, announced over the radio: "It looks like the hour has come when we all have to decide the most important decision facing Lithuania: Either independence or eternal slavery."...

....

The seizure of the television tower was a classic failure. Moscow had succeeded militarily but had failed politically; it had won a little and lost a great deal. Pyrrhus reportedly said after his battle with the Romans, "One more such victory and we are lost," and on the other hand, the poet John Dryden wrote, "Successful crimes alone are justified." As a British commentator put it, "President Gorbachev may win the battle he started by sending paratroops and 'Black Berets' on to the streets of the Baltic states... he has now assuredly lost the war."

A major factor in the Lithuanians' triumph, and probably the reason that the Soviet forces chose not to attack the parliament, was the presence of the horde of foreign correspondents. During that long night, I, like many others, thought that Lithuania was isolated, cut off. In the morning it became clear that the correspondents, who had flocked to the city over the past week, were informing the world. The attack on the television tower was a worldwide public relations disaster for the Soviet government and of course for Gorbachev.

The Lithuanians' tactic of passive resistance thrust on the military, together with its local allies and agents, the responsibility for violence. Military spokespersons in Vilnius and in Moscow objected to correspondents' reference to an "offensive" against the Landsbergis government, but the military and the Edinstvo demonstrators caused all the property damage and all the deaths involved. The Lithuanians had been defending "law and order"; the pro-Moscow forces had attempted a coup d'état and had failed.

Alfred Erich Senn (b. 1932), American professor of history, describing, in his 1995 book *Gorbachev's Failure in Lithuania*, the struggle of the Lithuanians for their independence in January 1991, Lithuania having declared its independence on March 11, 1990.

*Source:* Alfred Erich Senn, *Gorbachev's Failure in Lithuania* (New York: St. Martin's Press, 1995), pp. 130-131, 137 (reference to footnote omitted).

*Explanations:* ▸ *Black Berets:* Soviet internal ministry forces. ▸ *John Dryden* (1631-1700): English poet, dramatist and critic. ▸ *Edinstvo:* a pro-Soviet organization opposing the Lithuanian government. ▸ *Gorbachev:* Mikhail Sergeyevich Gorbachev (b. 1931), Soviet official, born in Russia, general secretary of the Communist Party of the Soviet Union (1985-1991), president of the Soviet Union (1990-1991), recipient of the 1990 Nobel Peace Prize. ▸ *Gorbachev's telegram:* a telegram arriving in Vilnius on January 10, 1991. ▸ *Landsbergis:* Vytautas Landsbergis (b. 1932), Lithuanian political leader and musicologist, president of Lithuania (1990-1992). ▸ *Motieka:* Kazimieras Motieka (b. 1929), Lithuanian attorney, deputy presidium chairman of the Supreme Council of Lithuania (1990-1993). ▸ *Pyrrhus* (ca. 318-272 B.C.): king of Epirus in ancient Greece, now northwestern Greece and southern Albania (ruled 307-303 and 297-272 B.C.).

*Remark:* The 1990 Nobel Peace Prize recipient using military force, winning a battle, losing a war.

## 172 INHUMANITY
Man's inhumanity to man
  Makes countless thousands mourn!

Robert Burns (1759-1796), Scottish national poet, in his 1785 poem "Man Was Made to Mourn."
*Source:* Robert Burns, *The Life and Works of Robert Burns*, ed. Robert Chambers, Library Edition, vol. I (Edinburgh and London: W. & R. Chambers, 1856), pp. 158, 159.
*Remark:* Humanity or inhumanity, even crimes against humanity. Making the right or wrong choices as to following others, following orders.

## 173 INITIATIVE
The tree which fills the arms grew from the tiniest sprout; the tower of nine storeys rose from a (small) heap of earth; the journey of a thousand lî commenced with a single step.

Lao-tzu or Lao-tze ("Master Lao") (Lao Tan) [Laozi] (from 604 to at least 517 B.C.), Chinese philosopher, founder of the mystical philosophy called Taoism, in his work *The Way and Its Power* (Chinese, *Tao-te Ching*) (part (book) II, chapter 64, paragraph 2).
*Source:* James Legge, trans., *The Sacred Books of China: The Texts of Tâoism*, Sacred Books of the East, vol. XXXIX (London: Oxford University Press (Humphrey Milford), 1891), pp. 45, 107-108.
*Explanation: Lî (li):* about 1/3 mile or 1/2 kilometer (varies).
*Notes:* ▶ The last sentence has been translated:
A journey of a thousand miles
Starts from beneath one's feet.
(Lao Tzu, *Tao te ching*, trans. D. C. Lau, Penguin Classics (1963; reprint, Harmondsworth, England: Penguin Books, 1971), p. 125)
  ▶ Legge calls the work *Tâo Teh King*.
*See* Walk (Satish Kumar, on his peace pilgrimage).

## 174 INTERVENTION
[T]he occasion has been judged proper for asserting, as a principle in which the rights and interests of the United States are involved, that the American continents, by the free and independent condition which they have assumed and maintain, are henceforth not to be considered as subjects for future colonization by any European powers.
    ....
    .... We owe it ... to candor and to the amicable relations existing between the United States and those powers to declare that we should consider any attempt on their part to extend their system to any portion of this hemisphere as dangerous to our peace and safety. With the existing colonies or dependencies of any European power we have not interfered and shall not interfere. But with the Governments who have declared their independence and maintained it, and whose independence we have, on great consideration and on just principles, acknowledged, we could not view any interposition for the purpose of oppressing

them, or controlling in any other manner their destiny, by any European power in any other light than as the manifestation of an unfriendly disposition toward the United States....

.... Our policy in regard to Europe, which was adopted at an early stage of the wars which have so long agitated that quarter of the globe, nevertheless remains the same, which is, not to interfere in the internal concerns of any of its powers; to consider the government *de facto* as the legitimate government for us; to cultivate friendly relations with it, and to preserve those relations by a frank, firm, and manly policy, meeting in all instances the just claims of every power, submitting to injuries from none.

James Monroe (1758-1831), president of the United States (1817-1825), in his seventh annual message to Congress on December 2, 1823, wherein he promulgated the Monroe Doctrine directed against European intervention in the political affairs of the American continents.

*Source:* James D. Richardson, comp., *A Compilation of the Messages and Papers of the Presidents, 1789-1897*, vol. II (Washington: Government Printing Office, 1896), pp. 207, 209, 218, 218-219.

*Remark:* The most famous doctrine of intervention.

### 175 INVASION

No one who saw this panoply of overwhelming might could doubt that the Allies would triumph in the battle to come. An English Coastguardsman in his lookout high up on the Dorset cliffs at Saint Alban's Head watched in disbelief as more than a thousand ships streamed by. Below him were soldiers and tanks in landing craft; above were barrage balloons; on the horizon were flotillas of landing craft to the east and lines of battleships to the west and a whole fleet silhouetted against the white cliffs of the Isle of Wight to the south. When the last of the ships had disappeared southward over the horizon, the Coastguardsman turned for home. "A lot of men are going to die tonight," he told his wife. "We should pray for them."

Douglas Botting (Douglas Scott Botting) (b. 1934), British writer and independent producer for television, born in England, describing, in his book *The Second Front*, the beginning of the seaborne journey from England which ended in the June 6, 1944 D-day Allied invasion at Normandy, northwestern France.

*Source:* Douglas Botting, *The Second Front*, ed. the editors of Time-Life Books, World War II (1978; rev. reprint, Alexandria, Virginia: Time-Life Books, 1980), p. 90.

*Remark:* Invasion of invasions?

### 176 INVENTION

Accurst be he that first invented war.

Christopher Marlowe (1564-1593), English dramatist, in his play *Tamburlaine the Great*, dating from about 1587 and published in 1590 (part I, act II, scene IV, line 664; Mycetes, king of Persia, speaking).

*Source:* Christopher Marlowe, *The Works of Christopher Marlowe*, ed. C. F. Tucker Brooke (Oxford: Clarendon Press, 1910), pp. 1, 9, 24, 26 (inuented modernized to invented; comma replaced by period at the end).

### 177 ISSUE

The problem of avoiding war is usually seen as one of establishing an alternative means of settling the important questions over which countries fight. Cures are designed not to alter the character of the dispute but to provide a substitute for armed conflict. Governments are urged to adjudicate or arbitrate those issues over which they would otherwise go to war.

.... Little issues can be adjudicated, but big issues appear to be different.

....

The danger inherent in big disputes and the difficulty of settling them suggests that, rather than spend our time looking for peaceful ways of resolving big issues, we might better explore the possibility of turning big issues—even issues like Hitler and Communism—into little ones....

....

A few examples show that the United States does have a choice in defining issues. In August, 1961, a civil aviation agreement between the United States and the Soviet Union was negotiated. The United States might have signed the agreement, treating it as a separate matter. We chose, however, to decline to sign it, and considered the matter related to Berlin. Sometimes, as has been the case with cultural exchange agreements, we agree to treat a particular problem between us and the Soviet Union as a matter that can be settled independently of other outstanding issues.

Another way in which an issue can be fractionated was illustrated after Brazil expropriated an American-owned telephone company in 1962. There were suggestions in Congress that if Latin America treated the United States in this way, we should give no further aid to the Alliance for Progress. The president, however, at a press conference defined the dispute as one between the governor of a province and a single American company over the form and amount of compensation due. A potentially big issue was turned into a small one. The way in which a government defines a dispute obviously does make a difference.

....

Within the last few years, it has been recognized that bigger military weapons do not necessarily mean better ones. Study of the complex questions involved in determining the military restraint which a country should exercise has developed the field of arms control. It is obvious that with international disputes, as with weapons, the bigger does not necessarily mean the better. Yet little study has been devoted to the criteria and methods by which a country should formulate and expand or contract issues in controversy. Arms are used only over issues. Perhaps more important than the field of arms control is the field of "issue control."

....

Fractionating conflict would ... seem to be a promising strategy not only for reducing the risk of war but also for promoting victory for our values.

Roger Fisher (Roger Dummer Fisher) (b. 1922), American lawyer, professor of international law at Harvard Law School, in a paper of a conference held by the American Academy of Arts and Sciences at Craigville, Massachusetts, in 1962.

*Source:* Roger Fisher, "Fractionating Conflict," in *International Conflict and Behavioral Science: The Craigville Papers*, ed. Roger Fisher (New York: Basic Books, 1964), pp. 91, 91-94, 108-109 (first paragraph indented).

*Explanation: Hitler:* Adolf Hitler (1889-1945), chancellor of the Third Reich of Nazi Germany (1933-1945).

*Remark:* Turning big issues into little ones—to adjudicate them, to improve relations.

### 178 JEW

No monument stands over Babii Yar.

....
I am
    each old man
        here shot dead.
I am
    every child
        here shot dead.
Nothing in me
        shall ever forget!

Yevgeny Yevtushenko (Yevgeny Aleksandrovich Yevtushenko) (b. 1933), Soviet-Russian poet, in his poem "Babii Yar," published on September 19, 1961, in *Literaturnaya Gazeta.*

*Source:* Yevgeny Yevtushenko, *The Poetry of Yevgeny Yevtushenko, 1953 to 1965,* ed. and trans. George Reavey (London: Calder and Boyars, 1966), pp. 145, 145, 149.

*Explanation: Babii Yar* (also spelled Babiy Yar, Babi Yar or Baby Yar, meaning women's cliff): "large ravine on the northern edge of the city of Kiev in Ukraine, the site of a mass grave of more than 100,000 victims, mostly Jews, who were killed by German Nazi SS squads between 1941 and 1943. The site became a symbol of Jewish suffering in the Holocaust." *Encyclopædia Britannica Online* (2001), under "Baby Yar" (underlining of the word "Holocaust" omitted). In the *same place* (on the Internet) it is stated that Yevtushenko wrote the poem "in protest against plans to build a sports stadium on the site." And also: "A small obelisk was constructed at Baby Yar in 1966, and in 1976 a 50-foot (15-metre) memorial statue was unveiled. Neither the statue nor the obelisk, however, made any reference to the Jewish dead."

*Additional explanation: SS:* an abbreviation of the German word Schutzstaffel (Protective Echelon), a Nazi Party corps responsible for, among other things, the administration of concentration (extermination) camps in World War II, declared a criminal organization by the International Military Tribunal in Nuremberg, Germany, in 1946.

*See* the same poem in Yevgeny Yevtushenko, comp., *Twentieth-Century Russian Poetry,* ed. Albert C. Todd and Max Hayward (with Daniel Weissbort) (London: Fourth Estate, 1993), pp. 805, 805-807.

*Remark:* The poem stands over Babii Yar.

### 179 JOURNALIST

Journalists engaged in dangerous professional missions in areas of armed conflict shall be considered as civilians....

Article 79, paragraph 1, of the Protocol Additional to the Geneva Conventions of 12 August 1949, and Relating to the Protection of Victims of International Armed

Conflicts (Protocol I), which was adopted at Geneva on June 8, 1977, and entered into force on December 7, 1978.

*Source:* United Nations, *Treaty Series*, vol. 1125, pp. 3, 40.

## 180 KILLING

Chî K'ang asked Confucius about government, saying, 'What do you say to killing the unprincipled for the good of the principled?' Confucius replied, 'Sir, in carrying on your government, why should you use killing at all? Let your *evinced* desires be for what is good, and the people will be good. The relation between superiors and inferiors, is like that between the wind and the grass. The grass must bend, when the wind blows across it.'

Confucius (K'ung Fu-tzu ("Master K'ung"), [Kongfuzi]) (551-479 B.C.), Chinese philosopher and political theorist, whose teachings became the basis of Confucianism, the main philosophical system in China, sometimes called a religion.

*Source:* James Legge, trans., *The Chinese Classics*, 2nd ed. rev., vol. I, *Confucian Analects, the Great Learning, and the Doctrine of the Mean* (Oxford: Clarendon Press, 1893), pp. 258-259 (book XII, chapter XIX).

*Explanation: Chî K'ang:* K'ang, a gentleman in Lu, the native state of Confucius (eastern China); *same source*, pp. 442-443.

## 181 LANDMINE

Landmines distinguish themselves because once they have been sown, once the soldier walks away from the weapon, the landmine cannot tell the difference between a soldier or a civilian—a woman, a child, a grandmother going out to collect firewood to make the family meal. The crux of the problem is that while the use of the weapon might be militarily justifiable during the day of the battle, or even the two weeks of the battle, or maybe even the two months of the battle, once peace is declared the landmine does not recognize that peace. The landmine is eternally prepared to take victims. In common parlance, it is the perfect soldier, the "eternal sentry." The war ends, the landmine goes on killing.

....

.... Landmines have been used since the U.S. Civil War, since the Crimean War, yet we are taking them out of arsenals of the world. It is amazing. It is historic. It proves that civil society and governments do not have to see themselves as adversaries. It demonstrates that small and middle powers can work together with civil society and address humanitarian concerns with breathtaking speed. It shows that such a partnership is a new kind of "superpower" in the post-Cold War world.

Jody Williams (b. 1950), American peace activist, recipient of the 1997 Nobel Peace Prize along with the International Campaign to Ban Landmines (ICBL), which she helped found in 1992 and for which she acted as a campaign coordinator, giving her Nobel lecture in Oslo on December 10, 1997.

*Source:* The Nobel Foundation, *Les Prix Nobel (The Nobel Prizes), 1997* (Stockholm: Almqvist & Wiksell International, 1998), pp. 32, 401, 401-402, 406.

*Explanations:* ▶ *Crimean War:* the Crimean War (1854-1856). ▶ *U.S. Civil War:* the American Civil War (1861-1865).

*Note:* The official announcement from the Norwegian Nobel Committee read as follows:

The Norwegian Nobel Committee has decided to award the Nobel Peace Prize for 1997, in two equal parts, to the International Campaign to Ban Landmines (ICBL) and to the campaign's coordinator Jody Williams for their work for the banning and clearing of anti-personnel mines.

There are at present probably over one hundred million anti-personnel mines scattered over large areas on several continents. Such mines maim and kill indiscriminately and are a major threat to the civilian populations and to the social and economic development of the many countries affected.

The ICBL and Jody Williams started a process which in the space of a few years changed a ban on anti-personnel mines from a vision to a feasible reality. The Convention which will be signed in Ottawa in December this year is to a considerable extent a result of their important work.

There are already over 1,000 organizations, large and small, affiliated to the ICBL, making up a network through which it has been possible to express and mediate a broad wave of popular commitment in an unprecedented way. With the governments of several small and medium-sized countries taking the issue up and taking steps to deal with it, this work has grown into a convincing example of an effective policy for peace.

The Norwegian Nobel Committee wishes to express the hope that the Ottawa process will win even wider support. As a model for similar processes in the future, it could prove of decisive importance to the international effort for disarmament and peace.

(*Same source*, pp. 32, 32-33; first paragraph indented)

*See* the Convention on the Prohibition of the Use, Stockpiling, Production and Transfer of Anti-Personnel Mines and on Their Destruction, concluded at Oslo on September 18, 1997, open for signature at Ottawa from December 3 to 4, 1997, and at the United Nations headquarters in New York from December 5, 1997, until its entry into force, on March 1, 1999. The text was soon published in *International Legal Materials*, vol. XXXVI, no. 6 (November 1997), pp. 1507-1519, and later in United Nations, *Treaty Series*, vol. 2056, p. 211.

*Remark:* A new kind of superpower, small and middle powers working together to ban landmines, the "eternal sentries."

### 182 LAW
[T]he cave men believed in killing—in the law of the jungle.

Thomas Craven (1889-1969), American writer, critic and lecturer on art, writing, in his 1943 book *The Story of Painting, from Cave Pictures to Modern Art*, about the cave men of the early Stone Age who, in northern Spain and southern France, produced cave pictures as far back as 30,000-50,000 years ago.

*Source:* Thomas Craven, *The Story of Painting, from Cave Pictures to Modern Art* (New York: Simon and Schuster, 1943), p. 16.

*Remark:* Some cave men still live, hiding everywhere.

### 183 LAW
In cases not covered by this Protocol or by other international agreements, civilians and combatants remain under the protection and authority of the

principles of international law derived from established custom, from the principles of humanity and from the dictates of public conscience.

Article 1, paragraph 2, of the Protocol Additional to the Geneva Conventions of 12 August 1949, and Relating to the Protection of Victims of International Armed Conflicts (Protocol I), which was adopted at Geneva on June 8, 1977, and entered into force on December 7, 1978.

*Source:* United Nations, *Treaty Series,* vol. 1125, pp. 3, 7.

*Remark:* Everyone should study international law, at the very least basic international humanitarian law. Otherwise, a normal conscience could serve as a guiding light. Those who are without conscience should not participate in war.

### 184 LEADER
Lead others, not by violence, but by law and equity.

From *The Gospel of Buddha according to Old Records,* first published in 1894, chapter XLVIII [48], "The Dharmapada," verse 40.

*Source:* Paul Carus, *The Gospel of Buddha according to Old Records,* 12th ed. (Chicago: Open Court Publishing Co., 1909), pp. 111, 115.

*Explanations:* ▸ *Buddha* (the Enlightened One): Gautama Buddha (Siddhartha Gautama) (ca. 563-ca. 483 B.C.), Indian prince, born in the district Nepal, founder of Buddhism. ▸ *The Dharmapada:* "the path of religion pursued by those who are Buddha's followers"; *same source,* p. 111 (verse 1).

### 185 LEADER
[F]irst in war, first in peace, and first in the hearts of his countrymen.

From resolutions adopted by the United States Congress on December 19, 1799, on the occasion of the death, on December 14, of George Washington (1732-1799), former commander in chief of the Continental Army (1775-1783) and president of the United States (1789-1797), the quoted words being written by Henry Lee (1756-1818), congressman from 1799 to 1801.

*Source:* United States, Congress, *The Debates and Proceedings in the Congress of the United States* [other titles: *The Annals of the Congress of the United States* and *History of Congress*], 6th Congress (December 2, 1799-March 3, 1801) (Washington: Gales and Seaton, 1851), pp. 203, 204 (text), 206.

### 186 LEADER
Never in the field of human conflict was so much owed by so many to one man.

Göran Liljestrand (1886-1968), Swedish physician, scientist and educator, member of the Royal Academy of Sciences in Sweden, in his December 10, 1953 remarks on the role of Sir Winston Churchill (Winston Leonard Spencer Churchill) (1874-1965), British statesman, orator and author, prime minister of the United Kingdom in World War II (1940-1945; also 1951-1955), on the occasion of Churchill being awarded the 1953 Nobel Prize in Literature in Stockholm the same day.

*Source:* Horst Frenz, ed., *Nobel Lectures Including Presentation Speeches and Laureates' Biographies: Literature, 1901-1967* (Amsterdam: Elsevier Publishing Company, for the Nobel Foundation, 1969), p. 494.

*Note:* Churchill received the Nobel Prize in Literature "for his mastery of historical and biographical description as well as for brilliant oratory in defending exalted human values." *Same source*, p. 487.

*See* Gratitude (Winston S. Churchill, on fighter pilots).

### 187 LIBERTY

Let every nation know, whether it wishes us well or ill, that we shall pay any price, bear any burden, meet any hardship, support any friend, oppose any foe to assure the survival and the success of liberty.

John F. Kennedy (John Fitzgerald Kennedy) (1917-1963), president of the United States (1961-1963), in his January 20, 1961 inaugural address.

*Source:* John F. Kennedy, *Public Papers of the Presidents of the United States: John F. Kennedy ... 1961* (Washington: United States Government Printing Office, 1962), p. 1, 1.

### 188 LIE

In the longest time of peace man does not speak as much nonsense, and tell as many a lie, as in the shortest time of war.

Jean Paul (Johann Paul Friedrich Richter) (1763-1825), German author, in his booklet *Friedens-Predigt an Deutschland* [Peace Sermon to Germany], published in 1808.

*Source:* Jean Paul, *Jean Pauls Sämtliche Werke*, part 1, vol. 14, *Politische Schriften* (Weimar: Hermann Böhlaus Nachfolger, 1939), pp. 1, 27 (semicolon replaced by period at the end; translation from German mine).

*Note:* The German text is as follows: Im längsten Frieden spricht der Mensch nicht so viel Unsinn und Unwahrheit als im kürzesten Kriege.

### 189 LIFE

Egypt! Noble are thy children,
Loyal, and guardians of thy soil.
In war and peace
We give our lives for thy sake.

From the national anthem of Egypt, "My Homeland" (Arabic, "Biladi"), adopted in 1979, lyrics and music by Sayed Darwish (1892-1923), Egyptian composer and singer.

*Source:* W. L. Reed and M. J. Bristow, eds., *National Anthems of the World*, 6th ed. (1985; reprint, Poole, Dorset, England: Blandford Press, 1986), pp. 153, 155.

*Compare with* Greatness, that is, with the words of a man on the other side of the Mediterranean Sea, the Roman statesman, orator and writer Marcus Tullius Cicero (106-43 B.C.), in his work *The Offices* (Latin, *De officiis*), finished in 44 B.C.: It is no less great and commendable to manage affairs of peace than of war.

*Remarks:* ▶ A life of peace—for one's country, for all nations, even the United Nations, as in the case of Boutros Boutros-Ghali (b. 1922), Egyptian

scholar and statesman, secretary-general of the United Nations (1992-1996).
▸ To give one's life in time of peace. Is there a nobler thought in any of our national anthems?

### 190 LIFESAVING

Dawn, August 2, 1940. A long line of Jews—ragtag, homeless, desperate—waits outside the Japanese consulate in Kovno, Lithuania....

....

.... The lives of many Jews could have been saved not only by countries with more lenient immigration policies but by a diplomat here, a border guard there, who understood the dangers facing a fellow human being and merely stretched a rule or two.

....

Sugihara is certainly not the only official to have become a mass rescuer during the Holocaust....

....

Yet he *did* act. He started issuing Japanese transit visas, many, many visas, visas with long strings of characters dancing down and around the page, crowned by several official-looking seals. Sugihara ultimately granted them to anyone who applied, with whatever documents, and with whatever explanation for not having whatever documents! The more visas he would issue, the more Jews there would be in line. And when his hand tired from all that writing and signing, he allowed his assistants to produce rubber stamps. He even invited Jewish representatives inside to process the documents, with conveyor-belt efficiency.

He kept the consulate open longer than he should and missed no opportunity—even from the moving train window as he and his family finally left Kovno—to issue still a few *more* life-saving documents....

....

.... By statistical extrapolation, we can estimate that he helped as many as ten thousand escape; those who actually survived are probably no more than half that number.

....

.... Why did he not do what virtually all the other diplomats across Europe were doing—shut the door?

....

Standing in front of the old consulate, I imagine the elusive Sugihara. His indefatigable hand is scribbling his life-saving bureaucratic formulas on scraps of paper. As the image comes into focus, I conjure up another hand, that of the infamous Dr. Josef Mengele, soon to be moving with the same precision at Auschwitz, sorting out Jews between immediate and attenuated dying....

....

.... As for motives, this is all he has to say: "I acted according to my sense of human justice, out of love for mankind."

Chiune Sugihara (Chiune "Sempo" Sugihara) (1900–1986), Japanese vice-consul in the town of Kaunas (formerly Kovno), Lithuania, from 1939 to 1940, according to Hillel Levine (b. 1946), American professor of sociology and religion, in his 1996 book *In Search of Sugihara*.

*Source:* Hillel Levine, *In Search of Sugihara: The Elusive Japanese Diplomat Who Risked His Life to Rescue 10,000 Jews from the Holocaust* (New York: Free Press, 1996), pp. 1, 3-5, 7, 9, 11, 14 (first paragraph indented; reference to footnote omitted).

*Explanation: Mengele:* Josef Mengele (1911-1979), chief German Nazi doctor at the Auschwitz (Auschwitz-Birkenau) concentration camp (1943-1945), notorious for medical experiments on inmates in the infamous German Nazi concentration camp, operated in the province of Cracow in southern Poland from 1940 to 1945, now the site of a state museum.

*Note:* The widow of the Japanese diplomat and humanitarian, Yukiko Sugihara, was in 1994 quoted as having said:

He couldn't stand by and watch this inhuman thing happen—that's why he chose humanity over his career.

(Kathlyn Gay and Martin K. Gay, *Heroes of Conscience: A Biographical Dictionary* (Santa Barbara, California: ABC-CLIO, 1996), pp. 375, 376)

*Remark:* Stretching a rule or two, "out of love for mankind," honoring Japan.

### 191 LIFESAVING

I cannot stay in Sweden beyond the beginning of July. Every day costs human lives. I will get myself ready to travel as soon as I can.

Raoul Wallenberg (Raoul Gustav Wallenberg) (1912-1947?), Swedish business-man and diplomat, in the summer of 1944, on the eve of his departure as a diplomat to Hungary where he managed to save the lives of one hundred thousand or more Hungarian Jews in Budapest, through Swedish protection passports and Swedish houses. He was arrested in January 1945 by the Soviet army fighting for Budapest and never reappeared.

*Source:* John Bierman, *Righteous Gentile: The Story of Raoul Wallenberg, Missing Hero of the Holocaust* (New York: Viking Press, 1981), p. 36.

*Note:* On the Internet (2004), under "Bergen-Belsen and the Hungarian Jews," one may read that on August 18, 1944, "a minimum of 437,685 Hungarian Jews had been transported to Auschwitz on 148 trains, mostly the Jews living in the villages and smaller towns.... According to the US Holocaust Museum, there were 200,000 Jews still living in Budapest after these deportations."

*See* Protection (John Bierman, on Raoul Wallenberg).

### 192 LIFESAVING

In those years, millions of Jews died in Nazi death camps, but Oscar Schindler's Jews miraculously survived. Even on the days when the air was black with the ashes from bodies on fire, there was hope in Crakow because Oscar Schindler was there. He spent millions to protect and save his Jews, everything he possessed. He died penniless.

From an Internet description of the World War II work undertaken by the Austrian-born German industrialist and humanitarian Oskar Schindler (1908-1974) to save Jews during World War II.

*Source:* The Internet (2003), under "The Schindler story" (text in bold letters in source).

*Notes:* ▸ In another source one may read:

Schindler's story was virtually unknown to the world until Thomas Keneally wrote a factually based but fictional version of his life, which was published in 1982. *Schindler's List* became an international bestseller. However, in 1993, it was indelibly stamped on the worldwide consciousness when Steven Spielberg transformed the story into an award-winning movie....

.... Schindler was ... a Nazi spy. Yet this "scoundrel savior," at great personal risk, saved approximately 1,200 Jews from Nazi extermination.

.... He ... joined the Nazi Party because it was good for business....

....

.... Schindler convinced the Nazis that the Jews he recruited for his factories were necessary for the German war effort.

....He also managed to obtain hundreds more Jewish "workers" from other labor camps, such as Auschwitz and Goleszow....

....

When the Nazi regime collapsed in 1945, Schindler's workers were freed, but he was in danger of being captured and executed as a Nazi war criminal.... Then they helped Schindler escape to Switzerland.

....

Schindler visited Jerusalem, Israel, in 1962, and the *Schindlerjuden* (Schindler's Jews) received him as a hero. With their financial support, he was able to live in Frankfurt, Germany, until his death in 1974. He was buried in a Catholic cemetery in Jerusalem. By 1993, when *Schindler's List* was filmed, about 6,000 survivors and descendants were still alive because of the efforts of one highly flawed hero.

Many have wondered why such a man risked so much to save so many. Years after the war, Schindler commented that because he believed that the Jews were being destroyed, "there was no choice...."

(Kathlyn Gay and Martin K. Gay, *Heroes of Conscience: A Biographical Dictionary* (Santa Barbara, California: ABC-CLIO, 1996), pp. 355, 355-357)

▸ On the Internet one has written:

Perhaps the most moving image in Steven Spielberg's film "Schindler's List" is the little girl in the red coat, the only color image in the three-hour black and white film. However, most people do not know that this image is based upon a true story, a story told at the trial of Adolf Eichmann.

Assistant Prosecutor (now Supreme Court Judge) Gavriel Bach tells this story from the trial. When asked if there was any one moment in the trial that affected him more than any other, this is the moment he describes.

Bach was questioning Dr. Martin Foldi, a survivor of Auschwitz, about the selection process at the train station in the shadows of the famous "Arbeit Macht Frei" sign at Auschwitz. Foldi described how he and a son went to the right while a daughter and his wife went to the left. His little daughter wore the red coat. When an SS officer sent the son to join the mother and daughter, Foldi describes his panic. How would the boy, only twelve, find them among the thousands of people there? But then he realized the red coat would be like a signpost for the boy to find his mother and sister.

He then ends his testimony with the chilling phrase, "I never saw them again."

While telling the story, thirty-five years after it happened, Judge Bach wells up with emotion. As Dr. Foldi retold the incident, Bach became frozen and unable to continue. All he could do was think about his own daughter for whom he had by chance just bought a red coat. He then adds that to this day he can be at the theater or a restaurant and he will feel his heart beating faster when he sees a little girl in a red coat.

Over one million children under the age of sixteen died in the Holocaust—she was one of them.

(The Internet (2005), under "Holocaust lesson plans" (paragraphs indented; three periods replaced by one at the end))

*Explanations:* ▸ *"Arbeit Macht Frei":* German for "Work Makes You Free." ▸ *Auschwitz:* German Nazi concentration camp at Auschwitz (Auschwitz-Birkenau) in the province of Cracow in southern Poland (operated 1940-1945). ▸ *Bach:* Gabriel Bach (b. 1927), German-born Israeli prosecutor and judge. ▸ *Eichmann:* Adolf Eichmann (Karl Adolf Eichmann) (1906-1962), German Nazi official, head of section for the extermination of Jews, later tried, sentenced and hanged in Israel. ▸ *Foldi:* Martin Földi (twentieth century), Hungarian advocate, a survivor of Auschwitz, who appeared as a witness in the 1961 trial of Adolf Eichmann. ▸ *Goleszow:* Goleszów, a Polish town that housed a subcamp of Auschwitz during World War II. ▸ *Keneally:* Thomas Keneally (Thomas Michael Keneally) (b. 1935), Australian author who wrote the book *Schindler's List*, published in 1982. ▸ *Spielberg:* Steven Spielberg (b. 1947), American motion-picture director and producer.

*Remark:* Even a Nazi saving a Jew.

## 193 LIMITATION

*Article 35.* BASIC RULES. 1. In any armed conflict, the right of the Parties to the conflict to choose methods or means of warfare is not unlimited.

2. It is prohibited to employ weapons, projectiles and material and methods of warfare of a nature to cause superfluous injury or unnecessary suffering.

3. It is prohibited to employ methods or means of warfare which are intended, or may be expected, to cause widespread, long-term and severe damage to the natural environment.

*Article 36.* NEW WEAPONS. In the study, development, acquisition or adoption of a new weapon, means or method of warfare, a High Contracting Party is under an obligation to determine whether its employment would, in some or all circumstances, be prohibited by this Protocol or by any other rule of international law applicable to the High Contracting Party.

....

*Article 75.* FUNDAMENTAL GUARANTEES....

2. The following acts are and shall remain prohibited at any time and in any place whatsoever, whether committed by civilian or by military agents:

(a) Violence to the life, health, or physical or mental well-being of persons, in particular:
   (i) Murder;
   (ii) Torture of all kinds, whether physical or mental;
   (iii) Corporal punishment; and
   (iv) [Mutilation];
(b) Outrages upon personal dignity, in particular humiliating and degrading treatment, enforced prostitution and any form of indecent assault;
(c) The taking of hostages;

*(d)* Collective punishments; and

*(e)* Threats to commit any of the foregoing acts.

Articles 35, 36 and 75, paragraph 2, of the Protocol Additional to the Geneva Conventions of 12 August 1949, and Relating to the Protection of Victims of International Armed Conflicts (Protocol I), which was adopted at Geneva on June 8, 1977, and entered into force on December 7, 1978.

*Source:* United Nations, *Treaty Series*, vol. 1125, pp. 3, 21, 37 (parentheses in italics in some cases).

*Remark:* "Unnecessary suffering."

### 194 LOSS

The Thirty Years War (1618-1648) left Germany a shatter belt of hundreds of often tiny states, and in many areas between two-thirds and three-quarters of the German population perished. So great was the loss and consequent shortage of men in many areas that polygamy had to be permitted....

Christie Davies (John Christopher Hughes Davies) (b. 1941), British professor of sociology, born in England, writing, in his 1990 book *Ethnic Humor around the World*, on some of the effects of the Thirty Years' War, primarily a religious war waged in Germany from 1618 to 1648.

*Source:* Christie Davies, *Ethnic Humor around the World: A Comparative Analysis* (Bloomington: Indiana University Press, 1990), p. 190 (reference to footnote omitted).

*Compare with* the Thirty Years' Truce in Greece, agreed to in 445 B.C., which lasted until 431 B.C. and has been described as follows:

In the winter of 446-445 [B.C.] a treaty of peace "for 30 years" was concluded between Athens on the one side and the Spartans and their allies on the other.

(*Encyclopædia Britannica* (1964), under "Greece" (vol. 10, pp. 785, 800))

*Note:* The Peloponnesian War between Athens and Sparta (Lacedaemon) was fought intermittently from 431 to 404 B.C., so that, instead of thirty years of peace, there were almost thirty years of war.

*See* Religion (Élie Ducommun).

*Remark:* Religion and politics, a bad mixture.

### 195 LOSS

THE EFFECTS of the first world war were vast. The four-year reign of destructiveness cost hundreds of billions of dollars. The United States alone spent a million dollars for every hour from its entrance into the war to six months after the armistice. The destruction of ships and cargoes, and the devastation of vast areas of prosperous country by the ravages of war, added to the frightful loss. It is impossible to calculate how much material wealth was lost through converting factories and machines from useful production to the manufacturing of war materials.

Human losses were even greater than this material destruction. Ten million soldiers were killed. Twenty millions were wounded, and six million were reported missing. The human cost did not stop there. The rest of the sixty million who fought in the holocaust carried mental pictures which had profound physiological and psychological consequences. Civilians also suffered from starvation, disease, and violent death. At least thirteen million civilians perished during the conflict.

Fay-Cooper Cole (1881-1961), American anthropologist, and Harris Gaylord Warren (1906-1988), American historian, on some of the effects of World War I.

*Source:* Fay-Cooper Cole and Harris Gaylord Warren, *An Illustrated Outline History of Mankind*, vol. II (Chicago: Spencer Press, 1955), p. 651 (first paragraph indented).

*Remark:* Almost as many civilians as soldiers perished in World War I.

### 196 LOSS

The USSR lost 20,000,000 of its sons and daughters—fighting men who fell on the battlefield, and civilians and prisoners of war killed or tortured to death by the nazis on occupied Soviet territory. Huge losses were also suffered by the population of the Soviet rear as a result of the siege of cities and air raids. Hundreds of thousands of Soviet people were exterminated in concentration camps in Germany herself. The nazis destroyed 1,710 Soviet towns and town-type settlements and more than 70,000 villages, 32,000 factories, 98,000 collective farms and 1,876 state farms. They blew up 65,000 kilometres of railways and damaged or removed from the country 16,000 locomotives and 428,000 railway carriages. The country's national wealth diminished by 30 per cent. The Soviet Union's material losses amounted to the astronomical sum of nearly 2,600,000 million rubles.

....

.... In the war against the USSR Germany lost 10 million men, which is three-fourths of her total World War II loss of 13,600,000 men.

From the book *Great Patriotic War of the Soviet Union, 1941-1945*, on Soviet losses in World War II.

*Source:* M. M. Minasyan, editor in chief, *Great Patriotic War of the Soviet Union, 1941-1945: A General Outline*, trans. David Skvirsky and Vic Schneierson (Moscow: Progress Publishers, 1974), pp. 434, 438 (abridged translation from the Russian edition of 1970; a 1965 Russian edition exists).

*Remark:* "The country's national wealth diminished by 30 per cent."

### 197 LOVE

[A]gainst these human frailties there stood out the man of infinite goodness, a seeker all his life of Truth, which he equated with God, a pilgrim who believed that love was the greatest gift of man and that love and understanding and tolerance and compassion and non-violence, if they were only practiced, would liberate mankind from much of the burden, oppression and evil of life.

William L. Shirer (William Lawrence Shirer) (1904-1993), American writer and journalist-historian, writing on Mahatma Gandhi (Mohandas Karamchand Gandhi) (1869-1948), Indian political and religious leader and "architect of India's freedom through a nonviolent revolution," in an introduction to his 1979 book *Gandhi: A Memoir*.

*Source:* William L. Shirer, *Gandhi: A Memoir* (New York: Simon and Schuster, 1979), p. 13.

*Explanation: Mahatma:* "great soul."
*Remark:* Love, liberation.

## 198 LOVE

Love is the most durable power in the world. This creative force, so beautifully exemplified in the life of our Christ, is the most potent instrument available in mankind's quest for peace and security. Napoleon Bonaparte, the great military genius, looking back over his years of conquest, is reported to have said: "Alexander, Caesar, Charlemagne and I have built great empires. But upon what did they depend? They depended on force. But centuries ago Jesus started an empire that was built on love, and even to this day millions will die for him." Who can doubt the veracity of these words. The great military leaders of the past have gone, and their empires have crumbled and burned to ashes. But the empire of Jesus, built solidly and majestically on the foundation of love, is still growing. It started with a small group of dedicated men, who, through the inspiration of their Lord, were able to shake the hinges from the gates of the Roman empire, and carry the gospel into all the world. Today the vast earthly kingdom of Christ numbers more than 900,000,000 and covers every land and tribe.

Martin Luther King (1929-1968), American clergyman and civil rights leader, in his sermon "Loving Your Enemies," written while jailed in Georgia, United States, rewritten "for the eye" and published in 1963.
*Source:* Martin Luther King, Jr., *Strength to Love* (New York: Harper & Row, Publishers, 1963), pp. 34, 40-41, cf. pp. ix-x.
*Explanations:* ▸ *Alexander:* Alexander III or Alexander the Great (356-323 B.C.), king of Macedonia (336-323 B.C.). ▸ *Caesar:* Julius Caesar (Gaius Julius Caesar) (100-44 B.C.), Roman general and statesman. ▸ *Charlemagne:* Charlemagne (Charles I or Charles the Great) (ca. 742-814), king of the Franks (768-814), later emperor of the West (Holy Roman emperor) (800-814). ▸ *Napoleon:* Napoleon I (Napoleon Bonaparte) (1769-1821), emperor of France (1804-1814, 1815).
*Note:* King received the 1964 Nobel Peace Prize.
*Remark:* On Christian love.

## 199 MADNESS

"I myself," continued Attila, "will throw the first javelin, and the wretch who refuses to imitate the example of his sovereign is devoted to inevitable death." The spirit of the barbarians was rekindled by the presence, the voice, and the example of their intrepid leader;... The nations from the Volga to the Atlantic were assembled on the plain of Châlons; but many of these nations had been divided by faction, or conquest, or emigration; and the appearance of similar arms and ensigns, which threatened each other, presented the image of a civil war.

.... The number of the slain amounted to one hundred and sixty-two thousand or, according to another account, three hundred thousand persons; and these incredible exaggerations suppose a real and effective loss, sufficient to justify the historian's remark that whole generations may be swept away by the madness of kings in the space of a single hour.

Edward Gibbon (1737-1794), English historian, describing, in his work *The History of the Decline and Fall of the Roman Empire*, published from 1776 to 1788 (chapter XXXV), the Battle of Châlons, northeastern France, in the year 451, where the Romans and the Visigoths defeated Attila (ca. 400-453), king of the Huns (434-453), known in western Europe as "the Scourge of God."

*Source:* Edward Gibbon, *The History of the Decline and Fall of the Roman Empire*, ed. William Smith, vol. IV (London: John Murray, 1862), pp. 236-237 (additional quotation marks in the beginning of lines omitted; reference to footnote omitted).

*Remark:* More deaths than in Hiroshima and Nagasaki.


## 200 MANKIND

For this cause have we ordained to the children of Israel that he who slayeth any one, unless it be a person guilty of manslaughter, or of spreading disorders in the land, shall be as though he had slain all mankind; but that he who saveth a life, shall be as though he had saved all mankind alive.

The Qur'an (Koran), chapter (sura) V, "The Table," verse 35.

*Source: The Koran*, trans. J. M. Rodwell, Everyman's Library (1909; reprint, London: J. M. Dent & Sons, 1918), pp. 485, 489.

*Explanation: The Qur'an* (Arabic, "recitation, reading"): the sacred book of Islam, the Muslim religion (Arabic, "submission to the will of God"), founded by the Arab prophet Mohammed (Muhammad, meaning "praised" or "praiseworthy") (ca. 570-632).

*Note:* The reference is to the first murder on earth, the slaying by Cain, the son of Adam and Eve, of his brother Abel.

*See* Lifesaving.


## 201 MARCH

The Red Army fears not the trials of a distant march;
To them a thousand mountains, ten thousand rivers are nothing.

Mao Tse-tung [Mao Zedong] (1893-1976), Chinese political leader, later chairman (chief of state) of the People's Republic of China (1949-1959), in his poem "The Long March," written in 1935. The poem is on the Red Army's eight-thousand-mile (thirteen-thousand-kilometer) march from the Kiangsi [Jiangxi] province in southeastern China to the northwestern province of Shensi [Shaanxi] in 1934-1935 (during the Chinese-Japanese War (1931-1945)).

*Source:* Mao Tse-tung, *Nineteen Poems* (Peking [Beijing]: Foreign Languages Press, 1958), p. 18 (semicolon replaced by period at the end; translator of the poem: Andrew Boyd).

*Note:* "In October 1934, the Red Army set out from the Kiangsi base and marched for 25,000 *li* or about 8,000 miles.... In October 1935, it reached the anti-Japanese base in north Shensi." *Same place* (note 1).

*See* Walk (Satish Kumar; an Indian peace pilgrimage).


## 202 MARRIAGE

[M]arriage is like life in this—that it is a field of battle, and not a bed of roses.

Robert Louis Stevenson (Robert Louis Balfour Stevenson) (1850-1894), Scottish novelist, essayist and poet, in his 1881 collection of essays *Virginibus Puerisque* (end of part I).

*Source:* Robert Louis Stevenson, *Virginibus Puerisque and Other Papers* (London: C. Kegan Paul & Co., 1881), pp. 1, 26.

### 203 MARTYR

The non-commissioned officer was Franciszek Gajowniczek. When the sentence of doom had been pronounced, Gajowniczek had cried out in despair, 'O my poor wife, my poor children. I shall never see them again.' It was then that the unexpected happened, and that from among the ranks of those temporarily reprieved, prisoner 16670 had stepped forward and offered himself in the other man's place. Then the ten condemned men were led off to the dreaded Bunker, to the airless underground cells where men died slowly without food or water.

Bruno Borgowiec was an eye-witness of those last terrible days for he was an assistant to the janitor and an interpreter in the underground Bunkers. He tells us what happened: '.... Two weeks passed in this way. Meanwhile one after another they died, until only Fr Kolbe was left. This, the authorities felt was too long; the cell was needed for new victims. So one day they brought in the head of the sick-quarters, a German, a common criminal named Bock, who gave Fr Kolbe an injection of carbolic acid in the vein of his left arm. Fr Kolbe, with a prayer on his lips, himself gave his arm to the executioner. Unable to watch this I left under the pretext of work to be done. Immediately after the SS men with executioner had left I returned to the cell, where I found Fr Kolbe leaning in a sitting position against the back wall with his eyes open and his head drooping sideways. His face was calm and radiant.'

....

The heroism of Father Kolbe went echoing through Auschwitz. In that desert of hatred he had sown love....

....

On 17 October 1971 Maximilian Kolbe was beatified by Pope Paul VI. Eleven years later on 10 October 1982 Pope John Paul II celebrated the Mass of Canonisation in St Peter's Square before a vast assembly,.... Like his master Jesus Christ he had loved his fellow men to the point of sacrificing his life for them.

Mary Craig (b. 1928), British writer and broadcaster, born in England, referring, in her article "Maximilian Kolbe," to the 1941 sacrifice of the Polish Franciscan priest Maximilian Kolbe (1894-1941), from 1982 St. Maximilian Maria Kolbe, in the German Nazi concentration camp at Auschwitz (Auschwitz-Birkenau) in the province of Cracow in southern Poland (operated 1940-1945).

*Source:* Catholic Truth Society, *Victims of the Nazis* (London: Catholic Truth Society, 1997), pp. 5, 18-21.

*Explanations:* ▸ *Bruno Borgowiec* (b. 1905): Polish political prisoner, assistant to the janitor and interpreter in the underground bunkers at Auschwitz. ▸ *Franciszek Gajowniczek* (1900-1995): Polish army sergeant, sent to Auschwitz for helping the Polish Resistance. ▸ *John Paul II* (Karol Józef Wojtyla) (1920-2005): Polish pope (1978-2005). ▸ *Paul VI* (Giovanni Battista Montini) (1897-1978): Italian pope (1963-1978).

*Notes:*  ▶  "As a reprisal for the escape of a prisoner in July 1941, 10 prisoners were indiscriminately chosen to die of starvation in the cellars of Block II, among them a young Pole, Gajowniczek, the father of a family. Kolbe volunteered to take his place. He was the only one of the 10 condemned to withstand a month without food in the darkness, and was finally put to death with a phenol injection."

(*The Encyclopedia of the Third Reich* (1991), under "Kolbe, Maximilian"; the dates are July 31 (most probably) and August 14, 1941)

  ▶  "For a long time I felt remorse when I thought of Maximilian. By allowing myself to be saved, I had signed his death warrant. But now, on reflection, I understood that a man like him could not have done otherwise. Perhaps he thought that as a priest his place was beside the condemned men to help them keep hope. In fact he was with them to the last."

(The words of Franciszek Gajowniczek who, after his release from Auschwitz, found his wife at home but his two sons had been killed during World War II. The Internet (2003), under "Kolbe, The Saint from Auschwitz")

  ▶  "The dreadful irony of the situation is that the escaped prisoner was later found drowned in a camp latrine, so the terrible reprisals had been exercised without cause."

(The words of Bruno Borgowiec; *last source*)

*Remark:* Flower of charity in the middle of a desert.

## 204 MASSACRE

Midway through the war there was one act of retribution against the gangster masters of the New Order for their slaughtering of the conquered people. Reinhard Heydrich, chief of the Security Police and the S.D., deputy chief of the Gestapo, this long-nosed, icy-eyed thirty-eight-year-old policeman of diabolical cast, the genius of the "final solution," Hangman Heydrich, as he became known in the occupied lands, met a violent end.

....

But of all the consequences of Heydrich's death the fate of the little village of Lidice near the mining town of Kladno not far from Prague will perhaps be longest remembered by the civilized world. For no other reason except to serve as an example to a conquered people who dared to take the life of one of their inquisitors a terrible savagery was carried out in this peaceful little rural place.

....

.... Four of the Lidice women who were about to give birth were first taken to a maternity hospital in Prague where their newly born infants were murdered and they themselves then shipped to Ravensbrueck.

....

Actually Lidice itself had been wiped off the face of the earth. As soon as the men had been massacred and the women and children carted off, the Security Police had burned down the village, dynamited the ruins and leveled it off.

Lidice, though it became the most widely known example of Nazi savagery of this kind, was not the only village in the German-occupied lands to suffer such a barbaric end....

But on June 10, 1944, two years to a day after the massacre of Lidice, a terrible toll of life was taken at the French village of Oradour-sur-Glane, near Limoges....

Nine years later, in 1953, a French military court established that 642 inhabitants—245 women, 207 children and 190 men—had perished in the massacre at Oradour. Ten survived. Though badly burned they had simulated death and thus escaped it.

Oradour, like Lidice, was never rebuilt. Its ruins remain a monument to Hitler's New Order in Europe. The gutted church stands out against the peaceful countryside as a reminder of the beautiful June day, just before the harvest, when the village and its inhabitants suddenly ceased to exist. Where once a window stood is a little sign: "Madame Rouffance, the only survivor from the church, escaped through this window."

William L. Shirer (William Lawrence Shirer) (1904-1993), American writer and journalist-historian, writing, in his 1960 book *The Rise and Fall of the Third Reich*, on German Nazi atrocities in World War II, and the assassination of the German Nazi Reinhard Heydrich (Reinhard Tristan Eugen Heydrich) (1904-1942), Reich protector (governor) of Bohemia-Moravia (in occupied Czechoslovakia, now in the Czech Republic) (assassination attempt on May 27, death on June 4, 1942).

*Source:* William L. Shirer, *The Rise and Fall of the Third Reich: A History of Nazi Germany* (New York: Simon and Schuster, 1960), pp. 991-993 (chapter 27; reference mark omitted).

*Explanations:* ▸ *Gestapo:* an abbreviation of Geheime Staatspolizei (Secret State Police), the political police of Nazi Germany. ▸ *Hitler:* Adolf Hitler (1889-1945), chancellor of the Third Reich of Nazi Germany (1933-1945). ▸ *Limoges:* a city of south central France, famous for porcelain manufacture. ▸ *Ravensbrueck:* German Nazi concentration camp for women, about 50 miles (80 kilometers) north of Berlin (operated from 1939 to 1945). ▸ *S.D.:* an abbreviation of the German word Sicherheitsdienst (Security Service), an intelligence and surveillance division of the SS, which was in turn an abbreviation of the German word Schutzstaffel (Protective Echelon), used for a Nazi Party corps, which was, among other things, responsible for the administration of concentration (extermination) camps in World War II, both declared criminal organizations by the International Military Tribunal in Nuremberg, Germany, in 1946.

*Note:* The children of Lidice (in Bohemia) were deported to a concentration camp.
*Remark:* Barbaric order, barbaric orders, "barbaric end."

### 205 MEDICAL UNIT
Medical units shall be respected and protected at all times and shall not be the object of attack.

Article 12, paragraph 1, of the Protocol Additional to the Geneva Conventions of 12 August 1949, and Relating to the Protection of Victims of International Armed Conflicts (Protocol I), which was adopted at Geneva on June 8, 1977, and entered into force on December 7, 1978.
*Source:* United Nations, *Treaty Series*, vol. 1125, pp. 3, 12.

### 206 MEMORY
[T]he rejection of memory becomes a divine curse, one that would doom us to repeat past disasters, past wars.

Elie Wiesel (Eliezer Wiesel) (b. 1928), Romanian-born American novelist and professor, recipient of the 1986 Nobel Peace Prize, in his Nobel lecture, "Hope, Despair and Memory," given in Oslo on December 11, 1986.
*Source:* Tore Frängsmyr, ed.-in-charge, Irwin Adams, ed., *Nobel Lectures Including Presentation and Acceptance Speeches and Laureates' Biographies: Peace, 1981-1990* (Singapore: World Scientific Publishing Co., for the Nobel Foundation, 1997), pp. 157, 174, 176.

### 207 MERCENARY
1. States Parties shall not recruit, use, finance or train mercenaries and shall prohibit such activities in accordance with the provisions of the present Convention.
....
3. They shall make the offences set forth in the present Convention punishable by appropriate penalties which take into account the grave nature of those offences.

Article 5, paragraphs 1 and 3, of the International Convention against the Recruitment, Use, Financing and Training of Mercenaries contained in an annex to resolution 44/34 adopted by the General Assembly of the United Nations on December 4, 1989 (International Convention against the Recruitment, Use, Financing and Training of Mercenaries). The Convention entered into force on October 20, 2001.
*Source:* United Nations, *Resolutions and Decisions Adopted by the General Assembly during Its Forty-fourth Session*, vol. I (General Assembly, Official Records: Forty-fourth Session, Supplement No. 49 (A/44/49)), pp. 306, 307.

### 208 MERCY
Buddha does not always appear as a Buddha.... In a war he preaches forbearance and mercy for the sufferings of people;...

Buddha (the Enlightened One), Gautama Buddha (Siddhartha Gautama) (ca. 563-ca. 483 B.C.), Indian prince, born in the district Nepal, founder of Buddhism, according to *The Teaching of Buddha*.
*Source: The Teaching of Buddha: A Compendium of Many Scriptures Translated from the Japanese*, 4th ed. (Tokyo: Bukkyo Dendo Kyokai, 1966), p. 31.
*Remark:* Buddha as usual.

### 209 MESSAGE
My centre is giving way, my right retreats, situation excellent. I am attacking!

Ferdinand Foch (1851-1929), French commander, former instructor in military history, later marshal of France (in August 1918) and supreme commander of the Allied armies on the western front at the end of World War I (as from April 1918), in his World War I message, sent to Joseph Joffre (Joseph Jacques Césaire Joffre) (1852-1931), French commander in chief, during the First Battle of the Marne, in northern France, from September 6 to 9, 1914.

*Source:* George Acton, *The Biography of the Late Marshal Foch* (New York: Macmillan Company, 1929), p. 155 (translation from the French text in the source: Mon centre cède, ma droite recule, situation excellente. J'attaque!).
*Remark:* Calculated risk.

## 210 MIGHT
Let us have faith that right makes might, and in that faith let us, to the end, dare to do our duty as we understand it.

Abraham Lincoln (1809-1865), American statesman, later president of the United States (1861-1865), ending his speech at Cooper Institute, New York, on February 27, 1860.
*Source:* Abraham Lincoln, *The Writings of Abraham Lincoln*, ed. Arthur Brooks Lapsley, vol. 5, *1852-1862*, Works of Abraham Lincoln, Federal Edition (New York: G. P. Putnam's Sons, 1906), pp. 121, 149 (sentence not capitalized here).
*Remark:* Lincolnesque.

## 211 MILITARY ESTABLISHMENT
A vital element in keeping the peace is our military establishment. Our arms must be mighty, ready for instant action, so that no potential aggressor may be tempted to risk his own destruction.

Our military organization today bears little relation to that known by any of my predecessors in peacetime, or indeed by the fighting men of World War II or Korea.

Until the latest of our world conflicts, the United States had no armaments industry. American makers of plowshares could, with time and as required, make swords as well. But now we can no longer risk emergency improvisation of national defense; we have been compelled to create a permanent armaments industry of vast proportions. Added to this, three and a half million men and women are directly engaged in the defense establishment. We annually spend on military security more than the net income of all United States corporations.

This conjunction of an immense military establishment and a large arms industry is new in the American experience. The total influence—economic, political, even spiritual—is felt in every city, every State house, every office of the Federal government. We recognize the imperative need for this development. Yet we must not fail to comprehend its grave implications. Our toil, resources and livelihood are all involved; so is the very structure of our society.

In the councils of government, we must guard against the acquisition of unwarranted influence, whether sought or unsought, by the military-industrial complex. The potential for the disastrous rise of misplaced power exists and will persist.

We must never let the weight of this combination endanger our liberties or democratic processes. We should take nothing for granted. Only an alert and knowledgeable citizenry can compel the proper meshing of the huge industrial and military machinery of defense with our peaceful methods and goals, so that security and liberty may prosper together.

Dwight D. Eisenhower (Dwight David Eisenhower) (1890-1969), president of the United States (1953-1961), formerly supreme commander of the Allied forces in western Europe during World War II, in his farewell radio and television address to the American people on January 17, 1961.

*Source:* Dwight D. Eisenhower, *Public Papers of the Presidents of the United States: Dwight D. Eisenhower, 1960-61* (Washington: U.S. Government Printing Office, 1961), pp. 1035, 1037-1038.

*Explanation: Korea:* the reference is to the Korean War (1950-1953).

*Remark:* A few words on the military-industrial complex.

### 212 MONUMENT

Though Lutyens drew on classical forms, he tended to reduce them to simpler and simpler outline or notation. This process has no better expression than in the Monument to the Missing of the Battle of the Somme at Thiepval. The hill dominated the battlefield. The terrifying and murderous task of taking it and the surrounding terrain was one of the most appalling chapters in the history of the war. Total casualties on both sides exceeded 1 million men; perhaps 600,000 died among the British and French forces. Of the British and Allied losses, the bodies of approximately 73,000 of these men were never found. It is their names which are inscribed on the internal walls of Lutyens' memorial.

....

In the centre of the monument is a simple sarcophagus, from which one sees two small cemeteries of French and British soldiers, whose names are 'known to God', as the British inscription reads.

Jay Winter (Jay Murray Winter) (b. 1945), American lecturer of history, writing, in his 1995 book *Sites of Memory, Sites of Mourning*, on one of the World War I monuments by the English architect Edwin Lutyens (Edwin Landseer Lutyens) (1869-1944), designed in the 1920s, commemorating the 1916 Battle of the Somme.

*Source:* Jay Winter, *Sites of Memory, Sites of Mourning: The Great War in European Cultural History*, Studies in the Social and Cultural History of Modern Warfare (Cambridge: Cambridge University Press, 1995), p. 105 (first paragraph indented).

*Explanations:*  ▶ *Somme:* a river and department of northwestern France, the site of a series of battles in 1916. ▶ *Thiepval:* a village on the Somme.

*Note:* The Monument to the Missing of the Battle of the Somme has been described as "romantic in inspiration, classic in discipline, yet 'abstract' in design." *The Dictionary of National Biography, 1941-1950*, under "Lutyens, Sir Edwin Landseer" (pp. 537, 540).

*Remark:* The green fields of France, and a black hole, not in space, swallowing stars, but on earth, swallowing fathers and sons. But do we learn?

### 213 MOTHER

Executive Mansion,
Washington, November 21, 1864.

Mrs. Bixby, Boston, Massachusetts.

Dear Madam:— I have been shown in the files of the War Department a statement of the Adjutant-General of Masschusetts that you are the mother of five sons who have died gloriously on the field of battle. I feel how weak and fruitless must be any words of mine which should attempt to beguile you from the grief of a loss so overwhelming. But I cannot refrain from tendering to you the consolation that may be found in the thanks of the Republic they died to save. I pray that our Heavenly Father may assuage the anguish of your bereavement, and leave you only the cherished memory of the loved and lost, and the solemn pride that must be yours to have laid so costly a sacrifice upon the altar of freedom.

Yours very sincerely and respectfully,

ABRAHAM LINCOLN.

Abraham Lincoln (1809-1865), president of the United States (1861-1865), in a November 21, 1864 letter of condolence addressed to his fellow countryman, the widow and mother Lydia Bixby (Lydia Parker Bixby) (1801?-1878).

*Source:* Abraham Lincoln, *The Writings of Abraham Lincoln*, ed. Arthur Brooks Lapsley, vol. 7, *1863-1865*, Works of Abraham Lincoln, Federal Edition (New York: G. P. Putnam's Sons, 1906), pp. 238, 238-239.

*Note:* It was later found out that the correct number of sons killed "on the field of battle" was two. Abraham Lincoln, *The Collected Works of Abraham Lincoln*, ed. Roy P. Basler, vol. VIII (New Brunswick, New Jersey: Rutgers University Press, 1953), pp. 116, 117.

*Remark:* And Lincoln too laid his life "upon the altar of freedom."

## 214 MOURNING

When he was now near his end, the best of the citizens and those of his friends who were left alive, sitting about him, were speaking of the greatness of his merit, and his power, and reckoning up his famous actions and the number of his victories; for there were no less than nine trophies, which, as their chief commander and conqueror of their enemies, he had set up for the honour of the city. They talked thus together among themselves, as though he were unable to understand or mind what they said, but had now lost his consciousness. He had listened, however, all the while, and attended to all, and, speaking out among them, said that he wondered they should commend and take notice of things which were as much owing to fortune as to anything else, and had happened to many other commanders, and, at the same time, should not speak or make mention of that which was the most excellent and greatest thing of all. "For," said he, "no Athenian, through my means, ever wore mourning."

Plutarch (ca. 46-120), Greek biographer, writing, in his work *Parallel Lives* (the biography of Pericles), on the Athenian statesman and general Pericles (ca. 490-429 B.C.).

*Source:* Plutarch, *Plutarch's Lives: The "Dryden Plutarch,"* rev. Arthur Hugh Clough, Everyman's Library, vol. I (1910; reprint, London: J. M. Dent & Sons; New York: E. P. Dutton & Co., 1914), pp. 226, 262.

*Remark:* No unnecessary wars.

## 215 MURDER

You shall not murder.

The Bible, Exodus 20:13 (the Fifth Commandment).

*Source: The Holy Bible Containing the Old and New Testaments*, New Revised Standard Version (New York: Oxford University Press, 1989).

### 216 MURDER
The murder of one person is called unrighteous and incurs one death penalty. Following this argument, the murder of ten persons will be ten times as unrighteous and there should be ten death penalties; the murder of a hundred persons will be a hundred times as unrighteous and there should be a hundred death penalties. All the gentlemen of the world know that they should condemn these things, calling them unrighteous. But when it comes to the great unrighteousness of attacking states, they do not know that they should condemn it. On the contrary, they applaud it, calling it righteous. And they are really ignorant of its being unrighteous. Hence they have recorded their judgment to bequeath to their posterity. If they did know that it is unrighteous, then why would they record their false judgment to bequeath to posterity?

Mo Ti, Motse or Mo-Tzu ("Master Mo") [Mozu] (470?-391? B.C.), Chinese philosopher and founder of a religion, according to his first essay on "Condemnation of Offensive War," considered to be written by his disciples.
*Source:* Motse, *The Ethical and Political Works of Motse*, trans. Yi-Pao Mei, Probsthain's Oriental Series, vol. XIX (London: Arthur Probsthain, 1929), pp. 98, 99.
*Remark:* Condemnation of offensive war in the fifth century B.C., about 2,400 years before Nuremberg.

### 217 MUSIC
Be embraced, millions all;
This kiss for the world is meant!

Words from the "Ode to Joy" ("An die Freude"), a poem written in 1785 by the German poet, dramatist and philosopher Friedrich von Schiller (Johann Cristoph Friedrich von Schiller) (1759-1805), part of the ode forming the final chorus of the Ninth Symphony (opus 125) of the German composer Ludwig van Beethoven (1770-1827), composed from 1815 to 1824 when the symphony was first performed (Beethoven's interest in the ode goes at least as far back as 1792).
*Source:* Philip H. Goepp, *Symphonies and Their Meaning*, 2nd series, 4th ed. (Philadelphia: J. P. Lippincott Company, 1902), pp. 153, 174 (quotation marks in the beginning omitted).
*Notes:* ▸ "[T]he work is *not* called a 'Choral Symphony' but 'Symphony No. 9 in D minor, with final chorus on Schiller's Ode to Joy'. In other words it was conceived first and foremost as an instrumental work, a true symphony. There are those ... who remain unconvinced by what all must accept as a gigantic work: they find the finale in every sense a strain. Others bow down before it, hailing it as the greatest of symphonies."
(Antony Hopkins, *The Nine Symphonies of Beethoven* (London: Heinemann, 1981), p. 250)
   ▸ Beethoven used the 1803 revision of the "Ode to Joy" as a basis for the final chorus. David Benjamin Levy, *Beethoven: The Ninth Symphony* (New York: Schirmer Books, 1995), p. 8. The text of that version, in German and the English translation of David Benjamin Levy, is on pp. 9-12 (*Seid umschlungen Millionen! / Diesen Kuß der ganzen Welt!*—Be embraced you millions! / This kiss is for the entire world!; p. 9, 9).

*Explanation: Antony Hopkins* (b. 1921): English composer, pianist and conductor.
*Compare with* Nuclear weapon (the cobalt bomb).
*Remark:* Kisses, not cobalt bombs, for our world.

### 218 MUSIC

The success of the First Symphony had been surpassed only by *Finlandia*, which focused, from the Russian point of view, unwelcome attention on the plight of the Finns. So as not to seem unduly provocative, it was thought wiser not to bill it as *Finlandia*; indeed Kajanus was even doubtful about doing so in Paris, and when Sibelius himself conducted it in Estonia in 1903 (another part of the Tsarist Empire) it went under the title 'Impromptu for orchestra'.

Robert Layton (b. 1930), English writer, describing the difficulties, in 1903, in connection with the use of the name *Finlandia* for the tone poem of the Finnish composer Johan Julius Sibelius (1865-1957), known as Jean Sibelius.
*Source:* Robert Layton, *The Master Musicians: Sibelius*, rev. ed. (London: J. M. Dent & Sons, 1992), p. 36 (comma after 1903 omitted).
*Explanations:* ▸ *Impromptu:* improvised. ▸ *Kajanus:* Robert Kajanus (1856-1933), Finnish conductor and composer. ▸ *Paris:* the reference is to Kajanus conducting a Finnish orchestra at the Paris World Exhibition in 1900.
*Remark:* Musical oppression.

### 219 MUSIC

For me the life of a single child is worth more than all my music; but, in the midst of the war's madness, it was perhaps mainly through music that I maintained my sanity. Music remained for me an affirmation of the beauty man was capable of producing—yes, man who was now causing such havoc and agony. I recalled how when Europe was ravaged a century before by the Napoleonic wars, Beethoven—tormented as he was by the savage conflict—continued to create his great masterpieces. Perhaps at such a time, when evil and ugliness are rampant, it is more important than ever to cherish what is noble in man.

Pablo Casals (Pau Carlos Salvador Defilló de Casals) (1876-1973), Spanish cellist and conductor, opponent of fascism and crusader for peace, reflecting on World War I during that war.
*Source:* Pablo Casals, *Joys and Sorrows: Reflections by Pablo Casals, as Told to Albert E. Kahn* (London: Macdonald and Co. (Publishers), 1970), p. 147.
*Explanations:* ▸ *Beethoven:* Ludwig van Beethoven (1770-1827), German composer. ▸ *Napoleonic wars:* the Napoleonic Wars (1800-1815). The wars followed the French Revolutionary Wars (1792-1799) and were waged mainly during the rule of Napoleon I (Napoleon Bonaparte) (1769-1821), emperor of France (1804-1814, 1815).
*Remark:* The life of a single child, or the music of the masters, that is, Bach, Beethoven, Mozart and the others.

### 220 NATION

We have recently passed through a great world war. That war has not brought peace and freedom, but it should teach us many lessons. It brought the downfall of what had been called fascism and nazism. Both of these creeds were narrow and overbearing and based on hatred and violence. I watched their growth in their respective countries as well as elsewhere. They brought a certain prestige to their people for a while, but they also killed the spirit and destroyed all values and standards of thought and behaviour. They ended by ruining the nations they sought to exalt.

Jawaharlal Nehru (1889-1964), Indian statesman, prime minister (1947-1964), referring specifically, in his 1949 book *Mahatma Gandhi*, to the downfall of Italian fascism in 1943 and German nazism in 1945.

*Source:* Jawaharlal Nehru, *Mahatma Gandhi* (1949; reprint, Bombay: Asia Publishing House, 1966), pp. 147-148.

*Remark:* Nehru speaking about fascism and nazism, two creeds which "ended by ruining the nations they sought to exalt."

### 221 NATIONALISM

Nationalism of the worst sort was displayed in the last two wars, and it may be regarded today as the greatest obstacle to mutual understanding between peoples.

Albert Schweitzer (1875-1965), Alsatian-German (later French) philosopher, theologian, organist, physician and mission doctor in French Equatorial Africa (later Gabon), recipient of the 1952 Nobel Peace Prize (awarded in 1953), in his Nobel lecture, "The Problem of Peace," given in Oslo on November 4, 1954.

*Source:* Frederick W. Haberman, ed., *Nobel Lectures Including Presentation Speeches and Laureates' Biographies: Peace*, vol. 3, *1951-1970* (Amsterdam: Elsevier Publishing Company, for the Nobel Foundation, 1972), pp. 35, 46, 55.

*Remark:* Nationalism in World War I, nationalism in World War II, "nationalism of the worst sort."

### 222 NATURE

No one is so foolish as to prefer to peace war, in which, instead of sons burying their fathers, fathers bury their sons.

Croesus (d. 525 B.C. or later), last king of the country Lydia in Asia Minor (ca. 560-ca. 546 B.C.), in an answer to Cyrus II the Great (590 or 580-ca. 529 B.C.), ruler of the Persian Empire, which he founded in 550 B.C. and ruled until his death, upon Cyrus's conquest of Lydia in or about 546 B.C., according to Herodotus (ca. 484-ca. 425 B.C.), Greek historian, known as "the Father of History." Herodotus's *History*, on the Greco-Persian Wars waged intermittently from about 546 to about 448 B.C., is believed to have been published before 425 B.C. (book I, entitled "Clio," chapter 87).

*Source:* Herodotus, *The History of Herodotus*, ed. George Rawlinson, vol. I (New York: D. Appleton & Company, 1859), p. 174.

*See* Oracle (Herodotus, on the ambiguous answers of the oracles at Delphi).

*Remark:* Croesus himself preferred war to peace because he believed in oracles, and victory.

### 223 NATURE

The [tendency of] man's nature to goodness is like the [tendency of] water to flow downwards.

Mencius or Meng-tzu ("Master Meng") [Mengzi] (372-289 B.C.), Chinese philosopher, according to the *Book of Mencius*, compiled by his disciples after his death (book VI, part I, chapter II, section 2).

*Source:* James Legge, trans., *The Chinese Classics*, vol. II, *The Life and Works of Mencius* (London: Trübner & Co., 1875), p. 307.

## 224 NAVAL BATTLE

Then, aboard the *Hood*, the worst happened: a shell struck the magazine. As Knight and the others on the *Prince of Wales* watched in horror, "a great spouting explosion issued from the center of the *Hood*, enormous reaching tongues of pale-red flame shot into the air, while dense clouds of whitish-yellow smoke burst upwards, gigantic pieces of brightly burning debris being hurled hundreds of feet in the air. I just did not believe what I saw—*Hood* had literally been blown to pieces." Of 1,419 men on the *Hood*, only three survived.

....

".... A pause—then *Bismarck* turned keel-up, slowly, the bows rose in the air, and, stern first, *Bismarck* slid down to the bottom."

Of the more than 2,000 officers and men who had sailed from Gotenhafen nine days earlier, only 110 were rescued. Neither Admiral Lütjens nor Captain Lindemann was among these survivors.

Thus ended Operation *Rheinübung*, and with it the major effort of Germany's surface navy in the Battle of the Atlantic....

....

.... [N]ever again would the big ships venture into the Atlantic to sink Allied vessels.

That was left to the submarines.

Barrie Pitt (Barrie William Edward Pitt) (1918-2006), British military historian and editor, born in Ireland, writing, in his book *The Battle of the Atlantic*, originally published in 1977, about the sinking, on May 24, 1941, of the 42,100 ton British battle cruiser *Hood*, in the Denmark Strait between Greenland and Iceland (in 1939 the largest warship in the world), and the sinking, on May 27, 1941, of the German battleship *Bismarck*, at that time the largest and newest of German warships (officially 35,000 tons but said, by the British, to be 50,000 tons and, by the Germans, unsinkable).

*Source:* Barrie Pitt, *The Battle of the Atlantic*, ed. the editors of Time-Life Books, World War II (Alexandria, Virginia: Time-Life Books, 1980), pp. 47-49 (the first sentence on *Bismarck*, within quotation marks, written by Gerhard Junack, German lieutenant, *Bismarck*'s chief turbine engineer, who ordered the men to abandon ship).

*Explanations:* ▶ *Gotenhafen:* Gdynia (Poland). ▶ *Lindemann:* Ernst Lindemann (1894-1941), German captain of *Bismarck* (August 1940-May 1941). ▶ *Lütjens:* Günther Lütjens (1889-1941), German admiral, commander of the German High-Sea Fleet (1940-1941). ▶ *Prince of Wales:* British battleship.

*Notes:* ▶ According to one source the final death toll for *Hood* was 1,415 and for *Bismarck* 2,131, altogether 3,546.

(David Mearns and Rob White, *Hood and Bismarck* (London: Channel 4 Books (Pan Macmillan), 2001), p. 221)

▶ In the preface to the *last source*, on p. 4, cf. p. 5, Eric Grove (Eric John Grove) (b. 1948), British military analyst, writes as follows:

Then came the final act in the tragedy. The cruiser HMS *Dorsetshire* (which had inflicted the final damage on the German ship) was reluctantly forced to leave most of the hundreds of German survivors to their fate because of the threat to the would-be rescuers from German U-boats.

*Remark:* How likely was it that rescuers of Germans, from the "unsinkable" *Bismarck*, would be attacked by German submarines?

### 225 NAVY

About this time, the religious animosity between Catholics and Protestants was greater than ever in the west of Europe; and whilst the former placed all their hopes upon Philip of Spain, the latter received assistance either private or open from Elizabeth of England. She sent her favorite, Leicester, with an army into the Netherlands, to prevent Parma's complete triumph; she assisted the Huguenots against Philip's allies, the Leaguists and Jesuits ... and consented to the execution of Mary Stuart, when she found that her own life was threatened by the daggers of fanatics.... Upon this, Philip determined to annihilate all the enemies of the Catholic Church by a mighty blow, and above all, to chastise heretical England and her excommunicated queen. With this view, he fitted out the Armada or "Invincible Fleet," consisting of 130 large ships of war, and sent them into the Channel, under the command of Medina Sidonia, to the end that, supported by Parma's land force, they might subject, at the same time, England, France, and the Netherlands. But the undertaking ended in the shame and ruin of Spain. The "Invincible Fleet" was destroyed by storms, and the skill and courage of the English; the greater part of that which escaped the fire-ships, the rocks, and the enemy, in the Channel, was wrecked upon the Hebrides and Shetland islands, when Sidonia attempted to return to Spain by sailing round Scotland. It was a fatal blow. Philip admitted this, when he composed the fears of the trembling admiral with the words, "I sent you against men, not against rocks and storms." This event destroyed Spain's supremacy at sea, and secured the independence of the Netherlands.

Georg Weber (1808-1888), German historian and educator, writing on the Spanish Armada in 1588 in his book *Outlines of Universal History*, first published in German in 1851 (*Weltgeschichte in übersichtlicher Darstellung*).

*Source:* George Weber, *Outlines of Universal History, from the Creation of the World to the Present Time*, trans. M. Behr, rev. Francis Bowen, 6th ed. (Boston: Hickling, Swan and Brown, 1856), p. 245.

*Explanations:* ▸ *Elizabeth of England:* Elizabeth I (1533-1603), queen of England and Ireland (1558-1603). ▸ *Huguenots:* the name given to the French Protestants of the sixteenth and seventeenth centuries. ▸ *Jesuits:* members of the Society of Jesus, a Catholic religious order, founded in 1540. ▸ *Leaguists:* members of an influential association of Catholics in France during the sixteenth century (organized in 1576). ▸ *Leicester:* Robert Dudley (1532 or 1533-1588), earl of Leicester (from 1564), English courtier, sent as a general with English forces to the United Provinces (the Netherlands) in 1585. ▸ *Mary Stuart:* Mary, Queen of Scots (1542-1587), Scottish queen (1542-1567), executed in 1587. ▸ *Medina Sidonia:* Don Alonso Perez de Guzman El Bueno, duke of Medina Sidonia (1550-1615), commander in chief of the Spanish Armada. ▸ *Parma:* Alessandro Farnese (1545-1592), duke of Parma (1586-1592), Italian statesman and general, regent of the Spanish Netherlands (1578-1592).  ▸ *Philip of Spain:* Philip II (1527-1598): king of Spain (1556-1598).

*Note:* "The Spanish Armada (Sp. *Armada Invencible*) was the great fleet sent in 1588 by Philip II of Spain, leader of Catholic Europe, to assist in the attempted invasion of England....

....

On every count the Armada's defeat was epoch-making. It probably saved the Reformation and it certainly saved England; and it taught England that the sea would be the instrument of its future greatness. It was also of great significance in the history of war as the first gun duel between fleets propelled exclusively by sail; the prototype of all naval actions up to and including the battle of Trafalgar (1805)."

(*Encyclopædia Britannica* (1964), under "Armada")

*Remark:* The end of an "invincible" fleet, the beginning of the independent Netherlands.

### 226 NAVY

In the gray predawn light of June 5, while the airborne troops who would spearhead the D-Day invasion were still asleep, the ground forces were already starting their slow seaborne journey to Normandy. Nearly 5,000 ships of all kinds—battleships and cruisers, frigates and sloops, tank landing craft and gunboats, troop transports and assault boats, repair ships, hospital ships, ammunition ships, ships to lay smoke screens, to direct aircraft and to be sunk as tide breakers off the Normandy coast—put out to sea that blustery morning. From the overcrowded harbors of the English south coast, from as far west as Falmouth and as far east as Felixstowe, the components of the greatest fleet that ever sailed butted through wind and swell toward the assembly point, Area Z, off the southern tip of the Isle of Wight.

Douglas Botting (Douglas Scott Botting) (b. 1934), British writer and independent producer for television, born in England, describing, in his book *The Second Front*, the beginning of the seaborne journey from England which ended in the June 6, 1944 D-day Allied invasion at Normandy, northwestern France.

*Source:* Douglas Botting, *The Second Front*, ed. the editors of Time-Life Books, World War II (1978; rev. reprint, Alexandria, Virginia: Time-Life Books, 1980), p. 90.

*Explanations:*  ▸ *Falmouth:* a seaport in Cornwall, the westernmost part of southern England.  ▸ *Felixstowe:* a seashore town near Ipswich, England, to the north of London.

*Remark:* "The greatest fleet that ever sailed," nearly five thousand ships.

### 227 NEGOTIATION

Let us never negotiate out of fear. But let us never fear to negotiate.

John F. Kennedy (John Fitzgerald Kennedy) (1917-1963), president of the United States (1961-1963), in his January 20, 1961 inaugural address.

*Source:* John F. Kennedy, *Public Papers of the Presidents of the United States: John F. Kennedy ... 1961* (Washington: United States Government Printing Office, 1962), pp. 1, 2.

### 228 NEIGHBOR

An ill neighbour is a bane, even as a good neighbour is a great blessing.

Hesiod (flourished ca. 800 B.C.), Greek poet, in his epic poem *Works and Days*.
*Source:* Hesiod, *Hesiod: The Poems and Fragments*, trans. A. W. Mair (Oxford: Clarendon Press, 1908), pp. 1, 13.

### 229 NEUTRALITY

The Governments of the American republics meeting at Panamá, have solemnly ratified their neutral status in the conflict which is disrupting the peace of Europe, but the present war may lead to unexpected results which may affect the fundamental interests of America and there can be no justification for the interests of the belligerents to prevail over the rights of neutrals causing disturbances and suffering to nations which by their neutrality in the conflict and their distance from the scene of events, should not be burdened with its fatal and painful consequences.

   ....

For these reasons the Governments of the American Republics RESOLVE AND HEREBY DECLARE:

1. As a measure of continental self-protection, the American Republics, so long as they maintain their neutrality, are as of inherent right entitled to have those waters adjacent to the American continent, which they regard as of primary concern and direct utility in their relations, free from the commission of any hostile act by any non-American belligerent nation, whether such hostile act be attempted or made from land, sea or air.

From the preamble to and part of operative paragraph 1 of the Declaration of Panama, approved on October 3, 1939, at the "Consultative Meeting of Foreign Ministers of the American Republics" held in Panama City from September 23 to October 3, 1939, at which the American republics declared a safety belt of 300 nautical miles around the American continents.
*Source:* United States, Department of State, *Department of State Bulletin*, vol. I, no. 15, publication 1389 (October 7, 1939), pp. 321, 331, 331-332.
*Remark:* A signal from Panama, and not only from Panama, to the effect that "there can be no justification for the interests of the belligerents to prevail over the rights of neutrals."

### 230 NEWS

When the Persians fled to their ships, Miltiades called for Pheidippides, the famous Athenian runner, and ordered him to carry the good news of victory with all speed to the city fathers of Athens.

Though he had fought through the battle as a common soldier and endured the heat and the hardships of the day, Pheidippides tossed aside his shield, stripped himself of his armor and set off over the hills toward the distant city. It was about eight leagues from the plain of Marathon to the market-place at Athens, but Pheidippides, spurred by the good news he was bringing, ran doggedly up and down the slopes and along the level stretches. As he went on his lips became parched and his breath came in painful stabs. His feet were cut and bleeding. But the Acropolis loomed in the distance. Pheidippides plunged ahead. He entered the city streets. The elders of Athens heard a great shout and saw an exhausted runner staggering toward them. "Rejoice; we conquer!" gasped Pheidippides and, his message carried and his goal attained, he dropped to the ground and died.

The modern marathon is a commemorative event in honor of the feat of the Athenian soldier and athlete, the story of whose last great race still goes echoing down the corridors of Time.

John Kieran (John Francis Kieran) (1892-1981), American sportswriter, on the run of the Athenian long-distance runner Pheidippides (Phidippides, Philippides) (d. 490 B.C.) from Marathon, Greece, to Athens in 490 B.C. bringing the news of victory of the Greek forces under the Athenian general Miltiades (d. ca. 488 B.C.), fighting against the forces of Darius I (ca. 549-486 B.C.), king of Persia (522-486 B.C.).

*Source:* John Kieran, *The Story of the Olympic Games, 776 B.C.-1936 A.D.* (New York: Frederick A. Stokes Company, 1936), p. 15.

*Explanations:* ▸ *Acropolis:* a citadel in Athens, in its present form from the second half of the fifth century B.C., with ancient temples and other buildings including the Parthenon, the chief temple of Athena, the ancient Greek protectress of cities, goddess of war, handicraft and wisdom. ▸ *The modern marathon:* the Olympic marathon, the distance of which has, since 1908, been 26 miles, 385 yards (42 kilometers, 195 meters) (standardized in 1924).

### 231 NEWS
Many of them fell there, and many more were drowned in attempting to pass the Nile.... The number of Mamelukes drowned in this battle has been estimated as high as 5000. Their numerous bodies carried the news of our victory, in a few days, to Damietta and Rosetta, and all along the banks.

Napoleon Bonaparte (1769-1821), French military leader, formerly Napoleon I, emperor of France (1804-1814, 1815), writing, in his memoirs, of the July 21, 1798 Battle of the Pyramids, where his army defeated an army of the Mamelukes, the ruling race in Egypt.

*Source:* Napoleon, *Memoirs of the History of France during the Reign of Napoleon, Dictated by the Emperor at Saint Helena to the Generals Who Shared His Captivity; and Published from the Original Manuscripts, Corrected by Himself,* vol. 2 (London: Henry Colburn and Co. and Martin Bossange and Co., 1823), pp. 236, 246.

*Explanation: Damietta and Rosetta:* towns in Egypt (Dumyat and Rashid).
*Remark:* A flow of tragic news.

### 232 NOBEL PEACE PRIZE
Some themes have been recurrent among most of the laureates: on the one hand, some remind us of the ever-present dangers of nationalism, xenophobia and exclusion as a continuous obstacle and threat to peace; others of the importance of building bridges, friendship and practical links between the members of all nations in the world society.

....

In the post-war period, and particularly during the last three decades, the concern with human rights has become one of the most prominent themes for the Nobel Peace Prize laureates. It illustrates the fact that we cannot stop at making peace between states,...

In the meantime, however, the laureates reflect the importance of alleviating the suffering of the millions of victims of meaningless violence in a world which is still very far from the rule of law. From the time of Jean-Henri Dunant, the first recipient of the Nobel Peace Prize, the humanitarian concern with the victims has been a major thread.

Asbjørn Eide (b. 1933), Norwegian lawyer, director of the Norwegian Institute of Human Rights in Oslo, referring to the themes in the addresses of Nobel Peace Prize recipients, in an introduction to a 1995 book, *Peace!*, published by the United Nations Educational, Scientific and Cultural Organization (UNESCO).

*Source:* Marek Thee, ed., *Peace!, by the Nobel Peace Prize Laureates: An Anthology*, Cultures of Peace (Paris: UNESCO Publishing, 1995), p. 20.

*Explanations:*  ▸ *Dunant:* Jean Henri Dunant (1828-1910), Swiss humanitarian who promoted the founding of the International Committee for the Relief of the Wounded in 1863 (now the International Committee of the Red Cross), recipient of the first Nobel Peace Prize in 1901 along with Frédéric Passy (1822-1912), French economist, founder and president of the first French peace society.  ▸ *Nobel:* Alfred Nobel (Alfred Bernhard Nobel) (1833-1896), Swedish chemist and engineer, inventor of dynamite and other explosives, founder of the Nobel prizes (since 1901 distributed for physics, chemistry, physiology or medicine, literature and peace, since 1969 also for economic sciences).

*Remark:* Victims, victims, victims of meaningless, meaningless, meaningless violence—"in a world which is still very far from the rule of law."

### 233 NONCOOPERATION

[T]here can be no violence simultaneously with non-co-operation. The greatest obstacle to the launching of all-out non-co-operation is the fear of violence breaking out. Those who are ready with arms or are eager to be so should also put them by while non-co-operation is going on.

To me, on the day when brute force gains ascendancy in India, all distinctions of East and West, of ancient and modern, will have disappeared. That day will be the day of my test. I take pride in looking upon India as my country because I believe that she has it in her to demonstrate to the world the supremacy of soul-force. When India accepts the supremacy of brute force, I should no longer be happy to call her my motherland.

Mahatma Gandhi (Mohandas Karamchand Gandhi) (1869-1948), Indian political and religious leader, "architect of India's freedom through a nonviolent revolution," in an August 15, 1920 article, "Doctrine of the Sword," published in the weekly he started, *Navajivan*.

*Source:* Mahatma Gandhi, *The Collected Works of Mahatma Gandhi*, vol. XVIII (New Delhi: Ministry of Information and Broadcasting, 1965), pp. 155, 158.

*Explanation: Mahatma:* "great soul."

*Remark:* Noncooperation means nonviolence.

### 234 NONINTERNATIONAL ARMED CONFLICT

*Article 4.* Fundamental guarantees. 1. All persons who do not take a direct part or who have ceased to take part in hostilities, whether or not their liberty has been restricted, are entitled to respect for their person, honour and convictions and religious practices. They shall in all circumstances be treated humanely, without any adverse distinction. It is prohibited to order that there shall be no survivors.

2. Without prejudice to the generality of the foregoing, the following acts against the persons referred to in paragraph 1 are and shall remain prohibited at any time and in any place whatsoever:

- *(a)* Violence to the life, health and physical or mental well-being of persons, in particular murder as well as cruel treatment such as torture, mutilation or any form of corporal punishment;
- *(b)* Collective punishments;
- *(c)* Taking of hostages;
- *(d)* Acts of terrorism;
- *(e)* Outrages upon personal dignity, in particular humiliating and degrading treatment, rape, enforced prostitution and any form of indecent assault;
- *(f)* Slavery and the slave trade in all their forms;
- *(g)* Pillage;
- *(h)* Threats to commit any of the foregoing acts.

Article 4, paragraphs 1 and 2, of the Protocol Additional to the Geneva Conventions of 12 August 1949, and Relating to the Protection of Victims of Non-International Armed Conflicts (Protocol II), which was adopted at Geneva on June 8, 1977, and entered into force on December 7, 1978.

*Source:* United Nations, *Treaty Series*, vol. 1125, pp. 609, 612 (italics added in parentheses).

*Remark:* Read the Geneva conventions or risk becoming a war criminal.

### 235 NONPARTICIPATION

It has come to us first as individuals—what shall I do, what is my duty? If an individual thinks that war is evil, we are so simpleminded, so naive, as to say: «If war is evil, then I do not take part in it», just as one might say, if drunkenness is evil, then I do not drink; if slaveholding is evil, then I do not hold slaves. I know that sounds too simple—almost foolish. I admit that that is our point of view, and this means, of course, that in every war some Friends have suffered not only fines, torture, punishment, or exile, but even the threat of death which, of course, is no more than the soldier faces, but in a different cause. William Penn has described the Quaker position in these few words: «Not fighting but suffering.»

Henry J. Cadbury (Henry Joel Cadbury) (1883-1974), American biblical scholar, professor of divinity at Harvard University, founder of the American Friends Service Committee (the Quakers) in 1917 and chairman thereof, describing the Quaker position in a Nobel lecture, "Quakers and Peace," given in Oslo on December 12, 1947, on behalf of the committee that shared the 1947 Nobel Peace Prize with the Friends Service Council, London.

*Source:* Frederick W. Haberman, ed., *Nobel Lectures Including Presentation Speeches and Laureates' Biographies: Peace*, vol. 2, 1926-1950 (Amsterdam:

Elsevier Publishing Company, for the Nobel Foundation, 1972), pp. 371, 391, 393 (reference to footnote omitted).

*Explanation: William Penn* (1644-1718): English religious leader (Quaker), founder, in 1682, of the colony of Pennsylvania which became one of the thirteen original states of the United States.

*See* Prevention (Henry J. Cadbury, on the lessons of over three hundred years).

*Remark:* The Quakers, "not fighting but suffering."

### 236 NONVIOLENCE

Q. Do you think the League of Nations will succeed in exterminating war?

A. War will never be exterminated by any agency until men and the nations become more spiritual, and adopt the principle of brotherhood and concord rather than antagonism, competition, and brute force. Those in the West do not recognize the power of spiritual things, but some day they will and then they will be free from war, crimes of violence and things that go with these evils. The West is too materialistic, selfish and narrowly nationalistic. What we want is an international mind, embracing the welfare and spiritual advancement of all mankind.

Q. How would you cure the evil of armaments?

A. By non-violence, which will eventually be the weapon of all nations. I say 'eventually' deliberately, because we shall have wars and armaments for a very long time. It is two thousand years since Christ preached His Sermon on the Mount and the world has adopted only a fragment of the imperishable lofty precepts therein enunciated for the conduct of man toward man. Until we take all Christ's principles to our hearts, war, hatred and violence will continue.

Mahatma Gandhi (Mohandas Karamchand Gandhi) (1869-1948), Indian political and religious leader, "architect of India's freedom through a nonviolent revolution," in an interview to the press in New Delhi, published in the daily *Hindu* on March 22, 1931.

*Source:* Mahatma Gandhi, *The Collected Works of Mahatma Gandhi*, vol. XLV [45] (New Delhi: Ministry of Information and Broadcasting, 1971), pp. 318, 319.

*Explanation: Mahatma:* "great soul."

*Remark:* Nonviolence, eventually "the weapon of all nations."

### 237 NUCLEAR ACCIDENT

At four A.M. on March 28, 1979, the worst accident in the history of the U.S. nuclear industry began and, within several hours, the badly damaged radioactive core of the nuclear reactor at Three Mile Island in Harrisburg, Pennsylvania, had partially melted down....

A normally operating 1000-megawatt reactor contains fifteen billion curies of radiation, the equivalent of the long-lived isotopes released by the explosion of 1,000 Hiroshima bombs....

....

Economically, a meltdown would cost tens of billions of dollars in property damage, but even more horrifying is the fact that it could contaminate an area the size of Pennsylvania for hundreds to thousands of years making it uninhabitable.

....

.... Presently, our medical education does not include the decontamination and treatment of radioactive patients; neither is the issue addressed in medical journals....

....

.... But throughout the accident, as evacuation plans were being discussed by the NRC, the radioactive plume had already moved over the population.

....

But despite this overall reassuring information, nuclear power is an unforgiving technology, and an accident could still occur by human or mechanical error. We, and future generations, still have to deal with the shockingly hazardous radioactive waste emanating from these radioactive mausoleums, which all must be closed down thirty to forty years after startup; these dates are rapidly approaching for many of the old reactors. But the NRC now wants to implement a twenty-year "life extension" for all U.S. reactors. And in their Generic Environmental Impact Statement for automatic twenty-year license extension, they evaluate a TMI or Chernobyl-level accident as "low" impact. The NRC still routinely allows plants to operate even with generic safety problems, as well as with TMI safety issues that are still unresolved.

Helen Caldicott (Helen Mary Broinowski Caldicott) (b. 1938), Australian physician (pediatrician), antinuclear activist and environmentalist, writing, in her 1994 book *Nuclear Madness*, on the partial meltdown of a nuclear reactor which began at Three Mile Island in Harrisburg, Pennsylvania, United States, on March 28, 1979.
*Source:* Helen Caldicott, *Nuclear Madness: What You Can Do*, rev. ed. (New York: W. W. Norton & Company, 1994), pp. 114-116, 122, 125.
*Explanations:* ▸ *Chernobyl:* the reference is to the serious nuclear accident which occurred on April 25-26, 1986, at the Chernobyl nuclear power station in the Soviet Union, 65 miles (104 kilometers) north of Kiev, the Soviet Union (now Ukraine). ▸ *Hiroshima bombs:* the reference is to the first American atomic bomb, dropped on Hiroshima, Japan, on August 6, 1945 (local time). ▸ *NRC:* Nuclear Regulatory Commission. ▸ *TMI:* Three Mile Island.
*Remark:* Ticking time bombs in our midst, even thousand-year bombs.

### 238 NUCLEAR AGE
Even little wars are dangerous in a nuclear world.

John F. Kennedy (John Fitzgerald Kennedy) (1917-1963), president of the United States (1961-1963), in his September 20, 1963 address before the General Assembly of the United Nations.
*Source:* John F. Kennedy, *Public Papers of the Presidents of the United States: John F. Kennedy ... 1963* (Washington: United States Government Printing Office, 1964), pp. 693, 694.

### 239 NUCLEAR WEAPON
Arnold had long maintained that conventional strategic bombing by itself could compel the Japanese to surrender. In late June, when invasion was being decided, he had rushed LeMay to Washington to work the numbers. LeMay figured he could complete the destruction of the Japanese war machine by October 1.

"In order to do this," writes Arnold, "he had to take care of some 30 to 60 large and small cities." Between May and August LeMay took care of fifty-eight. But Marshall disagreed with the Air Force assessment. The situation in the Pacific, he had told Truman in June, was "practically identical" to the situation in Europe after Normandy. "Airpower alone was not sufficient to put the Japanese out of the war. It was unable alone to put the Germans out." He explained his reasoning at Potsdam to an interviewer after the war:

We regarded the matter of dropping the [atomic] bomb as exceedingly important. We had just gone through a bitter experience at Okinawa [the last major island campaign, when the Americans lost more than 12,500 men killed and missing and the Japanese more than 100,000 killed in eighty-two days of fighting]. This had been preceded by a number of similar experiences in other Pacific islands, north of Australia. The Japanese had demonstrated in each case they would not surrender and they would fight to the death.... It was expected that resistance in Japan, with their home ties, would be even more severe. We had had the one hundred thousand people killed in Tokyo in one night of [conventional] bombs, and it had had seemingly no effect whatsoever. It destroyed the Japanese cities, yes, but their morale was not affected as far as we could tell, not at all. So it seemed quite necessary, if we could, to shock them into action.... We had to end the war; we had to save American lives.

Richard Rhodes (Richard Lee Rhodes) (b. 1937), American journalist and author, on the choice of roads to victory over Japan in 1945, in his 1986 book *The Making of the Atomic Bomb*, for which he received the Pulitzer Prize for General Nonfiction in 1988.

*Source:* Richard Rhodes, *The Making of the Atomic Bomb* (New York: Simon & Schuster, 1986), pp. 687-688.

*Explanations:* ▶ *Arnold:* Henry Harley Arnold (Hap Arnold) (1886-1950), American air force general whose principal campaign was the strategic bombing of Japan (1944-1945). ▶ *LeMay:* Curtis E. Lemay (Curtis Emerson Lemay) (1906-1990), American air force officer, major general from 1943. ▶ *Marshall:* George C. Marshall (George Catlett Marshall) (1880-1959), American general, chief of staff (1939-1945), later secretary of state (1947-1949) and recipient of the 1953 Nobel Peace Prize. ▶ *Normandy:* the reference is to the aftermath of the June 6, 1944 D-day Allied invasion at Normandy, northwestern France. ▶ *Potsdam:* a town in Germany, near Berlin, where the Potsdam Conference was held from July 17 to August 2, 1945. There, the Potsdam Declaration, "Proclamation Defining Terms for Japanese Surrender," was issued on July 26, 1945, by the heads of government of China, the United Kingdom and the United States. ▶ *Truman:* Harry S. Truman (1884-1972), president of the United States (1945-1953).

*Remark:* "Marshall disagreed with the Air Force assessment."

## 240 NUCLEAR WEAPON

[B]y repeated warnings, emphasised by heavy bombing attacks, an endeavour was made to procure the general exodus of the civil population from the threatened cities. Thus everything in human power, short of using the atomic bomb, was done to spare the civil population of Japan, though there are voices which assert that the bomb should never have been used at all. I cannot associate myself with such ideas. Six years of total war have convinced most people that had the Germans or Japanese discovered this new weapon, they would have used it upon us to our complete destruction with the utmost alacrity. I am surprised that very worthy people, but people who in most cases had no intention of proceeding to the Japanese front themselves, should adopt the position that rather than throw this bomb, we should have sacrificed a million American and a quarter of a million British lives in the desperate battles and massacres of an invasion of Japan. Future generations will judge these dire decisions, and I believe that if they find themselves dwelling in a happier world from which war has been banished, and where freedom reigns, they will not condemn those who struggled for their benefit amid the horrors and miseries of this gruesome and ferocious epoch.

The bomb brought peace, but men alone can keep that peace, and henceforward they will keep it under penalties which threaten the survival, not only of civilisation, but of humanity itself.

Winston S. Churchill (Winston Leonard Spencer Churchill) (1874-1965), British statesman, orator and author, prime minister of the United Kingdom (1940-1945, 1951-1955), reflecting, in a speech given on August 16, 1945, to the House of Commons on the use of the atomic bomb against Japan in order to end World War II.

*Source: Parliamentary Debates*, Commons, 5th series, vol. 413, pp. 76, 79.

*Remark:* Churchill putting emphasis on "a million American and a quarter of a million British lives."

### 241 NUCLEAR WEAPON

Years earlier an experience of my own had given me a striking example of the truth that conflicting judgments about the nation's security could be forcefully expressed without carrying the implication that either side deserved the charge of "security risk."

The incident took place in 1945 when Secretary of War Stimson, visiting my headquarters in Germany, informed me that our government was preparing to drop an atomic bomb on Japan. I was one of those who felt that there were a number of cogent reasons to question the wisdom of such an act. I was not, of course, called upon, officially, for any advice or counsel concerning the matter, because the European theater, of which I was the commanding general, was not involved, the forces of Hitler having already been defeated. But the Secretary, upon giving me the news of the successful bomb test in New Mexico, and of the plan for using it, asked for my reaction, apparently expecting a vigorous assent.

During his recitation of the relevant facts, I had been conscious of a feeling of depression and so I voiced to him my grave misgivings, first on the basis of my belief that Japan was already defeated and that dropping the bomb was completely unnecessary, and secondly because I thought that our country should avoid shocking world opinion by the use of a weapon whose employment was, I thought, no longer mandatory as a measure to save American lives. It was my belief that Japan was, at that very moment, seeking some way to surrender with a minimum loss of "face." The Secretary was deeply perturbed by my attitude, almost angrily refuting the reasons I gave for my quick conclusions.

But in spite of his instant rejection of my opinion, it never occurred to Secretary Stimson to question my loyalty to America, or for me to think that anyone else would or could do so.

Dwight D. Eisenhower (Dwight David Eisenhower) (1890-1969), former president of the United States (1953-1961) and supreme commander of the Allied forces in western Europe during World War II, referring, in his 1963 book *The White House Years: Mandate for Change, 1953-1956,* to his discussions, after July 16, 1945, with Henry L. Stimson (Henry Lewis Stimson) (1867-1950), American secretary of war (1940-September 1945).

*Source:* Dwight D. Eisenhower, *The White House Years: Mandate for Change, 1953-1956* (Garden City, New York: Doubleday & Company, 1963), pp. 312-313 (chapter XIII).

*Explanation: Hitler:* Adolf Hitler (1889-1945), chancellor of the Third Reich of Nazi Germany (1933-1945).

*Remark:* "I was one of those who felt that there were a number of cogent reasons to question the wisdom of such an act."

## 242 NUCLEAR WEAPON

We returned to the hill. In the evening began a ghostly, hellish parade of the wounded. Naked, burned, flayed, and bleeding they came. It was impossible to know whether some of them were men or women. One man glittered with countless slivers of glass embedded in his body. One attempted to keep his internal organs inside his split body with his hand. A mother, aimlessly wandering with a vacant expression on her face, held her dead child in her arms. Throughout the crowd ran other people in search of their relatives and loved ones. Their frenzied calls for mother, father, children, wives, and husbands echoed over the hillside.

Kakuji Miyazaki, referring, in a 1978 article, to his experience, as a sixteen-year old Japanese student, on the day of the American atomic bombing of the city of Nagasaki, Japan, August 9, 1945 (local time).

*Source:* Kakuji Miyazaki, "Hopeless Attempts to Help," in *Cries for Peace: Experiences of Japanese Victims of World War II,* comp. The Youth Division of Soka Gakkai, ed. Richard L. Gage, 1st English ed. (Tokyo: Japan Times, 1978), pp. 203, 205.

*Note:* "Nagasaki was successfully bombed." Harry S. Truman, *Memoirs by Harry S. Truman,* vol. 1, *Year of Decisions* (Garden City, New York: Doubleday & Company, 1955), p. 426.

*Explanation: Truman:* Harry S. Truman (1884-1972), former president of the United States (1945-1953).

*See* Human being (Toge Sankichi, on Hiroshima in 1945).

*Remark:* Can you read this again?

## 243 NUCLEAR WEAPON

Our school reopened in borrowed quarters in October, 1945; and I was well enough to attend. Only forty of the former nearly two thousand pupils appeared the first day.

Masaki Morimoto (b. 1932?), Japanese student, referring, in a 1978 article, to his experience as a result of the American atomic bombing of the city of Nagasaki, Japan, on August 9, 1945 (local time).

*Source:* Masaki Morimoto, "Sad Reunion," in *Cries for Peace: Experiences of Japanese Victims of World War II*, comp. The Youth Division of Soka Gakkai, ed. Richard L. Gage, 1st English ed. (Tokyo: Japan Times, 1978), pp. 207, 208.

*Remark:* Autumn leaves falling in Nagasaki, or did they fall that year?

### 244 NUCLEAR WEAPON

This one bomb, the 1954 superbomb, contained less than one ton of nuclear explosive. The energy released in the explosion of this bomb was greater than that of all the explosives used in all of the wars that have taken place during the entire history of the world, including the First World War and the Second World War.

....

A single 25-megaton bomb could largely destroy any city on earth and kill most of its inhabitants. Thousands of these great bombs have been fabricated, together with the vehicles to deliver them.

Precise information about the existing stockpiles of nuclear weapons has not been released. The participants in the Sixth Pugwash Conference, in 1960, made use of the estimate 60,000 megatons. This is 10,000 times the amount of explosive used in the whole of the Second World War.

Linus Pauling (Linus Carl Pauling) (1901-1994), American chemist, recipient of the 1962 Nobel Peace Prize, awarded in 1963, talking, in his Nobel lecture, "Science and Peace," given in Oslo on December 11, 1963, about the hydrogen bomb tested by the United States on March 1, 1954.

*Source:* Frederick W. Haberman, ed., *Nobel Lectures Including Presentation Speeches and Laureates' Biographies: Peace*, vol. 3, *1951-1970* (Amsterdam: Elsevier Publishing Company, for the Nobel Foundation, 1972), pp. 257, 271, 271-272, 279.

*Explanation: Pugwash:* The Pugwash Conferences on Science and World Affairs, the first one held in 1957 in the village of Pugwash, Nova Scotia, Canada, series of meetings of scientists from many countries to discuss nuclear weapons and world security, the reduction of armaments and the tempering of the arms race. The Pugwash Conferences on Science and World Affairs and Joseph Rotblat (1908-2005), Polish-born British physicist and pacifist who worked on the atom bomb in Liverpool, England, and Los Alamos, United States, the Pugwash organization's secretary-general (1957-1973) and president (1988-1997), jointly received the 1995 Nobel Peace Prize.

*Note:* Linus Pauling had protested against the production of the hydrogen bomb. He also worked for a nuclear test ban, the Treaty Banning Nuclear Weapon Tests in the Atmosphere, in Outer Space and under Water (the Nuclear Test Ban Treaty, the Partial Test Ban Treaty). The treaty, signed at Moscow on August 5, 1963, entered into force on October 10, 1963, the same day it was announced that he had been awarded the Nobel Peace Prize. *Same source*, pp. 290-291. He had received the Nobel Prize in Chemistry in 1954, making him the only person to win two undivided Nobel prizes.

*See* Government (A. P. Herbert, in his poem "Too Much!").

*Remark:* Successfully sold to governments, number concealed by governments, top priority of governments, thereunder even "government of the people, by the people, for the people."

### 245 NUCLEAR WEAPON
The explosion of perhaps less than two dozen C-bombs might be sufficient to destroy all life on the earth's surface.

Fay-Cooper Cole (1881-1961), American anthropologist, and Harris Gaylord Warren (1906-1988), American historian, on cobalt bombs.
*Source:* Fay-Cooper Cole and Harris Gaylord Warren, *An Illustrated Outline History of Mankind,* vol. II (Chicago: Spencer Press, 1955), p. 719.
*Remark:* Bombs—or life on earth.

### 246 NUCLEAR WEAPON
I had hoped—like countless millions of others—that the victory over fascism in the Second World War would bring great changes to the world. I had looked to a time of new freedom and amity among the nations. Instead, the cold war came with its atom bomb tests, rearmament and bitter strife. When I visited the United States a decade and a half after the defeat of the Axis—after a war in which some fifty million human beings had perished—people were building private air-raid shelters. I read with horror about atom bomb drills in the schools—drills in which children were taught to crouch in corners and hide under desks. To me all this was madness—I knew that the only defense against atom bombs was peace.

Pablo Casals (Pau Carlos Salvador Defilló de Casals) (1876-1973), Spanish cellist and conductor, opponent of fascism and crusader for peace, reflecting, in or about 1960, on the defense against atom bombs.
*Source:* Pablo Casals, *Joys and Sorrows: Reflections by Pablo Casals, as Told to Albert E. Kahn* (London: Macdonald and Co. (Publishers), 1970), pp. 281, 283.
*Explanation: Axis:* the reference is mainly to the defeat of Germany and Japan in 1945.
*Remark:* "I knew that the only defense against atom bombs was peace."

### 247 NUCLEAR WEAPON
*The General Assembly,*

    ....
*1. Declares* that:
*(a)* The use of nuclear and thermo-nuclear weapons is contrary to the spirit, letter and aims of the United Nations and, as such, a direct violation of the Charter of the United Nations;
*(b)* The use of nuclear and thermo-nuclear weapons would exceed even the scope of war and cause indiscriminate suffering and destruction to mankind and civilization and, as such, is contrary to the rules of international law and to the laws of humanity;
*(c)* The use of nuclear and thermo-nuclear weapons is a war directed not against an enemy or enemies alone but also against mankind in general, since

the peoples of the world not involved in such a war will be subjected to all the evils generated by the use of such weapons;

(d) Any State using nuclear and thermo-nuclear weapons is to be considered as violating the Charter of the United Nations, as acting contrary to the laws of humanity and as committing a crime against mankind and civilization.

From the preamble to and operative paragraph 1 of United Nations General Assembly resolution 1653 (XVI) of November 24, 1961 (Declaration on the Prohibition of the Use of Nuclear and Thermo-Nuclear Weapons).

*Source:* United Nations, *Resolutions Adopted by the General Assembly during Its Sixteenth Session*, vol. I, *19 September 1961-23 February 1962* (General Assembly, Official Records: Sixteenth Session, Supplement No. 17 (A/5100)), pp. 4, 4-5 (semicolon replaced by period at the end).

*Note:* To name examples, India, Japan and the Soviet Union voted for, China, France, South Africa, the United Kingdom and the United States against, and Denmark, Finland, Iceland, Israel, Norway, Pakistan and Sweden abstained.

*See also* Richard A. Falk, *Legal Order in a Violent World* (Princeton, New Jersey: Princeton University Press, 1968), pp. 425-426, 432 (on declaring nuclear weapons illegitimate).

*Remark:* Expression of international law or the seed of future international law?

### 248 NUCLEAR WEAPON

An objective of a no-first-use proposal is to make less likely the introduction of nuclear weapons into armed conflict between states. In so doing, this policy seeks primarily to encourage the perception of these weapons as illegitimate instruments of conflict, and thus to promote a concept of defense planning that satisfies security interests without relying upon nuclear weapons, save in the instance when the enemy uses them first....

....

.... It is doubtful that the United States would have introduced atomic bombs into World War II under the claim of military necessity if their status as weapons had been previously declared, with some formality, to be illegitimate. Would we, for instance, have been willing to attain an equivalent impact upon the course of World War II (assuming the same quantum of damage) by the use of poison gas against Hiroshima and Nagasaki? I ask this question to suggest that the status of a weapon does appear to have some bearing upon the decision to use it....

....

.... A no-first–use proposal might contribute to the safety of the existing security system and, at the same time, foster a transition to a new system of international relations in which national military capabilities were drastically reduced.

Richard A. Falk (Richard Anderson Falk) (b. 1930), American professor of international law and practice, in his 1968 book *Legal Order in a Violent World.*

*Source:* Richard A. Falk, *Legal Order in a Violent World* (Princeton, New Jersey: Princeton University Press, 1968), pp. 425-426, 432.

*Explanation: Hiroshima and Nagasaki:* Japanese cities upon which American atomic bombs were dropped at the end of World War II, on August 6 and 9, 1945, respectively (local time).

*Remark:* No first use of nuclear weapons. No nuclear weapons would be even better.

### 249 NUCLEAR WEAPON

Today's nuclear arsenals contain the combined potential firepower of over one million Hiroshimas.

Norman Myers (b. 1934), English environmental scientist, conservationist, writer and photographer, in the 1984 book *Gaia*.

*Source:* Norman Myers, Uma Ram Nath and Melvin Westlake, *Gaia: An Atlas of Planet Management*, Norman Myers, gen. ed. (Garden City, New York: Anchor Press/Doubleday and Company, 1984), p. 248.

*Remark:* Only one million Hiroshimas in 1984.

### 250 NUMBER

Mankind has fought over 14,000 large and small wars. These have carried away nearly 4,000,000,000 human lives—that is to say about the same number as there are people living in the world today.

Yuri Kashlev (Yuri Borisovich Kashlev) (b. 1934), Soviet-Russian diplomat, in his book *After 14,000 Wars*, first published in Russian in 1976.

*Source:* Yu. Kashlev, *After 14,000 Wars*, trans. David Sinclair-Loutit (Moscow: Progress Publishers, 1979), p. 5.

*Remark:* The book has only the number of wars until 1976.

### 251 NURSE

This remarkable woman was in truth performing the function of an administrative chief. How had this come about? Was she not in reality merely a nurse? Was it not her duty simply to tend the sick? And indeed, was it not as a ministering angel, a gentle "lady with a lamp" that she actually impressed the minds of her contemporaries? No doubt that was so; and yet it is no less certain that, as she herself said, the specific business of nursing was "the least important of the functions into which she had been forced."... For to those who watched her at work among the sick, moving day and night from bed to bed, with that unflinching courage, with that indefatigable vigilance, it seemed as if the concentrated force of an undivided and unparalleled devotion could hardly suffice for that portion of her task alone. Wherever, in those vast wards, suffering was at its worst and the need for help was greatest, there, as if by magic, was Miss Nightingale. Her superhuman equanimity would, at the moment of some ghastly operation, nerve the victim to endure and almost to hope. Her sympathy would assuage the pangs of dying and bring back to those still living something of the forgotten charm of life. Over and over again her untiring effort rescued those whom the surgeons had abandoned as beyond the possibility of cure. Her mere presence brought with it a strange influence. A passionate idolatry spread among the men: they kissed her shadow as it passed. They did more. "Before she came," said a soldier, "there was cussin' and swearin', but after that it was as 'oly as a church."...

....

.... One simple comparison of figures was enough to reveal the extraordinary change: the rate of mortality among the cases treated had fallen from 42 per cent. to 22 per thousand. But still the indefatigable lady was not satisfied. The main problem had been solved—the physical needs of the men had been provided for; their mental and spiritual needs remained.

Lytton Strachey (Giles Lytton Strachey) (1880-1932), English biographer, writing, in his 1918 book *Eminent Victorians*, on the work of the English nurse Florence Nightingale (1820-1910), "founder of modern nursing," during the Crimean War (1854-1856).
*Source:* Lytton Strachey, *Eminent Victorians: Cardinal Manning, Florence Nightingale, Dr. Arnold, General Gordon* (London: Chatto & Windus, 1918), pp. 117, 135-137, 141.
*Remark:* A "lady with a lamp," a lady with a pen.

### 252 OFFER
I would say to the House, as I said to those who have joined this Government: "I have nothing to offer but blood, toil, tears and sweat."

We have before us an ordeal of the most grievous kind. We have before us many, many long months of struggle and of suffering. You ask, what is our policy? I will say: It is to wage war, by sea, land and air, with all our might and with all the strength that God can give us; to wage war against a monstrous tyranny, never surpassed in the dark, lamentable catalogue of human crime. That is our policy. You ask, what is our aim? I can answer in one word: It is victory, victory at all costs, victory in spite of all terror, victory, however long and hard the road may be; for without victory, there is no survival.

Winston S. Churchill (Winston Leonard Spencer Churchill) (1874-1965), British statesman, orator and author, prime minister of the United Kingdom (1940-1945, 1951-1955), speaking in the House of Commons, on May 13, 1940, for the first time after having become prime minister three days earlier, on May 10.
*Source: Parliamentary Debates,* Commons, 5th series, vol. 360, pp. 1501, 1502.
*Remark:* Also hope.

### 253 OLYMPIC GAMES
The holding of the games was a religious feast for all Greece. Though those were the days of almost incessant warring among neighboring towns and states, hostilities were suspended during the "Hieromenia," the sacred month during which athletes and spectators were allowed to journey to and from the games with safety under the protection of tradition and the watchful eyes of the gods.

....
For centuries the Olympic Games were the great peaceful events of the civilization that centered around the Mediterranean Sea. Then the glory that was Greece began to fade before the grandeur that was Rome. As Greece lost power and prestige, the games lost their ancient significance. They lost the spirit of the older days.

John Kieran (John Francis Kieran) (1892-1981), American sportswriter, on the Olympic Games in ancient times (776-394 B.C.).

*Source:* John Kieran, *The Story of the Olympic Games, 776 B.C.-1936 A.D.* (New York: Frederick A. Stokes Company, 1936), pp. 8, 12.

*Note:* The Olympic Games were revived in 1896.

*See also* Truce (the Olympic Truce).

*Remark:* "Great peaceful events."

### 254 OPINION

Let the public continue to regard me as the blood-thirsty beast, the cruel sadist and the mass murderer; for the masses could never imagine the commandant of Auschwitz in any other light.

They could never understand that he, too, had a heart and that he was not evil.

Rudolf Höss (Rudolf Franz Ferdinand Höss) (1900-1947), former German commandant (from May 1, 1940, to November 1943) of the Auschwitz (Auschwitz-Birkenau) concentration camp, operated by the German Nazis in the province of Cracow in southern Poland from 1940 to 1945, at the end of his autobiography, finished in February 1947.

*Source:* Rudolf Hoess, *Commandant of Auschwitz: The Autobiography of Rudolf Hoess,* trans. Constantine FitzGibbon (London: Weidenfeld and Nicolson, 1959), p. 181.

*Notes:* ▶ In *The Encyclopedia of the Third Reich* (1976), under "Hoess, Rudolf Franz," the following words are, among other things, sadly to be read:

At Auschwitz Hoess was responsible for the execution of more than 2.5 million inmates, not counting a half million who were allowed to starve to death. He performed his job so well that he was commended in a 1944 SS report that called him "a true pioneer in this area because of his new ideas and educational methods."...

.... "I must admit," he said later, "that the gassing process had a calming effect on me. I always had a horror of the shootings, thinking of the number of people, the women and children. I was relieved that we were spared these blood baths."...

....

.... Most of all, his orders relieved him in his own mind of any personal responsibility.

▶ Höss was sentenced to death by the Supreme National Tribunal in Warsaw on April 2, 1947, and hanged later that month, on April 16, in Auschwitz.

*Remark:* Even the evil consider themselves good. Some goodness, my goodness!

### 255 OPPONENT

I tell you Wellington is a bad general, the English are bad soldiers; we will settle the matter by lunch time.

Napoleon I (Napoleon Bonaparte) (1769-1821), emperor of France (1804-1814, 1815), speaking to Nicolas Jean de Dieu Soult, duc de Dalmatie [duke of Dalmatia] (1769-1851), a marshal in his army, at 8.30 A.M., June 18, 1815, at the battlefield of Waterloo, Belgium, where he was defeated by the combined British and Allied forces under Field Marshal Arthur Wellesley, duke of Wellington (1769-1852), and the Prussian forces under Field Marshal Gebhard Leberecht von Blücher (1742-1819).

*Source:* Napoleon, *The Corsican: A Diary of Napoleon's Life in His Own Words,* comp. R. M. Johnston [Robert Matteson Johnston] (London: Macmillan and Co., 1910), p. 459.

*Compare with* Plan (Josef Goebbels, on Adolf Hitler's plan to invade the Soviet Union).

*Remark:* The "bad" may win.

### 256 ORACLE

"Crœsus, king of the Lydians and of other nations, esteeming these to be the only oracles among men, sends these presents in acknowledgment of your discoveries; and now asks whether he should lead an army against the Persians, and whether he should join any auxiliary forces with his own." Such were their questions; and the opinions of both oracles concurred, foretelling "that if Crœsus should make war on the Persians, he would destroy a mighty empire;" and they advised him to engage the most powerful of the Grecians in his alliance.

Herodotus (ca. 484-ca. 425 B.C.), Greek historian, known as "the Father of History," describing, in his *History,* on the Greco-Persian Wars waged intermittently from about 546 to about 448 B.C., a work believed to have been published before 425 B.C. (book I, entitled "Clio," chapter 53), the ambiguous answer, in about 546 B.C., of the oracles at Delphi, Greece, to an inquiry by the messengers of Croesus (d. 525 B.C. or later), last king of Lydia and other countries in Asia Minor (ca. 560-ca. 546 B.C.).

*Source:* Herodotus, *Herodotus,* trans. Henry Cary (New York: Harper & Brothers, Publishers, 1881), p. 21.

*Note:* The empire that came to be overthrown in or about 546 B.C. turned out to be, not the Persian Empire under Cyrus II the Great (590 or 580-ca. 529 B.C.), which he founded in 550 B.C. and ruled until his death, but the Lydian one under Croesus who had ruled from or from about 560 B.C.

*Remark:* Are the oracles of today to be trusted?

### 257 ORDER

R. Höss declared that the annihilation operation was to embrace twelve million Jews in Europe, and described its preparation as follows:

"In the summer of 1941 (...) I was suddenly summoned to the *SS Reichsführer* in Berlin, directly by his adjutant's office. Himmler who, quite exceptionally, spoke to me without his A. D. C. being present, said: 'The *Führer* has ordered that the Jewish question be solved once and for all. We, the *SS,* are to implement that order. (...) So I have earmarked Oswiecim, both because of its good location as regards communication, and because the area can easily be isolated and camouflaged....'

"Although the order was something unprecedented and monstrous, the reasons advanced were such that I agreed to undertake the extermination operation. In any case, I did not then reflect on it; I simply received an order and had to carry it out. I could not allow myself to consider whether mass extermination of Jews was or was not necessary: I could not look so far ahead. If the *Führer* himself ordered that the 'Jewish question be solved once and for all', a veteran national socialist, and an *SS* officer at that, could not question it".

Jan Sehn (1909-1965), Polish judge, on the description of the preparation for the extermination of Jews by Rudolf Höss (Rudolf Franz Ferdinand Höss) (1900-1947), the German commandant (from May 1, 1940, to November 1943) of the Auschwitz (Auschwitz-Birkenau) concentration camp, operated by the German Nazis in the province of Cracow in southern Poland from 1940 to 1945, and in particular Höss's conversation in the summer of 1941 with Heinrich Himmler (1900-1945), German Nazi leader, head of the SS, a Nazi Party corps responsible for the enforcement of extermination policies.

*Source:* Jan Sehn, *Concentration Camp Oswiecim-Brzezinka (Auschwitz-Birkenau)*, trans. Klemens Keplicz, The Chief Commission for the Investigation of Nazi Crimes in Poland (Warsaw: Wydawnictwo Prawnicze, 1957), pp. 111-112 (reference to footnote omitted; Sehn's earlier writings on the subject in 1946 and 1955: *same source*, p. 5).

*Explanations:* ▸ *A.D.C.:* aide-de-camp. ▸ *Führer:* in English "leader," a reference to Adolf Hitler (1889-1945), chancellor of the Third Reich of Nazi Germany (1933-1945). ▸ *Oswiecim:* Auschwitz (Auschwitz-Birkenau), the site of a German Nazi concentration camp in the province of Cracow in southern Poland (1940-1945), now the site of a state museum. ▸ *SS:* an abbreviation of the German word Schutzstaffel (Protective Echelon), a Nazi Party corps responsible for, among other things, the administration of concentration (extermination) camps in World War II, declared a criminal organization by the International Military Tribunal in Nuremberg, Germany, in 1946.

*Note:* In the autobiography of Rudolf Höss the following text can be found:

When in the summer of 1941 he himself gave me the order to prepare installations at Auschwitz where mass exterminations could take place, and personally to carry out these exterminations, I did not have the slightest idea of their scale or consequences. It was certainly an extraordinary and monstrous order. Nevertheless the reasons behind the extermination programme seemed to me right. I did not reflect on it at the time: I had been given an order, and I had to carry it out. Whether this mass extermination of the Jews was necessary or not was something on which I could not allow myself to form an opinion, for I lacked the necessary breadth of view.

If the Führer had himself given the order for the 'final solution of the Jewish question', then, for a veteran National-Socialist and even more so for an SS officer, there could be no question of considering its merits. 'The Führer commands, we follow' was never a mere phrase or slogan. It was meant in bitter earnest.

(Rudolf Hoess, *Commandant of Auschwitz: The Autobiography of Rudolf Hoess*, trans. Constantine FitzGibbon (London: Weidenfeld and Nicolson, 1959), pp. 144-145. *See also* p. 183.)

*See* Opinion (Rudolf Höss; death sentence).

*Remark:* "I simply received an order and had to carry it out." Well, it is not that simple.

### 258 ORDER

The real liberator of Paris was the destroyer of Rotterdam and Sebastopol, von Choltitz the German commander; he dared to disobey an order to burn it down.

M. R. D. Foot (Michael Richard Daniell Foot) (b. 1919), English historian, at a symposium in the University of Salford, England, held from February 27 to March 2, 1973.

*Source:* M. R. D. Foot, "What Good Did Resistance Do?", in *Resistance in Europe, 1939-1945,* ed. Stephen Hawes and Ralph White (London: Allen Lane, 1975), pp. 204, 217.

*Explanations:* ▸ *Choltitz:* Dietrich von Choltitz (1894-1966), German general who oversaw the destruction of Rotterdam in 1940 and Sevastopol (Sebastopol) in 1942 but surrendered, as the last German governor of Paris, to Allied forces in France in August 1944. ▸ *Rotterdam:* a city in the Netherlands, subjected to heavy German air raids on May 14, 1940, after the Dutch had surrendered. ▸ *Sebastopol:* Sevastopol, a city in the Crimea, the Soviet Union (now in Ukraine).

*Remark:* Who is not in love with Paris?

## 259 ORGANIZATION

Each catastrophe apparently teaches mankind to set up institutions that might have prevented it, though they usually do not prevent the next catastrophe. Just as the generals are always supposed to be prepared to fight the last war, so the international institutions are designed to prevent it. The slow learning process nevertheless goes on, and the institutions themselves can be regarded as repositories of political skill and knowledge. Indeed, for the meagre resources that we devote to the international order, we get a remarkable return. This becomes apparent when we consider that the combined budget for all the international agencies is less than that of the Ford Foundation.

Kenneth E. Boulding (Kenneth Ewart Boulding) (1910-1993), English-born American professor of economics, educator, author, poet and pacifist who received Nobel Prize nominations for both economics and peace, in a 1967 article.

*Source:* Kenneth E. Boulding, "The Learning and Reality-Testing Process in the International System," *Journal of International Affairs,* vol. XXI, no. 1 (1967), pp. 1, 12.

*Remark:* Which come first—wars or institutions?

## 260 PAINTING

*Guernica* is generally considered to be a painting of war. It became commonplace to compare it with Goya's work on the subject. Art history does not offer another case like this. The work has been compared with the most significant paintings having war as their theme: those of Ucello, Velázquez, Goya and Delacroix; from the old mosaic depicting the confrontation of Darius and Alexander to the canvas by Manet showing the shooting of Maximilian.

....

*Guernica* is not a painting of war—in the traditional sense. The obstinacy of such a characterization does not alter its real meaning. An attentive look at the painting would suffice to conclude that it contains not a single element for validating such an interpretation.

....

The military theme attributed to *Guernica* comes from a confusion. The error derives from introducing the bellicose source of the renowned name of Guernica into the pictorial plane. That is to say, we bring what we know to what we see. The identification of the title of the painting with the name of the historic Basque town and the event of its bombardment is what, obliquely, contributes to the notion that this canvas shows a theme of war. We know beforehand that Guernica was destroyed by Nazi aviation; that it was an episode during the Spanish Civil War; that Picasso, indignant after reading the description of the bombardment in the Paris newspapers, rushed to his study to begin painting the work the Spanish Government had already commissioned him to do in January of that year—a work that was destined to decorate the pavilion of the Spanish Republic at the International Fair taking place in the French capital.

Eugenio F. Granell (Eugenio Fernandez Granell) (1912-2001), Spanish writer, professor of Spanish literature and painter, evaluating *Guernica*, a mural painted by the Spanish artist Pablo Picasso (Pablo Ruiz y Picasso) (1881-1973) from May to early June, 1937, to protest the destruction, by German airplanes flying for General Francisco Franco, of the Basque village Guernica in the province of Biscay, northern Spain, on April 26, 1937, during the Spanish Civil War of 1936-1939.

*Source:* E. F. Granell, *Picasso's Guernica: The End of a Spanish Era* (Ann Arbor, Michigan: UMI Research Press, 1981), pp. 4, 7-8 (reference to footnote omitted; revision of a doctoral thesis from 1967).

*Explanations:* ▸ *Darius and Alexander:* the reference is to Alexander III or Alexander the Great (356-323 B.C.), king of Macedonia (336-323 B.C.), and the Battle of Gaugamela (Arbela, now the town of Irbil in northeastern Iraq, near the city of Mosul), fought on October 1, 331 B.C., wherein Darius III Codommanus (ca. 380-330 B.C.), king of Persia (336 or 335-330 B.C.), was defeated. ▸ *Delacroix:* Eugène Delacroix (Ferdinand Victor Eugène Delacroix) (1798-1863), French Romantic painter who painted, for instance, *Liberty Guiding the People* in 1830 to commemorate the rising of that year. ▸ *Francisco Franco* (Francisco Paulino Hermenegildo Teódulo Franco Bahamonde) (1892-1975), Spanish general, leader of the Nationalist forces, head of state after the Spanish Civil War until his death, or from 1939 to 1975. ▸ *Goya:* Francisco Goya (Francisco José de Goya y Lucientes) (1746-1828), Spanish painter and engraver, famous for his series of etchings *The Disasters of War* (Spanish, *Los Desastres de la Guerra*), produced in 1810-1823 but published in 1863, inspired by the French occupation of and war against Spain during the Peninsular War of 1808-1814. ▸ *Manet:* Édouard Manet (1832-1883), French painter and engraver who influenced the impressionists and painted, for instance, *The Execution of Maximilian* in 1867. ▸ *Maximilian:* Maximilian (Ferdinand Joseph Maximilian) (1832-1867), emperor of Mexico (1864-1867). ▸ *Spanish Civil War:* 1936-1939. ▸ *Ucello:* Paolo Uccello (Paolo di Dono) (1397-1475), Italian (Florentine) painter who painted *The Rout of San Romano* in about 1456. ▸ *Velázquez:* Diego Rodríguez de Silva Velázquez or Velásquez (1599-1660), Spanish painter, famous, for instance, for his painting *The Surrender of Breda* (a town in the Netherlands surrendering to the Spaniards in 1625).

*Notes:* ▸ In his 1958 book *Picasso: His Life and Works*, Roland Penrose (Roland Algernon Penrose) (1900-1984), British author, painter, collector and exhibition organizer, born in England, writes as follows:

To others the horse and its rider are the heroic victims of a brutal attack from the bull; but on examination we find, particularly in the early versions, nothing to suggest that the bull is in this case the villain. On the contrary he appears to be searching the horizon for the enemy, who is in fact not present in the scene at all. His enemy is the common enemy of all mankind, too vile and too universal to be contained in a single image. What we see in the painting is the effect of his enormity: the dead child, the house in flames, lacerated bodies, hysterical cries of agony and looks of astonishment that such things are possible. The omission of the evil spirit that has caused this disaster is a more effective insult than its introduction ... in the shape of a loathsome monster. Also it makes prophetic reference to the impersonality of modern warfare which allows the victims increasingly little chance of knowing who is their aggressor.

Roland Penrose, *Picasso: His Life and Works* (New York: Harper & Brothers, Publishers, 1958), pp. 265, 272 (reference to footnote omitted).

▸ Furthermore Penrose writes:

One thing must be certain—that his 'Guernica' will always speak its inspired and powerful message. If this is his great painting with 'war' as its theme, some of his later paintings ... express a remarkable sense of peace.

(Roland Penrose, "Guernica," in *War and Peace*, ed. Anil de Silva, Otto von Simson and Roger Hinks, Man through His Art, vol. I (London: Educational Productions, 1963), p. 63, 63)

▸ *Guernica* is now kept in the Prado Museum in Madrid.

*Remark:* A masterpiece without the enemy but with his destruction.

### 261 PAINTING

When Prime Minister Churchill and Gen. Charles de Gaulle met at Marrakesh, the general politely asked the Prime Minister whether he was still painting.

"I am too weak for that sort of thing," Mr. Churchill replied, "but I am still strong enough to wage war."

A news report, dated January 16, 1944, to the *New York Times* on a meeting in January 1944 in the city of Marrakesh, Morocco, between Winston S. Churchill (Winston Leonard Spencer Churchill) (1874-1965), British statesman, orator and author, prime minister of the United Kingdom (1940-1945 and 1951-1955), and Charles de Gaulle (Charles André Joseph Marie de Gaulle) (1890-1970), French general.

*Source: New York Times*, January 17, 1944, p. 3 (late edition).

*Note:* De Gaulle later served as president of France (1959-1969).

*Remark:* Painting the globe, though.

### 262 PATRIOTISM

I only regret that I have but one life to lose for my country.

Nathan Hale (1755-1776), American revolutionary officer, captured by the British after having volunteered to enter their lines to obtain information, uttered these words before being hanged on September 22, 1776.

*Source:* Henry Phelps Johnston, *Nathan Hale 1776: Biography and Memorials*, rev. ed. (New Haven: Yale University Press, 1914), p. 129 (capitals changed to lowercase letters).

*Remark:* Why not "I only regret that I have but one life to *live* for my country"?

### 263 PEACEFUL STRUGGLE

[T]he Christian doctrine of love, operating through the Gandhian method of nonviolence, is one of the most potent weapons available to an oppressed people in their struggle for freedom.

Martin Luther King (1929-1968), American clergyman and civil rights leader, in a revised 1963 article.

*Source:* Martin Luther King, Jr., "Pilgrimage to Nonviolence," in *Strength to Love* (New York: Harper & Row, Publishers, 1963), pp. 135, 138, cf. pp. ix-x.

*Explanations:*  ▸ *Gandhian:* the reference is to Mahatma Gandhi (Mohandas Karamchand Gandhi) (1869-1948), Indian political and religious leader and "architect of India's freedom through a nonviolent revolution."  ▸ *Mahatma:* "great soul."

*Note:* King received the 1964 Nobel Peace Prize.

*Remark:* Love is a patient, profitable weapon.

## 264 PEACEMAKER

It is reported that two kingdoms were on the verge of war, the possession of a certain embankment being disputed by them.

And Buddha seeing the kings with their armies ready to fight, requested them to tell him the cause of their quarrels. Having heard the complaints on both sides, he said:

"I understand that the embankment has value for some of your people, has it any intrinsic value aside from its service to your men?"

"It has no intrinsic value whatever," was the reply. The Tathâgata continued: "Now when you go to battle is it not sure that many of your men will be slain and you yourselves, O kings, are liable to lose your lives?"

And they said: "Verily, it is sure that many will be slain and our own lives be jeopardised."

"The blood of men, however," said Buddha, "has it less intrinsic value than a mound of earth?"

"No," the kings said, "the lives of men and above all the lives of kings, are priceless."

Then the Tathâgata concluded: "Are you going to stake that which is priceless against that which has no intrinsic value whatever?"

The wrath of the two monarchs abated, and they came to a peaceable agreement.

From *The Gospel of Buddha according to Old Records*, first published in 1894, chapter LXXVII [77], "The Peacemaker" (produced here in full).

*Source:* Paul Carus, *The Gospel of Buddha according to Old Records*, 12th ed. (Chicago: Open Court Publishing Co., 1909), pp. 175, 175-176.

*Explanations:*  ▸ *Buddha* (the Enlightened One): Gautama Buddha (Siddhartha Gautama) (ca. 563-ca. 483 B.C.), Indian prince, born in the district Nepal, founder of Buddhism.  ▸ *Tathâgata* (Tathagata): the Perfect One (Buddha); *same source*, pp. 17, 34.

*Remark:* Saving priceless lives was Buddha's advice.

## 265 PEACEMAKER

Mo-tzu was a teacher who took his own teachings seriously. For example, in the *Mo-tzu*, the work that bears the philosopher's name and contains records of his sayings and doings, there is a chapter on "Condemnation of Offensive War." In the same volume there are also records of his journeying to distant states to prevent the outbreak of a war when he had heard of such a possibility. On one of these journeys, the record tells, he had to walk for ten days and ten nights and tear pieces of cloth from his garments to wrap round his feet. An ancient critic said of Mo-tzu, "Despite all personal hardships, he held fast to his ideas—a man of distinction indeed!"

Mo Ti, Motse or Mo-Tzu ("Master Mo") [Mozu] (470?-391? B.C.), Chinese philosopher and founder of a religion, according to *Encyclopœdia Britannica* (1964).
*Source: Encyclopœdia Britannica* (1964), under "Mo Ti (Mo-tzu)."
*See* Walk (Satish Kumar).
*Remark:* Mo Ti, an active peacemaker.

### 266 PEACEMAKER
Blessed are the peacemakers, for they will be called children of God.

The Bible, Matthew 5:9 (Jesus in the Sermon on the Mount).
*Source: The Holy Bible Containing the Old and New Testaments*, New Revised Standard Version (New York: Oxford University Press, 1989).

### 267 PEACEMAKER
They call us romantics, weak, stupid, sentimental idealists, perhaps because we have some faith in the good which exists even in our opponents and because we believe that kindness achieves more than cruelty. It may be that we are simpleminded, but I do not think that we are dangerous. Those, however, who stagnate behind their political programs, offering nothing else to suffering mankind, to starving, dying millions—they are the scourge of Europe.

Fridtjof Nansen (1861-1930), Norwegian explorer, scientist (zoologist, oceanographer), artist, statesman and humanitarian, recipient of the 1922 Nobel Peace Prize, in his Nobel lecture, "The Suffering People of Europe," given in Christiania (Oslo) on December 19, 1922.
*Source:* Frederick W. Haberman, ed., *Nobel Lectures Including Presentation Speeches and Laureates' Biographies: Peace*, vol. 1, *1901-1925* (Amsterdam: Elsevier Publishing Company, for the Nobel Foundation, 1972), pp. 351, 361, 372.
*Remark:* Some need for excuses? Who is simpleminded, a peacemaker or an aggressor?

### 268 PEACEMAKER
Peace is a daily, a weekly, a monthly process, gradually changing opinions, slowly eroding old barriers, quietly building new structures. And however undramatic the pursuit of peace, that pursuit must go on.

John F. Kennedy (John Fitzgerald Kennedy) (1917-1963), president of the United States (1961-1963), in his September 20, 1963 address before the General Assembly of the United Nations.
*Source:* John F. Kennedy, *Public Papers of the Presidents of the United States: John F. Kennedy ... 1963* (Washington: United States Government Printing Office, 1964), pp. 693, 694.
*Remark:* Writing a drama may also be undramatic at times.

### 269 PEOPLE

People throughout the world may look different or have a different religion, education or position, but they are all the same. They are the people to be loved. They are all hungry for love.

Mother Teresa (Agnes Gonxha Bojaxhiu) (1910-1997), Roman Catholic nun, baptized in Shkup, Albania, within the Ottoman Empire (now Skopje in Macedonia), citizen of India and recipient of the 1979 Nobel Peace Prize, in the book *The Joy in Loving*, published in 1996.

*Source:* Mother Teresa, *The Joy in Loving: A Guide to Daily Living with Mother Teresa*, comp. Jaya Chaliha and Edward Le Joly, Viking (New Delhi: Penguin Books India, 1996), p. 151.

*Note:* Mother Teresa worked in Calcutta, India, for the poorest of the poor and became "Saint of the Gutter." She was beatified in 2003.

*Remark:* Let them have love and peace.

### 270 PEOPLE'S WAR

According to our idea of a people's war, it should, like a kind of nebulous vapoury essence, never condense into a solid body; otherwise the enemy sends an adequate force against this core, crushes it, and makes a great many prisoners; their courage sinks, every one thinks the main question is decided, any further effort useless, and the arms fall from the hands of the people. Still, however, on the other hand, it is necessary that this mist should collect at some points into denser masses, and form threatening clouds from which now and again a formidable flash of lightning may burst forth. These points are chiefly on the flanks of the enemy's theatre of war, as already observed.

Karl von Clausewitz (Karl Marie von Clausewitz) (1780-1831), Prussian general and military strategist, in his work *On War* (German, *Vom Kriege*), written from 1818 to 1830 and published posthumously in German in 1832 (book VI, chapter XXVI).

*Source:* Carl von Clausewitz, *On War*, trans. J. J. Graham, three volumes in one, vol. II (London: N. Trübner & Co., 1873), pp. 175-176.

### 271 PHOTOGRAPHY

In a strange way, these two ordinary Americans did as much as many great and famous men to hasten the end of World War II. Their pictures of Old Glory taken that day, 23 February 1945, lifted the war-weary spirits of not only their nation but those of others united against powerful enemies in Europe and Asia. The war, which had already cost many millions of lives, was in its sixth horrendous year, and it was projected to go on for two, perhaps three more years.

....

On the fourth day, 23 February, Rosenthal and Genaust made the 556-foot climb that would take them into the history books. Earlier that day, Mount Suribachi had been captured by a patrol of forty Marines who had fought their way up against Japanese gunfire and grenades. When they reached the top, the Marines had raised a small flag.

This was a historic moment, the first time in World War II that an American flag was raised over Japanese territory.

Genaust and Rosenthal arrived too late to film the flag raising, but they decided to make the climb up Suribachi anyway. That was the first of their lucky decisions that day. Avoiding paths that were mined and finding no enemy opposition, they reached the top to discover that the Marines were preparing to raise a second, much larger flag.

Joe Rosenthal, small and pudgy, piled up some rocks and stood on them to get a better view of the scene. Bill Genaust, a six-footer, stood at his elbow. As five Marines and one Navy corpsman raised the heavy pipe and the flying colors, both men followed the action simultaneously. Joe's camera was a big, heavy Speed Graphic that shot a four-by-five-inch negative. Bill's motion picture camera was a heavy but compact 16-mm Bell & Howell Automaster.

Afterward, Rosenthal described his shot as a one-in-a-billion lucky break that unexpectedly turned out to be a masterpiece.

Because Genaust was at the end of his movie reel, he was not sure that he had filmed the whole scene. He was killed in combat nine days later and never knew that he had also shot a masterpiece almost identical to Rosenthal's.

Their pictures and the Stars and Stripes immortalized that day were a unique inspiration to the nation. The photo and motion picture of our nation's flag being raised above that brutal and bloody battle impressed upon Americans the greatness of their country and, because of men like the six flag raisers, reaffirmed their knowledge that the United States would win its greatest war.

....

Today more than half a century later, the photos of the Iwo Jima flag raising are still an inspiration to millions of Americans of all ages. It has been predicted that these pictures will live forever in the hearts and minds of the American people.

Perhaps they will. But what will be said about the two men who took them? What kind of man is Joe Rosenthal? What kind of man was Bill Genaust? They are my friends, and this is their story.

It always will be part of that legend of nearly 7,000 Americans who died on that ugliest of islands.

After he tripped his shutter at noon on that February day in 1945, Joe Rosenthal's life was never the same. Although he escaped unhurt from Iwo Jima, he was badly damaged by the furor and controversy that erupted around his photo in the weeks, months, and even years afterward.

He suffered the curse of instant celebrity. The press gave him no peace. Because he avoided publicity, particularly the ordeal of being interviewed, some reporters wrote lies about him and his unique photo. They claimed that his photo was a fake. They accused him of organizing the raising of the second flag and posing the men who hoisted it into the air because he had missed the first flag raising.

Rosenthal was so hurt by the lies, accusations, and unfairness of such people that, for ten years, he remained silent, avoided the media, and kept the details of his achievement to himself. Not until 1955 did he consent to reveal the facts of how, just by luck, he happened to be at the right place at the right time—on top of Mount Suribachi at noon on 23 February 1945.

Tedd Thomey (b. 1920), American writer and columnist, writing, in his 1996 book *Immortal Images*, on the February 23, 1945 unofficial raising of a big American flag by six American soldiers on the Japanese island of Iwo Jima, the second unofficial flag raising that day.

*Source:* Tedd Thomey, *Immortal Images: A Personal History of Two Photographers and the Flag Raising on Iwo Jima* (Annapolis, Maryland: Naval Institute Press, 1996), pp. xi, xv-xvii.

*Explanations:*  ▶  *Genaust:* William H. Genaust (William Homer Genaust, Bill Genaust) (1907-1945), United States Marine movie cameraman, a sergeant.  ▶ *Old Glory:* the national flag of the United States.  ▶  *Rosenthal:* Joe Rosenthal (Joseph J. Rosenthal) (1911-2006), American civilian photographer who worked as a war photographer for Associated Press from 1941 to 1946, the World War II photographer who "took probably the most famous photograph of the war during the Battle of Iwo Jima." *Historical Dictionary of War Journalism* (1997), under "Rosenthal, Joe."  ▶  *The Stars and Stripes:* the national flag of the United States.

*Note:* The Battle of Iwo Jima took place from February to March 1945, the casualties of Japan and the United States being over 20, 000 troops, respectively.

*Remark:* A photo and a movie of six soldiers, by two men "at the right place at the right time."

### 272 PILOT

With wave after wave of escorted bombers Hitler tried to smash British ports, airfields and industrial centres, but he was denied victory by the resolute pilots of Hurricanes and Spitfires. Small Australian squadrons shared with distinction in this fearsome air fighting, and many more served later, not only with Fighter Command, but also in the flying boats that waged war on enemy submarines. By 1942 Australia had seventeen squadrons in Britain, some of them active in the heavy bombers that were beginning to spread nightly devastation in Germany. Before war ended the R.A.A.F. in Britain lost more than 5000 lives.

Douglas Pike (Douglas Henry Pike) (1908-1974), Australian professor of history, on the Battle of Britain, a series of air battles between British and German planes during German bombing raids on the United Kingdom, mainly waged in August and September 1940 but lasting until the early summer of 1941.

*Source:* Douglas Pike, *Australia: The Quiet Continent* (Cambridge: Cambridge University Press, 1962), pp. 193-194.

*Explanations:*  ▶  *Hitler:* Adolf Hitler (1889-1945), chancellor of the Third Reich of Nazi Germany (1933-1945).  ▶ *R.A.A.F.:* the Royal Australian Air Force (RAAF).

*Note:* In *Encyclopædia Britannica* (1964), under "Britain, Battle of," one may read that the battle "frustrated the German plan for the invasion of Great Britain" and that it "may have saved Great Britain from conquest and so changed the course of World War II." Furthermore, one may read there: Between July 10 and Oct. 31 (the official British dates for the battle), the Germans lost 1,733 aircraft and the British 915.

*Remark:* A Canadian pilot in World War I, Australian pilots in World War II.

### 273 PILOT

The use of the helicopter for medical evacuation was one of the major advances in emergency medical care pioneered in the Korean War. Nearly every major medical center in the United States today is equipped for helicopter transport of patients from accident sites or crime scenes for emergency medical care. With names like Lifeline, Lifeflight, or AirStar, these modern "medevacs" can trace their lineage to the helicopters used in the MASH units of the Korean War.

....

Although the helicopter made its debut in World War II, it saw broader—if still limited by today's standards—action in Korea. Korea was helicopter country: the entire nation was marked by poor roads ruined by tank traffic, railroads with bombed-out track and bridges, mountainous terrain with ridges up to six thousand feet. Conditions deteriorated in rainy weather, which washed out roads, and winter weather, which covered roads with snow and iced over bridges. Tactical positions in those mountains became impassable for ground vehicles. The helicopter was the only solution.

....

.... One lieutenant told Henderson, "Doctor, I was wounded when a mortar blew up. I was taken to the First Aid Station in 5 minutes, and within 55 minutes I was on a plane heading for a hospital. When they take care of you like that, a man doesn't mind fighting."

....

When the helicopters transported the wounded to the MASH and could fly no longer because of nightfall or weather restrictions, our pilots did not call it a day. They did not mix martinis when there was work to be done. They continued on wherever they were needed. The work of the pilots and the surgeons was inseparable. They helped us and we helped them. We always worked as different parts of the same unit. Eight-hour flying days were common, and in the evenings the pilots often went into the operating tents to assist in any way they could.

....

The pilots with the 8076th were indeed intrepid. They were the lifeline between the battlefield and the operating table. They were strong and brave and risked their lives many times to help the young men in the field. We saw in these pilots the same courage we saw in the young men they brought to us. I considered it an honor to serve with them. It was an honor that our peers in the fixed hospitals in the rear did not have.

.... They had the mission to come to the battlefield like mechanized angels and carry away the dying and the wounded. It was a thankless job, but they did it well.

Otto F. Apel (1923-2000), American surgeon, and Pat Apel (b. 1948), American lawyer, writing, in their 1998 book *MASH: An Army Surgeon in Korea*, on the pilots of helicopters for medical evacuation in the Korean War (1950-1953).
*Source:* Otto F. Apel, Jr., and Pat Apel, *MASH: An Army Surgeon in Korea* (Lexington, Kentucky: University Press of Kentucky, 1998), pp. 67-68, 70, 84, 90.
*Explanation:* MASH: Mobile Army Surgical Hospital.
*Note:* M*A*S*H* was the name of a popular American film and television series which began in the 1970s. *Same source*, p. x.
*Remark:* "Lady with a lamp," Crimea in the 1850s. "Mechanized angels," Korea in the 1950s.

### 274 PLAN
The Führer estimates that the operation will take four months, I reckon on fewer. Bolshevism will collapse like a house of cards. We face victories unequalled in human history.

Josef Goebbels (Paul Josef Goebbels) (1897-1945), German propaganda minister during Nazi rule (1933-1945), referring in his diary, on June 16, 1941, six days before Germany's invasion of the Soviet Union in World War II, to the invasion plan of Adolf Hitler (1889-1945), chancellor of the Third Reich of Nazi Germany (1933-1945).

*Source:* [Josef] Goebbels, *The Goebbels Diaries, 1939-1941,* ed. and trans. Fred Taylor (London: Hamish Hamilton, 1982), p. 414.

*Explanation: Führer:* in English "leader," a reference to Adolf Hitler.

*Compare with* Opponent.

*Remark:* The result of the German Nazi aggression plan: Not victory in four months but defeat in four years.

### 275 PLAN

An immense armada of upwards of 4,000 ships, together with several thousand smaller craft, crossed the Channel. Massed airborne landings have been successfully effected behind the enemy lines and landings on the beaches are proceeding at various points at the present time. The fire of the shore batteries has been largely quelled. The obstacles that were constructed in the sea have not proved so difficult as was apprehended. The Anglo-American Allies are sustained by about 11,000 first-line aircraft, which can be drawn upon as may be needed for the purposes of the battle. I cannot, of course, commit myself to any particular details. Reports are coming in in rapid succession. So far the Commanders who are engaged report that everything is proceeding according to plan. And what a plan! This vast operation is undoubtedly the most complicated and difficult that has ever occurred. It involves tides, wind, waves, visibility, both from the air and the sea standpoint, and the combined employment of land, air, and sea forces in the highest degree of intimacy and in contact with conditions which could not and cannot be fully foreseen.

Winston S. Churchill (Winston Leonard Spencer Churchill) (1874-1965), British statesman, orator and author, prime minister of the United Kingdom (1940-1945 and 1951-1955), in a speech given on June 6, 1944, to the House of Commons, on the day of the Allied invasion at Normandy, northwestern France.

*Source: Parliamentary Debates,* Commons, 5th series, vol. 400, pp. 1207, 1209.

*Explanation: The Channel:* the English Channel, between the southern coast of England and the northern coast of France.

*Remark:* A plan against aggression.

### 276 POVERTY

Today continuing poverty and distress are a deeper and more important cause of international tensions, of the conditions that can produce war, than previously.

Lester B. Pearson (Lester Bowles Pearson) (1897-1972), Canadian statesman and diplomat, recipient of the 1957 Nobel Peace Prize, later prime minister (1963-1968), in his Nobel lecture, "The Four Faces of Peace," given in Oslo on December 11, 1957.

*Source:* Frederick W. Haberman, ed., *Nobel Lectures Including Presentation Speeches and Laureates' Biographies: Peace,* vol. 3, *1951-1970* (Amsterdam: Elsevier Publishing Company, for the Nobel Foundation, 1972), pp. 117, 129, 132.

*Note:* In the presentation of the Norwegian Nobel Committee the following was stated:

Therefore, it may well be said that the Suez crisis was a victory for the United Nations and for the man who contributed more than anyone else to save the world at that time. That man was LESTER PEARSON.

(The Nobel Foundation, *Les Prix Nobel en 1957* (The Nobel Prizes in 1957) (Stockholm: Imprimerie Royale P. A. Norstedt & Söner, 1958), pp. 57, 66, 71-72)

*Explanation: Suez:* the reference is to the Suez crisis of 1956 relating to the Suez Canal, an about 100-mile (160-kilometer) long artificial waterway traversing Egypt connecting the Mediterranean Sea and the Red Sea.

*Remark:* Not only the arms race creates international tensions.

### 277 POWER
Two persons will hereafter be exalted
Above the heavens—the man with boundless power
Who yet forbears to use it indiscreetly,
And he who is not rich and yet can give.

From the great national epic of the Hindus, *Mahabharata* (The great poem of the Bharatas), compiled gradually for centuries in India and probably completed about 200 (book V, verse 1028).

*Source:* Monier Monier-Williams, *Indian Wisdom; or, Examples of the Religious, Philosophical, and Ethical Doctrines of the Hindus*, 4th ed., enlarged and improved (London: Luzac & Co., 1893), p. 445; translator of the verse: Monier Monier-Williams).

*Compare with* Power (Acton).

*Remark:* A guideline for rulers (a must for those who want to be extraordinary rulers).

### 278 POWER
Power tends to corrupt and absolute power corrupts absolutely.

Acton, known as Lord Acton (John Emerich Edward Dalberg-Acton) (1834-1902), English historian, in his letter of April 5, 1887, addressed to Mandell Creighton (1843-1901), British priest and historian, born in England, later bishop of London.

*Source:* John Emerich Edward Dalberg-Acton, *Essays on Freedom and Power*, comp. Gertrude Himmelfarb (Boston: Beacon Press, 1948), pp. 357, 358, 364.

*Remark:* Often quoted, often misquoted.

### 279 PREFERENCE
We are now Friends with England and with all Mankind. May we never see another War! for in my opinion *there never was a good War, or a bad Peace.*

Benjamin Franklin (1706-1790), American statesman, scientist and writer who helped draft the Declaration of Independence of July 4, 1776, writing a letter on September 11, 1783, to Josiah Quincy (1709-1784), American merchant, a few days after the negotiation, in which Franklin participated, of the Definite Treaty of Peace, between the United States and Britain.

*Source:* Benjamin Franklin, *The Writings of Benjamin Franklin*, comp. and ed. Albert Henry Smyth, vol. IX, *1783-1788* (1906; reprint, New York: Macmillan Company, 1907), pp. 93, 96.

*Note:* The text of the treaty, which was signed on September 3, 1783, and ratified by the Continental Congress on January 14, 1784, can be found in William M. Malloy, comp., *Treaties, Conventions, International Acts, Protocols and Agreements between the United States of America and Other Powers, 1776-1909,* vol. I (Washington: Government Printing Office, 1910), pp. 586-590.

*Remark:* "May we never see another War!"

### 280 PREVENTION

They have been met with the argument that war is the lesser of two evils. I will not admit the validity of that argument. We have heard time and time again for over three hundred years that «this war is different», that this time it really is for a purpose which was not successful in the last war. In thinking this over, we have mostly learned that war could have been prevented.

Henry J. Cadbury (Henry Joel Cadbury) (1883-1974), American biblical scholar, professor of divinity at Harvard University, founder of the American Friends Service Committee (the Quakers) in 1917 and chairman thereof, giving the Quakers' view on prevention of wars in a Nobel lecture, "Quakers and Peace," given in Oslo on December 12, 1947, on behalf of the committee that shared the 1947 Nobel Peace Prize with the Friends Service Council, London.

*Source:* Frederick W. Haberman, ed., *Nobel Lectures Including Presentation Speeches and Laureates' Biographies: Peace,* vol. 2, *1926-1950* (Amsterdam: Elsevier Publishing Company, for the Nobel Foundation, 1972), pp. 371, 391, 395-396.

*See* Arbitration (*The Christ of the Andes*).

*Remark:* Why wage wars instead of preventing them?

### 281 PREVENTION

Conflict prevention must be made the cornerstone of collective security in the twenty-first century.

Kofi Annan (Kofi Atta Annan) (b. 1938), Ghanaian economist and international civil servant, secretary-general of the United Nations (1997-2006), speaking to the Security Council of the United Nations on July 20, 2000.

*Source:* The Internet (2005) (www.un.org; United Nations, Security Council, press release SC/6892 (July 20, 2000) (period added at the end)).

*Note:* Annan shared the 2001 Nobel Peace Prize with the United Nations.

*Remark:* Twenty-first-century priority.

### 282 PRINCE

For unto us a child is born, unto us a son is given: and the government shall be upon his shoulder: and his name shall be called Wonderful, Counsellor, The mighty God, The everlasting Father, The Prince of Peace.

The Bible, Isaiah 9:6 (a reference to the coming king).

*Source: The Holy Bible Containing the Old and New Testaments*, The Authorized (King James) Version (Nashville, Tennessee: Gideons International, 1979).
*Explanation: Isaiah:* Jewish prophet (flourished from about 738 to at least 701 B.C.).

### 283 PRISONER

The main solution to the problem of persecuting persons with deviant views must be liberation on the basis of international agreements—a liberation of all political prisoners, of all prisoners of conscience in prisons, internment camps, and psychiatric clinics, if necessary on the basis of a resolution passed by the General Assembly of the United Nations. This proposal involves no intervention in the internal affairs of any country. After all, it would apply to every country on the same basis....

Andrei Sakharov (Andrei Dmitrievich Sakharov) (1921-1989), Soviet-Russian nuclear physicist and "the Father of the Soviet H-bomb," dissident and advocate of human rights, recipient of the 1975 Nobel Peace Prize, in his Nobel lecture, "Peace, Progress, Human Rights," read on his behalf in Oslo on December 11, 1975, by his wife Elena Bonner (Elena Georgievna Bonner, Elena Bonner Sakharov) (1923-2011), Soviet-Russian physician and human rights activist.
*Source:* Tore Frängsmyr, ed.-in-charge, Irwin Adams, ed., *Nobel Lectures Including Presentation and Acceptance Speeches and Laureates' Biographies: Peace, 1971-1980* (Singapore: World Scientific Publishing Co., for the Nobel Foundation, 1997), pp. 103, 122, 131 (translation).

### 284 PRISONER OF WAR

In September 1941 the deputy commander of Auschwitz, Karl Fritzsch, took approximately six hundred Soviet POWs (who had been brought to Auschwitz by the Einsatzkommandos as "intolerable" elements to undergo "special treatment" there) and experimented on them with ZYKLON B pesticide. The method was thus found that would kill millions of people with minimal effort.

From the *Encyclopedia of the Holocaust*, on illegal German Nazi experiments on Soviet prisoners of war in 1941.
*Source: Encyclopedia of the Holocaust* (1990), under "prisoners of war" (vol. 3, pp. 1188, 1192, 1195).
*Explanations:* ▸ *Einsatzkommandos:* Einsatzgruppen (Task Forces), mobile SS killing squads that in World War II "followed the German regular army into Poland and Russia for the purpose of killing Jews and other "undesirables" there." ▸ *Karl Fritzsch* (1903-1945): German Nazi deputy commandant (1940-1941) at the Auschwitz (Auschwitz-Birkenau) concentration camp, operated by the German Nazis in the province of Cracow in southern Poland from 1940 to 1945 (came from the Dachau camp, near Munich, Germany). ▸ *SS:* an abbreviation of the German word Schutzstaffel (Protective Echelon), a Nazi Party corps responsible for, among other things, the administration of concentration (extermination) camps in World War II, declared a criminal organization by the International Military Tribunal in Nuremberg, Germany, in 1946.
*Notes:* ▸ In the *same source*, p. 1192, the following is stated:

Second only to the Jews, Soviet prisoners of war (POWs) were the largest group of victims of Nazi extermination policy.... Some 5.7 million Red Army personnel fell into German hands between June 22, 1941, and the end of World War II.... The remaining 3.3 million (57.5 percent of the total) had perished.

Comparable figures for Anglo-American POWs are 8,348 dead by the end of the war, out of 235,000 (3.6 percent). Of the 3,155,000 German POWs taken prisoner by the Soviets, 1,185,000, or 37.5 percent, died in captivity, according to the finding of a Federal German commission of historians.

▶ According to another source, the said Task Forces "murdered almost one million Soviet and Polish Jews in the occupied territories." *Encyclopædia Britannica Online* (2001), under "Heydrich, Reinhard."

▶ The following has been written on the widow of Karl Fritzsch:

Fanny Fritsch was 67 years old when I visited her in her apartment in Regensburg; she was a small woman who lived in her memories. It was not hard for her to explain to herself the atrocities attributed to her husband: she decided that they had never occurred. Her husband, she said, was "the best man in the world" and never harmed a soul.

(Tom Segev, *Soldiers of Evil: The Commandants of the Nazi Concentration Camps*, trans. Haim Watzman (New York: McGraw-Hill Book Company, 1987), p. 141)

*See* Restriction (the Geneva Protocol of 1925 to which Germany became a party).

## 285 PRISONER OF WAR

Prisoners of war must at all times be humanely treated. Any unlawful act or omission by the Detaining Power causing death or seriously endangering the health of a prisoner of war in its custody is prohibited, and will be regarded as a serious breach of the present Convention. In particular, no prisoner of war may be subjected to physical mutilation or to medical or scientific experiments of any kind which are not justified by the medical, dental or hospital treatment of the prisoner concerned and carried out in his interest.

Likewise, prisoners of war must at all times be protected, particularly against acts of violence or intimidation and against insults and public curiosity.

Measures of reprisal against prisoners of war are prohibited.

....

No physical or mental torture, nor any other form of coercion, may be inflicted on prisoners of war to secure from them information of any kind whatever. Prisoners of war who refuse to answer may not be threatened, insulted, or exposed to unpleasant or disadvantageous treatment of any kind.

Article 13 and Article 17, paragraph 4, of the Geneva Convention Relative to the Treatment of Prisoners of War of August 12, 1949, which was signed at Geneva on August 12, 1949, and entered into force on October 21, 1950, replacing the Geneva Convention Relative to the Treatment of Prisoners of War of July 27, 1929, in relations between the high contracting parties.

*Source:* United Nations, *Treaty Series*, vol. 75, pp. 135, 146, 150.

*See* Prisoner of war (*Encyclopedia of the Holocaust*, on illegal German experiments on Soviet prisoners of war in 1941).

*Remark:* Humane treatment, period.

## 286 PROFIT

There was a city in expectation of being besieged, and a council was called accordingly to discuss the best means of fortifying it. A Bricklayer gave his opinion that no material was so good as brick for the purpose. A Carpenter begged leave to suggest that timber would be far preferable. Upon which a Currier started up, and said, "Sirs, when you have said all that can be said, there is nothing in the world like leather."

Aesop (ca. 620-ca. 564 B.C.), author of Greek fables (a slave who was later freed, presumably a native of the country Phrygia in Asia Minor), in his fable "The Three Tradesmen" (produced here in full).
*Source: Æsop, Æsop's Fables: An Anthology of the Fabulists of All Countries* (London: J. M. Dent & Sons, 1919), p. 80, 80.
*Remark:* History repeats itself?

## 287 PROTECTION

When the Russians entered the General Ghetto two days later they found 69,000 Jews alive there. In the International Ghetto they were to find 25,000 survivors, and later on, when they captured the Buda side of the twin city, another 25,000 or so Jews emerged from their hiding places in Gentile homes, in monasteries, convents, and church cellars. In all some 120,000 had survived the Final Solution—the only substantial Jewish community left in Europe.

In the view of Per Anger, Wallenberg's closest colleague, Wallenberg must take the credit for the deliverance of the Jews in the General Ghetto as well as those in the International Ghetto. "He was the only foreign diplomat to stay behind in Pest, with the sole purpose of protecting these people. And he succeeded beyond all expectations. If you add them all up, 100,000 or more people owed their lives to him."

John Bierman (1929-2006), English journalist, writing, in his 1981 book *Righteous Gentile*, on the Swedish diplomat Raoul Wallenberg (Raoul Gustav Wallenberg) (1912-1947?) who served in Budapest during World War II, from July 1944 to January 1945 when he was arrested by the Soviet army fighting for Budapest and never reappeared.
*Source:* John Bierman, *Righteous Gentile: The Story of Raoul Wallenberg, Missing Hero of the Holocaust* (New York: Viking Press, 1981), p. 116.
*Explanations:* ▶ *Per Anger:* Per Johan Valentin Anger (1913-2002), Swedish diplomat who served in Budapest from 1942 to 1945. ▶ *Buda and Pest:* towns forming Budapest. ▶ *Russians:* Soviet military forces, which liberated the general ghetto in Budapest on January 16, 1945, the international ghetto on January 18 and the city as a whole on February 13.
*Notes:* ▶ Browsing on the Internet (2005), http//www.raoul-wallenberg.org.ar/english/visaslife2.htm and, furthermore, http//www.raoul-wallenberg.net/english/carlutz.htm, one could find a description of the remarkable feats of the consular and diplomatic corps in Budapest and other places, Red Cross people and the future Pope John XXIII, including the story of Carl Lutz (1895-1975), the Swiss vice-consul in Budapest (1942-1945). "Carl Lutz helped 62,000 Jews to survive." ▶ Budapest is on the World Heritage List.

*Additional explanation: Pope John XXIII:* Angelo Giuseppi Roncalli (1881-1963), Italian pope (1958-1963).
*See* Achievement (Tommy Lapid).
*See also* Lifesaving.

### 288 PROVOCATION
Wound not another, though by him provoked,
Do no one injury by thought or deed,
Utter no word to pain thy fellow-creatures.

From an Indian collection of laws and precepts, the Code of Manu (the Hindu Noah), dating in its present form back to about the fifth century B.C. (dates vary greatly) (book II, verse 161).
*Source:* Monier Monier-Williams, *Indian Wisdom; or, Examples of the Religious, Philosophical, and Ethical Doctrines of the Hindus,* 4th ed., enlarged and improved (London: Luzac & Co., 1893), pp. 213, 279 (period added at the end; translator of the verse: Monier Monier-Williams).
*Remark:* Old and new wisdom from India.

### 289 PURCHASE
The First Consul of the French Republic desiring to give to the United States a strong proof of his friendship doth hereby cede to the said United States in the name of the French Republic forever and in full sovereignty the said territory....

From Article I of the Treaty for the Cession of Louisiana to the United States concluded on April 30, 1803, between the French Republic and the United States of America, ratifications being exchanged on October 21, 1803.
*Source:* William M. Malloy, comp., *Treaties, Conventions, International Acts, Protocols and Agreements between the United States of America and Other Powers, 1776-1909,* vol. I (Washington: Government Printing Office, 1910), pp. 508, 509.
*Note:* In a convention concluded the same day the purchase price was fixed at sixty million francs. *Same source,* pp. 511, 512.

### 290 PURGE
Whatever his reasons, Stalin set about with a vengeance—literally—to remake the Army to his own satisfaction. On June 11, 1937, Marshal Mikhail N. Tukhachevsky, one of the master builders of the Red Army, and seven other leading officers were arrested and charged with treason. They were tried and convicted that same day and executed the next. Thus began the Great Purge of the Red Army. It was to last a year and a half, during which Stalin eliminated 35,000 of the Red Army's most talented commanders—in all, half its senior officer corps. The victims included three out of five marshals, 13 of 15 commanders of armies and 220 of 406 brigade commanders. At the very top Stalin liquidated or imprisoned 75 members of the 80-man Supreme Military Council and all 11 Vice Commissars of Defense. Considered by ranks, the toll appears even more incredible: the Purge cost the country 54 per cent of the Red Army's generals and 80 per cent of its colonels. Few wars could have caused such high-level casualty figures.

Nicholas Bethell (Nicholas William Bethell) (1938-2007), British writer and politician, born in England, member of the House of Lords (1967-1999), describing, in his 1977 book *Russia Besieged*, the purge of commanders of the Red Army of the Soviet Union in the 1930s by Joseph Stalin (Joseph Vissarionovich Dzhugashvili) (1879-1953), Soviet political leader, born in Georgia, general secretary of the Central Committee of the Communist Party (1922-1953), later premier of the Soviet Union (1941-1953).

*Source:* Nicholas Bethell, *Russia Besieged*, ed. the editors of Time-Life Books, World War II (Alexandria, Virginia: Time-Life Books, 1977), p. 63.

*Explanation: Mikhail N. Tukhachevsky:* Mikhail Nicolaevich Tukhachevsky (1893-1937), Russian marshal, "cleared judicially and rehabilitated" in 1988.

*Remark:* One ruler in history.

### 291 QUARANTINE

To halt this offensive buildup, a strict quarantine on all offensive military equipment under shipment to Cuba is being initiated. All ships of any kind bound for Cuba from whatever nation or port will, if found to contain cargoes of offensive weapons, be turned back. This quarantine will be extended, if needed, to other types of cargo and carriers. We are not at this time, however, denying the necessities of life as the Soviets attempted to do in their Berlin blockade of 1948.

John F. Kennedy (John Fitzgerald Kennedy) (1917-1963), president of the United States (1961-1963), in his "Radio and Television Report to the American People on the Soviet Arms Buildup in Cuba," delivered from the president's office on October 22, 1962.

*Source:* John F. Kennedy, *Public Papers of the Presidents of the United States: John F. Kennedy ... 1962* (Washington: United States Government Printing Office, 1963), pp. 806, 807-808.

### 292 QUEEN

Though German by birth, she became probably the most beloved citizen of her adopted country after her marriage to Prince Albert—they were married at the turn of the century. She was especially concerned about the problems of the working people. She dedicated herself to every sort of social cause; and she founded a medical clinic, at which she herself taught nursing. When the First World War came and the Germans invaded Belgium, she refused to leave. She stayed in Brussels until the Germans were at the gates of the city. Then she retreated with the Belgian army, serving as a nurse. "As long as a single foot of free Belgian soil remains," she said, "I will be on it." When only a few miles of unconquered territory were left, she stayed there, living with King Albert in a little house in a coastal town that was under heavy bombardment—her life was in constant danger. She set up a hospital in an old hotel, where she helped care for the sick and wounded, and she organized a school for the children of refugees. When the Germans at last began to withdraw, she followed on the heels of their retreating army.

In the years after the war, Queen Elisabeth championed all kinds of liberal causes. Sometimes her conduct shocked the aristocrats, but she did not care. Her greatest concern was world peace, and after the Second World War, she helped sponsor the Stockholm Peace Appeal, calling for the banning of all atomic weapons.

Pablo Casals (Pau Carlos Salvador Defilló de Casals) (1876-1973), Spanish cellist and conductor, opponent of fascism and crusader for peace, reflecting mainly on the struggle of Elisabeth (1876-1965), daughter of the duke of Bavaria, Germany, queen of the Belgians (1909-1934), in World War I.

*Source:* Pablo Casals, *Joys and Sorrows: Reflections by Pablo Casals, as Told to Albert E. Kahn* (London: Macdonald and Co. (Publishers), 1970), pp. 130-131.

*Explanations:* ▸ *Albert:* Albert I (1875-1934), king of the Belgians (1909-1934). ▸ *Stockholm Peace Appeal:* the reference is to the Stockholm Appeal of 1950 adopted by the World Congress of the Defenders of Peace.

*Note:* What she did in the World War II is partly described in the following words: "She was a formidable woman and on many occasions intervened on behalf of Jews and other Belgians arrested by the Germans."

(*Obituaries from the Times* (1961-1970), pp. 65, 66)

*Remark:* What a German! What a Belgian! What a woman! What a queen!

## 293 RACE

The little-minded ask: Belongs this man
To our own family? The noble-hearted
Regard the human race as all akin.

From a collection of Indian fables, *Panchatantra* [Five Books], probably composed about 200 B.C. (book V, verse 38).

*Source:* Monier Monier-Williams, *Indian Wisdom; or, Examples of the Religious, Philosophical, and Ethical Doctrines of the Hindus,* 4th ed., enlarged and improved (London: Luzac & Co., 1893), p. 536 (period added at the end; translator of the verse: Monier Monier-Williams).

*Remark:* Family of man.

## 294 RADIO

I know that most governments thoroughly dislike the international radio broadcasts conducted by those to whom they are opposed. However, these external radio services have become a regular feature; they are a fact of life. Why not accept them and why not try to use them in order to promote the ideals of the United Nations, of Unesco and of world peace?

....

There is nothing that can be done to stop or to alter the course of these broadcasts. But is it not surprising that there is not one single station broadcasting in the name of the United Nations and Unesco, advocating an end to the arms race and urging the achievement of general and complete disarmament?

Séan MacBride (1904-1988), Irish attorney and statesman, recipient of the 1974 Nobel Peace Prize, president of the International Peace Bureau, Geneva, in a 1981 paper, based on a statement made at a Peace Forum organized by the United Nations Educational, Scientific and Cultural Organization (UNESCO) in November 1979.

*Source:* Séan MacBride, "The Role of the Mass Media in the Search for Peace," *Armaments, Arms Control and Disarmament: A Unesco Reader for Disarmament Education,* ed. Marek Thee (Paris: Unesco Press, 1981), pp. 315, 318-319.

*Remark:* "This is United Nations Radio!"—or more bombs, bangs and blunders?

### 295 RAPE

Women shall be especially protected against any attack on their honour, in particular against rape, enforced prostitution, or any form of indecent assault.

Article 27, paragraph 2, of the Geneva Convention Relative to the Protection of Civilian Persons in Time of War of August 12, 1949, which was signed at Geneva on August 12, 1949, and entered into force on October 21, 1950.

*Source:* United Nations, *Treaty Series,* vol. 75, pp. 287, 306.

*Note:* Article 76, paragraph 1, of the Protocol Additional to the Geneva Conventions of 12 August 1949, and Relating to the Protection of Victims of International Armed Conflicts (Protocol I), which was adopted at Geneva on June 8, 1977, and entered into force on December 7, 1978, reads as follows:

Women shall be the object of special respect and shall be protected in particular against rape, forced prostitution and any other form of indecent assault.

*Source:* United Nations, *Treaty Series,* vol. 1125, pp. 3, 38.

*Remark:* The ordeal of civilians in time of war.

### 296 RAPE

Actions to be taken

....

145. By Governments and international and regional organizations:

....

(d) Reaffirm that rape in the conduct of armed conflict constitutes a war crime and under certain circumstances it constitutes a crime against humanity and an act of genocide as defined in the Convention on the Prevention and Punishment of the Crime of Genocide; take all measures required for the protection of women and children from such acts and strengthen mechanisms to investigate and punish all those responsible and bring the perpetrators to justice.

From, in particular, paragraph 145 of the Platform for Action adopted on September 15, 1995, by the Fourth World Conference on Women held at Peking [Beijing] from September 4 to 15, 1995.

*Source:* United Nations, *The Beijing Declaration and the Platform for Action: Fourth World Conference on Women, Beijing, China, 4-15 September 1995* (New York: United Nations, Department of Public Information, 1996), pp. 13, 88-89 (beginning, in bold letters in source, indented; reference to footnote omitted; semicolon replaced by period at the end).

*Explanation: Genocide:* certain "acts committed with intent to destroy, in whole or in part, a national, ethnical, racial or religious group, as such." The definition in full is in Article II of the Convention on the Prevention and Punishment of the Crime of Genocide, which was annexed to resolution 260 (III) (Prevention and Punishment of the Crime of Genocide), adopted on December 9, 1948, by the General Assembly of the United Nations, and entered into force on January 12, 1951. For the text of the resolution and convention, *see* United Nations, *Resolutions, 21 September-12 December 1948* (General Assembly, Official Records: Third Session, Part I (A/810)), p. 174, 174. For the text of the convention, *see also* United Nations, *Treaty Series*, vol. 78, p. 277. *See also* Genocide (the full text of the definition).

*See* Genocide (Roy Gutman, quoting Simon Wiesenthal: "You don't have to kill everyone to have genocide.").

*Remark:* Rape is not only a crime. It can be a war crime, a crime against humanity and genocide.

### 297 RECONSTRUCTION
With malice toward none, with charity for all, with firmness in the right as God gives us to see the right, let us strive on to finish the work we are in, to bind up the nation's wounds, to care for him who shall have borne the battle and for his widow and his orphan, to do all which may achieve and cherish a just and lasting peace among ourselves and with all nations.

Abraham Lincoln (1809-1865), president of the United States (1861-1865), in his second inaugural address on March 4, 1865.

*Source:* James D. Richardson, comp., *A Compilation of the Messages and Papers of the Presidents, 1789-1897*, vol. VI (Washington: Government Printing Office, 1897), pp. 276, 277.

*Remark:* A lot to do after a war.

### 298 RECRUITMENT
Daddy, what did you do in the Great War?

English recruiting poster in World War I (daughter to father).

*Source: The Oxford Dictionary of Quotations*, 5th ed. (New York: Oxford University Press, 1999), p. 647.

*Note:* Under the picture the word "you" was in capital letters and underlined. The Internet (2003), under "Daddy, what did you do in the Great War?"

*Remark:* Daddy, what did you do to prevent the war?

### 299 REFUGEE
Bring water to the thirsty,
meet the fugitive with bread,
    O inhabitants of the land of
       Tema.
For they have fled from the
       swords,
from the drawn sword,
from the bent bow,
and from the stress of battle.

The Bible, Isaiah 21:14-15 (the oracle concerning the desert plain).

*Source: The Holy Bible Containing the Old and New Testaments*, New Revised Standard Version (New York: Oxford University Press, 1989) (verse numbering omitted).

*Explanation: Isaiah:* Jewish prophet (flourished from about 738 to at least 701 B.C.).
*Remark:* Neighbors on earth.

## 300 REGIONAL ORGANIZATION

We, the Heads of African States and Governments assembled in the City of Addis Ababa, Ethiopia;

....

INSPIRED by a common determination to promote understanding among our peoples and co-operation among our States in response to the aspirations of our peoples for brotherhood and solidarity, in a larger unity transcending ethnic and national differences;

CONVINCED that, in order to translate this determination into a dynamic force in the cause of human progress, conditions for peace and security must be established and maintained;

....

PERSUADED that the Charter of the United Nations and the Universal Declaration of Human Rights, to the principles of which we reaffirm our adherence, provide a solid foundation for peaceful and positive co-operation among states;

....

HAVE agreed to the present Charter.

ESTABLISHMENT
*Article I*

1. The High Contracting Parties do by the present Charter establish an Organization to be known as the *Organization of African Unity.*

....

PURPOSES
*Article II*

1. The Organization shall have the following purposes:
a. to promote the unity and solidarity of the African States;
b. to coordinate and intensify their co-operation and efforts to achieve a better life for the peoples of Africa;
c. to defend their sovereignty, their territorial integrity and independence;
d. to eradicate all forms of colonialism from Africa; and
e. to promote international co-operation, having due regard to the Charter of the United Nations and the Universal Declaration of Human Rights.

....

COMMISSION OF MEDIATION, CONCILIATION AND ARBITRATION
*Article XIX*

Member States pledge to settle all disputes among themselves by peaceful means and, to this end decide to establish a Commission of Mediation, Conciliation and Arbitration, the composition of which and conditions of service shall be defined by a separate Protocol to be approved by the Assembly of Heads of State and Government. Said Protocol shall be regarded as forming an integral part of the present Charter.

From the preamble to, and Article I, paragraph 1, Article II, paragraph 1, and Article XIX of, the Charter of the Organization of African Unity (OAU), which was signed at Addis Ababa on May 25, 1963, and entered into force on September 13, 1963.

*Source:* United Nations, *Treaty Series*, vol. 479, pp. 39, 70, 72, 80.

*Explanations:* ▸ *Charter of the United Nations:* Charter of the United Nations, which was signed at San Francisco, United States, on June 26, 1945, and entered into force on October 24, 1945. ▸ *Universal Declaration of Human Rights:* Universal Declaration of Human Rights adopted and proclaimed by United Nations General Assembly resolution 217 (III) of December 10, 1948 (International Bill of Human Rights; part A, Universal Declaration of Human Rights).

*Notes:* ▸ The Organization of African Unity was succeeded in 2001 by the African Union (AU) after amalgamation of OAU with the African Economic Community (AEC) established in 1991.

▸ In the constitutive act of the union one may read:

We, Heads of State and Government of the Member States of the Organization of African Unity (OAU):

....

INSPIRED by the noble ideals, which guided the founding fathers of our Continental Organization and generations of Pan-Africanists in their determination to promote unity, solidarity, cohesion and cooperation among the peoples of Africa and African States;

CONSIDERING the principles and objectives stated in the Charter of the Organization of African Unity and the Treaty establishing the African Economic Community;

RECALLING the heroic struggles waged by our peoples and our countries for political independence, human dignity and economic emancipation;

....

GUIDED by our common vision of a united and strong Africa and by the need to build a partnership between governments and all segments of civil society, in particular women, youth and the private sector, in order to strengthen solidarity and cohesion among our peoples;

CONSCIOUS of the fact that the scourge of conflicts in Africa constitutes a major impediment to the socio-economic development of the continent and of the need to promote peace, security and stability as a prerequisite for the implementation of our development and integration agenda;

DETERMINED to promote and protect human and peoples' rights, consolidate democratic institutions and culture, and to ensure good governance and the rule of law;

....

HAVE AGREED AS FOLLOWS:

....

Article 2
Establishment

The African Union is hereby established in accordance with the provisions of this Act.

Article 3
Objectives

The objectives of the Union shall be to:

(a) achieve greater unity and solidarity between the African countries and the peoples of Africa;

(b) defend the sovereignty, territorial integrity and independence of its Member States;

(c) accelerate the political and socio-economic integration of the continent;

(d) promote and defend African common positions on issues of interest to the continent and its peoples;

(e) encourage international cooperation, taking due account of the Charter of the United Nations and the Universal Declaration of Human Rights;

(f) promote peace, security, and stability on the continent;

(g) promote democratic principles and institutions, popular participation and good governance;

(h) promote and protect human and peoples' rights in accordance with the African Charter on Human and Peoples' Rights and other relevant human rights instruments;

....

## Article 4
### Principles

The Union shall function in accordance with the following principles:

(a) sovereign equality and interdependence among Member States of the Union;

(b) respect of borders existing on achievement of independence;

....

(g) non-interference by any Member State in the internal affairs of another;

(h) the right of the Union to intervene in a Member State pursuant to a decision of the Assembly in respect of grave circumstances, namely: war crimes, genocide and crimes against humanity;

(i) peaceful co-existence of Member States and their right to live in peace and security;

....

(o) respect for the sanctity of human life, condemnation and rejection of impunity and political assassination, acts of terrorism and subversive activities:

(p) condemnation and rejection of unconstitutional changes of governments.

....

## Article 9
### Powers and Functions of the Assembly

1. The functions of the Assembly shall be to:

....

(g) give directives to the Executive Council on the management of conflicts, war and other emergency situations and the restoration of peace;

....

## Article 24
### The Headquarters of the Union

1. The Headquarters of the Union shall be in Addis Ababa in the Federal Democratic Republic of Ethiopia.

....

## Article 30
### Suspension

Governments which shall come to power through unconstitutional means shall not be allowed to participate in the activities of the Union.

(Organization of African Unity, *Constitutive Act of the African Union* ([Addis Ababa], Organization of African Unity, 2001, pp. 2-7, 9, 14, 16 (the uppercase words in the preamble and the articles and headlines thereunder in bold letters in source; indentation harmonized).

*Remark:* Peaceful settlement of disputes.

### 301 RELATIONS

A war of aggression constitutes a crime against the peace, for which there is responsibility under international law.

In accordance with the purposes and principles of the United Nations, States have the duty to refrain from propaganda for wars of aggression.

....

States have a duty to refrain from acts of reprisal involving the use of force.

Every State has the duty to refrain from any forcible action which deprives peoples referred to in the elaboration of the principle of equal rights and self-determination of their right to self-determination and freedom and independence.

Every State has the duty to refrain from organizing or encouraging the organization of irregular forces or armed bands, including mercenaries, for incursion into the territory of another State.

Every State has the duty to refrain from organizing, instigating, assisting or participating in acts of civil strife or terrorist acts in another State or acquiescing in organized activities within its territory directed towards the commission of such acts, when the acts referred to in the present paragraph involve a threat or use of force.

.... No territorial acquisition resulting from the threat or use of force shall be recognized as legal....

....

States shall ... seek early and just settlement of their international disputes by negotiation, inquiry, mediation, conciliation, arbitration, judicial settlement, resort to regional agencies or arrangements or other peaceful means of their choice. In seeking such a settlement the parties shall agree upon such peaceful means as may be appropriate to the circumstances and nature of the dispute.

The parties to a dispute have the duty, in the event of failure to reach a solution by any one of the above peaceful means, to continue to seek a settlement of the dispute by other peaceful means agreed upon by them.

....

States have the duty to co-operate with one another, irrespective of the differences in their political, economic and social systems, in the various spheres of international relations, in order to maintain international peace and security and to promote international economic stability and progress, the general welfare of nations and international co-operation free from discrimination based on such differences.

....

All States enjoy sovereign equality....

In particular, sovereign equality includes the following elements:

....

(f) Each State has the duty to comply fully and in good faith with its international obligations and to live in peace with other States.

From the Declaration on Principles of International Law concerning Friendly Relations and Co-operation among States in accordance with the Charter of the United Nations contained in an annex to resolution 2625 (XXV) adopted by the General Assembly of the United Nations on October 24, 1970 (Declaration on Principles of International Law concerning Friendly Relations and Co-operation among States in accordance with the Charter of the United Nations).

*Source:* United Nations, *Resolutions Adopted by the General Assembly during Its Twenty-fifth Session* (General Assembly, Official Records: Twenty-fifth Session, Supplement No. 28 (A/8028)), pp. 121, 122-124.

*Remark:* "No territorial acquisition resulting from the threat or use of force shall be recognized as legal." So why try?

### 302 RELIGION
And God calleth to the abode of peace; and He guideth whom He will into the right way.

Goodness itself and an increase of it for those who do good! neither blackness nor shame shall cover their faces! These shall be the inmates of Paradise, therein shall they abide for ever.

And as for those who have wrought out evil, their recompense shall be evil of like degree, and shame shall cover them—no protector shall they have against God: as though their faces were darkened with deep murk of night! These shall be inmates of the fire: therein they shall abide for ever.

The Qur'an (Koran), chapter (sura) X, "Jonah, Peace Be on Him!", verses 26-28.

*Source: The Koran,* trans. J. M. Rodwell, Everyman's Library (1909; reprint, London: J. M. Dent & Sons, 1918), pp. 275, 277-278 (reference to footnotes omitted).

*Explanations:* ▸ *Abode of peace:* Paradise. ▸ *God:* Allah (Arabic). ▸ *The Qur'an* (Arabic, "recitation, reading"): the sacred book of Islam, the Muslim religion (Arabic, "submission to the will of God"), founded by the Arab prophet Mohammed (Muhammad, meaning "praised" or "praiseworthy") (ca. 570-632).

*Remark:* Paradise for those who do good.

### 303 RELIGION
Requite evil with good, and he who is your enemy will become your dearest friend.

The Qur'an (Koran), chapter (sura) XLI [41], "Revelations Well Expounded," verse 19.

*Source: The Koran,* trans. N. J. Dawood, Penguin Classics, revised ed. (1959; reprint, Harmondsworth, England: Penguin Books, 1961), pp. 155, 157.

*Explanation: The Qur'an* (Arabic, "recitation, reading"): the sacred book of Islam, the Muslim religion (Arabic, "submission to the will of God"), founded by the Arab prophet Mohammed (Muhammad, meaning "praised" or "praiseworthy") (ca. 570-632).

*Compare with* the Qur'an, chapter (sura) XLII [42], "Counsel," verse 34: Those who avenge themselves when wronged incur no guilt. *Same source,* pp. 150, 153.

*Remark:* Turning enemies into friends.

### 304 RELIGION
In his fortieth year, Mohámmed came forth with his doctrine, "There is but one god, and Mohámmed is his prophet."... In Medína he composed a part of the

sentences of which the holy book of the Koran consists. Mecca soon acknowledged him as a prophet, and his doctrine, called Islam, was soon predominant all over Arabia. He combined in it the fundamental doctrines of Judáism and Christianity, with maxims that were adapted to the East.... A chief commandment of the Koran was, to diffuse Islam by every means, and to compel the nations to receive it by fire and sword. Those who fell bravely in battle were promised a paradise of sensual enjoyments.

Georg Weber (1808-1888), German historian and educator, writing, in his book *Outlines of Universal History*, first published in German in 1851 (*Weltgeschichte in übersichtlicher Darstellung*), on Mohammed and the Qur'an (Koran).
*Source:* George Weber, *Outlines of Universal History, from the Creation of the World to the Present Time*, trans. M. Behr, rev. Francis Bowen, 6th ed. (Boston: Hickling, Swan and Brown, 1856), p. 126.
*Explanations:* ▸ *The Koran:* The Qur'an (Arabic, "recitation, reading"), the sacred book of Islam, the Muslim religion founded by Mohammed. ▸ *Mecca:* a city in Arabia (now Saudi Arabia), the holiest city of Islam, the Muslim religion. ▸ *Medína:* Medina, a city in Arabia (now Saudi Arabia), "the city of the apostle of God." ▸ *Mohammed:* Mohammed (Muhammad, meaning "praised" or "praiseworthy") (ca. 570-632), Arab prophet, founder of Islam, the Muslim religion (Arabic, "submission to the will of God").

### 305 RELIGION

The year 1618 saw the outbreak of the Thirty Years' War, waged by the German States, Austria, Sweden, and France under the pretext of religion. Massacre, pillage, the burning of villages and of whole lands, famine and demoralization—such is the sinister record of over a quarter of a century's folly. After the population of Germany had been decimated, a peace was signed in Westphalia which did no more than reaffirm the original state of affairs except for granting some concessions to princes who did not even know how to preserve them. It was certainly not worth the trouble of tearing one another apart for thirty years just to arrive at the conclusion that nobody knew for what or for whom he had been fighting.

Élie Ducommun (1833-1906), Swiss writer and editor, commenting on the Thirty Years' War (1618-1648) in his Nobel lecture, "The Futility of War Demonstrated by History," given in Christiania (Oslo) on May 16, 1904, on the occasion of receiving the 1902 Nobel Peace Prize jointly with the Swiss philanthropist and worker for international peace Charles Albert Gobat (1843-1914), secretary-general of the Interparliamentary Union.
*Source:* Frederick W. Haberman, ed., *Nobel Lectures Including Presentation Speeches and Laureates' Biographies: Peace*, vol. 1, *1901-1925* (Amsterdam: Elsevier Publishing Company, for the Nobel Foundation, 1972), pp. 13, 17, 22 (translation from French).
*Explanation: Westphalia:* a region in northwestern Germany (German, Westfalen) where the Thirty Years' War was brought to an end in 1648, with two peace treaties (the Peace of Westphalia).
*See* Loss (Christie Davies, on the effects of the Thirty Years' War).
*Remark:* Unholy warfare.

### 306 RELIGION
The founders of all religions have affirmed that they appeared for the benefit of all beings, and all have spoken out against excessive consumption.

Buddhadasa Bhikkhu (Nguam Phanich) (1906-1993), Thai Buddhist interpreter, preacher and campaigner for world peace, in a 1988 article.

*Source:* Buddhadasa Bhikkhu, "Dhammic Socialism," in *Treasury of Thai Literature: The Modern Period,* ed. Prasert na Nagara and others (Bangkok: National Identity Board, Office of the Prime Minister, 1988), pp. 212, 216.

*Explanation:* ▸ *Bhikkhu:* "in Buddhism, one who has renounced worldly life and joined the mendicant and contemplative community." *Encyclopædia Britannica Online* (2005), under "bhikku." ▸ *Buddha* (the Enlightened One): Gautama Buddha (Siddhartha Gautama) (ca. 563-ca. 483 B.C.), Indian prince, born in the district Nepal, founder of Buddhism. ▸ *Buddhadasa:* Servant of the Buddha.

*Remark:* Listen to them.

### 307 RELOCATION
Between July and November 1941 as many as 1,523 factories, including 1,360 large, chiefly war-industrial plants, were shifted to and restarted in the Urals, Siberia, the Volga area and Kazakhstan. In a little over five months nearly 1,500,000 carloads of freight was transported by rail.

From the book *Great Patriotic War of the Soviet Union, 1941-1945,* on the relocation of factories in the Soviet Union after the German invasion of June 22, 1941.

*Source:* M. M. Minasyan, editor in chief, *Great Patriotic War of the Soviet Union, 1941-1945: A General Outline,* trans. David Skvirsky and Vic Schneierson (Moscow: Progress Publishers, 1974), p. 77 (abridged translation from the Russian edition of 1970; a 1965 Russian edition exists).

*Note:* "During the second half of 1941 ... over 10,000,000 people were evacuated to the eastern regions from the threatened areas." *Same source,* p. 440.

*Remark:* Moving cities.

### 308 REPARATION
1. Germany must pay in kind for the losses caused by her to the Allied nations in the course of the war. Reparations are to be received in the first instance by those countries which have borne the main burden of the war, have suffered the heaviest losses and have organised victory over the enemy.

2. Reparation in kind is to be exacted from Germany in three following forms:

*a)* Removals within 2 years from the surrender of Germany or the cessation of organised resistance from the national wealth of Germany located on the territory of Germany herself as well as outside her territory (equipment, machine-tools, ships, rolling stock, German investments abroad, shares of industrial, transport and other enterprises in Germany etc.), these removals to be carried out chiefly for purpose of destroying the war potential of Germany.

*b)* Annual deliveries of goods from current production for a period to be fixed.

*c)* Use of German labour.

From the Protocol of the Proceedings of the Crimea Conference, points 1 and 2 of a protocol concerning German reparation in kind, approved at the Crimea (Yalta) Conference of February 4 to 11, 1945, by the "Big Three," Winston S. Churchill (Winston Leonard Spencer Churchill) (1874-1965), prime minister of the United Kingdom (1940-1945, 1951-1955), Franklin D. Roosevelt (Franklin Delano Roosevelt) (1882-1945), president of the United States (1933-1945), and Joseph Stalin (Joseph Vissarionovich Dzhugashvili) (1879-1953), premier of the Soviet Union (1941-1953) and general secretary of the Central Committee of the Communist Party (1922-1953).

*Source:* United States, Department of State, *Treaties and Other International Agreements of the United States of America, 1776-1949,* comp. Charles I. Bevans, vol. 3, *Multilateral, 1931-1945,* publication 8484 (November 1969), pp. 1013, 1016.

*Remark:* Take two.

### 309 REPATRIATION
Subject to the provisions of the third paragraph of this Article, Parties to the conflict are bound to send back to their own country, regardless of number or rank, seriously wounded and seriously sick prisoners of war, after having cared for them until they are fit to travel,...

....

No sick or injured prisoner of war who is eligible for repatriation under the first paragraph of this Article, may be repatriated against his will during hostilities.

From Article 109, paragraphs 1 and 3, of the Geneva Convention Relative to the Treatment of Prisoners of War of August 12, 1949, which was signed at Geneva on August 12, 1949, and entered into force on October 21, 1950, replacing the Geneva Convention Relative to the Treatment of Prisoners of War of July 27, 1929, in relations between the high contracting parties.

*Source:* United Nations, *Treaty Series,* vol. 75, pp. 135, 218.

### 310 RESISTANCE
We desire peace—and that is why we have never resorted to physical force. We crave for justice—and that is why we are so persistent in the struggle for our rights. We seek freedom of convictions—and that is why we have never attempted to enslave man's conscience nor shall we ever attempt to do so.

....

When I recall my own path of life I cannot but speak of the violence, hatred and lies. A lesson drawn from such experiences, however, was that we can effectively oppose violence only if we ourselves do not resort to it.

....

.... My most ardent desire is that my country will recapture its historic opportunity for a peaceful evolution and that Poland will prove to the world that even the most complex situations can be solved by a dialogue and not by force.

....

May I repeat that the fundamental necessity in Poland is now understanding and dialogue. I think that the same applies to the whole world: we should go on talking, we must not close any doors or do anything that would block the road to an understanding. And we must remember that only peace built on the foundations of justice and moral order can be a lasting one.

Lech Walesa (b. 1943), Polish trade union leader, recipient of the 1983 Nobel Peace Prize, later president of Poland (1990-1995), in his December 10, 1983 acceptance speech (the first paragraph of the quotation), read in Oslo by his wife Danuta Walesa (Miroslawa "Danuta" Golos Walesa), and in his December 11, 1983 Nobel lecture, "Solidarity in the Spirit of Peace and Justice," read by Bogdan Cywinski (b. 1939), Polish historian.

*Source:* Tore Frängsmyr, ed.-in-charge, Irwin Adams, ed., *Nobel Lectures Including Presentation and Acceptance Speeches and Laureates' Biographies: Peace, 1981-1990* (Singapore: World Scientific Publishing Co., for the Nobel Foundation, 1997), pp. 71, 87, 87, 89, 90, 92, 93.

*Remark:* The antidote to violence, nonviolence.

### 311 RESPONSIBILITY

The principle that violations of the laws or customs of war are international crimes has far-reaching implications. In the first place, it means that persons violating, in their individual capacity, these rules are liable to punishment. But, furthermore, it implies that individuals performing acts of State are criminally responsible under international law, when such acts constitute violations of duties incumbent on the State according to the laws or customs of war. It has already been seen that the Court refused to admit, in regard to international crimes, the plea that individuals are not responsible under international law for acts of State.

From the memorandum on the September 30 and October 1, 1946 judgment of former German Nazi leaders by the International Military Tribunal in Nuremberg, Germany (the Nuremberg Tribunal), submitted in 1949 by Trygve Lie (Trygve Halvdan Lie) (1896-1968), Norwegian lawyer and statesman, secretary-general of the United Nations (1946-1953).

*Source:* United Nations, Secretary-General, *The Charter and Judgment of the Nürnberg Tribunal: History and Analysis* (Lake Success, New York: United Nations, General Assembly, International Law Commission, 1949), p. 62.

*Notes:* ▶ The following conclusion is quoted from the judgment of the Nuremberg Tribunal:

That they were assigned to their tasks by a dictator does not absolve them from responsibility for their acts. The relation of leader and follower does not preclude responsibility here any more than it does in the comparable tyranny of organized domestic crime.

*(Same source, p. 52)*

▶ The following argument was not accepted by the Nuremberg Tribunal:

"Statesmen", it was argued by counsel for Ribbentrop, "are committed to take care of their people's interests. If they fail in their politics, then the countries they were acting for have to bear the consequences, and they themselves are judged by the judgment of history. But in a legal sense they were responsible only to their proper country for acts which their country was charged with, acts looked upon as infringing international law. The foreign country injured by the action in question could not hold responsible the acting individual."

*(Same source, p. 39)*

*Explanation: Ribbentrop:* Joachim von Ribbentrop (1893-1946), German Nazi, former foreign minister of Germany (1938-1945), sentenced to hanging by the

International Military Tribunal in Nuremberg, Germany, in 1946, and hanged there on October 16, 1946.

*See* Order (Jan Sehn, on Adolf Hitler and Rudolf Höss, the commandant of the Auschwitz concentration camp).

*Remark:* There is follower's responsibility in international crimes and domestic crimes. Crimes under orders are crimes too. Orders may create dilemmas of conscience (alas, only for some) but international and noninternational armed conflicts create a lot of dilemmas, and the crimes committed should as a rule not go unpunished.

### 312 RESTRICTION

THE UNDERSIGNED PLENIPOTENTIARIES, in the name of their respective Governments:

Whereas the use in war of asphyxiating, poisonous or other gases, and of all analogous liquids materials or devices, has been justly condemned by the general opinion of the civilised world; and

Whereas the prohibition of such use has been declared in Treaties to which the majority of Powers of the world are Parties; and

To the end that this prohibition shall be universally accepted as a part of International Law, binding alike the conscience and the practice of nations;

DECLARE:

That the High Contracting Parties, so far as they are not already Parties to Treaties prohibiting such use, accept this prohibition, agree to extend this prohibition to the use of bacteriological methods of warfare and agree to be bound as between themselves according to the terms of this declaration.

From the Protocol for the Prohibition of the Use in War of Asphyxiating, Poisonous or Other Gases, and of Bacteriological Methods of Warfare (Geneva Protocol of 1925), which was signed at Geneva on June 17, 1925, and entered into force on February 8, 1928.

*Source:* League of Nations, *Treaty Series*, vol. XCIV [94], pp. 65, 67, 69.

*Note:* Germany deposited its ratification on April 25, 1929.

*See* Prisoner of war (German Nazi experiments on Soviet prisoners of war in Auschwitz).

*Remark:* What is the antidote to poison gas? "Charters and covenants alone?"

### 313 RETALIATION

*Socrates* Again, Crito, may we do evil?

*Crito* Surely not, Socrates.

*Socrates* And what of doing evil in return for evil, which is the morality of the many—is that just or not?

*Crito* Not just.

*Socrates* For doing evil to another is the same as injuring him?

*Crito* Very true.

*Socrates* Then we ought not to retaliate or render evil for evil to any one, whatever evil we may have suffered from him. But I would have you consider, Crito, whether you really mean what you are saying. For this opinion has never been held, and never will be held, by any considerable number of persons; and those who are agreed and those who are not agreed upon this point have no common ground, and can only despise one another when they see how widely they differ.

Socrates (ca. 470-399 B.C.), Greek philosopher, talking to his visiting friend, Crito, in a prison at Athens in 399 B.C. while awaiting the execution of a death sentence, according to the Greek philosopher Plato (428 or 427-348 or 347 B.C.), a disciple of Socrates, in his dialogue *Crito* (section 49).

*Source:* Plato, *The Dialogues of Plato*, trans. B. Jowett, 2nd ed. rev., vol. I (Oxford: Clarendon Press, 1875), pp. 377, 383, 390 (names written in full above instead of *Soc.* and *Cr.*).

*Remark:* Many people follow the Golden Rule.

### 314 RETURN

When we arrived at Batchelor Field, reporters pressed me for a statement. I said: "The President of the United States ordered me to break through the Japanese lines and proceed from Corregidor to Australia for the purpose, as I understand it, of organizing the American offensive against Japan, a primary object of which is the relief of the Philippines. I came through and I shall return."

I spoke casually enough, but the phrase "I shall return" seemed a promise of magic to the Filipinos. It lit a flame that became a symbol which focused the nation's indomitable will and at whose shrine it finally attained victory and, once again, found freedom. It was scraped in the sands of the beaches, it was daubed on the walls of the *barrios*, it was stamped on the mail, it was whispered in the cloisters of the church. It became the battle cry of a great underground swell that no Japanese bayonet could still.

Douglas MacArthur (1880-1964), American general, in a statement made after his arrival at Batchelor Field, near Darwin in Australia, on March 17, 1942, coming from the Philippines.

*Source:* Douglas MacArthur, *Reminiscences* (New York: McGraw-Hill Book Company, 1964), p. 145.

*Explanations:* ▸ *Barrios:* town districts. ▸ *Corregidor:* a rocky island near Manila, the last point of organized resistance against Japanese forces in World War II, until May 6, 1942.

*Note:* On February 5, 1945, the chair of the United States House of Representatives sent the following message to General MacArthur:

At the suggestion of the House of Representatives, unanimously expressed, I send to you and the valiant officers and men who serve with you our grateful thanks for the courage and effectiveness in bringing freedom to the Philippines and further glory to American arms.

SAM RAYBURN,
*Speaker.*

(United States, Congress, *Congressional Record*, 79th Congress, 1st session (1945), vol. 91, part 1, p. 839)

*Remark:* For the general, retreat, return and reward. For the aggressor, a temporary victory and permanent defeat.

### 315 REVOLUTION

Sire, it is not a Revolt, it is a Revolution; and truly no rose-water one!

François Alexandre Frédéric, duc de [duke of] Liancourt (1747-1827) (duc de la Rochefoucauld-Liancourt from September 1792), French social reformer, to Louis

XVI (1754-1793), king of France (1774-1792), after the fall of the Bastille, a state prison in Paris, on July 14, 1789, according to Thomas Carlyle (1795-1881), Scottish essayist and historian, in his work *The French Revolution*, written from 1834 to 1837 and first published in 1837.

*Source:* Thomas Carlyle, *The French Revolution: A History*, vol. II (New York: Harper & Brothers, Publishers, 1860), p. 72 (book II, chapter 1).

### 316 REVOLUTION

[A] revolution is not a dinner party, or writing an essay, or painting a picture, or doing embroidery; it cannot be so refined, so leisurely and gentle, so temperate, kind, courteous, restrained and magnanimous. A revolution is an insurrection, an act of violence by which one class overthrows another.

Mao Tse-tung [Mao Zedong] (1893-1976), Chinese political leader, later chairman (chief of state) of the People's Republic of China (1949-1959), in his Report on an Investigation of the Peasant Movement in Hunan, of March 1927.

*Source:* Mao Tse-tung, *Selected Works of Mao Tse-tung*, vol. I (Peking [Beijing]: Foreign Languages Press, 1965), pp. 23, 28 (reference to footnote omitted).

*Remark:* Remember Lincoln, saying "Do not mistake that the ballot is stronger than the bullet."

### 317 RIDICULE

At this point they came in sight of thirty or forty windmills that there are on that plain, and as soon as Don Quixote saw them he said to his squire, 'Fortune is arranging matters for us better than we could have shaped our desires ourselves, for look there, friend Sancho Panza, where thirty or more monstrous giants present themselves, all of whom I mean to engage in battle and slay, and with whose spoils we shall begin to make our fortunes; for this is righteous warfare, and it is God's good service to sweep so evil a breed from off the face of the earth.'

....

So saying, and commending himself with all his heart to his lady Dulcinea, imploring her to support him in such a peril, with lance in rest and covered by his buckler, he charged at Rocinante's fullest gallop and fell upon the first mill that stood in front of him; but as he drove his lance-point into the sail the wind whirled it round with such force that it shivered the lance to pieces, sweeping with it horse and rider, who went rolling over on the plain, in a sorry condition. Sancho hastened to his assistance as fast as his ass could go, and when he came up found him unable to move, with such a shock had Rocinante fallen with him.

'God bless me!' said Sancho, 'did I not tell your worship to mind what you were about, for they were only windmills? and no one could have made any mistake about it but one who had something of the same kind in his head.'

Miguel de Cervantes Saavedra (1547-1616), Spanish novelist, playwright and poet, in his novel *Don Quixote* (Spanish, *El Ingenioso Hidalgo Don Quixote de la Mancha*), part I, published in 1605 (chapter VIII; Don Quixote, the knight-errant and adventurer, in the Battle of the Windmills).

*Source:* Miguel de Cervantes Saavedra, *The Ingenious Gentleman Don Quixote of la Mancha*, trans. John Ormsby, vol. I (New York: Macmillan and Co.;

London: Smith, Elder & Co., 1885), pp. 176-178 (first paragraph indented; reference to footnote omitted).

*Explanation: Dulcinea:* Don Quixote's sweetheart.

*Remark:* Too much eagerness in attacking enemies, anytime, anywhere, even inventing them for that purpose.

### 318 RIGHT

*The General Assembly,*

....

*Convinced* that life without war serves as the primary international prerequisite for the material well-being, development and progress of countries, and for the full implementation of the rights and fundamental human freedoms proclaimed by the United Nations,

....

*Recognizing* that the maintenance of a peaceful life for peoples is the sacred duty of each State,

1. *Solemnly proclaims* that the peoples of our planet have a sacred right to peace;

....

3. *Emphasizes* that ensuring the exercise of the right of peoples to peace demands that the policies of States be directed towards the elimination of the threat of war, particularly nuclear war, the renunciation of the use of force in international relations and the settlement of international disputes by peaceful means on the basis of the Charter of the United Nations.

From the preamble to, and operative paragraphs 1 and 3 of, the Declaration on the Right of Peoples to Peace, contained in an annex to United Nations General Assembly resolution 39/11 of November 12, 1984 (Declaration on the Right of Peoples to Peace).

*Source:* United Nations, *Resolutions and Decisions Adopted by the General Assembly during its Thirty-ninth Session* (General Assembly, Official Records: Thirty-ninth Session, Supplement No. 51 (A/39/51)), p. 22, 22 (semicolon replaced by period at the end).

*See* Human rights (the Declaration of Independence and Federico Mayor).

*Remark:* A right to peace.

### 319 RISK

A man should ever strive to be at peace
Even with those who equal him in strength;
The victory in war is always doubtful.
Who but a silly person would commit
His friends, his army, realm, renown, and self
To the uncertain balance of a battle?

From a medieval collection of Indian tales, *Hitopadesa* [Friendly Advice], composed by one Narayana (book IV, verses 22, 23).

*Source:* Monier Monier-Williams, *Indian Wisdom; or, Examples of the Religious, Philosophical, and Ethical Doctrines of the Hindus,* 4th ed., enlarged and improved

(London: Luzac & Co., 1893), p. 550 (translator of the verses: Monier Monier-Williams).

*See* Peacemaker (Buddha's advice on a territorial dispute).

*Remark:* Some rush to join the group of the silly persons of history.

### 320 RISK

Today there are millions of men in nearly every great nation who have taken part in war and they still believe that that war, or their part in it, was justified. As long as they hold that view they seem to me to be a risk against world peace. Those people who have once believed that war is justified can readily be persuaded that it will be justified again. While I am not mentioning the names of any nations, whether victor or vanquished, I believe it is true that this tendency to believe that war is justified creates in itself a danger to peace, and it is not lessened by what men have learned or experienced of the terrible damage that war can do materially, morally, or spiritually, or by what we know now that another war could do. I believe the greatest risk of war is in the minds of men who have an unrepentant and unchanging view of the justification of past wars. So perhaps in a world like this there is room for a few thousand persons like Quakers who take the opposite view, who begin with the assumption that war is not and has not been and will not be justified, on either practical or moral grounds. Such persons may have time, interest, and desire to put their minds on alternative ways.

Henry J. Cadbury (Henry Joel Cadbury) (1883-1974), American biblical scholar, professor of divinity at Harvard University, founder of the American Friends Service Committee (the Quakers) in 1917 and chairman thereof, in a Nobel lecture, "Quakers and Peace," given in Oslo on December 12, 1947, on behalf of the committee that shared the 1947 Nobel Peace Prize with the Friends Service Council, London.

*Source:* Frederick W. Haberman, ed., *Nobel Lectures Including Presentation Speeches and Laureates' Biographies: Peace,* vol. 2, *1926-1950* (Amsterdam: Elsevier Publishing Company, for the Nobel Foundation, 1972), pp. 371, 391, 395.

*See* Prevention (Henry J. Cadbury, on the lessons of over three hundred years).

*Remark:* "Quakers ... begin with the assumption that war is not and has not been and will not be justified, on either practical or moral grounds." So why justify it?

### 321 SACRIFICE

Susanin was a peasant from the village of Dereven'ki, near the village of Domnino, Kostroma district. In the winter of 1612-13, he was forced by a detachment of Polish noblemen to lead them to Domnino, a Romanov estate, where the newly elected tsar Mikhail Fedorovich was residing at the time. Susanin deliberately led the Poles astray in a dense, swampy forest, an act for which he was later tortured to death.

Susanin's heroic deed has been preserved in folklore and fiction and is the subject of M. I. Glinka's opera *Ivan Susanin.* A monument to Susanin was erected in the city of Kostroma.

From a description in the *Great Soviet Encyclopedia* of the sacrifice of the Russian peasant Ivan Susanin (d. 1613), a hero in the struggle of the Russians against Polish invaders at the beginning of the seventeenth century.

*Source: Great Soviet Encyclopedia* (1980), under "Susanin, Ivan."

*Explanations:* ▸ *Glinka:* Mikhail Ivanovich Glinka (1804-1857), Russian composer whose first opera, *A Life for the Tsar*, performed for the first time on December 9, 1836, in St. Petersburg, was re-named *Ivan Susanin* after the Russian Revolution of 1917 (as the composer called it before the 1836 performance). ▸ *Kostroma district:* a region in central Russia, northeast of Moscow. ▸ *Mikhail Fedorovich:* Michael (Mikhail Fedorovich Romanov) (1596-1645), the first Russian czar of the Romanov Dynasty (1613-1645).

*Remark:* Invaders tricked.

### 322 SATIRE

The 1920s ... saw the publication in Czech of Jaroslav Hašek's *The Good Soldier Švejk*, one of the funniest satires on militarism in general and on German militarism in particular ever written.

Christie Davies (John Christopher Hughes Davies) (b. 1941), British professor of sociology, born in England, in his 1990 book *Ethnic Humor around the World*.

*Source:* Christie Davies, *Ethnic Humor around the World: A Comparative Analysis* (Bloomington: Indiana University Press, 1990), p. 212.

*Explanation: Hašek:* Jaroslav Hašek (Jaroslav Matej Frantisek Hašek) (1883-1923), Czech novelist and short-story writer, born in Prague, Bohemia, Austria-Hungary (now in the Czech Republic), whose satirical novel *The Good Soldier Schweik* was written after World War I (appearing in four volumes from 1920 to 1923; magazine stories collected in a short-story volume in 1912).

### 323 SCULPTURE

No. 1 Pit is a military formation. The chambers are arranged in the battle order of an infantry regiment, which faces eastwards. Altogether it is estimated that there are 3,210 terracotta foot soldiers....

....
The statues in Pit No. 1 are made from the heavy clay found in the vicinity of Mount Li. The advantage for the Ch'in potter-sculptor was that this type of clay was strong enough for large-scale pieces. Although some people find this difficult to believe, no two faces are alike....

....
.... Pit No. 3 is the controlling one for the entire 7,000-piece force....

.... Passing into the heat of the Shensi afternoon, we mounted the wide steps of the museum building, and entered through a small side entrance into the gigantic chamber of Pit No. 1. The initial impact was unforgettable. Five metres (sixteen feet) below where we stood were the ranks of the terracotta army, a sea of faces, eyes staring hard ahead. Although obviously static, the restored figures gave the impression that they were poised to charge. The alertness of the crossbowmen in the vanguard was matched by the boldness of the infantrymen crowded behind. One was conscious of the coiled strength, the shattering force inherent in this infantry regiment.

The Ch'in reputation on the battlefield was swiftly understood. Here is an exact representation of the First Emperor's crack troops,...

Arthur Cotterell (b. 1942), [British] writer, on the mausoleum of Shih-huang-ti [Shi Huangdi] ("First Sovereign Emperor") (259-210 B.C.), the first emperor of China (221-210 B.C.), previously King Cheng of the state Ch'in in northwestern China (246-221 B.C.).

*Source:* Arthur Cotterell, *The First Emperor of China* (London: Macmillan London, 1981), pp. 22, 28, 39-40.

*Explanation: Shensi* [Shaanxi]: also Shen-hsi Sheng, a province in northwestern China.

*Notes:* ▶ The tomb is on Mount Li in Shensi, the total area being almost two square kilometers (three quarters of a square mile). The work on the tomb was begun already in 246 B.C. After 221 B.C. more than 700,000 conscripts from all over China labored there. The emperor also completed the Great Wall of China. *Same source*, pp. 16-18, 37. ▶ The mausoleum is on the World Heritage List.

*Remark:* Will war as an institution belong to antiquities in the future, as the terracotta soldiers?

### 324 SELF-DEFENSE

Nothing in the present Charter shall impair the inherent right of individual or collective self-defense if an armed attack occurs against a Member of the United Nations, until the Security Council has taken the measures necessary to maintain international peace and security. Measures taken by Members in the exercise of this right of self-defense shall be immediately reported to the Security Council and shall not in any way affect the authority and responsibility of the Security Council under the present Charter to take at any time such action as it deems necessary in order to maintain or restore international peace and security.

Article 51 of the Charter of the United Nations, which was signed at San Francisco, United States, on June 26, 1945, and entered into force on October 24, 1945.

*Source:* United States, Department of State, *Treaty Series*, vol. 993, *Charter of the United Nations and Statute of the International Court of Justice*, pp. 3, 14-15 (a photocopy of a certified copy).

*Remark:* Observe the wording "until the Security Council has taken the measures necessary to maintain international peace and security."

### 325 SELF-DETERMINATION

All peoples have the right of self-determination. By virtue of that right they freely determine their political status, and freely pursue their economic, social and cultural development.

Taking into account the particular situation of peoples under colonial or other forms of alien domination or foreign occupation, the World Conference on Human Rights recognizes the right of peoples to take any legitimate action, in accordance with the Charter of the United Nations, to realize their inalienable right of self-determination. The World Conference on Human Rights considers the denial of the right of self-determination as a violation of human rights and underlines the importance of the effective realization of this right.

Paragraph 2 (1-2) of part I of the Vienna Declaration and Programme of Action adopted by the World Conference on Human Rights on June 25, 1993.

*Source:* United Nations, *Vienna Declaration and Programme of Action*, General Assembly document A/CONF.157/23, July 12, 1993, p. 4.

*See also* United Nations, Department of Public Information, *The United Nations and Human Rights, 1945-1995*, United Nations Blue Books, vol. VII (New York: United Nations, 1995), pp. 448, 449.

*Remark:* Denial of the right of self-determination, denial of human rights.

### 326 SETTLEMENT

Benevolence subdues its opposite just as water subdues fire. Those, however, who now-a-days practice benevolence [do it] as if with a cup of water they could save a whole waggon-load of faggots which was on fire, and when the flames were not extinguished were to say that water cannot subdue fire. Such a course, moreover, is the greatest aid to what is not benevolent.

Mencius or Meng-tzu ("Master Meng") [Mengzi] (372-289 B.C.), Chinese philosopher, according to the *Book of Mencius*, compiled by his disciples after his death (book VI, part I, chapter XVIII, section 1).

*Source:* James Legge, trans., *The Chinese Classics*, vol. II, *The Life and Works of Mencius* (London: Trübner & Co., 1875), p. 323 (reference to footnote omitted).

*Remark:* Attitude has effect.

### 327 SETTLEMENT

The Israelis and the Palestinians have now agreed upon a declaration of principles on interim self-government that opens the door to a comprehensive and lasting settlement.

This declaration represents an historic and honorable compromise between two peoples who have been locked in a bloody struggle for almost a century. Too many have suffered for too long. The agreement is a bold breakthrough. The Palestinian Liberation Organization openly and unequivocally has renounced the use of violence and has pledged to live in peace with Israel. Israel, in turn, has announced its recognition of the PLO.

....

.... Yesterday Yasser Arafat wrote to Prime Minister Rabin, committing the PLO to accept Israel's right to exist in peace and security, to renounce terrorism, to take responsibility for the actions of its constituent groups, to discipline those elements who violate these new commitments, and to nullify key elements of the Palestinian covenant that denied Israel's right to exist.

....

.... Throughout this century, bitterness between the Palestinian and Jewish people has robbed the entire region of its resources, its potential, and too many of its sons and daughters....

....

.... Now the efforts of all who have labored before us bring us to this moment, a moment when we dare to pledge what for so long seemed difficult even to imagine: that the security of the Israeli people will be reconciled with the hopes of the Palestinian people and there will be more security and more hope for all.

....

.... And the Koran teaches that if the enemy inclines toward peace, do thou also incline toward peace.

....

.... Above all, let us dedicate ourselves today to your region's next generation. In this entire assembly, no one is more important than the group of Israeli and Arab children who are seated here with us today.

.... For too long, the young of the Middle East have been caught in a web of hatred not of their own making. For too long, they have been taught from the chronicles of war. Now we can give them the chance to know the season of peace.

....

On behalf of the American people I wish to extend congratulations to Prime Minister Yitzhak Rabin, Chairman Yasser Arafat, and Foreign Minister Shimon Peres on being selected as the Nobel Peace Prize laureates for 1994.

It was with great pride that we welcomed these leaders to the White House on September 13 last year to sign the historic Israel[i]-Palestinian Declaration of Principles. It is fitting that this achievement be recognized by award of the Nobel Peace Prize and that the presentation take place in Norway, the country which contributed so much to making it possible.

There is still much work to be done by all who support and share with this year's Nobel laureates the goal of a just, comprehensive, and lasting peace in the Middle East. The ceremony in the Oslo City Hall not only marks a great achievement, it encourages all of us to redouble our efforts to realize the promise of peace for all the people of the Middle East.

Bill Clinton (William Jefferson Clinton, original name William Jefferson Blythe IV) (b. 1946), president of the United States (1993-2001), in his "Remarks on the Israeli-Palestinian Declaration of Principles," on September 10, 1993, and at the signing ceremony for the declaration, on September 13, 1993, as well as in his "Statement Congratulating the Nobel Peace Prize Recipients," on December 11, 1994.

*Source:* William J. Clinton, *Public Papers of the Presidents of the United States: William J. Clinton ... 1993*, book II (Washington: United States Government Printing Office, 1994), pp. 1463, 1463-1464, 1475, 1475-1476, 2181, 2181.

*Explanations:* ▸ *Arafat:* Yasser Arafat (Yasir 'Arafat or Mu̱hammad 'Abd ar-Ra'u̱f al-Qudwah al-H̱usayni,) (1929-2004), chairman of the Palestine Liberation Organization (PLO). ▸ *The Koran:* The Qur'an (Arabic, "recitation, reading"), the sacred book of Islam, the Muslim religion (Arabic, "submission to the will of God") founded by the Arab prophet Mohammed (Muhammad, meaning "praised" or "praiseworthy") (ca. 570-632). ▸ *Peres:* Shimon Peres (b. 1923), Israeli foreign minister (1986-1988, 1992-1995, 2001-2002; prime minister 1984-1986 and 1995-1996). ▸ *Rabin:* Yitzhak Rabin (1922-1995), Israeli soldier and statesman, prime minister (1974-1977, 1992-1995).

*Notes:* ▸ The reference to the Qur'an (Koran) is to chapter (sura) VIII, "The Spoils," verse 62 (And if they incline towards peace, incline thou also towards it,...; *The Holy Quran*, vol. 2 (Surrey: Islam International Publications, 1988), pp. 868, 898.).
▸ Peres was elected president of Israel in 2007 for a seven-year term.

*Remark:* An "honorable compromise" for the "next generation."

### 328 SIEGE

According to the report prepared by the Extraordinary State Commission, 641,803 people died of hunger during the blockade. Many of them are buried in common graves at the Piskarev Cemetery....

....

The battle for Leningrad had ended. For 900 days Leningraders and Soviet troops, supported and aided by the whole country, heroically defended the cradle of the proletarian revolution in battle and in persevering labour. Nothing broke their will, neither hunger, nor frost, nor bombing, nor shelling.

From the book *Great Patriotic War of the Soviet Union, 1941-1945*, on the Siege of Leningrad, the Nine-hundred-day Siege, actually lasting 872 days, from September 8, 1941, to January 27, 1944.

*Source:* M. M. Minasyan, editor in chief, *Great Patriotic War of the Soviet Union, 1941-1945: A General Outline*, trans. David Skvirsky and Vic Schneierson (Moscow: Progress Publishers, 1974), p. 244 (abridged translation from the Russian edition of 1970; a 1965 Russian edition exists).

*Explanation: Leningrad:* the second largest city of the Soviet Union, with a population of 3,191,304 in 1939. In 1991 its name was changed back to Saint Petersburg (St. Petersburg). The city is in northwestern Russia.

*Notes:* ▶ Nicholas Bethell (Nicholas William Bethell) (1938-2007), British writer and politician, born in England, member of the House of Lords (1967-1999), has written as follows:

Most Western scholars believe that the number of deaths from starvation during the entire siege exceeded one million, and that several hundred thousand more were killed by bombs, shells or gunfire. By contrast, the United States and Britain together suffered fewer than 800,000 deaths during all of World War II.

(Nicholas Bethell, *Russia Besieged*, ed. the editors of Time-Life Books, World War II (Alexandria, Virginia: Time-Life Books, 1977), p. 113)

▶ John Shaw (1931-2004), Australian-based English-born correspondent, wrote as follows:

The siege of Leningrad dragged on and on. More than three million citizens had been cut off by the surging German armies in August of 1941, and ever since then the city and the Soviet troops defending it had refused to surrender in spite of bombing raids, incessant artillery shelling, heavy snows, temperatures as low as 61° below zero and mass starvation. By December the city's plight was desperate. Leningrad was then struggling along without fuel, running water or electric lights. The survivors had consumed all their pets and were subsisting on a tiny ration—a few mouthfuls of bread a day.

January of 1942 was the blackest month for Leningrad. Countless citizens fell dead in the snow-covered streets, and children dragged sleds bearing the dead to the burial grounds. The Germans continued to close in, driving to within three miles of the city on its southern perimeter. Luftwaffe planes dropped millions of leaflets urging the Leningraders to save themselves by accepting the status of an open city. The city council called a meeting and composed Leningrad's answer: "Death will be afraid of us before we are afraid of death."

....

By April, the worst was over, and the home front breathed a transcontinental sigh of relief. No one knew how many Leningraders had died of all causes by then; guesses ran from a half million to a million and more, and an Extraordinary State Commission finally placed at exactly 641,803 the number of citizens who had died of starvation during the blockade. And hundreds of thousands of citizens were barely alive. At the end of March, when the Leningrad city council ordered everyone who could walk to clean up the wreckage and look for unburied dead, less than a quarter of a million emaciated people were strong enough to turn out.

(John Shaw, *Red Army Resurgent*, ed. the editors of Time-Life Books, World War II (Alexandria, Virginia: Time-Life Books, 1979), p. 83)

*Additional explanation: Luftwaffe:* the German air force (1935-1945).

*See* Diary (Nicholas Bethell, on Tanya Savicheva).

*Remark:* Note John's words, "children dragged sleds bearing the dead to the burial grounds."

### 329 SLAVERY

[O]n the first day of January, in the year of our Lord one thousand eight hundred and sixty-three, all persons held as slaves within any state or designated part of a state, the people whereof shall then be in rebellion against the United States, shall be then, thenceforward, and forever, free;...

From the Emancipation Proclamation, issued on January 1, 1863, by Abraham Lincoln (1809-1865), president of the United States (1861-1865) (a preliminary proclamation was issued on September 22, 1862).

*Source:* George P. Sanger, ed., *The Statutes at Large, Treaties, and Proclamations, of the United States of America, from December 5, 1859, to March 3, 1863,* vol. XII (Boston: Little, Brown and Company, 1863), p. 1268, 1268.

*Remark:* A country of liberty.

### 330 SLAVERY

He was fighting the slave trade single-handed, and was ringed around by cruel and unscrupulous enemies, whose dark deeds had only him to fear. He is almost beaten in the unequal strife; almost, but never quite. No man was ever yet quite beaten who is as sure of Christ as he was. He has one thing to rely on, as he said before—"the word of a Gentleman of the strictest honour"—and it is enough. So he will remain and outwit the slave-traders if he can. And yet it is a misnomer to call it a "trade"; "it is not a trade, but a system of consecutive murders."

....

.... To his daughter Agnes, whose courage he never failed to praise, he writes: "The death knell of American slavery was rung by a woman's hand. We great he-beasts say Mrs. Stowe exaggerated. From what I have seen of slavery I say exaggeration is a simple impossibility. I go with the sailor who, on seeing slave-traders, said: 'If the devil don't catch those fellows we might as well have no devil at all.'"

C. Silvester Horne (Charles Silvester Horne) (1865-1914), English clergyman, on the struggle against slavery in Africa of David Livingstone (1813-1873), Scottish missionary and explorer in Africa who started working in Bechuanaland (now Botswana), north of South Africa, in 1841, and worked mostly in Africa from that time until his death in 1873. Here, a special attention is drawn to the slave-trade problem of the late 1860s.

*Source:* C. Silvester Horne, *David Livingstone* (New York: Macmillan Company, 1913), pp. 163-164, 167.

*Explanations:* ▸ *Agnes:* Agnes Livingstone, later Agnes Livingstone Bruce (1847-1912), Scottish housewife and missionary worker. ▸ *Stowe:* Harriet Elizabeth Beecher Stowe (1811-1896), American writer and philanthropist, the author of *Uncle Tom's Cabin; or, Life among the Lowly,* which appeared in serial form in an antislavery paper in Washington, the *National Era,* in 1850, and was published in book form in 1852, selling very well and influencing public opinion in the northern states against slavery.

*Notes:* ▸ "The publication in book form (1852) was a factor which must be reckoned in summing up the causes of the Civil War." *Encyclopædia Britannica* (1964), under "Stowe, Harriet Elizabeth Beecher."

▸ Stowe's work has been described as follows:

It is not the simple sentimental tract it is often held to be but a powerful analysis of every aspect of racialism, including a good understanding of the sexuality of slavery and a fair range of Yankee and Southern slaveholders. Mrs Stowe knew exactly how slavery degenerates, even if her death of Little Eva is sentimental and her integratable Negro rather crude. Her book undoubtedly contributed to national resistances to slavery which led to the Civil War, as Lincoln himself recognized.

(*The Penguin Companion to American Literature* (1971), under "Stowe, Harriet Beecher")

*Remark:* African slavery, a man's hand. American slavery, a woman's hand.

## 331 SOLDIER

China marches its men down Po-têng Road
While Tartar troops peer across blue waters of the bay ...
And since not one battle famous in history
Sent all its fighters back again,
The soldiers turn round, looking toward the border,
And think of home, with wistful eyes,
And of those tonight in the upper chambers
Who toss and sigh and cannot rest.

Li Po (Li Tai Po) [Li Bo] (701-762), Chinese poet, referring, in his poem "The Moon at the Fortified Pass," to an impending battle between Chinese and Tatar troops, in the time of the T'ang Dynasty (618-906).

*Source:* Witter Bynner, *The Jade Mountain: A Chinese Anthology Being Three Hundred Poems of the T'ang Dynasty, 618-906* (New York: Alfred A. Knopf, 1929), pp. 60, 61 (translated by Witter Bynner from the text of Kiang Kang-hu, taken from "T'ang shih san pai shou," an anonymous compilation of 311 poems, published in the eighteenth century).

*Explanation: Tartar:* relating to Tartars, more correctly Tatars, a word originally used for a tribe living in northeastern Mongolia in the fifth century, and later, for instance, for the Mongols of Genghis Khan (1167?-1227), khan (chieftain) of the Mongols (1206 or 1207-1227) who, in the end, ruled from the Yellow Sea to the Black Sea.

*Remark:* Even friendly fire.

## 332 SOLDIER

The world has turned over many times since I took the oath on the plain at West Point, and the hopes and dreams have long since vanished. But I still remember the refrain of one of the most popular barrack ballads of that day which proclaimed most proudly that—

"Old soldiers never die; they just fade away."

And like the old soldier of that ballad, I now close my military career and just fade away—an old soldier who tried to do his duty as God gave him the light to see that duty.

Good-by.

Douglas MacArthur (1880-1964), American general, in his Old Soldiers Never Die Address, delivered at a joint meeting of the two houses of Congress on April 19, 1951, shortly after his recall as commander of United States and United Nations forces in the Korean War (1950-1953).

*Source:* United States, *Congressional Record,* 82nd Congress, 1st session (1951), vol. 97, part 3, pp. 4123, 4125.

*Explanations:* ▸ *"Old soldiers never die"* : the chorus of this old army ballad reads as follows:

Old soldiers never die,

Never die, never die,

Old soldiers never die

They just fade away.

(The Internet (2002), under "Old Soldiers Never Die" )

▸ *West Point:* a military academy in the state of New York established in 1802.

*See* Solution (John F. Kennedy: Our problems are manmade—therefore, they can be solved by man.).

*See also* United States, *Senate Documents,* 82nd Congress, 1st session (1951), vol. 10, *Miscellaneous,* Senate document no. 36, pp. 1, 6.

*Remark:* Old soldiers fade away but must hopes and dreams vanish? Some things can change. The American and British Quakers said good-bye to slavery.

### 333 SOLIDARITY

All free men, wherever they may live, are citizens of Berlin, and, therefore, as a free man, I take pride in the words *"Ich bin ein Berliner."*

John F. Kennedy (John Fitzgerald Kennedy) (1917-1963), president of the United States (1961-1963), in his remarks on the steps of the Schöneberger Rathaus, West Berlin's city hall, on June 26, 1963.

*Source:* John F. Kennedy, *Public Papers of the Presidents of the United States: John F. Kennedy ... 1963* (Washington: United States Government Printing Office, 1964), pp. 524, 525.

*Remark:* The quotable Kennedy.

### 334 SOLUTION

Gerald Fleming, a tireless researcher, single-mindedly has pursued evidence of all kinds not only in British, American, and German archives, but also in the closely guarded Russian archives at Riga; and he has traced and questioned now-obscure German eyewitnesses in order to complete his inquiry. The result is an impressive work which proves that the Final Solution was deliberately designed and personally willed and ordered by Hitler. Fleming reveals the elaborate precautions taken not only to disguise the nature of the operation but also to ensure that it could not be connected with Hitler, whose orders were always verbal and indirect, although given the force of law. He also shows that Himmler was at first reluctant to go so far as to exterminate the Jews but accepted the task as a "heavy duty" imposed on him by the Führer, and that Himmler stopped the operation when faced with the certain defeat of Germany, while Hitler continued to the very end to demand its completion.

From the front flap of the book *Hitler and the Final Solution*, written by Gerald Fleming (1921-2006), German-born British historian, and originally published in 1982 in German (*Hitler und die Endlösung*), in 1984 in English.

*Source:* Gerald Fleming, *Hitler and the Final Solution* (London: Hamish Hamilton, 1985), front flap.

*Explanations:* ▸ *Final Solution:* "Nazi plan to destroy the Jews of Europe"; Louis L. Snyder, *Louis L. Snyder's Historical Guide to World War II* (Westport, Connecticut: Greenwood Press, 1982), p. 235, 235. ▸ *Führer:* in English "leader," a reference to Adolf Hitler. ▸ *Himmler:* Heinrich Himmler (1900-1945), German Nazi leader, head of the Nazi Party corps SS, responsible for the enforcement of extermination policies. ▸ *Hitler:* Adolf Hitler (1889-1945), chancellor of the Third Reich of Nazi Germany (1933-1945).

*See* Order (Jan Sehn, on Adolf Hitler and Rudolf Höss, commandant of the Auschwitz concentration camp).

*Remark:* The Hitler connection.

### 335 SOLUTION

Let us examine our attitude toward peace itself. Too many of us think it is impossible. Too many think it unreal. But that is a dangerous, defeatist belief. It leads to the conclusion that war is inevitable—that mankind is doomed—that we are gripped by forces we cannot control.

We need not accept that view. Our problems are manmade—therefore, they can be solved by man.

John F. Kennedy (John Fitzgerald Kennedy) (1917-1963), president of the United States (1961-1963), in his June 10, 1963 commencement address at the American University in Washington.

*Source:* John F. Kennedy, *Public Papers of the Presidents of the United States: John F. Kennedy ... 1963* (Washington: United States Government Printing Office, 1964), pp. 459, 460-461.

*Remark:* Mankind is not doomed, according to Kennedy. Peace is possible. Let us commence.

### 336 SONG

JOHN LENNON AND YOKO ONO married in March, 1969, moved into the Amsterdam Hilton for their honeymoon, and announced that a happening was about to take place in their bed.... When the newsmen entered, John and Yoko were sitting in bed, wearing pajamas. "I hope it's not a let-down," John said. "We wouldn't make love in public—that's an emotionally personal thing."

He announced that they would stay in bed for a week, "our protest against all the suffering and violence in the world." They conducted interviews ten hours a day, starting at ten in the morning. John explained, "We're sending out a message, mainly to youth, or to anybody interested in protesting against any form of violence.... Things like the Grosvenor Square marches in London, the end product of it all was just newspaper stories about riots and fighting. We did the bed-in in Amsterdam ... just to give people the idea that there are many ways of protest.... Protest for peace in any way, but peacefully, 'cause we think that peace is only got by peaceful methods, and that to fight the establishment with their own weapons is no good because they always win, and they've been winning for thousands of years. They know how to play the game of violence. But they don't know how to handle humor, and peaceful humor—and that's our message really."

    ....

.... They settled on Montreal as the city closest to the U.S. media to stage their second bed-in for peace, arrived in May, 1969, and did more than 60 radio interviews.

    ....

The last night of the Montreal bed-in John taught everyone in the room the new song he had written, and recorded it on an eight-track portable tape recorder he had installed. On John's first non-Beatles recording, the back-up singers were Yoko, Dick Gregory, Timothy Leary, Tommy Smothers, Murray the K, Petula Clark, a rabbi, a priest, and the Canadian chapter of the Radha Krishna temple. The song, the musical product of the bed-ins, was "Give Peace a Chance."

Released a single in the U.S. in July, 1969, the song reached number 14 on the American charts in September and number two on the British charts. It received top-40 radio play for nine weeks, and became a million-seller worldwide.

John sang the song with a cheerful enthusiasm; it bounced along over rich cross-rhythms. And he sang verses filled with words, apparently whimsical nonsense lyrics: "everybody's talking 'bout madism, bagism, shagism, dragism." On closer examination, the song had clear politics. John's verses called on people to put aside political differences and factionalism within the antiwar movement, to unite around the simple demand for "peace." John treated political positions as "isms":

Everybody's talking 'bout ...
This-ism, that-ism, ism-ism-ism.
All we are saying
Is give peace a chance.
Revolution, evolution ...
United nations, congratulations,
All we are saying ...

Jon Wiener (Jonathan M. Wiener) (b. 1944), American history educator, in his 1983 article on John Lennon (John Winston Lennon) (1940-1980), English rock singer, guitarist, songwriter and poet, one of the Beatles, the British musical quartet (1962-1970), his wife Yoko Ono (b. 1933), Japanese performance artist, songwriter, singer and campaigner for peace, and the song "Give Peace a Chance," written by John Lennon in 1969.

Source: Jon Wiener, "Give Peace a Chance: An Anthem for the Anti-War Movement," in Give Peace a Chance: Music and the Struggle for Peace, ed. Marianne Philbin, A Catalog of the Exhibition at the Peace Museum, Chicago

(Chicago: Chicago Review Press, 1983), pp. 11, 11-12, 14-16 (first paragraph indented; Grovesnor Square corrected to Grosvenor Square).

*Explanation: Montreal:* a large city in eastern Canada.

*Notes:* ▸ Marianne Philbin (1955-2010), American curator of the aforementioned Peace Museum in Chicago and the editor of the catalog, writes in her introduction thereto as follows:

Music will continue to play a major role in inspiring efforts for peace as new musicians step onto the tightrope, taking real risks for the sake of conscience.

....

John Lennon and Yoko Ono were often accused of using peace as a way of getting free publicity. They were criticized for their bed-ins—turning their honeymoon into a press conference, giving statements to the media about the need for peace in the world. They received, as they knew they would, huge amounts of publicity. And for that week, instead of our television screens and newspaper headlines being filled with stories of war and violence, we heard the Lennons telling us that "War is over, if you want it." This media blitz gave many the opportunity to attack the already controversial couple, it gave others the opportunity to ridicule them, and it allowed all of us to hear their very clear and simple message—a plea to "give peace a chance."

(*Same source*, pp. 8-9)

▸ And, another quotation, from an interview with John Lennon:

*What do you think of "Give Peace a Chance"?*

I thought it was beautiful.

*Did you ever see the Moratorium Day in Washington?*

That's what it was for, you know.

*Did you see that scene?*

I think I heard it, I don't know. I just remember hearing them all sing it ... I don't know whether it was on the radio or TV. You know, it was a very big moment for me, that's what the song was about. You see I'm shy and aggressive, so I have great hopes for what I do with my work and I also have great despair that it's all pointless and it's shit. How can you beat Beethoven or Shakespeare, or whatever? I go through all that, and in my secret heart I wanted to write something that would take over "We Shall Overcome." I don't know why. Maybe because that was the one they always sang. I thought why doesn't somebody write one for the people now, you know, that's what my job is, our job is, to write for the people now, the songs that they go and sing on the buses even, and not just love songs.

(Jann Wenner, *Lennon Remembers: The Rolling Stone Interviews*, Rolling Stone Press Book (New York: Fawcett Popular Library, 1972), pp, 109-110 ("me secret heart" corrected to "my secret heart")).

▸ The following has been written on Zilphia Mae Horton and the Highlander Folk School established in 1932 in Monteagle, Tennessee:

[S]he encouraged students to share the songs of their home communities and to adapt the lyrics to contemporary situations. Until her sudden death in 1956, she collected songs and mimeographed song sheets for picket lines and protest marches. The most famous song she uncovered was a hymn, "I Will Overcome," that striking tobacco workers adapted as "We Will Overcome," on picket lines in Charleston, South Carolina in 1945. At Highlander, it became the anthem of the civil rights movement: We Shall Overcome.

(Waldo E. Martin, Jr., and Patricia Sullivan, eds., *Civil Rights in the United States*, vol. 1 (New York: Macmillan Reference USA, 2000), p. 349)

▸ And they continued. On October 9, 2007, on Lennon's birthday, Ono unveiled in his memory her outdoor work of art, *Imagine Peace Tower*, on the island of Videy, Reykjavík. In the book *Imagine Peace Tower* one may read:

IMAGINE PEACE TOWER was lit for the first time. IMAGINE PEACE TOWER is essentially a beam of light that streams up from a wishing well inscribed with the words "IMAGINE PEACE" in 24 different languages....

....

In a newspaper interview, Yoko Ono said she had long nurtured the idea of creating a peace light, but that she had considered Iceland as a potential location only three years before. With the peace light she wanted to urge people to think about peace. People had to be able to envision peace before it could become a reality and she had greater faith that the grassroots movement, as opposed to the politicians, could carry out the task. A light tower in Videy would not create peace on Earth, but it might make people think. The more people thought about peace, the sooner it would surely move from being a dream to being a reality.

IMAGINE PEACE TOWER, Yoko Ono's outdoor artwork, was raised on the island of Videy to honor the memory of John Lennon. It was unveiled on October 9, 2007, on what would have been Lennon's 67th birthday. IMAGINE PEACE TOWER is intended to be a beacon for world peace. It symbolizes the struggle for peace begun by Ono and Lennon in the late 1960s....Each year, IMAGINE PEACE TOWER will shine between October 9 and December 8—the day Lennon was killed....

....

.... The concept of peace in Yoko Ono's work is no accident. The peace ideal is interwoven with her entire life. Together, she and John Lennon made the struggle for world peace into their struggle. A struggle that is still ongoing.

....

.... Nostrodamus described a land in the north that would play a major role in the reconstruction of the world. A light of hope shone from that place.

....

IMAGINE PEACE TOWER has risen, John and Yoko have made their contribution, and it is now up to us to foster and nurture a culture of peace in the world.

(Haukur Haraldsson, ed., *Imagine Peace Tower* ([Reykjavík]: Iceland Post, 2008), pp. 13, 15 (Pétur Blöndal), 21 (Edvard T. Jónsson), 35, 74 (Sigtryggur Magnason), 95 (Gunnar Hersveinn) (paragraphs indented)).

*Additional explanations:* ▸ *Beethoven:* Ludwig van Beethoven (1770-1827), German composer. ▸ *Moratorium Day:* October 15, 1969, "Vietnam Moratorium Day," the day upon which the largest antiwar demonstration in American history took place. ▸ *Nostrodamus:* Nostrodamus (Michael de Notredame or Nostrodame) (1503-1566), French astrologer and physician. ▸ *Shakespeare:* William Shakespeare (1564-1616), English poet, player and playwright. ▸ *We Shall Overcome:* "the anthem of the American Civil Rights Movement," the basis for which was the gospel song "I'll Overcome Someday," composed in 1901 by a well-known American composer of gospel songs, the Reverend C. A. Tindley (Charles Albert Tindley) (1851 or 1859-1933); new lyrics and arrangements in 1956 by Zilphia Horton (Zilphia Mae Johnson) (1913-1956), American social activist and educator, Guy Carawan (Guy H. Carawan) (b. 1927), American folk singer, Pete

Seeger (Peter R. Seeger) (b. 1919), American folk singer and songwriter, and Frank S. Hamilton (Frank Strawn Hamilton) (b. 1934), American composer and musician.
*Remark:* "Give Peace a Chance," according to the circumstances.

### 337 SPACE
*The States Parties to this Agreement,*

....
*Desiring* to prevent the moon from becoming an area of international conflict,

....
*Have agreed* on the following:
#### Article 1
1. The provisions of this Agreement relating to the moon shall also apply to other celestial bodies within the solar system, other than the earth, except in so far as specific legal norms enter into force with respect to any of these celestial bodies.

....
#### Article 3
1. The moon shall be used by all States Parties exclusively for peaceful purposes.

....
#### Article 11
1. The moon and its natural resources are the common heritage of mankind,...

From the preamble to, and Article 1, paragraph 1, Article 3, paragraph 1, and part of Article 11, paragraph 1, of, the Agreement Governing the Activities of States on the Moon and Other Celestial Bodies contained in an annex to United Nations General Assembly resolution 34/68 of December 5, 1979 (Agreement Governing the Activities of States on the Moon and Other Celestial Bodies). The agreement was opened for signature on December 18, 1979, and entered into force on July 11, 1984.
*Source:* United Nations, *Resolutions and Decisions Adopted by the General Assembly during Its Thirty-fourth Session* (General Assembly, Official Records: Thirty-fourth Session, Supplement No. 46 (A/34/46)), pp. 77, 77-79.
*See also* United Nations, *Treaty Series,* vol. 1363, p. 3.
*Remark:* Why except the earth in Article 3?

### 338 SPOILS
The leaders of the three Great Powers—the Soviet Union, the United States of America and Great Britain—have agreed that in two or three months after Germany has surrendered and the war in Europe has terminated the Soviet Union shall enter into the war against Japan on the side of the Allies on condition that:

....
2. The former rights of Russia violated by the treacherous attack of Japan in 1904 shall be restored, viz:

    (a) the southern part of Sakhalin as well as all the islands adjacent to it shall be returned to the Soviet Union,

....
3. The Kuril islands shall be handed over to the Soviet Union.

From the Agreement regarding Japan, signed on February 11, 1945, at the end of the Crimea (Yalta) Conference, by the "Big Three," Winston S. Churchill (Winston

Leonard Spencer Churchill) (1874-1965), prime minister of the United Kingdom (1940-1945, 1951-1955), Franklin D. Roosevelt (Franklin Delano Roosevelt) (1882-1945), president of the United States (1933-1945), and Joseph Stalin (Joseph Vissarionovich Dzhugashvili) (1879-1953), premier of the Soviet Union (1941-1953) and general secretary of the Central Committee of the Communist Party (1922-1953).

*Source:* United States, Department of State, *Executive Agreement Series*, vol. 498, publication 2505 (1946), pp. 1, 3.

*Explanations:* ▸ *Kuril islands:* Kurile Islands, a chain of small islands in the North Pacific, southwest of the peninsula of Kamchatka, the Soviet Union (now Russia).
▸ *Sakhalin:* a large island off the Pacific coast of the Soviet Union (now Russia).

*Remark:* We shall return.

### 339 SPORT

O Sport, you are Peace! You forge happy bonds between the peoples by drawing them together in reverence for strength which is controlled, organised and self-disciplined. Through you the young of all the world learn to respect one another, and thus the diversity of national traits becomes a source of generous and peaceful emulation.

Pierre de Coubertin (1863-1937), French educator and scholar who proposed the revival of the Olympic Games and was the first president of the International Olympic Committee (1896-1925), in his 1912 Ode to Sport, for which he received a gold medal in the poetry competition at the Olympic Games in Stockholm the same year.

*Source:* Pierre de Coubertin, *The Olympic Idea: Discourses and Essays*, ed. Carl-Diem–Institut an der Deutschen Sporthochschule Köln, rev. L. Diem and O. Andersen, trans. John G. Dixon (from French) (Lausanne: Éditions Internationales Olympia; Stuttgart: Olympischer Sport-Verlag, 1966), pp. 39, 40 (published under a pseudonym).

*Remark:* Sport is beautiful.

### 340 STARVATION

Starvation of civilians as a method of combat is prohibited. It is therefore prohibited to attack, destroy, remove or render useless, for that purpose, objects indispensable to the survival of the civilian population, such as foodstuffs, agricultural areas for the production of foodstuffs, crops, livestock, drinking water installations and supplies and irrigation works.

Article 14 of the Protocol Additional to the Geneva Conventions of 12 August 1949, and Relating to the Protection of Victims of Non-International Armed Conflicts (Protocol II), which was adopted at Geneva on June 8, 1977, and entered into force on December 7, 1978.

*Source:* United Nations, *Treaty Series*, vol. 1125, pp. 609, 615.

*Remark:* Starvation of prisoners of war too.

### 341 STATE

A thousand years scarce serve to form a state;
An hour may lay it in the dust: and when
Can Man its shattered splendour renovate,
Recall its virtues back, and vanquish Time and Fate?

George Gordon Byron, more commonly known as Lord Byron (1788-1824), English poet, referring to Greece in his poem *Childe Harold's Pilgrimage*, published from 1812 to 1818 (canto II, completed in 1810, stanza LXXXIV [84], lines 6-9).

*Source:* [George Gordon] Byron, *The Works of Lord Byron*, Poetry, vol. II, ed. Ernest Hartley Coleridge, 2nd ed. rev. (1904; reprint, London: John Murray, 1922), pp. 9, 98, 155.

*Remark:* A state in Byron's age, a world in the nuclear age.

### 342 STATESMAN

[N]o one can be a true statesman, whether he aims at the happiness of the individual or state, who looks only, or first of all, to external warfare; nor will he ever be a sound legislator who orders peace for the sake of war, and not war for the sake of peace.

Plato (428 or 427-348 or 347 B.C.), Greek philosopher, in his dialogue *Laws*, supposedly composed in his later years (book I, section 628; an Athenian stranger speaking to Cleinias, a Cretan, and Megillus, a Lacedaemonian (Spartan)).

*Source:* Plato, *The Dialogues of Plato*, trans. B. Jowett, 2nd ed. rev., vol. V (Oxford: Clarendon Press, 1875), pp. 1, 193, 197-198.

*See* Glory (Demetrius Charles Boulger, on the policy of Yung-chen, emperor of China).

*See also* Self-defense (Charter of the United Nations).

### 343 STEP

On a small scale, my approach eight years ago as the Governing Mayor of Berlin was that small steps are better than no steps at all. When hundreds of thousands of people, after years of separation, were given passes to visit their relatives over Christmas, this, in a nutshell, was the application of the knowledge that there could be a new, only apparent, paradox—and that is improving the situation by recognising it for what it is.

Willy Brandt (Herbert Ernst Karl Frahm) (1913-1992), German statesman, chancellor of the Federal Republic of Germany (1969-1974), recipient of the 1971 Nobel Peace Prize, in his Nobel lecture, "Peace Policy in Our Time," given in Oslo on December 11, 1971.

*Source:* Tore Frängsmyr, ed.-in-charge, Irwin Adams, ed., *Nobel Lectures Including Presentation and Acceptance Speeches and Laureates' Biographies: Peace, 1971-1980* (Singapore: World Scientific Publishing Co., for the Nobel Foundation, 1997), pp. 1, 20, 23.

*Note:* Brandt who for years lived in exile from Nazi Germany and for some time was a Norwegian citizen was mayor of Berlin from 1957 to 1966.

*See* Solidarity (John F. Kennedy, "Ich bin ein Berliner.").

*Remark:* "Small steps" or "no steps."

### 344 STRENGTH

The great fish eats the little one.

Greek proverb.

*Source:* Alexander Negris, ed. and trans., *A Dictionary of Modern Greek Proverbs* (Edinburgh: Thomas Clark, 1831), p. 131 (italics omitted).

### 345 SUPERIORITY

The Persians marched through the island, burning and destroying; and at length, under the command of Híppias, landed on the coast of Attica, and encamped on the plain of Márathon. The Athenians sent in haste to the Spartans for assistance; but these not appearing at the proper time, in consequence of an ancient law of their religion, which forbade them to march to battle before a full moon, the Athenians, under the command of ten leaders, advanced upon the enemy. The most esteemed among these leaders was Miltíades, who had formerly served in the Persian army, and was thoroughly acquainted with its qualities and tactics. By his direction, 10,000 Athenians, and 1,000 Platœans, attacked the army of Persians, of ten times their number, in a place unfavorable for cavalry, and gave them a complete overthrow in the battle of Márathon. The victors gained a rich booty, and placed the fetters they discovered, and which were intended for themselves, on the bodies of their enemies. Great was the renown acquired by the Athenians, who here for the first time proved that they were worthy of the democratic freedom they had lately introduced among themselves; and centuries later, patriotic orators would excite the enthusiasm of the people, by calling to their remembrance the victory of Márathon. Híppias was one of the slain.

Georg Weber (1808-1888), German historian and educator, describing, in his book *Outlines of Universal History*, first published in German in 1851 (*Weltgeschichte in übersichtlicher Darstellung*), the Battle of Marathon, Greece, in 490 B.C.

*Source:* George Weber, *Outlines of Universal History, from the Creation of the World to the Present Time*, trans. M. Behr, rev. Francis Bowen, 6th ed. (Boston: Hickling, Swan and Brown, 1856), p. 40.

*Explanations:* ▸ *Híppias:* Hippias (ca. 570-ca. 490 B.C.), Greek tyrant of Athens (528 or 527-510 B.C.) who later sided with the Persians and accompanied them in the 490 B.C. Battle of Marathon. ▸ *Márathon:* Marathon, a plain in Attica, Greece, about 25 miles (40 kilometers) northeast of Athens. ▸ *Miltíades:* Miltiades (d. ca. 488 B.C.), Athenian general, the victor of Marathon in 490 B.C., fighting there against the forces of Darius I (ca. 549-486 B.C.), king of Persia (522-486 B.C.).

*See* News (John Kieran).

### 346 SUPERPOWER

Today, should total war ever break out again—no matter how—our two countries would become the primary targets. It is an ironic but accurate fact that the two strongest powers are the two in the most danger of devastation. All we have built, all we have worked for, would be destroyed in the first 24 hours. And even in the cold war, which brings burdens and dangers to so many countries, including this Nation's closest allies—our two countries bear the heaviest burdens.

John F. Kennedy (John Fitzgerald Kennedy) (1917-1963), president of the United States (1961-1963), referring, in his June 10, 1963 commencement address at the American University in Washington, to the two superpowers, the Soviet Union and the United States.

*Source*: John F. Kennedy, *Public Papers of the Presidents of the United States: John F. Kennedy ... 1963* (Washington: United States Government Printing Office, 1964), pp. 459, 462.

*See* State (George Gordon Byron, 1810):

A thousand years scarce serve to form a state;

An hour may lay it in the dust....

*Remark*: "24 hours."

### 347 SURPRISE ATTACK

YESTERDAY, December 7, 1941—a date which will live in infamy—the United States of America was suddenly and deliberately attacked by naval and air forces of the Empire of Japan.

The United States was at peace with that Nation and, at the solicitation of Japan, was still in conversation with its Government and its Emperor looking toward the maintenance of peace in the Pacific. Indeed, one hour after Japanese air squadrons had commenced bombing in the American Island of Oahu, the Japanese Ambassador to the United States and his colleague delivered to our Secretary of State a formal reply to a recent American message. And while this reply stated that it seemed useless to continue the existing diplomatic negotiations, it contained no threat or hint of war or of armed attack.

It will be recorded that the distance of Hawaii from Japan makes it obvious that the attack was deliberately planned many days or even weeks ago. During the intervening time the Japanese Government has deliberately sought to deceive the United States by false statements and expressions of hope for continued peace.

....

But always will our whole Nation remember the character of the onslaught against us.

Franklin D. Roosevelt (Franklin Delano Roosevelt) (1882-1945), president of the United States (1933-1945), in his address to Congress, on December 8, 1941, asking for a declaration of war against Japan after its surprise attack the day before on Pearl Harbor, situated on the island Oahu in the American territory of the Hawaiian Islands (the fiftieth state since 1959).

*Source*: Franklin D. Roosevelt, *The Public Papers and Addresses of Franklin D. Roosevelt*, comp. Samuel I. Rosenman, 1941 volume, *The Call to Battle Stations* (New York: Harper & Brothers Publishers, 1950), pp. 514, 514-515.

*Remark*: The moonscape of Hiroshima not on the chessboard.

### 348 TANK

The Battle of the Kursk Salient, one of the greatest operations of the Second World War, lasted for fifty days. Like the battles at Moscow and Stalingrad, it falls into two phases. The first was the defensive action in the southern and northern legs of the Kursk Salient and it was started on July 5. Compared with the preceding battles it did not last long. The second phase was the counter-offensive, in which five fronts took part: the Western, Bryansk, Central, Voronezh and Steppe. It was mounted on July 12 in the direction of Orel and on August 3 in the direction of Belgorod and Kharkov. The Battle of Kursk ended on August 23. The counter-offensive developed into a colossal strategic offensive in an area stretching from

Velikiye Luki to the Black Sea. Its victorious outcome showed that GHQ had been right in deliberately deciding on defence.

The German Army suffered a defeat from which it never recovered. Soviet forces smashed almost 30 enemy divisions, including seven panzer divisions, and destroyed over 3,500 aircraft. Soviet pilots won air supremacy and held it firmly till the end of the war. After Kursk the nazi Command was compelled to abandon its offensive strategy and go over to the defensive along the entire Soviet-German front. This meant that the backbone of the German Army had been broken. The strategic initiative was now unequivocally in the hands of the Soviet Armed Forces. This finally turned the tide of the war.

From the book *Great Patriotic War of the Soviet Union, 1941-1945*, on the Battle of Kursk, Russia, from July 5 to August 23, 1943, during World War II, the greatest tank battle ever fought.

*Source:* M. M. Minasyan, editor in chief, *Great Patriotic War of the Soviet Union, 1941-1945: A General Outline*, trans. David Skvirsky and Vic Schneierson (Moscow: Progress Publishers, 1974), p. 191 (abridged translation from the Russian edition of 1970; a 1965 Russian edition exists).

*Explanations:* ▸ *GHQ*: General Headquarters. ▸ *Velikiye Luki*: a city half way between Moscow and the Baltic Sea.

*Remark:* From the offensive to the defensive in an aggressive war.

### 349 TELEGRAM

As men and women have died in American wars since then—in Korea, Vietnam, and the Persian Gulf—memories of the scope of World War II tend to dim, but it was, by far, the Gargantua of all wars ever fought by the United States. We had 16 million men and women in our armed forces from 1941 to 1946. U.S. casualties were the worst this country has experienced. Battle deaths were nearly 300,000. Almost 700,000 military personnel were wounded. In a million American homes, mothers, fathers, wives, and young brothers and sisters read telegrams from Washington that broke their hearts.

Tedd Thomey (b. 1920), American writer and columnist, writing, in his 1996 book *Immortal Images*, on American casualties in World War II.

*Source:* Tedd Thomey, *Immortal Images: A Personal History of Two Photographers and the Flag Raising on Iwo Jima* (Annapolis, Maryland: Naval Institute Press, 1996), pp. xi-xii (reference to footnote omitted).

*Explanations:* ▸ *Gargantua*: a voracious giant in the work *Gargantua*, written by the French author François Rabelais (ca. 1495-1553) and first published in 1535. ▸ *Korea*: the reference is to the Korean War (1950-1953). ▸ *Persian Gulf*: the Persian Gulf War or the Gulf War (1990-1991) is being referred to. ▸ *Vietnam*: the reference is to the Vietnam War (1955-1975).

*Remark:* Wars break hearts.

### 350 TELEVISION

I stared edgily at two freshly dug graves ten meters down one of the burial rows. From past experience I knew they would be the safest places to crouch if the shelling began in earnest. That was always a distinct possibility since the Serb forces in the hills surrounding the city had made something of a specialty of firing on mourners as they buried their dead.

.... Until the cease-fire in February 1994, every part of Sarajevo was dangerous, and almost no place out of reach either of mortar or artillery fire, or of the ubiquitous snipers. At least shelling is relatively impersonal. Gunners aim at a neighborhood or, often, at a particular building. But what is especially frightening and degrading about being under sniper fire is that the sniper is picking and choosing from among the people who pass through the cross hairs of his gunsights. He is saying to himself, "I think I will shoot the girl in the red parka." Or he is saying, "I think I will let the tall man cross the road, but try to bring down his friend, the short unshaven guy in the wool coat, when he tries to follow."

.... A European city was being reduced to nothing; Carthage in slow motion, but this time with an audience and a videotaped record. Nothing, not the complex history of the region, nor the errors and crimes of the Bosnians themselves, nor the sometimes justified fears of the Bosnian Serbs, can mitigate the crime that took place. Nothing. Nothing. Nothing.

....

.... There was a "CNN effect," in the broad sense that without CNN, the BBC, and the others showing it all the time, the Bosnian tragedy would have faded from people's minds after the first few months of fighting, even though it was taking place a couple of hundred miles from Italy. And, in a narrower sense, it really was the television cameras and not NATO, let alone the United Nations, that saved Sarajevo after the massacre in the Central Market in early February 1994....

....

What was true was that, because what was happening in Bosnia was genocide, most of the journalists did come to sympathize with the Bosnian cause, in exactly the way one hopes that if representatives of the foreign press had been stationed in the Warsaw ghetto in 1943, they would have sympathized with the Jews....

....

.... In the future, no one will be able to say, as many Germans legitimately said after the Second World War, that he or she did not know what was going on in Bosnia. The United Nations might console itself that the press was biased. In reality, no slaughter was more scrupulously and ably covered.

David Rieff (David Sontag Rieff) (b. 1952), American editor, writer and critic, on Sarajevo, the capital of Bosnia and Herzegovina, in 1994, during the war in that country (1992-1995).

*Source:* David Rieff, *Slaughterhouse: Bosnia and the Failure of the West* (New York: Simon & Schuster, 1995), pp. 215-218, 223.

*Explanations:*  ▶  *BBC:* British Broadcasting Corporation.  ▶  *Carthage:* an ancient city on the north coast of Africa (now a suburb of the city of Tunis).  ▶ *CNN:* Cable News Network, an American company broadcasting news live around the globe, around the clock.  ▶  *Genocide:* certain "acts committed with intent to destroy, in whole or in part, a national, ethnical, racial or religious group, as such." The definition in full is in Article II of the Convention on the Prevention and Punishment of the Crime of Genocide, which was annexed to resolution 260 (III) (Prevention and Punishment of the Crime of Genocide), adopted on December

9, 1948, by the General Assembly of the United Nations, and entered into force on January 12, 1951. For the text of the resolution and convention, see United Nations, *Resolutions, 21 September-12 December 1948* (General Assembly, Official Records: Third Session, Part I (A/810)), p. 174, 174. For the text of the convention, see also United Nations, *Treaty Series*, vol. 78, p. 277). *See also* Genocide (the full text of the definition).  ▸ *NATO:* North Atlantic Treaty Organization, a military defense organization established under the North Atlantic Treaty, which was signed at Washington on April 4, 1949, and entered into force on August 24, 1949.  ▸ *Warsaw ghetto:* the reference is to the Warsaw Ghetto Revolt (the Warsaw Ghetto Uprising) of April 19-May 16, 1943.

*See* Child (*Airlift to Biafra*, on "the first TV war").
*Remark:* A city saved by television cameras.

### 351 TEMPER
One who is slow to anger is better
    than the mighty,
and one whose temper is
    controlled than one who
    captures a city.

The Bible, Proverbs 16:32 (the proverbs of Solomon, king of Israel (ruled ca. 961-922 B.C.)).
*Source: The Holy Bible Containing the Old and New Testaments*, New Revised Standard Version (New York: Oxford University Press, 1989).

### 352 TERRITORY
Civilians shall not be compelled to leave their own territory for reasons connected with the conflict.

Article 17, paragraph 2, of the Protocol Additional to the Geneva Conventions of 12 August 1949, and Relating to the Protection of Victims of Non-International Armed Conflicts (Protocol II), which was adopted at Geneva on June 8, 1977, and entered into force on December 7, 1978.
*Source:* United Nations, *Treaty Series*, vol. 1125, pp. 609, 616.
*Compare with* Book title ("*Who's Living in My House?*", on the war in Bosnia and Herzegovina).

### 353 TERRORISM
*The Security Council,*
    ....
*Reaffirming also* its unequivocal condemnation of the terrorist attacks which took place in New York, Washington, D.C. and Pennsylvania on 11 September 2001, and expressing its determination to prevent all such acts,
*Reaffirming further* that such acts, like any act of international terrorism, constitute a threat to international peace and security,
    ....
2. *Decides also* that all States shall:
    ....

(b) Take the necessary steps to prevent the commission of terrorist acts, including by provision of early warning to other States by exchange of information;

....

3. *Calls upon* all States:

(a) To find ways to intensify and accelerate the exchange of operational information, especially regarding actions or movements of terrorist persons or networks; forged or falsified travel documents; traffic in arms, explosives or sensitive materials; use of communications technologies by terrorist groups; and the threat posed by the possession of weapons of mass destruction by terrorist groups;

....

5. *Declares* that acts, methods, and practices of terrorism are contrary to the purposes and principles of the United Nations and that knowingly financing, planning and inciting terrorist acts are also contrary to the purposes and principles of the United Nations.

From the preamble to, and operative paragraphs 2, 3 and 5 of, United Nations Security Council resolution 1373 (2001) of September 28, 2001, relating to threats to international peace and security caused by terrorist acts.

*Source:* United Nations, *Resolutions and Decisions of the Security Council, 1 January 2001-31 July 2002* (Security Council, Official Records (S/INF/57)), pp. 291, 291-293 (semicolon replaced by period at the end).

*Remark:* Terrorism, "a threat to international peace and security," "contrary to the purposes and principles of the United Nations."

### 354 TERRORISM

The 11 September attacks were assaults on humanity, and humanity must respond to them as one. Every nation and every people have a responsibility to fight against terrorism by ensuring that differences and disputes are resolved through political means, and not through violence.

For the United Nations, it is essential that the global response to terrorism be truly universal and not divisive. North, South, East and West must come together to forge a sense of human solidarity and unified purpose. To defeat terrorism, we need a sustained effort and a broad strategy that unite all nations, and address all aspects of the scourge we face. We are in a moral struggle to fight an evil that is anathema to all faiths. The struggle will be long, for there is much to do. Terrorists must not be given shelter and their financial mechanisms and logistical supports must be destroyed. The international community has at its disposal political, legal, diplomatic and financial means, which it must use in innovative ways to combat terrorism.

....

The victims of the attacks on 11 September were, first and foremost, the innocent civilians who lost their lives. The victims were also their families who now grieve for them. But peace, tolerance, mutual respect, human rights, the rule of law, and the global economy are all threatened by the terrorists' acts. In order to restore trust among peoples and cultures, a concerted international response can make the work of terrorists much harder to accomplish. The unity born out of this tragedy should bring all nations together in defence of the most basic right—the right of all peoples to live in peace and security. This is the challenge before us as we seek to eliminate terrorism in every part of the world.

Kofi Annan (Kofi Atta Annan) (b. 1938), Ghanaian economist and international civil servant, secretary-general of the United Nations (1997-2006), in a November 6, 2001 message, delivered by Vladimir Petrovsky (Vladimir Fyodorovich Petrovsky) (b. 1933), director-general of the United Nations Office in Geneva (1993-2002), to the Warsaw conference of heads of state from central and eastern Europe on combating terrorism.

*Source:* The Internet (2003) (www.un.org; United Nations, Secretary-General, Statements, press release SG/SM/8013 (November 6, 2001) (paragraphs indented)).

*Explanation: 11 September attacks:* terrorist acts on September 11, 2001, in New York, host city of the United Nations, Washington and the state of Pennsylvania.

*Note:* Annan shared the 2001 Nobel Peace Prize with the United Nations.

*Remark:* "Assaults on humanity" necessitate "a concerted international response."

### 355 THOUGHT

I am now convinced, that no great improvements in the lot of mankind are possible, until a great change takes place in the fundamental constitution of their modes of thought.

John Stuart Mill (1806-1873), British philosopher and economist, in his autobiography, published posthumously in 1873.

*Source:* John Stuart Mill, *Autobiography of John Stuart Mill* (1924; reprint, New York: Columbia University Press, 1944), p. 167.

*Note:* In the beginning of the preamble to the Constitution of the United Nations Educational, Scientific and Cultural Organization (UNESCO), which was signed at London on November 16, 1945, and entered into force on November 4, 1946, one may read that "since wars begin in the minds of men, it is in the minds of men that the defences of peace must be constructed." United Nations, *Treaty Series*, vol. 4, pp. 275, 276.

### 356 TIME

Human beings have existed on the earth for at least 300 000 years and there have been weapons for hunting for the past 200 000 of these. On the other hand, wars seem to have existed for only the last 9000 years and thus can be suggested to be cultural phenomena.... Youngsters could learn more about the non-violent solutions to conflict and less about the violent ones. This would also necessitate more research on non-violent conflict resolution and a rewriting of history books. In fact, there is a vast history of non-violent sanctions, that is, pressures that do not kill or threaten physical harm but which, nonetheless, thwart opponents' objectives and cause them to alter their behaviour.... Some 85 major cases have been described.... Yet the conflicts which have been solved through non-violent means are both inadequately researched and made invisible in history. When both a violent and a non-violent action have been used in a conflict, the violent one is the one which is described in history.... In the case of the uprising against the dictatorship of Maximiliano Hernandez Martínez in El Salvador in 1944, the violent action of 2 April was not successful in obtaining the resignation of the dictator whereas the non-violent one of 9 May was. Yet it is 2 April that is celebrated, not 9 May.

Birgit Brock-Utne (b. 1938), Norwegian professor, writing, in a 1988 article, about time, and the timely emphasis on more education about nonviolent resolutions to conflict.

*Source:* Birgit Brock-Utne, "Formal Education as a Force in Shaping Cultural Norms Relating to War and the Environment," in *Cultural Norms, War and the Environment*, ed. Arthur H. Westing (New York: Oxford University Press, 1988), pp. 83, 93.

*Explanations:* ▸ *Hernández Martínez:* Maximiliano Hernández Martínez (1882-1966), Salvadoran general, president of El Salvador (1931-1944). ▸ *9 May:* May 9, 1944, the date of entry into effect of the president's May 8 announcement of resignation, occasioned by the strike begun by a group of medical students on April 24.

*Note:* Further food for thought is to be found in another source, that is, Sue Mansfield, *The Gestalts of War: An Inquiry into Its Origins and Meanings as a Social Institution* (New York: Dial Press, 1982), pp. 20-21, as follows:

Though humans have unquestionably possessed the capacity to kill each other with some ease since, in the early Middle Pleistocene (200,000 years ago), they invented hunting tools such as hand axes and clubs, and though they have possessed the capacity to kill other humans with some safety and ease since, during the later stages of the Upper Pleistocene (about 35,000 years ago), they invented the bow and arrow and stone-tipped throwing spears, there is no clear evidence that they began manufacturing weapons deliberately (i.e., artifacts designed specifically for use against other human beings) as opposed to hunting tools until the Neolithic period (about 13,000 years ago). In other words, hunters have possessed for at least 190,000 years the technical capacity to create shock weapons and for 26,000 years the capacity to create missile weapons of outstanding effectiveness. But though they may sporadically and in anger have used hunting tools to kill one another, apparently the species did not deliberately make weapons in order to wage war during these long, early years of human evolution.

*Remark:* Were the animal hunters of older times wiser than the vote hunters of present times?

### 357 TORTURE

1. Each State Party shall take effective legislative, administrative, judicial or other measures to prevent acts of torture in any territory under its jurisdiction.

2. No exceptional circumstances whatsoever, whether a state of war or a threat of war, internal political instability or any other public emergency, may be invoked as a justification of torture.

3. An order from a superior officer or a public authority may not be invoked as a justification of torture.

Article 2 of the Convention against Torture and Other Cruel, Inhuman or Degrading Treatment or Punishment contained in an annex to resolution 39/46 adopted by the General Assembly of the United Nations on December 10, 1984 (Convention against Torture and Other Cruel, Inhuman or Degrading Treatment or Punishment). The convention entered into force on June 26, 1987.

*Source:* United Nations, *Resolutions and Decisions Adopted by the General Assembly during Its Thirty-ninth Session* (General Assembly, Official Records: Thirty-ninth Session, Supplement No. 51 (A/39/51)), p. 197, 197.

*Note:* For the text of the convention, *see also* United Nations, *Treaty Series*, vol. 1465, pp. 85, 113.

*Remark:* Torture? Under no circumstances.

### 358 TRICK

At this point a new factor emerged. Some shepherds had captured what appeared to be a badly frightened Greek. His name was Sinon....

When asked about the wooden horse, Sinon explained that it had been built to placate Athena. It had been constructed on such a large scale in order to prevent the Trojans from bringing it into their city, for were the horse to be sheltered within the citadel, not only would the city be protected, but the Trojans would have the power to attack the Greeks.

....

With the horse inside the citadel and the Greeks apparently departed, the Trojans rejoiced. They decked their temples with festive greenery, danced, sang and drank and finally, for the first time in years, fell into a deep untroubled sleep.

But, as the night wore on, fate closed its grip on the doomed city. The wooden horse was, in fact, no empty offering to the goddess. The huge hollow belly concealed the very pick of the Greek warriors and Sinon's story was a clever lie devised to deceive the Trojans and to lure them into doing just what they had done.

....

Although the Greeks had burned their camp, they had not gone far. They anchored behind the nearby island of Tenedos and waited there for a signal to return. While the city slept, Sinon released the men hidden within the horse and gave the signal. The rest of the Greeks sailed back to the Trojan shore, advanced unhindered into the citadel and fell upon the unwary citizens. Up until this moment Greek had met Trojan in armed combat. It was a fair fight. Now it simply became a massacre. There was nothing to stop the Greeks; the city lay open before them, defenceless.

Susan Woodford (b. 1938), American art historian, referring, in her book *The Trojan War in Ancient Art*, to the Trojan Horse (the Wooden Horse), brought into Troy, a city in northwestern Asia Minor (now Turkey), where the Trojan War was fought about 1200 B.C.

*Source:* Susan Woodford, *The Trojan War in Ancient Art* (London: Gerald Duckworth & Co., 1993), pp. 105, 107-108.

*Explanations:* ▶ *Athena:* the ancient Greek protectress of cities, goddess of war, handicraft and wisdom. ▶ *Sinon* (flourished ca. 1200 B.C.): a relation of Odysseus (also called Ulysses), the Greek hero who played an important role in the Trojan War and was king of the island of Ithaca, off the western coast of Greece (Greek, Itháki).

*Notes:* ▶ One of the nine Troys, discovered by archaeologists, has been described as follows:

Troy VIIa probably lasted little more than a generation. The crowding together of houses and the special measures to store up food supplies suggest that preparations had been made to withstand a siege. The town was destroyed in a devastating fire, and remnants of human bones found in some houses and streets strengthen the impression that the town was captured, looted, and burnt by enemies. Based on the evidence of imported Mycenaean pottery, the end of Troy VIIa can be dated to between 1260 and 1240 BC. The Cincinnati expedition under Blegen concluded that Troy VIIa was very likely the capital of King Priam described in Homer's *Iliad*, which was destroyed by the Greek armies of Agamemnon.

(*Encyclopædia Britannica Online* (2002), under "Troy")

▸ The archaeological site of Troy is on the World Heritage List.

*Additional explanations:*  ▸ *Agamemnon* (flourished ca. 1200 B.C.): Greek hero, king of the ancient city Mycenae or the city of Argos (both in the Peloponnesian peninsula in southern Greece) and commander in chief of the Greek forces in the Trojan War, brother of Menelaus, king of Sparta (Lacedaemon).  ▸ *Blegen:* Carl William Blegen (1887-1971), American archaeologist.

*See* Woman (A. P. Herbert, on Helen of Troy).

*Remark:* The Trojans, soon to be deceived, "for the first time in years, fell into a deep untroubled sleep."

### 359 TRUCE

The French clergy started the Peace of God which tried to enforce the following program: peaceful clergy were not to be attacked; animals were not to be carried off; peasants, women, children, and peaceful merchants were not to be molested; churches and Church property should not be violated; and all employees of the Church were to be safeguarded.

In order to make the Peace of God more effective, the Truce of God was instituted by the Church. There was to be no fighting from Friday to Monday out of respect to the days of Christ's death and resurrection; certain holy days and seasons were to be observed, as Advent (including Christmas), Epiphany, Lent, Whitsuntide, and certain of the important saints' days. If fighting could be eliminated on all these days, then there would be only a small fraction of the year in which to quarrel. Unfortunately for feudal society, even the Church could not enforce such an idealistic program. But the papacy was indebted to the French kings for their whole-hearted support of these policies.

Fay-Cooper Cole (1881-1961), American anthropologist, and Harris Gaylord Warren (1906-1988), American historian, on peace efforts by the Roman church in feudal times.

*Source:* Fay-Cooper Cole and Harris Gaylord Warren, *An Illustrated Outline History of Mankind*, vol. I (Chicago: Spencer Press, 1955), p. 239.

*See* Truce (United Nations General Assembly resolution (The Olympic Ideal)).

*Remark:* Idealism and optimism is needed in the search for peace, and courage to make mistakes.

### 360 TRUCE

*The General Assembly*,

....

*Recalling also* its resolution 48/11 of 25 October 1993, which, *inter alia*, revived the ancient Greek tradition of *ekecheria* or "Olympic Truce", calling for all hostilities to cease during the Games, thereby mobilizing the youth of the world in the cause of peace,

....

1. *Calls upon* Member States to reaffirm the observance of an Olympic Truce during the Games of the XXVI Olympiad, the Centennial Games, to be held at Atlanta, United States of America, from 19 July to 4 August 1996, and also calls upon them to reaffirm the observance of the Olympic Truce in advance of each Summer and Winter Olympic Games;

2. *Commends* the International Olympic Committee, now in its one-hundred-and-first year, for promoting international understanding and equality among nations and thereby serving the cause of peace and the well-being of humankind by providing assistance for the development of sport and the Olympic Ideal;

....

6. *Decides* to include in the provisional agenda of its fifty-second session the item entitled "Building a peaceful and better world through sport and the Olympic Ideal" and to biennialize this item so that it will be considered in advance of each Summer and Winter Olympic Games.

From the preamble to, and operative paragraphs 1, 2 and 6 of, United Nations General Assembly resolution 50/13 of November 7, 1995 (The Olympic Ideal).

*Source:* United Nations, *Resolutions and Decisions Adopted by the General Assembly during Its Fiftieth Session*, vol. I, *19 September-23 December 1995* (General Assembly, Official Records: Fiftieth Session, Supplement No. 49 (A/50/49)), p. 20, 20.

*See* Olympic Games (the suspension of hostilities during the sacred month in Greece).

*Remark:* Olympic Games, feudal times, Olympic Games.

### 361 TRUTH

[I]n war truth is the first casualty.

Dictum.
*Source:* Jon Silkin, *Out of Battle: The Poetry of the Great War* (Oxford: Oxford University Press, 1978), p. 51 (period added at the end).
*Explanation:* The *Great War:* World War I (1914-1918).

### 362 TYPE

These two kinds of war are: the one in which the object is *the overthrow of our adversary*, whether we wish to destroy him politically or merely to disarm him and thus force him to accept whatever peace we will; and the other in which we want *merely to make some conquests on the frontier of his country*, either to retain them or to avail ourselves of them as useful bargaining points in settling the terms of peace. The two kinds must, no doubt, continue to blend into one another, but the wholly different characters of the two efforts must everywhere prevail, and things which are irreconcilable must be kept in their separate categories.

Karl von Clausewitz (Karl Marie von Clausewitz) (1780-1831), Prussian general and military strategist, in a note, dated July 10, 1827, on his work *On War* (German, *Vom Kriege*), written from 1818 to 1830 and published posthumously in German in 1832.

*Source:* Karl von Clausewitz, *On War*, Modern Library, trans. O. J. Matthijs Jolles (New York: Random House, 1943), p. xxix.

*See* Peacemaker (Buddha's advice on a territorial dispute).

### 363 TYRANT

[H]e is always stirring up some war or other, in order that the people may require a leader.

Socrates (ca. 470-399 B.C.), Greek philosopher, referring to tyrants, according to his disciple, the Greek philosopher Plato (428 or 427-348 or 347 B.C.), in the latter's dialogue *The Republic*, supposedly composed in his first period of literary activity (book VIII, section 567).
*Source:* Plato, *The Dialogues of Plato*, trans. B. Jowett, 2nd ed. rev., vol. III (Oxford: Clarendon Press, 1875), pp. 1, 193, 459.
*Remark:* Peaceful leaders sought, Solomon, Numa, Augustus, etc.

### 364 UNION

"United we stand—divided we fall!"

George Pope Morris (1802-1864), known as General Morris, American journalist and poet, in his poem "The Flag of Our Union," published in sheet music form in 1851.
*Source:* George Pope Morris, *The Deserted Bride, and Other Productions* (New York: Charles Scribner, 1853), p. 41, 41.
*Notes:* ▸ "By *uniting* We stand, by *dividing* We fall" were the words which the American statesman, lawyer and writer John Dickinson (1732-1808) used in "A New Song," published in July 1768 (called "The Liberty Song").
(John Dickinson, *Life and Writings of John Dickinson*, vol. II (Philadelphia: Historical Society of Philadelphia, 1895), pp. 419, 431, 432)
▸ In an address to Philadelphia merchants early the same year Dickinson had ended with the exhortation "United we conquer, divided we die." *Last source*, p. 421.
*Remark:* The nations of the world also?

### 365 UNITED NATIONS

WE THE PEOPLES OF THE UNITED NATIONS
DETERMINED

> to save succeeding generations from the scourge of war, which twice in our lifetime has brought untold sorrow to mankind, and

> to reaffirm faith in fundamental human rights, in the dignity and worth of the human person, in the equal rights of men and women and of nations large and small, and

> to establish conditions under which justice and respect for the obligations arising from treaties and other sources of international law can be maintained, and

> to promote social progress and better standards of life in larger freedom,

AND FOR THESE ENDS

> to practice tolerance and live together in peace with one another as good neighbors, and

> to unite our strength to maintain international peace and security, and

> to ensure, by the acceptance of principles and the institution of methods, that armed force shall not be used, save in the common interest, and

> to employ international machinery for the promotion of the economic and social advancement of all peoples,

HAVE RESOLVED TO COMBINE OUR EFFORTS
TO ACCOMPLISH THESE AIMS.

Accordingly, our respective Governments, through representatives assembled in the city of San Francisco, who have exhibited their full powers found to be in good and due form, have agreed to the present Charter of the United Nations and do hereby establish an international organization to be known as the United Nations.

The preamble to the Charter of the United Nations, which was signed at San Francisco, United States, on June 26, 1945, and entered into force on October 24, 1945.

*Source:* United States, Department of State, *Treaty Series*, vol. 993, *Charter of the United Nations and Statute of the International Court of Justice*, pp. 3, 5 (a photocopy of a certified copy).

*Remark:* Is it too often overlooked that "armed force shall not be used, save in the common interest"?

### 366 UNITED NATIONS

CHAPTER I

PURPOSES AND PRINCIPLES

*Article 1*

The Purposes of the United Nations are:

1. To maintain international peace and security, and to that end: to take effective collective measures for the prevention and removal of threats to the peace, and for the suppression of acts of aggression or other breaches of the peace, and to bring about by peaceful means, and in conformity with the principles of justice and international law, adjustment or settlement of international disputes or situations which might lead to a breach of the peace;

2. To develop friendly relations among nations based on respect for the principle of equal rights and self-determination of peoples, and to take other appropriate measures to strengthen universal peace;

3. To achieve international cooperation in solving international problems of an economic, social, cultural, or humanitarian character, and in promoting and encouraging respect for human rights and for fundamental freedoms for all without distinction as to race, sex, language, or religion; and

4. To be a center for harmonizing the actions of nations in the attainment of these common ends.

*Article 2*

The Organization and its Members, in pursuit of the Purposes stated in Article 1, shall act in accordance with the following Principles.

....

3. All Members shall settle their international disputes by peaceful means in such a manner that international peace and security, and justice, are not endangered.

4. All Members shall refrain in their international relations from the threat or use of force against the territorial integrity or political independence of any state, or in any other manner inconsistent with the Purposes of the United Nations.

Article 1 (purposes) and part of Article 2 (principles) of the Charter of the United Nations, which was signed at San Francisco, United States, on June 26, 1945, and entered into force on October 24, 1945.

*Source:* United States, Department of State, *Treaty Series*, vol. 993, *Charter of the United Nations and Statute of the International Court of Justice*, pp. 3, 7 (a photocopy of a certified copy).

*Remark:* Remarkable words, "effective collective measures," "justice," "international law," "settlement," "friendly relations," "equal rights," "self-determination," "cooperation," "human rights" and "center for harmonizing the actions of nations."

### 367 UNITED NATIONS

We meet in an hour of grief and challenge. Dag Hammarskjold is dead. But the United Nations lives. His tragedy is deep in our hearts, but the task for which he died is at the top of our agenda. A noble servant of peace is gone. But the quest for peace lies before us.

The problem is not the death of one man—the problem is the life of this organization. It will either grow to meet the challenges of our age, or it will be gone with the wind, without influence, without force, without respect. Were we to let it die, to enfeeble its vigor, to cripple its powers, we would condemn our future.

For in the development of this organization rests the only true alternative to war—and war appeals no longer as a rational alternative. Unconditional war can no longer lead to unconditional victory. It can no longer serve to settle disputes. It can no longer concern the great powers alone. For a nuclear disaster, spread by wind and water and fear, could well engulf the great and the small, the rich and the poor, the committed and the uncommitted alike. Mankind must put an end to war—or war will put an end to mankind.

John F. Kennedy (John Fitzgerald Kennedy) (1917-1963), president of the United States (1961-1963), in his September 25, 1961 address before the General Assembly of the United Nations.

*Source:* John F. Kennedy, *Public Papers of the Presidents of the United States: John F. Kennedy ... 1961* (Washington: United States Government Printing Office, 1962), pp. 618, 618-619.

*Explanation: Hammarskjold:* Dag Hammarskjöld (Dag Hjalmar Agne Carl Hammarskjöld) (1905-1961), Swedish economist and statesman, secretary-general of the United Nations (1953-1961), who was posthumously awarded the 1961 Nobel Peace Prize.

*Remark:* "A noble servant of peace is gone."... "Mankind must put an end to war—or war will put an end to mankind."

### 368 UNITED NATIONS

Since the eighth World Health Assembly, held in Mexico City in 1955, WHO has been engaged in a world-wide campaign to root out malaria, a disease to which more than 1,400 million people were exposed. By the end of 1965, over 55 per cent of the population living in the world's original malarious areas had been freed from the threat of the disease.

The United Nations, on the World Health Organization's (WHO's) campaign against malaria by the end of 1965.

*Source:* United Nations, Office of Public Information, *Everyman's United Nations: A Complete Handbook of the Activities and Evolution of the United Nations during Its First Twenty Years, 1945-1965*, 8th ed. (New York: United Nations, 1968), p. 511.

*Remark:* Just one example of the achievements of the United Nations.

### 369 UNITED NATIONS

The entire UN system could run for nearly two centuries on only one year's world military spending.

Norman Myers (b. 1934), English environmental scientist, conservationist, writer and photographer, in the 1984 book *Gaia*.

*Source:* Norman Myers, Uma Ram Nath and Melvin Westlake, *Gaia: An Atlas of Planet Management*, Norman Myers, gen. ed. (Garden City, New York: Anchor Press/Doubleday & Company, 1984), p. 246.

*Remark:* Why military service? Why not peace service?

### 370 UNITED NATIONS

*The Security Council,*

....

2. *Authorizes* Member States co-operating with the Government of Kuwait, unless Iraq on or before 15 January 1991 fully implements ... the above-mentioned resolutions, to use all necessary means to uphold and implement resolution 660 (1990) and all subsequent relevant resolutions and to restore international peace and security in the area.

From the preamble to and operative paragraph 2 of United Nations Security Council resolution 678 (1990) of November 29, 1990, on Iraq's invasion of Kuwait on August 2, 1990, and the ensuing Persian Gulf War or the Gulf War (1990-1991).

*Source:* United Nations, *Resolutions and Decisions of the Security Council, 1990* (Security Council, Official Records: Forty-fifth Year (S/INF/46)), pp. 27, 27-28 (semicolon replaced by period at the end).

*Note:* In the *Observer*, an English Sunday newspaper, referring, on July 30, 2000, to a Kuwaiti by the name of Muhammad ben Naji, one could read what the resolution was intended to reverse:

'Every day for seven months I was expecting to die,' he says. 'They would come into our houses and search them. If they found a typewriter or a camera, everyone would be killed. Every house has bad memories of that time.'
(From the Internet (2001), under "The day Kuwait wants to forget")

### 371 UNITED NATIONS

Fifty years ago the United Nations was born out of the sufferings caused by the Second World War. The determination, enshrined in the Charter of the United Nations, "to save succeeding generations from the scourge of war" is as vital today as it was fifty years ago....

The United Nations has been tested by conflict, humanitarian crisis and turbulent change, yet it has survived and played an important role in preventing another global conflict and has achieved much for people all over the world....

....

On the occasion of the fiftieth anniversary of the United Nations, we, the Member States and observers of the United Nations, representing the peoples of the world:

....

— Will give to the twenty-first century a United Nations equipped, financed and structured to serve effectively the peoples in whose name it was established.

....

15. In order to carry out its work effectively, the United Nations must have adequate resources. Member States must meet, in full and on time, their obligation to bear the expenses of the Organization, as apportioned by the General Assembly.

From the preamble to and part of operative paragraph 15 of the Declaration on the Occasion of the Fiftieth Anniversary of the United Nations contained in United Nations General Assembly resolution 50/6 of October 24, 1995 (Declaration on the Occasion of the Fiftieth Anniversary of the United Nations).
*Source*: United Nations, *Resolutions and Decisions Adopted by the General Assembly during Its Fiftieth Session*, vol. I, *19 September-23 December 1995* (General Assembly, Official Records: Fiftieth Session, Supplement No. 49 (A/50/49)), pp. 13, 15.
*Remark*: Note that the words "played an important role in preventing another global conflict" undoubtedly refer to the work of the United Nations—and especially U Thant (1909-1974), educator and civil servant from Burma (now Myanmar), secretary-general of the United Nations (1962-1971)—to solve the October 1962 Cuban missile crisis with two nuclear superpowers involved, the Soviet Union and the United States.

### 372 VALUE

Work for the sake of the children is better than pilgrimage and the holy war.

Moroccan wisdom.
*Source*: Edward Westermarck and Shereef 'Abd-es-Salam el-Baqqali, *Wit and Wisdom in Morocco: A Study of Native Proverbs* (1930; reprint, London: George Routledge & Sons, 1980), p. 91.
*See* Music (Pablo Casals: For me the life of a single child is worth more than all my music;...).

### 373 VICTIM

We are aware that in order to eradicate nuclear illusions and impart hatred of war to the peoples, one should be based, like in our medical practice, on solid scientific data. I do not wish to dwell on the results of our studies confirmed by the authoritative expert group of the World Health Organization. Physicians have demonstrated to the whole world that not only would nuclear war spell the end of civilisation, it would also prejudice the existence of life on Earth. My conscience, and I am sure the same applies to many of my colleagues in IPPNW, was staggered primarily by the total number of victims in nuclear war. The human mind finds it difficult to comprehend the figure of 2,000 million victims. As they say, one death is death, but a million deaths are statistics. For us, physicians, life is the aim of our work and each death is a tragedy.

Yevgeny Chazov (Yevgeny Ivanovich Chazov) (b. 1929), Soviet physician (cardiologist) and politician, deputy-minister of public health (1967-1987), in a Nobel lecture, "Tragedy and Triumph of Reason," given in Oslo on December 11, 1985, on behalf of the recipient of the 1985 Nobel Peace Prize, International Physicians for the Prevention of Nuclear War (IPPNW), a movement Chazov helped found in 1980.

*Source:* Tore Frängsmyr, ed.-in-charge, Irwin Adams, ed., *Nobel Lectures Including Presentation and Acceptance Speeches and Laureates' Biographies: Peace, 1981-1990* (Singapore: World Scientific Publishing Co., for the Nobel Foundation, 1997), pp. 123, 140, 143.

*Note:* Following the Nobel lectures, Dr. Dagmar Sørbøe (Dagmar Karin Sørbøe) (b. 1945), Norwegian physician, "led the assembled physicians in reciting the amended oath of Hippocrates" a part of which reads as follows:

As a physician, I recognise that the only effective medical response to nuclear war is prevention. I believe that medical preparations for nuclear war increase its likelihood by strengthening the illusions of protection, survival, and recovery. Such measures promote the acceptability of a catastrophe which I will not accept. As a matter of individual conscience, I will refuse to participate in any medical preparations for nuclear war. I affirm my duty and willingness to provide care in all medical emergencies to the best of my ability. I commit myself to applying my medical knowledge and skills for the preservation of human life.

As a physician of the twentieth century, I recognise that nuclear weapons have presented my profession with a challenge of unprecedented proportions, and that a nuclear war would be the final epidemic for humankind. I will do all in my power to work for the prevention of nuclear war.

(*Same source*, p. 153)

*Explanation: Hippocrates:* Hippocrates (ca. 460-ca. 377 B.C.), Greek physician, known as "the Father of Medicine" and author of the medical profession's Hippocratic Oath.

*Remark:* In 1985, estimated two thousand million victims.

### 374 VICTIM

There may be times when we are powerless to prevent injustice, but there must never be a time when we fail to protest. The Talmud tells us that by saving a single human being, man can save the world. We may be powerless to open all the jails and free all the prisoners, but by declaring our solidarity with one prisoner, we indict all jailers. None of us is in a position to eliminate war, but it is our obligation to denounce it and expose it in all its hideousness. War leaves no victors, only victims.

Elie Wiesel (Eliezer Wiesel) (b. 1928), Romanian-born American novelist and professor, recipient of the 1986 Nobel Peace Prize, in his Nobel lecture, "Hope, Despair and Memory," given in Oslo on December 11, 1986.

*Source:* Tore Frängsmyr, ed.-in-charge, Irwin Adams, ed., *Nobel Lectures Including Presentation and Acceptance Speeches and Laureates' Biographies: Peace, 1981-1990* (Singapore: World Scientific Publishing Co., for the Nobel Foundation, 1997), pp. 157, 174, 178.

*Explanations:* ▶ *The Talmud:* "('Study'; an abbreviation of *Talmud Torah,* 'Study of the *Torah*'), collection of Jewish books, containing traditions, laws, rules, and institutions, by which, in addition to the Heb. Bible, the conduct of Jewry is regulated." *Everyman's Encyclopaedia* (1958), under "Talmud, The." ▶ *Torah:* the law of Moses, the Jewish lawgiver and prophet (thirteenth century B.C.), embodied in the Pentateuch (the first five books of the Bible).

*Note:* The Palestinian Talmud was completed late in the fourth century, the Babylonian Talmud about 499.

*See* Nuclear weapon (Fay-Cooper Cole and Harris Gaylord Warren, on cobalt bombs).

*Remark:* "War leaves no victors, only victims."

### 375 VICTORY
1. Now arms, however beautiful, are instruments of evil omen, hateful, it may be said, to all creatures. Therefore they who have the Tâo do not like to employ them.

2. The superior man.... uses them only on the compulsion of necessity. Calm and repose are what he prizes; victory (by force of arms) is to him undesirable. To consider this desirable would be to delight in the slaughter of men; and he who delights in the slaughter of men cannot get his will in the kingdom.

3. .... He who has killed multitudes of men should weep for them with the bitterest grief; and the victor in battle has his place (rightly) according to those rites [the rites of mourning].

Lao-tzu or Lao-tze ("Master Lao") (Lao Tan) [Laozi] (from 604 to at least 517 B.C.), Chinese philosopher, founder of the mystical philosophy called Taoism, in his work *The Way and Its Power* (Chinese, *Tao-te Ching*) (part (book) I, chapter 31, paragraphs 1-3).

*Source:* James Legge, trans., *The Sacred Books of China: The Texts of Tâoism,* Sacred Books of the East, vol. XXXIX (London: Oxford University Press (Humphrey Milford), 1891), pp. 45, 73-74 (text within brackets added).

*Explanation: Tâo:* the way.

*Note:* Legge calls the work *Tâo Teh King.*

*See* Weapon (*Kalevala*).

### 376 VICTORY
Pyrrhus replied to one that gave him joy of his victory that one other such would utterly undo him. For he had lost a great part of the forces he brought with him, and

almost all his particular friends and principal commanders; there were no others there to make recruits, and he found the confederates in Italy backward. On the other hand, as from a fountain continually flowing out of the city, the Roman camp was quickly and plentifully filled up with fresh men, not at all abating in courage for the losses they sustained, but even from their very anger gaining new force and resolution to go on with the war.

Plutarch (ca. 46-120), Greek biographer, referring, in his work *Parallel Lives* (the biography of Pyrrhus), to the very costly victory in 279 B.C. ("Pyrrhic victory") of Pyrrhus (ca. 318-272 B.C.), king of Epirus in ancient Greece, now northwestern Greece and southern Albania (ruled 307-303 and 297-272 B.C.), over Roman forces near the town of Asculum (now Ascoli di Satriano), southern Italy. The Roman forces were under the command of the consuls Gaius Fabricius (surnamed Luscinus) (d. 250? B.C.) and Quintus Aemilius (flourished ca. 280 B.C.).
*Source:* Plutarch, *Plutarch's Lives: The "Dryden Plutarch,"* rev. Arthur Hugh Clough, Everyman's Library, vol. II (1910; reprint, London: J. M. Dent & Sons; New York: E. P. Dutton & Co., 1914), pp. 41, 61.
*Note:* In 280 B.C. Pyrrhus had already gained a costly victory over the Roman army, under the consul Publius Valerius Laevinus, at the city of Heraclea (near the Gulf of Taranto, southern Italy). There he lost "the flower of his men, and amongst them his particular friends as well as officers whom he most trusted and made use of." *Same source*, pp. 41, 57.
*Remark:* Are more victories than we think "Pyrrhic victories"?

### 377 VICTORY
Thence he passed to Asia, where he heard that Domitius was beaten by Pharnaces, son of Mithridates, and had fled out of Pontus with a handful of men; and that Pharnaces pursued the victory so eagerly, that though he was already master of Bithynia and Cappadocia, he had a further design of attempting the Lesser Armenia, and was inviting all the kings and tetrarchs there to rise. Caesar immediately marched against him with three legions, fought him near Zela, drove him out of Pontus, and totally defeated his army. When he gave Amantius, a friend of his at Rome, an account of this action, to express the promptness and rapidity of it he used three words, I came, saw, and conquered, which in Latin, having all the same cadence, carry with them a very suitable air of brevity.

Plutarch (ca. 46-120), Greek biographer, describing, in his work *Parallel Lives* (the biography of Caesar), how Julius Caesar (Gaius Julius Caesar) (100-44 B.C.), Roman general and statesman, came to use the words "Veni, vidi, vici" ("I came, I saw, I conquered"). The occasion was his victory in 47 B.C., at Zela in Asia Minor (now Zile in central northern Turkey), over Pharnaces II (ca. 97-47 B.C.), king of Bosporus or Cimmerian Bosporus (63-47 B.C.). Bosporus was a state on the Kerch Strait that connects the Black Sea and the Sea of Azov (now in Ukraine).
*Source:* Plutarch, *Plutarch's Lives: The "Dryden Plutarch,"* rev. Arthur Hugh Clough, Everyman's Library, vol. II (1910; reprint, London: J. M. Dent & Sons; New York: E. P. Dutton & Co., 1914), pp. 530, 567.
*Explanations:* ▸ *Bithynia:* an ancient region of northwestern Asia Minor (now northwestern Turkey). ▸ *Cappadocia:* an ancient region of eastern Asia Minor

(now southeastern Turkey). ▸ *Domitius:* Lucius Domitius Ahenobarbus, Roman general and politician, consul in 54 B.C., killed in 48 B.C. ▸ *Mithridates:* Mithradates VI Eupator (Mithradates the Great) (ca. 132-63 B.C.), king of Pontus (120-63 B.C.), Asia Minor (now northeastern Turkey).
*Remark:* Not everybody conquers.

### 378 VICTORY
He knows to win that knows how to prevent.

English proverb.
*Source:* Selwyn Gurney Champion, *War Proverbs and Maxims, East and West* (London: Arthur Probsthain, 1945), p. 61 (the word "win" in bold letters in source).

### 379 VICTORY
Peace hath her victories
No less renowned than War.

John Milton (1608-1674), English poet, in sonnet XVI, "To the Lord General Cromwell," written in 1652.
*Source:* [John] Milton, *Milton's Sonnets*, ed. A. W. Verity, Pitt Press (1895; reprint, with additions, Cambridge: Cambridge University Press, 1916), p. 19, 19 (colon replaced by period at the end).
*Explanation: Cromwell:* Oliver Cromwell (1599-1658), English soldier and statesman, lord protector of the Commonwealth of England, Scotland and Ireland (1653-1658).
*Remark:* Wallenberg in Budapest.

### 380 VICTORY
All hearts resolved on victory or death.

End of the first verse of the French national anthem, known as "The Marseillaise" (French, "La Marseillaise"), written and composed by Claude-Joseph Rouget de Lisle (1760-1836), French officer, in Strasbourg, France, on April 24, 1792. Its original name was "Chant de guerre de l'armée du Rhin" ("War Song of the Army of the Rhine"). The song was adopted as national anthem on July 15, 1795.
*Source:* W. L. Reed and M. J. Bristow, eds., *National Anthems of the World*, 6th ed. (1985; reprint, Poole, Dorset, England: Blandford Press, 1986), pp. 173, 175 (translator of the verse: Percy Bysshe Shelley).

### 381 VICTORY
Then conquer we must, for our cause it is just.

From the national anthem of the United States since 1931, "The Star-Spangled Banner," lyrics by Francis Scott Key (1779-1843), American lawyer, written while witnessing the British bombardment of Fort McHenry, Baltimore, Maryland, United States, from the deck of the ship *Surprise* from September 13 to 14, 1814, during the War of 1812-1814 (the War of 1812, which actually ended in 1815).

*Source:* W. L. Reed and M. J. Bristow, eds., *National Anthems of the World*, 6th ed. (1985; reprint, Poole, Dorset, England: Blandford Press, 1986), pp. 451, 453 (comma replaced by period at the end).

### 382 VICTORY

On land and sea and in the air, American men and women have given their lives so that this day of ultimate victory might come and assure the survival of a civilized world. No victory can make good their loss.

Harry S. Truman (1884-1972), president of the United States (1945-1953), in a radio address from the White House on the evening of September 1, 1945, Washington time, after the Japanese signing of World War II terms of unconditional surrender aboard the American battleship *Missouri* in Tokyo Harbor on September 2, 1945, Tokyo time.
*Source:* Harry S. Truman, *Public Papers of the Presidents of the United States: Harry S. Truman ... 1945* (Washington: United States Government Printing Office, 1961), pp. 254, 255.
*Remark:* "No victory can make good their loss."

### 383 VICTORY

To summarize, it is not the case that the winner is the party who suffers less. Often the winner suffers more than the loser in terms of battle deaths. It is possible that this paradox is explained by the cost-tolerance factor.

What about our measure of wealth as an index of strength, the ability to harm? How great was the tendency for the wealthier or stronger party to win? If strength explains most of the variation in winning and losing, then the factor of cost-tolerance cannot be very important.

Our principal finding is that 70 percent ... of the wars were won by the wealthier party. There is an impressively strong relationship between wealth and victory. Only about 1 war in 5 was won by the party with less wealth. And ... there was a small tendency for wealth to be more important in large wars than small ones.

If strength predicts the outcome of 4/5 of all international wars, and is more important in large, costly wars than in small ones, then there is only a small range within which cost-tolerance factors could influence victory and defeat.

Steven Rosen (Steven Jack Rosen) (b. 1942), [American] political scientist, referring to international wars from 1815 to 1945 in a 1972 article on strength and cost-tolerance in wars.
*Source:* Steven Rosen, "War Power and the Willingness to Suffer," in *Peace, War, and Numbers*, ed. Bruce M. Russett (Beverly Hills, California: Sage Publications, 1972), pp. 167, 177, cf. p. 174.

### 384 VIKING

How he actually died is an academic question now. The fact of his fall signalled the end of the Battle of Hastings, the rout of the English.

And what an irony there is in that. Where the Vikings from the homelands had failed, the émigré descendants of the Vikings had succeeded. The Viking threat to England had been finally destroyed at Stamford Bridge by the grandson of a Viking—Harold Godwinsson. But it had been a Pyrrhic victory, which left England at the mercy of those other Viking descendants, the Northmen of Normandy, their traditional combative energy honed and disciplined by 150 years of feudal living in France. It was they who notched up the last—and the most lasting—achievement of the Viking Age: the military conquest and permanent occupation of a major European nation.

At 6 p.m. on Saturday 14 October 1066 the world changed. The Viking Age was effectively over.

Magnus Magnusson (1929-2007), Icelandic journalist, broadcaster and writer, resident of Scotland, writing, in his 1980 book on the Vikings, on the 1066 Battle of Hastings, southeastern England, and the death of Harold II Godwinsson (ca. 1022-1066), king of the English from January 6 to October 14, 1066, fighting the Normans under William (1027 or 1028-1087), duke of Normandy, France, who became king of England, William I the Conqueror (1066-1087).

*Source:* Magnus Magnusson, *Vikings!* (London: Bodley Head and British Broadcasting Corporation, 1980), pp. 312-313.

*Explanation: Stamford Bridge:* a village near the town of York in northeastern England where Harold II Godwinsson, on September 25, 1066, defeated his brother Tostig (Tosti) (d. 1066), earl of Northumbria, northeastern England, and his ally, Harald III Hardruler (Harald the Tyrant) (1015-1066), king of Norway (1045-1066).

*Remark:* Successful expeditions, from Normandy to England in 1066, from England to Normandy in 1944.

### 385 VIOLENCE

So in the past, or in human history, unfortunately, when we find some disagreement, some conflict, then we use force. In human history, warfare and violence have become part of human history....

....

.... destruction of your neighbor is destruction of yourself.

....

Translator: Using force under such circumstances, and finding some temporary solutions, is nothing but gaining some kind of emotional satisfaction rather than really solving the problem.

DL [Dalai Lama]: That is foolish. That's unwise, not human way. So, therefore, judging from that kind of situation, the concept of warfare, the concept of violence is out of date. It is quite clear. So, at the individual level, or family level, or national level, or global level, now we must find another effective human way to face the problem. That, I think, is dialogue.

Tenzin Gyatso (b. 1935), the Fourteenth Dalai Lama of Tibet, Tibetan Buddhist, spiritual and political leader of the Tibetan people, in exile since the Tibetan people's revolt in 1959, recipient of the 1989 Nobel Peace Prize, in his address at the National Mall in Washington on July 2, 2000.

*Source:* The Internet (2004), under "Address (Transcript) by His Holiness the Dalai Lama on the National Mall, Washington, D.C., July 2, 2000," pp. 7-8 (paragraphs indented).

*Note:* In other sources, on different occasions, his words may be somewhat different, such as:

The concept of violence is out of date. The destruction of your neighborhood is actually the destruction of yourself.

(Dalai Lama, *Words of Wisdom: Quotes from His Holiness the Dalai Lama*, comp. Margaret Gee (Kansas City: Andrews McMeel Publishing, 2001), p. 82 (no timing))

*See* Resistance (Lech Walesa: [E]ven the most complex situations can be solved by a dialogue and not by force.).

*Remark:* Another way, dialogue.

### 386 VIRTUE

The virtuous are honoured wherever they go, but a king is great only in his country.

Tibetan wisdom.

*Source:* J. Gergan, *A Thousand Tibetan Proverbs and Wise Sayings* (Kathmandu: Tiwari's Pilgrims Book House, 1991 reprint), p. 118 (translator: Walter Asboe).

### 387 WALK

We were taking our four steps to Moscow, Paris, London and Washington. In all the countries, politicians, soldiers and people in responsible jobs argued, 'We're all right, we are peaceful. The other party is the trouble-maker.' The Russians said, 'Go to the West'; the westerners said, 'Go to the communists'; the Pakistanis said, 'Go and sort out your own country.' Always the other, the other ...

We met no one on the walk who didn't want peace, but no one seemed to know how to achieve it. Politicians were as powerless as the common people....

....

IN WASHINGTON we had wanted to make an appeal to President Kennedy. However, when we eventually reached there on 9th January 1964, after walking eight thousand miles, President Kennedy had been killed, the victim of an assassin's bullet. It was to the cemetery and not to the White House that we went to look for him. And it was at his tomb, where the young President had ended his journey, that our walk also came to an end—a long walk, from Gandhi's grave to Kennedy's grave.

Satish Kumar (b. 1936), Indian educator, environmentalist and pacifist, writing, in his 1992 book *No Destination*, about his eight-thousand-mile (thirteen-thousand-kilometer) peace pilgrimage from India to America, from 1962 to 1964, protesting with his friend, Prabhakar Menon, against nuclear weapons in the capital cities of the nuclear powers and elsewhere.

*Source:* Satish Kumar, *No Destination*, Resurgence Book (Devon, England: Green Books, 1992), pp. 111, 113.

*Explanations:* ▶ *Gandhi:* Mahatma Gandhi (Mohandas Karamchand Gandhi) (1869-1948), Indian political and religious leader, "architect of India's freedom through a nonviolent revolution," assassinated on January 30, 1948. ▶ *Kennedy:* John F. Kennedy (John Fitzgerald Kennedy) (1917-1963), president of the United States (1961-1963), assassinated on November 22, 1963. ▶ *Mahatma:* "great soul."

*See* March (Mao Tse-tung [Mao Zedong]).

*Remark:* "The other party is the trouble-maker."

### 388 WALL

There had been earlier ramparts and sectional walls along the long northern frontier of China, but credit must be given to the First Emperor for building the mighty wall as it is known today. About 214 B.C. he united into one mighty rampart the sections that then existed in order to keep out the northern hordes who from time immemorial had regarded China as choice prey. The Great Wall winds in and out, over mountain and stream, for about 1,500 miles. It starts at the sea opposite Peiping at Shan-hai-kuan and travels inland almost to the Gobi Desert. It is faced with either brick or granite and is filled with earth. The wall has an average height of twenty feet and the roadway which runs on top is fifteen feet wide. As a means of additional protection there are fortified towers at every hundred yards.

Fay-Cooper Cole (1881-1961), American anthropologist, and Harris Gaylord Warren (1906-1988), American historian, on the Great Wall of China, mostly completed about 214 B.C.

*Source:* Fay-Cooper Cole and Harris Gaylord Warren, *An Illustrated Outline History of Mankind*, vol. I (Chicago: Spencer Press, 1955), p. 174.

*Explanations:* ▶ *The First Emperor:* Shih-huang-ti [Shi Huangdi] ("First Sovereign Emperor") (259-210 B.C.), first emperor of China (221-210 B.C.), previously King Cheng of the state Ch'in in northwestern China (246-221 B.C.). ▶ *The Gobi Desert:* one of the largest deserts in the world, in Mongolia and China. ▶ *Peiping:* Peking [Beijing].

*Note:* The Great Wall is on the World Heritage List.

*See* Defense (Lu Hsun).

### 389 WARRIOR

[N]obody is more pacific than I am.

Napoleon I (Napoleon Bonaparte) (1769-1821), emperor of France (1804-1814, 1815), addressing Jean-Jacques Régis de Cambacérès (1753-1824), French statesman and legal expert, on June 15, 1813.

*Source:* Napoleon, *The Corsican: A Diary of Napoleon's Life in His Own Words*, comp. R. M. Johnston [Robert Matteson Johnston] (London: Macmillan and Co., 1910), p. 388.

*Remark:* Therefore he visited Moscow.

### 390 WEAPON

[T]he sword is fine-looking but the sword is bad-mannered:
every day it killed a man, preferably two men.

From *Kalevala*, the great epic of Finland, which was compiled by the Finnish philologist Elias Lönnrot (1802-1884) from old national songs, folklore and legends and first published in 1835 (enlarged in 1849) (poem (Finnish, runo) 20 (the old *Kalevala*), on Ilmarinen, the craftsman).

*Source:* Elias Lönnrot, *The Old Kalevala and Certain Antecedents*, trans. Francis Peabody Magoun, Jr. (Cambridge, Massachusetts: Harvard University Press, 1969), pp. 117, 117-118.

*Explanation: Kalevala:* a poetical name for Finland, "land of heroes."

*Remark:* Bad-mannered weapons.

**391 WIDOW**

Well, the war is done,
Now I'm the only one.
I'm the husband, I'm the cow.
I'm the wife and I'm the plow.

A song by an unknown poet, "Well, the war is done," which was sung by soldiers' widows in Russian villages in World War II.

*Source:* Yevgeny Yevtushenko, comp., *Twentieth-Century Russian Poetry*, ed. Albert C. Todd and Max Hayward (with Daniel Weissbort) (London: Fourth Estate, 1993), p. 768 (translator of the poem: Bradley Jordan).

*See* Child (Jay Winter, on World War I orphans: "Six million children were deprived of their fathers by the Great War. How did they mourn and what became of them?").

*Remark:* What do men do unto women?

**392 WIFE**

My man
has gone to war. It's not
just a matter of going, then,
in a few days, a few months,
coming back—
oh, will there never be an end to war?

From an anonymous Chinese poem, "War has taken my husband," dating back to the Chou Dynasty and taken from the *Book of Odes* (*Shih Ching*), a collection of people's poems and songs, probably composed between the ninth and the seventh centuries B.C.

*Source:* Rewi Alley, trans., *Peace through the Ages: Translations from the Poets of China* (Peking [Beijing]: Rewi Alley, 1954), p. 4, 4.

*Explanation: The Chou dynasty:* about 1122-256 or 255 B.C., according to *Encyclopædia Britannica* (1964), under "China," 1066-403 B.C., according to Alley, pp. v, vii, 1.

*Remark:* Not yet an end to war, almost three thousand years later.

**393 WILL**

God knows that I wanted peace.

Adolf Hitler (1889-1945), chancellor of the Third Reich of Nazi Germany (1933-1945), concentrating on German conquests in Europe in his speech to the German parliament (German, Reichstag) in Berlin, on May 4, 1941.

*Source:* Lewis Copeland, ed., *The World's Great Speeches*, 2nd rev. ed. (New York: Dover Publications, 1958), pp. 474, 484, 487.

*Remark:* If the source is reliable, God was in his vocabulary, and peace too.

**394 WOMAN**

The story of Paris and Helen of Troy is perhaps the oldest love-story we all know. It has as much title to be called a "true" story as many of the accepted anecdotes of English history. Helen ran away with Paris about the 12th century B.C., but she is as real as Cleopatra or Queen Anne, and much more interesting.

....

.... Other young wives have run away with fascinating young men: but Helen is the only woman in history who was important and charming enough to cause a ten years' war by that proceeding. Perhaps, as Agamemnon hints, a beautiful woman is as good a reason for having a war as any other: but the ten years need some explaining away. We can understand the Greeks going after Helen; but what is more remarkable is the Trojans' refusal to give her up, though they disliked Paris, we are told, and probably did not much enjoy the last few years of the siege. She must have had charm.

....

If you imagine all the Kings of ancient Britain collecting their fleets, sailing across the North Sea and besieging Stockholm for ten years, with very hot weather in the summer and very cold weather in the winter, you will form some idea of Helen's charm.

....

AGAMEMNON (reverent).
Is that the face that launched a thousand ships,
The fatal grace, the killing eyes and lips?
No wonder, Helen, the fleets put out to sea,
No wonder nations fight and die for thee!
Beauty is magical and knows no laws,
And men have fought for many a meaner cause.
For who wants life if Beauty liveth not?
What worth has gold where Beauty can't be got?
No wonder, Helen, the fleets put out to sea,
No wonder nations fight and die for thee.

A. P. Herbert (Alan Patrick Herbert) (1890-1971), English novelist, poet and politician, in an introduction to the comic opera *Helen*, presented in London in 1932, and Agamemnon's words from act III, scene I. The libretto was based upon the comic opera *La Belle Hélène* of 1864 by Henri Meilhac (1831-1897), French dramatist, and Ludovic Halévy (1834-1908), French dramatist, librettist and novelist (music by the French composer Jacques Offenbach (1819-1880)).

*Source:* A. P. Herbert, *Helen: A Comic Opera in Three Acts Based Upon "La Belle Hélène" by Henri Meilhac and Ludovic Halévy* (London: Chappell & Co., 1932), pp. 9, 14-15, 104-105 (reference mark omitted).

*Explanations:* ▶ *Agamemnon:* Greek hero, king of the ancient city Mycenae or the city of Argos (both in the Peloponnesian peninsula in southern Greece) and commander in chief of the Greek forces in the Trojan War (ca. 1200 B.C.), brother of Menelaus, king of Sparta (Lacedaemon). ▶ *Anne* (1665-1714): queen of Great Britain and Ireland (1702-1714). ▶ *Cleopatra:* Cleopatra VII (69-30 B.C.), queen of Egypt (51-30 B.C.). ▶ *Helen* (flourished ca. 1200 B.C.): wife of Menelaus, king of Sparta (Lacedaemon), according to Greek legend the most beautiful woman of Greece, seduced by Paris with the help of Aphrodite, the Greek goddess of love, beauty and fertility. ▶ *Paris:* prince of Troy, a city in northwestern Asia Minor (now Turkey), where the Trojan War was fought about 1200 B.C., son of Priam, the last king of Troy.

*Remark:* A beautiful woman, an ugly war.

### 395 WOMAN

All the world has heard of the nation of Amazons, who inhabited the banks of the river Thermodoon in Cappadocia; who expelled their men by force of arms, defended themselves by their own prowess, managed the reins of government, prosecuted the operations in war, and held the other sex in the utmost contempt. We are informed by Homer, that Penthesilea, queen of the Amazons, acted as auxiliary to Priam, and fell, valiantly fighting in his cause, before the walls of Troy. Quintus Curtius tells us, that Thalestris brought one hundred armed Amazons in a present to Alexander the Great. Diodorus Siculus expressly says, there was a nation of female warriors in Africa, who fought against the Libyan Hercules. We read in the voyages of Columbus, that one of the Caribbee Islands was possessed by a tribe of female warriors, who kept all the neighbouring Indians in awe;...

....

.... The Amazons of old appeared with the left breast bare, an open jacket, and trowsers that descended no farther than the knee; the right breast was destroyed, that it might not impede them in bending the bow, or darting the javelin: but there is no occasion for this cruel excision in the present discipline, as we have seen instances of women who handle the musket without finding any inconvenience from that protuberance.

....

A female brigade, properly disciplined and accoutred, would not, I am persuaded, be afraid to charge a numerous body of the enemy, over whom they would have a manifest advantage; for if the barbarous Scythians were ashamed to fight with the Amazons who invaded them, surely the French, who pique themselves on their sensibility and devotion to the fair sex, would not act upon the offensive against a band of female warriors, arrayed in all the charms of youth and beauty.

Oliver Goldsmith (1728-1774), Anglo-Irish playwright, novelist and poet, in his essay on female warriors, originally published in the form of a letter addressed to the authors of the *British Magazine* in January 1762.

*Source:* Oliver Goldsmith, *The Works of Oliver Goldsmith*, with notes from various sources by J. W. M. Gibbs, Bohn's Standard Library, vol. I, *Life of Goldsmith: Vicar of Wakefield: Essays: Letters* (London: George Bell and Sons, 1884), pp. 315, 317, 319-320.

*Explanations:* ▸ *Alexander:* Alexander III or Alexander the Great (356-323 B.C.), king of Macedonia (336-323 B.C.). ▸ *Cappadocia:* an ancient region of eastern Asia Minor (now Turkey). ▸ *Columbus:* Christopher Columbus (Spanish, Cristóbal Colón) (1451-1506), Genoese explorer, possibly of a Spanish-Jewish family settled there, who in 1492 sailed west and discovered some of the West Indies, later part of mainland America, from Venezuela to Panama. This he did for "the Catholic sovereigns" in Spain, Ferdinand II of Aragon (Ferdinand V of Castile) (1452-1516), king of Aragon (1479-1516), and his wife Isabella of Castile (1451-1504), which they ruled jointly (1474-1504). ▸ *Quintus Curtius:* Curtius (Quintus Curtius Rufus) (flourished ca. the end of the first century), Roman historian, author of a history of Alexander the Great. ▸ *Diodorus Siculus* (90-21 B.C.): Greek historian, author of the universal history *Bibliotheca historica*. ▸ *Hercules* (Greek, Herakles): Greek legendary hero. ▸ *Homer* (flourished ca. eighth century B.C.): Greek epic poet, the author of the famous epic poems *Iliad* and *Odyssey*. ▸ *Penthesilea* (d. ca. 1200 B.C.): Amazon queen who is said to have come from Thrace (west of the Sea of Marmara, near modern Istanbul) to aid the Trojans, and was then killed in battle by the Greek hero Achilles, "Achilles of the vulnerable heel." ▸ *Priam:* the last king of Troy. ▸ *Scythians:* the nomadic Scythians living north and northeast of the Black Sea. ▸ *Thalestris* (fourth century B.C.): Amazon queen at Hyrcania, ancient province of northern Persia, contemporary of Alexander the Great. ▸ *Thermodoon:* Thermodon. ▸ *Troy:* a city in northwestern Asia Minor (now Turkey) where the Trojan War was fought about 1200 B.C.

### 396 WOMAN

O ladies! sisters! if we really mean
To make the men make Peace, there's but one way,

....

We must abstain—each—from the joys of Love.

....

For if we women will but sit at home,
Powdered and trimmed, clad in our daintiest lawn,
Employing all our charms, and all our arts
To win men's love, and when we've won it, then
Repel them, firmly, till they end the war,
We'll soon get Peace again, be sure of that.

Aristophanes (ca. 450-ca. 388 B.C.), Greek writer of comedy, in his play *Lysistrata*, written in 412 B.C., at "the very darkest period" of the Peloponnesian War (431-404 B.C.), and produced in 411 B.C. (lines 120-121,126,151-156).

*Source:* Aristophanes, *Aristophanes*, trans. Benjamin Bickley Rogers, Loeb Classical Library, vol. III (1924; reprint, London: William Heinemann; Cambridge, Massachusetts: Harvard University Press, 1972), pp. 7, 17, 19 (the Athenian woman Lysistrata speaking).

*Notes:* ▸ Aristophanes is considered to have advocated peace between his hometown Athens and Sparta (Lacedaemon) earlier in the Peloponnesian War, in his play *The Peace*, produced in 421 B.C. He wrote against war as well in his comedy *The Acharnians* (425 B.C.).

▸ "*Lysistrata* takes its name from the feminist protagonist, who decides that women can end the sad spectacle of war by resisting men's amorous advances. The play's risqué wit and humor make this one of the best comedies of manners and the most frequently produced Greek play of the modern theater."
(*Cyclopedia of World Authors* (1997), under "Aristophanes")
*Remark:* Overlooking no possibility for peace.

### 397 WOMAN

The English and their allies proclaimed Henry VI., who was scarcely a year old, the rightful ruler of the country, and retained their superiority in the field, so that they already held Orleans in siege.

.... In this necessity, the Maid of Orleans, a peasant girl of Dom Remy in Lorraine, who gave out that she had been summoned to the redemption of France by a heavenly vision, aroused the sinking courage of Charles and his soldiers. Under her banner, the town of Orleans was delivered, the king conducted to Rheims to be crowned, and the greater part of their conquests wrested from the English. The faith in her heavenly mission inspired the French with courage and self-confidence, and filled the English with fear and despair. This effect remained after Joan of Arc had fallen into the hands of the latter, and had been given up to the flames on a pretended charge of blasphemy and sorcery.

Georg Weber (1808-1888), German historian and educator, writing, in his book *Outlines of Universal History*, first published in German in 1851 (*Weltgeschichte in übersichtlicher Darstellung*), on Joan of Arc (1412-1431), later Saint Joan of Arc, French patriot and national heroine who led the army which raised the siege by the English of the French city of Orleans (French, Orléans) in May 1429, fought on, fell into the hands of the English in 1430 and was sentenced and burned at the stake in 1431.

*Source:* George Weber, *Outlines of Universal History, from the Creation of the World to the Present Time*, trans. M. Behr, rev. Francis Bowen, 6th ed. (Boston: Hickling, Swan and Brown, 1856), p. 179.

*Explanations:* ▸ *Charles:* Charles VII (1403-1461), king of France (1422-1461), crowned in the city of Rheims (French, Reims) on July 17, 1429, who drove the English out of France in 1453, thus ending the Hundred Years' War which was fought intermittently from 1337 to 1453. ▸ *Henry VI* (1421-1471): English king (1422-1461 and 1470-1471), proclaimed king of France in 1422.

*Remark:* The Maid of Orleans.

### 398 WOMAN

[T]he full and complete development of a country, the welfare of the world and the cause of peace require the maximum participation of women on equal terms with men in all fields.

From the preamble to the Convention on the Elimination of All Forms of Discrimination against Women contained in an annex to resolution 34/180 adopted by the General Assembly of the United Nations on December 18, 1979 (Convention on the Elimination of All Forms of Discrimination against Women). The convention entered into force on September 3, 1981.

*Source:* United Nations, *Resolutions and Decisions Adopted by the General Assembly during Its Thirty-fourth Session* (General Assembly, Official Records: Thirty-fourth Session, Supplement No. 46 (A/34/46)), pp. 193, 194 (comma replaced by period at the end). For the text of the convention, *see also* United Nations, *Treaty Series*, vol. 1249, p. 13.

*Remark:* Women of the world.

### 399 WOMAN

Women's rights are human rights.

Paragraph 14 of the Beijing Declaration adopted on September 15, 1995, by the Fourth World Conference on Women held at Peking [Beijing] from September 4 to 15, 1995.

*Source:* United Nations: *The Beijing Declaration and the Platform for Action: Fourth World Conference on Women, Beijing, China, 4-15 September 1995* (New

York: United Nations, Department of Public Information, 1996), pp. 5, 8 (semicolon replaced by period at the end).

### 400 WORLD

Socrates ... said ... he was not an Athenian or a Greek, but a citizen of the world....

Plutarch (ca. 46-120), Greek biographer, referring, in his work *Morals* (Latin, *Opera moralia* or *Moralia*), more particularly a part called "Of Banishment, or Flying One's Country," to the Greek philosopher Socrates (ca. 470-399 B.C.).
*Source:* Plutarch, *Plutarch's Essays and Miscellanies Comprising All His Works Collected under the Title of "Morals," Translated from the Greek by Several Hands,* corr. and rev. William W. Goodwin, vol. 3 (Boston: Little, Brown, and Company, 1906), pp. 1, 15, 19.
*Remark:* What are you?

### 401 WORLD

A world that does not offer a fair chance to all, and a world threatened by climate change and widespread environmental degradation, will be neither prosperous nor peaceful.

Kofi Annan (Kofi Atta Annan) (b. 1938), Ghanaian economist and international civil servant, secretary-general of the United Nations (1997-2006), in an October 19, 2003 message, delivered by Giandomenico Picco (b. 1948), Italian special adviser and personal representative of the secretary-general for the United Nations Dialogue among Civilizations, to the Pio Manzù international conference in Rimini, Italy.
*Source:* The Internet (2003) (www.un.org; United Nations, Secretary-General, Statements, press release SG/SM/8951 (October 20, 2003)).
*Note:* Annan shared the 2001 Nobel Peace Prize with the United Nations.
*See* Poverty (Lester B. Pearson).
*See also* United Nations, *Treaty Series,* vol. 1771, p. 107 (United Nations Framework Convention on Climate Change, which was adopted in New York on May 9, 1992, and entered into force on March 21, 1994).

### 402 WORLD WAR I

[I]t is highly probable that the war of 1914 would not have occurred if the international system had possessed a more objective, carefully sampled, and adequately processed information system, which could have given the makers of a number of disastrous decisions a different image of the system. A more realistic image might have prevented these decisions, even without any change in ultimate values.

Kenneth E. Boulding (Kenneth Ewart Boulding) (1910-1993), English-born American professor of economics, educator, author, poet and pacifist who received Nobel Prize nominations for both economics and peace, referring to World War I in a 1967 article.
*Source:* Kenneth E. Boulding, "The Learning and Reality-Testing Process in the International System," *Journal of International Affairs,* vol. XXI, no. 1 (1967), pp. 1, 13.

*Remark:* World War II could have been World War I, or might not have been started at all.

### 403 WORLD WAR II

The world looked back on years of fighting which had caused enormous casualties and vast destruction. The Soviet Union had suffered the largest number of deaths. Earlier estimates of 20 million, which were occasionally derided as too high, now turn out to have been too low. New research growing out of the more open atmosphere in recent years has been pointing to figures closer to, and possibly in excess of, 25 million deaths. Of these, at most one-third were military, thus demonstrating in this case what was true for the war as a whole: the civilian casualties exceeded the military. Chinese casualties are much more difficult to estimate than those of the Soviet Union, but 15 million dead is a reasonable approximation. In Poland, close to 6 million lost their lives, while Yugoslavia suffered between 1.5 and 2 million deaths. About 400,000 United Kingdom soldiers and civilians lost their lives; about 300,000 from the United States. Germany lost over 4 million and Japan over 2 million lives in the war. The total for the globe as a whole probably reached 60 million, a figure which includes the six million murdered because they were Jewish.

At the war's end, the movement of people caused by the great upheaval did not come to a halt. Millions had been displaced as refugees or deportees, and many of them found it difficult or impossible to go home.... One of the more dramatic instances of this was the fate of surviving Jewish Poles who, on attempting to return, were chased back out, sometimes to the accompaniment of pogroms....

    ....

The destruction caused by the war had been tremendous. It was worst in Eastern and Southeast Europe; in addition, bombing had affected numerous cities in Western Europe, Germany and Japan. There had been extensive damage in China, especially in the early years of fighting there; there had been great destruction in the Philippines, and much of Manila had been wrecked in the fighting for that city. Innumerable other cities, towns and villages in both the European and Pacific theaters had been dramatically and directly damaged during hostilities. Millions of tons of shipping had been sunk; factories destroyed or damaged; bridges and dams deliberately blown up by one side or the other.

    ....

.... If the costs of victory were immense, those of an alternative outcome would have been even more horrendous. And not only for the losers in the war; as the great theologian Dietrich Bonhoeffer and some other German opponents of Hitler recognized at the time, even for the peoples of the Axis, defeat would be better than a world dominated by evil.

Gerhard L. Weinberg (Gerhard Ludwig Weinberg) (b. 1928), German-born American professor of history, writing on the outcome of World War II in his 1994 work *A World at Arms.*

*Source:* Gerhard L. Weinberg, *A World at Arms: A Global History of World War II* (1994; reprint, Cambridge: Cambridge University Press, 1994), pp. 894-895, 897, 899 (reference to footnote omitted).

*Explanations:*  ▸  *Axis:* mainly Germany, Italy and Japan.  ▸  *Bonhoeffer:* Dietrich Bonhoeffer (1906-1945), German Lutheran minister and writer. He took part in German resistance during World War II and was hanged by the Nazis on April 9, 1945, for having supported, despite being in prison, a 1944 plot to kill Adolf Hitler (1889-1945), chancellor of the Third Reich of Nazi Germany (1933-1945).  ▸ *Pogrom:* a devastation of an ethnic group, mainly Jews.

*Remark:* Note that "because they were Jewish" they suffered twenty times the losses of the Americans.

### 404 WORLD WAR III
NEVER TO EXPERIENCE WAR is to be blessed; not to understand how murderous and hideous war is invites the danger of plunging the world into the kind of global blood bath it has already endured twice in this century.

Isao Nozaki, Japanese director of the youth division of the Soka Gakkai, a Buddhist lay association, in a preface to the 1978 book *Cries for Peace.*
*Source:* The Youth Division of Soka Gakkai, comp., Richard L. Gage, ed., *Cries for Peace: Experiences of Japanese Victims of World War II,* 1st English ed. (Tokyo: Japan Times, 1978), p. 9.
*Remark:* How to prevent a world war.

### 405 WORLD WAR IV
Now and then the professor gets angry, realizing how blind his contemporaries are in the face of the imminent danger. Asked what weapons would be used in a Third World War, he made this characteristic reply:
"I don't know. But I can tell you what they'll use in the fourth—rocks!"

Alfred Werner (1911-1979), Austrian-born American art critic, poet and author, in a 1949 interview with German-born American physicist Albert Einstein (1879-1955), recipient of the 1921 Nobel Prize in Physics and contributor to the development of the atomic bomb.
*Source:* Alfred Werner, "Albert Einstein at Seventy," *Liberal Judaism,* vol. 16 (1948-1949), April-May 1949 issue, pp. 4, 12.
*Remark:* Back to basics.

### 406 WOUND
I knew that I was hit and leaned over and put my hand on my knee. My knee wasn't there.

Ernest Hemingway (Ernest Miller Hemingway) (1899-1961), American novelist and short-story writer, in his 1929 novel on World War I, *A Farewell to Arms* (chapter IX; the reference is to the American lieutenant Frederic Henry, volunteer ambulance driver in the Italian army).
*Source:* Ernest Hemingway, *A Farewell to Arms* (New York: Charles Scribner's Sons, 1929), p. 59.
*Note:* Hemingway received the 1954 Nobel Prize in Literature "for his powerful mastery of the art of storytelling, most recently displayed in *The Old Man and the Sea,* and for his influence on contemporary style." Horst Frenz, ed., *Nobel Lectures*

*Including Presentation Speeches and Laureates' Biographies: Literature, 1901-1967*
(Amsterdam: Elsevier Publishing Company, for the Nobel Foundation, 1969), p. 496
(typeface changed).

### 407 WRONG
I would rather suffer wrong than do wrong.

Socrates (ca. 470-399 B.C.), Greek philosopher, speaking, according to the
Greek philosopher Plato (428 or 427-348 or 347 B.C.), in one of the latter's earlier
dialogues, *Gorgias*, to the teacher of rhetoric Polus (fifth century B.C.), that is, Polus
of Agrigentum (Greek, Akragas, now Agrigento), southern Sicily, a city founded by
the Greeks.
*Source:* Plato, *Gorgias*, trans. W. Hamilton, Penguin Classics (Harmondsworth,
England: Penguin Books, 1960), p. 53.
*Explanation: Gorgias:* Gorgias of Leontini (ca. 483-376 B.C.), Greek sophist and
rhetorician, a native of Leontini, Sicily.
*Notes:* ▸ Another translation: To do injustice is more disgraceful than to suffer
it. ▸ In one source it is said that the main thesis of the dialogue, which takes
place toward the end of Socrates' life, is that "it is better to suffer wrong than to
do wrong." Plato, *Gorgias*, trans. Walter Hamilton, Penguin Classics (1971; reprint,
Harmondsworth, England: Penguin Books, 1982), p. 48 (footnote).
*See* Nuclear age (John F. Kennedy: Even little wars are dangerous in a nuclear
world.).
*Remark:* Should a small wrong suffered by a state call for a wrong decision on
going to a war that may develop into a nuclear war?

### 408 YOUTH
[W]ar likes to hunt down men who are young.

Sophocles (ca. 496-406 B.C.), Greek dramatist and tragic poet, in his play *The
Men of Scyros*, of which fragments exist.
*Source:* Sophocles, *Sophocles*, [vol. 3], *Fragments*, ed. and trans. Hugh Lloyd-
Jones, Loeb Classical Library (Cambridge, Massachusetts: Harvard University Press,
1996), pp. 277, 279.
*Notes:* ▸ The play tells how the mother (Deidamia) and grandfather
(Lycomedes) of the Greek hero Neoptolemus, who according to Greek legend was
the son of Achilles and lived on the island of Scyros (Greek, Skíros) in the Aegean Sea,
unsuccessfully tried not to let Neoptolemus sail for the city of Troy in northwestern
Asia Minor (now Turkey) where he, at the end of the Trojan War (ca. 1200 B.C.),
slayed Priam, the last king of Troy. ▸ "Disguised there as a woman, in the palace of
Lycomedes, to keep him back from the Trojan War, he was discovered by Odysseus,
and accompanied him to Troy." *Encyclopædia Britannica* (1964), under "Scyros."
*Explanations:* ▸ *Achilles:* "Achilles of the vulnerable heel," Greek legendary
hero who took part in the Trojan War, killed by Priam's son, Paris, whose arrow was
guided by Apollo, the Greek god of light and archery. ▸ *Odysseus:* Greek hero
(also called Ulysses) who played an important role in the Trojan War, king of the
island of Ithaca, off the western coast of Greece (Greek, Itháki).
*Remark:* Have they protested?

# INDEX

Reference to selected numbered quotations

achievement, **1** (Great Pyramid), **2** (*Mona Lisa*), **3** (Taj Mahal), **4** (Wallenberg, Raoul, in Budapest)

Achilles (flourished ca. 1200 B.C.), 395 (Amazon)

Acton (Lord Acton) (Dalberg-Acton, John Emerich Edward) (1834-1902), 278 (power)

advantage, **5** (peaceful home)

*Adventures of the Good Soldier Schwejk during the World War, The*, 322 (satire)

Aesop (ca. 620-ca. 564 B.C.), 286 (profit)

Africa, 300 (African Union), 48 (Biafra), 40 (brotherhood), 8 (Carthage), 350 (destruction), 126 (flight), 129 (forgiveness), 395 (Libyan Hercules), 33 (sack of Rome), 221 (Schweitzer, Albert), 330 (slave trade)

Agamemnon (flourished ca. 1200 B.C.), 394 (Helen of Troy), 358 (Trojan Horse)

aggression, **6** (national socialism), **7** (Nuremberg Tribunal)

agitation, **8** (Cato the Elder)

agreement, **9** (scrap of paper)

Ainsztein, Reuben (1917-1981), 136 (Warsaw ghetto)

air raid, **10** (Guernica), **11** (Red Cross)

Albania, 85, 269 (Mother Teresa), 376 (Pyrrhic victory), 171 (Pyrrhus)

Alexander III (Alexander the Great) (356-323 B.C.), 395 (Amazon), 198 (empire), 122 (famine), 260 (mosaic)

alien, **12** (Egypt)

alliance, **13** (NATO)

Allied invasion, 130 (D-day)

*All Quiet on the Western Front*, 93 (destruction), 125 (film)

America, 17 (arbitration), 395 (Colombus, Christopher), 56 (exploration), 164 (human rights), 229 (interest), 174 (intervention), 13 (NATO), 262 (patriotism), 347 (surprise attack), 387 (walk)

American Civil War (1861-1865), 181 (landmine)

American Quaker, 332 (slavery)

Amnesty International, 38 (Bosnia and Herzegovina)

amusement, **14** (war)

anarchy, **15** (man)

animal, **16** (thinking animal)

Annan, Kofi (Annan, Kofi Atta) (b. 1938), 96 (diplomacy), 401 (fair chance), 281 (prevention), 354 (terrorism)

Apel, Otto F. (1923-2000), 273 (pilot)

Apel, Pat (b. 1948), 273 (pilot)

Arabia, 24 (attack), 327 (enemy), 151 (hatred), 200 (mankind), 303 (recompense), 302, 304 (religion)

Arafat, Yasser ('Arafat, Yasir, or 'Abd ar-Ra'uf al-Qudwah al-Husayni, Muhammad) (1929-2004), 327 (settlement)

arbitration, **17** (Argentina and Chile)

Argentina, 17 (arbitration), 70 (Eichmann, Adolf), 97 (enforced disappearance)

Aristophanes (ca. 450-ca. 388 B.C.), 396 (*Lysistrata*)

Armenia, 134 (genocide), 377 (victory)

armistice, **18** (Geneva convention of 1949)

arms, **19** (uranium 238)

arms race, **20** (security)

Arnold, Henry Harley (Arnold, Hap) (1886-1950), 239 (conventional bombing)

art, **21** (boundary)

Asia, 161 (Constantinople), 138 (glory), 271 (photography), 39 (River Kwai), 43 (Trojan War), 377 (victory)

assassination, 22 (history)

Athens, 81 (Acropolis), 15 (anarchy), 396 (Lysistrata), 230, 345 (Marathon), 214 (mourning), 35 (Peloponnesian War), 313 (Socrates), 194 (truce)

Atlantic Ocean, 97 (enforced disappearance), 224 (naval battle)

atrocity, **23** (German Nazi atrocities)

attack, **24** (Qur'an), **25** (weakness)

Attila (ca. 400-453), 199 (defeat)

attitude, **26** (culture of dialogue and peace)

Augustus (Octavius, Gaius, later Caesar, Gaius Julius, called Augustus since 27 B.C.) (63 B.C.-A.D. 14), 363 (peaceful leader)

Auschwitz, 135 (Bosnia and Herzegovina), 254 (commandant), 61 (crime), 85 (Father Kolbe), 257 (final-solution order), 154 (Frank, Anne), 63 (gas chamber), 191 (Hungarian Jews), 203 (martyr), 190 (Mengele, Josef), 62 (one way out), 284 (prisoner of war), 311 (responsibility), 192 (Schindler, Oskar), 136 (size)

Australia, 237 (Caldicott, Helen), 192 (Holocaust), 239 (island campaign), 272 (pilot), 314 (return), 19 (uranium 238)

Austria, 89 (Freud, Sigmund), 322 (Hašek [Hasek], Jaroslav), 154 (hero), 64 (Hitler's gas ovens), 325 (human rights), 192 (lifesaving), 4 (Mauthausen), 219 (music), 42 (Solferino), 41 (Suez), 305 (Thirty Years' War), 70, 135 (Wiesenthal, Simon), 56 (Zweig, Stefan)

Austria-Hungary, 322 (Hašek [Hasek], Jaroslav), 41 (Suez), 135 (Wiesenthal, Simon)

Austrian army, 42 (Solferino)

Baha'i Faith, 72 (country)

Baha'ullah (Husain 'Ali Nuri, Mirza) (1817-1892), 72 (country)

Balfour, Arthur James (1848-1930), 157 (declaration)

ballot, 27 (Lincoln, Abraham)

Baltic states, 64 (Hitler's gas ovens), 171 (independence)

battle, **28** (one battle)

battlefield, **29** (the road from Moscow)

Battle of Arbela (331 B.C.), 260 (mosaic)

Battle of Borodino (1812), 36 (*War and Peace*)

Battle of Britain (1940-1941), 147 (gratitude)

Battle of France (1940), 89 (world war)

Battle of Gaugamela (331 B.C.), 260 (mosaic)

Battle of Marathon (490 B.C.), 230 (news), 345 (superiority)

Battle of Moscow (1941-1942), 348 (comparison)

Battle of Salamis (480 B.C.), 88 (Thermopylae)

Battle of the Atlantic (World War II), 224 (*Hood* and *Bismarck*)

Battle of the Somme (1916), 212 (monument)

Battle of Thermopylae (480 B.C.), 88 (defeat), 90 (defense)

Bechuanaland, 330 (slavery)

Beethoven, Ludwig van (1770-1827), 219 (Casals, Pablo), 336 (Lennon, John), 217 (Ninth Symphony)

beginning, **30** (festive mood)

Beijing Declaration (1995), 399 (women's rights)

Belarus, 55 (Berezina), 100 (Niemen)

Belgium, 42 (battle), 57 (Caesar, Julius), 23 (German Nazi atrocities), 64 (Hitler's gas ovens), 158 (horror), 9 (neutrality), 292 (queen), 255 (Waterloo)

Belorussia, 55 (Berezina)

benefit, 31 (country)

Bethell, Nicholas (Bethell, Nicholas William) (1938-2007), 95 (diary), 290 (purge), 328 (Siege of Leningrad)

Bethmann Hollweg, Theobald von (1856-1921), 9 (scrap of paper)

Biafra, 48 (airlift)

Bible, 12 (alien), 101 (dispute resolution), 106 (duel), 106 (earth), 131 (future), 139 (Gideon), 142 (Golden Rule), 143 (good), 215 (murder), 266 (peacemaker), 169 (ploughshare), 282 (prince), 299 (refugee), 351 (temper)

Bierman, John (1929-2006), 4 (achievement), 191 (lifesaving), 287 (protection)

biological warfare (BW), **32** (Black Death)

bishop, **33** (sack of Rome)

blame, **34** (cause of war)

blessing, **35** (peace)

Blücher, Gebhard Leberecht von (1742-1819), 255 (opponent)

Bonaparte, Napoleon (1769-1821), 118 (exhortation), 231 (news)

book, **37** (*Farewell to Arms, A*), **36** (*War and Peace*)

*Book of Mencius*, 148 (greatness), 223 (nature), 326 (settlement)

*Book of Odes*, 392 (wife)

book title, **38** (house)

Bosnia and Herzegovina, 53 (civil war), 38 (ethnic cleansing), 135 (genocide), 350 (television), 352 (territory)

Botswana, 330 (slavery)

Botting, Douglas (Botting, Douglas Scott) (b. 1934), 226 (D-day), 175 (invasion)

Boulding, Kenneth E. (Boulding, Kenneth Ewart) (1910-1993), 259 (organization), 402 (World War I)

Boulger, Demetrius Charles (Boulger, Demetrius Charles von Kavanagh (de Kevenagh)) (1853-1928), 138 (glory)

Boutros-Ghali, Boutros (b. 1922), 189 (life)

Brandt, Willy (Frahm, Herbert Ernst Karl) (1913-1992), 343 (step)

Brazil, 56 (colonialism), 177 (issue)

Brett-James, Antony (Brett-James, Eliot Antony) (1920-1984), 100 (disaster)

Briand, Aristide (1862-1932), 7 (aggression)

Britain, 17 (arbitration), 73 (court), 99 (disarmament treaty), 147 (gratitude), 262 (patriotism), 279 (peace treaty), 272 (pilot), 9 (scrap of paper), 338 (spoils), 41 (Suez), 328 (war deaths), 394 (woman)

British Quaker, 332 (slavery)

brotherhood, **40** (national anthem)

Budapest, 379 (victory)

Buddha, Gautama Buddha (Gautama, Siddhartha) (ca. 563-ca. 483 B.C.), 34 (blame), 67 (conqueror), 112 (enemy), 144 (goodness), 184 (leader), 208 (mercy), 264 (peacemaker), 306 (religion)

Bulgaria, 76 (crime)

Bunche, Ralph J. (Bunche, Ralph Johnson) (1904-1971), 75 (crime)

Burma, 39 (River Kwai), 104, 371 (Thant, U)

Burns, Robert (1759-1796), 172 (inhumanity)

Byelorussia, 55 (Berezina)

Byington, Ezra Hoyt (1828-1901), 22 (assassination)

Byron, George Gordon (Lord Byron) (1788-1824), 341 (state)

Cadbury, Henry J. (Cadbury, Henry Joel) (1883-1974), 84 (custom), 235 (nonparticipation), 280 (prevention), 320 (risk)

Caesar, Julius (Caesar, Gaius Julius) (100-44 B.C.), 22 (assassination), 57 (commander), 198 (empire), 126 (flight), 158 (horror), 377 (victory)

Caldicott, Helen (Caldicott, Helen Mary Broinowski) (b. 1938), 237 (nuclear accident), 19 (uranium 238)

Canada, 19 (Hoskins, Eric), 181 (landmine), 111 (Niagara), 244 (Pugwash), 326 (song) canal, **41** (Suez)

care, **42** (Solferino)

Carlyle, Thomas (1795-1881), 315 (revolution)

Carthage, 8 (Cato the Elder), 33 (sack of Rome)

Casals, Pablo (Casals, Pau Carlos Salvador Defilló de) (1876-1973), 30 (beginning), 219 (music), 246 (nuclear weapon), 292 (queen)

cause, **44** (mistake), **43** (woman)

Central America, 56 (exploration), 174 (intervention)

central Asia, 138 (glory)

Cervantes Saavedra, Miguel de (1547-1616), 317 (ridicule)

chance, **45** (surprise)

Charlemagne (Charles I or Charles the Great) (ca. 742-814), 198 (empire)

Charter of the United Nations (1945), 365 (armed force), 94 (development), 103, 318 (dispute resolution), 165, 167 (human rights), 371 (lifesaving), 104 (preamble), 300 (principles), 97 (purposes), 366 (purposes and principles), 301 (relations), 13, 324, 342 (self-defense), 325 (self-determination), 247 (use of nuclear weapons)

Chazov, Yevgeny (Chazov, Yevgeny Ivanovich) (b. 1929), 373 (victim)

chemical warfare (CW), **46** (Chemical Weapons Convention)

child, **48** (airlift to Biafra), **49** (death), **19** (uranium 238), **47** (World War I)

Childe Harold's Pilgrimage, 341 (state)

Chile, 17 (arbitration)

China, 46 (Chemical Weapons Convention), 102 (dispute resolution), 121 (family), 132 (general), 138 (glory), 148 (greatness), 91 (Great Wall), 150 (harvest), 156 (home), 173 (initiative), 180 (killing), 316 (Mao Tse-tung), 201 (march), 216 (murder), 223 (nature), 5 (peaceful home), 265 (peacemaker), 323 (sculpture), 326 (settlement), 331

(soldier), 77 (statutory limitations), 31 (Sun Tzu), 247 (use of nuclear weapons), 375 (victory), 388 (wall), 392 (wife), 296, 399 (woman), 403 (World War II)

Chinese Classics, The, 148 (greatness), 180 (killing), 223 (nature), 326 (settlement)

Chinese-Japanese War (1931-1945), 201 (march)

Christ, 198 (love), 236 (principle)

Christianity, 50 (love)

Churchill, Winston S. (Churchill, Winston Leonard Spencer) (1874-1965) 147 (Battle of Britain), 45 (chance), 117 (evacuation), 124, 130 (fight), 23 (German Nazi atrocities), 186 (leader), 252 (offer), 261 (painting), 275 (plan), 308 (reparation), 240 (sacrifice), 338 (spoils)

Cicero, Marcus Tullius (106-43 B.C.), 189 (affairs of peace)

city, **51** (destruction)

civilian, **52** (attack)

civil war, **54** (city), **53** (of all wars the worst)

Clausewitz, Karl von (Clausewitz, Karl Marie von) (1780-1831), 28 (battle), 69 (conqueror), 92 (definition), 270 (people's war), 362 (type)

cold, 55 (Russia in 1812)

Cole, Fay-Cooper (1881-1961), 1 (achievement), 245 (cobalt bomb), 195 (loss), 359 (truce), 388 (wall)

Collected Works of Mahatma Gandhi, The, 233 (noncooperation), 236 (nonviolence)

colonialism, **56** (Brazil)

Columbus, Christopher (1451-1506), 395 (woman)

commander, **57** (Caesar, Julius)

communication, **58** (Cuban missile crisis)

comparison, **59** (peace and war)

compensation, **60** (Geneva conventions, Protocol I)

concentration camp, **61** (crime), **63** (gas chamber), **64** (Hitler's gas ovens), **62** (one way out of Auschwitz)

conciliation, **65** (small society)

conference, **66** (Treaty of Versailles)

Confucius (K'ung Fu-tzu ("Master K'ung"), [Kongfuzi]) (551- 479 B.C.), 121 (*Book of Poetry*), 180 (killing)

conqueror, **68** (life), **69** (lover of peace), **67** (self)

conscience, **70** (Eichmann, Adolf)

constitution, **71** (renunciation of war)

Constitution of the United Nations Educational, Scientific and Cultural Organization (1945), 98 (disarmament), 141 (mind), 108 (minds of men), 355 (thought)

Convention on the Prevention and Punishment of the Crime of Genocide (1948), 296 (rape)

Convention on the Rights of the Child (1989), 109 (education)

*Corsican: A Diary of Napoleon's Life in His Own Words, The*, 68 (conqueror), 255 (opponent), 389 (pacifist)

Cortés [Cortes], Hernán or Hernando (1485-1547), 141 (gold)

Coubertin, Pierre de (1863-1937), 339 (sport)

country, **72** (earth)

court, **74** (International Criminal Court), **73** (World War I)

Cowper, William (1731-1800), 110 (empire)

Craig, Mary (b. 1928), 203 (martyr)

Craven, Thomas (1889-1969), 182 (law), 2 (*Mona Lisa*)

Crete, 23 (German Nazi atrocities)

crime, **78** (grave breaches), **75** (the greatest of all crimes), **77** (period of limitation), **76** (the supreme international crime)

Crimean War (1854-1856), 161 (hospital), 181 (landmine), 251, 273 (nurse)

Croesus (d. 525 B.C. or later), 222 (nature)

Cromwell, Oliver (1599-1658), 379 (victory)

Crowder, Michael (1934-1988), 48 (Biafra)

Cuba, 58 (Cuban missile crisis), 371 (missile crisis), 291 (quarantine)

Cuban missile crisis, 58 (communication), 371 (United Nations)

culpability, **79** (enemy)

cultural exchange, **80** (prevention)

cultural heritage, **81** (Acropolis), **83** (Geneva conventions, Protocol I), **82** (return)

culture, **83** (hostility)

custom, **84** (war)

Cyrus II the Great (590 or 580-ca. 529 B.C.), 222 (nature), 256 (oracle)

Czechoslovakia, 23 (German Nazi atrocities), 322 (Hašek [Hasek], Jaroslav), 64 (Hitler's gas ovens), 204 (massacre)

Czech Republic, 322 (Hašek [Hasek], Jaroslav)

Dalai Lama XIV, 385 (violence)

Darius I (ca. 549-486 B.C.), 230, 345 (Marathon)

Darius III Codommanus (ca. 380-330 B.C.), 260 (mosaic)

David (ruled ca. 1000-ca. 961 B.C.), 131 (future)

Davies, Christie (Davies, John Christopher Hughes) (b. 1941), 194 (loss), 322 (satire)

death, **85** (fittest place), **87** (foreign field), **86** (Gettysburg)

Declaration on the Occasion of the Fiftieth Anniversary of the United Nations (1995), 371 (World War III)

defeat, **89** (battle), **88** (triumph)

defense, **90** (Battle of Thermopylae), **91** (wall)

definition, **92** (policy)

de Gaulle, Charles (de Gaulle, Charles André Joseph Marie) (1890-1970), 89 (defeat), 261 (painting)

Denmark, 23 (German Nazi atrocities), 224 (naval battle), 247 (use of nuclear weapons)

destruction, **93** (generation)

development, **94** (well-being)

*Dialogues of Plato, The,* 15 (anarchy), 53 (civil war), 342 (statesman)

diary, 154 (Amsterdam), **95** (Leningrad)

diplomacy, **96** (billion)

disappearance, **97** (enforced disappearance)

disarmament, **99** (aim), **98** (people)

disaster, **100** (Russia in 1812)

dispute resolution, 300 (Africa), 17 (arbitration), 362 (bargaining point), 264 (Buddha as peacemaker), 366 (Charter of the United Nations), **102** (Chinese silk), 58 (communication), 65, 168 (conciliation), 371 (Cuban missile crisis), 310, 385 (dialogue), 107 (economic sanction), 301 (friendly relations), 177 (issue), 50 (love for enemies), 75 (mediation), 108 (minds of men), 354 (nonviolence), 356 (nonviolent solution), 310 (right to peace), 343 (small steps), **101** (Solomon), **103**, 366, 367 (United Nations), 7, 71 (war)

diversity, **104** (safety)

*Don Quixote,* 317 (ridicule)

dream, **105** (peace bomb)

Dryden, John (1631-1700), 171 (crime)

Ducommun, Élie (1833-1906), 305 (Thirty Years' War)

Dunant, Jean Henri (1828-1910), 42 (care), 232 (Nobel Peace Prize)

earth, **106** (peace)

economic sanction, **107** (speed)

education, **109** (child), **108** (minds of men)

Egypt, 12 (alien), 394 (Cleopatra VII), 118 (exhortation), 1 (Great Pyramid), 189 (life), 231 (news), 41 (Suez), 276 (Suez crisis)

Eichmann, Adolf (Eichmann, Karl Adolf) (1906-1962), 70 (conscience), 192 (trial)

Eide, Asbjørn [Asbjorn] (b. 1933), 232 (Nobel Peace Prize)

*1812: Eyewitness Accounts of Napoleon's Defeat in Russia,* 29 (battlefield), 100 (disaster)

Einstein, Albert (1879-1955), 405 (World War IV)

Eisenhower, Dwight D. (Eisenhower, Dwight David) (1890-1969), 211 (military establishment), 241 (unnecessary atomic bombing)

El Salvador, 356 (dispute)

empire, **110** (fall)

end, **111** (Niagara)

enemy, **112** (happiness), **113** (opinion)

England, 278 (Acton (Lord Acton)), 17 (arbitration), 140 (Bacon, Francis), 95, 290, 328 (Bethell, Nicholas), 287 (Bierman, John), 341 (Byron, George Gordon), 100 (conqueror), 171 (crime), 379 (Cromwell, Oliver), 175 (D-day), 116, 258 (Foot, M. R. D.), 87 (foreign field), 33, 159, 199 (Gibbon, Edward), 395 (Goldsmith, Oliver), 146 (government), 155, 394 (history), 157 (home), 217 (Hopkins, Antony), 330 (Horne, C. Silvester), 397 (Joan of Arc), 128 (Kipling, Rudyard), 218 (Layton, Robert), 176 (Marlowe, Christopher), 212 (monument), 49, 249, 309 (Myers, Norman), 226 (navy), 119 (Nelson, Horatio), 161 (Nightingale, Florence), 235 (nonparticipation), 244 (nuclear research), 251 (nurse), 310 (*Observer*), 279 (peace treaty), 275 (plan), 79 (Ponsonby, Arthur), 298 (recruitment), 110 (revolt), 39 (River Kwai), 255 (soldier), 336 (song), 225 (Spanish Armada), 378 (victory), 160 (Wilson, Robert)

environment, **114** (care), **115** (destruction)

epic poem, 390 (*Kalevala*), 149, 277 (*Mahabharata*), 100 (*Paradise Lost*), 228 (*Works and Days*)

Erskine, John (1879-1951), 43 (Helen of Troy)

espionage, **116** (German attack)

Estonia, 64 (Hitler's gas ovens), 218 (music)

*Ethical and Political Works of Motse, The,* 216 (murder)

Ethiopia, 300 (Organization of African Unity)

Euripides (ca. 485-407 B.C.), 45 (decision)

Europe, 229 (American republics), 154 (Amsterdam), 68 (balance of power), 199 (Battle of Châlons [Chalons]), 32 (Black Death), 135 (Bosnia and Herzegovina), 239 (conventional bombing), 76 (crime), 190 (diplomat), 211 (Eisenhower, Dwight D.), 338 (end), 334 (final solution), 257 (final-solution order), 64 (Hitler's gas ovens), 166 (human rights), 23 (Hun), 174 (intervention), 204 (massacre), 219 (music), 13 (NATO), 271 (photography), 287 (protection), 225 (religion), 55 (Russia in 1812), 42 (Solferino), 267 (starvation), 98 (suffering), 350 (television), 354 (terrorism), 66 (Treaty of Versailles), 384 (Viking), 17 (warship), 393 (will), 44 (World War I), 124, 403 (World War II)

European Jew, 64 (Hitler's gas ovens)

evacuation, **117** (victory)

exhortation, **119** (England), **118** (forty centuries)

expansionism, **120** (failure)

eyewitness, 29 (Russia in 1812)

Falk, Richard A. (Falk, Richard Anderson) (b. 1930), 248 (no first use)

family, **121** (return)

famine, **122** (Alexander III's return from India)

Farewell to Arms, A, 37 (book), 406 (wound)

Fascist Italy, 220 (Nehru, Jawaharlal)

Fay, Sidney Bradshaw (1876-1967), 44 (cause)

fight, **124** (beach), **123** (Irishman)

film, **125** (antiwar themes)

Finland, 218 (music), 390 (sword), 247 (use of nuclear weapons)

Fisher, Roger (Fisher, Roger Dummer) (b. 1922), 177 (issue)

flight, **126** (enemy)

Foch, Ferdinand (1851-1929), 209 (attack)

folly, **127** (right to kill)

Foot, M. R. D. (Foot, Michael Richard Daniell) (b. 1919), 116 (espionage), 258 (order)

force, **128** (jungle)

forgiveness, **129** (self-interest)

France, 7 (aggression), 125 (antiwar novel), 29 (battlefield), 199 (Battle of Châlons [Chalons]), 89 (Battle of France), 32 (Black Death), 118 (Bonaparte, Napoleon), 71 (Briand-Kellogg Pact), 57 (Caesar, Julius), 182 (cave men), 46 (Chemical Weapons Convention), 51 (city), 55 (cold), 394 (comic opera), 68, 69 (conqueror), 73 (court), 161 (Crimean War), 130, 175 (D-day), 261 (de Gaulle, Charles), 100 (disaster), 198 (empire), 117 (evacuation), 119 (exhortation), 124 (fight), 23 (German Nazi atrocities), 260 (Guernica), 64 (Hitler's gas ovens), 158, 160 (horror), 166 (human rights), 397 (Joan of Arc), 2 (Louvre), 204 (massacre), 209 (message), 212 (monument), 218, 219 (music), 226 (navy), 231 (news), 232 (Nobel Peace Prize), 336 (Nostrodamus), 255 (opponent), 11 (Oradour), 389 (pacifist), 258 (Paris order), 127 (Pascal, Blaise), 275 (plan), 349 (Rabelais, François), 315 (revolution), 39 (River Kwai), 36 (Russia in 1812), 289 (sale), 221 (Schweitzer, Albert), 42 (Solferino), 225 (Spanish Armada), 339 (sport), 77 (statutory limitations), 41 (Suez), 305 (Thirty Years' War), 44, 66 (Treaty of Versailles), 359 (truce), 247 (use of nuclear weapons), 380 (victory), 384 (Viking), 75 (Voltaire), 387 (walk), 395 (woman), 30 (World War I)

Franco, Francisco (Franco Bahamonde, Francisco Paulino

Hermenegildo Teódulo) (1892-1975), 10, 260 (Guernica)

Frank, Anne (Frank, Annelies Marie) (1929-1945), 95 (diary), 154 (hero)

Franklin, Benjamin (1706-1790), 279 (preference)

freedom, **130** (D-day)

French Equatorial Africa, 221 (Schweitzer, Albert)

Freud, Sigmund (1856-1939), 80 (cultural development)

Fritzsch, Karl (1903-1945), 62 (one way out of Auschwitz)

future, **131** (peaceable men)

Gaiseric (ca. 390-477), 33 (bishop)

Gandhi, Mahatma (Gandhi, Mohandas Karamchand) (1869-1948), 170 (independence), 197 (love), 233 (noncooperation), 236 (nonviolence), 263 (peaceful struggle), 387 (walk)

Garfield, James A. (Garfield, James Abram) (1831-1881), 22 (assassination)

Gaul, 57 (Caesar), 158 (horror)

Geissler, Erhard (b. 1930), 32 (Black Death)

general, **132** (corpses)

General Assembly of the United Nations, 371 (anniversary), 337 (celestial bodies), 46 (chemical warfare), 99 (disarmament treaty), 97 (enforced disappearance), 115 (environment), 152 (environmental modification), 371 (fiftieth anniversary of the United Nations), 134, 135, 296, 350 (genocide), 165, 167, 168, 300 (human rights), 74 (International Criminal Court), 20, 238, 268, 367 (Kennedy, John F.), 207 (mercenary), 359, 360 (Olympic Ideal), 64 (Prevention and Punishment of the Crime of Genocide), 285 (prisoner), 301 (relations), 82 (return of cultural property), 109 (rights of the child), 318 (right to peace), 77 (statutory limitations), 357 (torture), 247 (use of nuclear weapons), 398 (woman)

General Assembly resolution, 371 (anniversary), 337 (celestial bodies), 99 (disarmament treaty), 97 (enforced disappearance), 115 (environment), 152 (environmental modification), 134, 135, 296, 350 (genocide), 165, 167, 168, 300 (human rights), 74 (International Criminal Court), 207 (mercenary), 359, 360 (Olympic Ideal), 64 (Prevention and Punishment of the Crime of Genocide), 283 (prisoner), 301 (relations), 82 (return of cultural property), 109 (rights of the child), 318 (right to peace), 77 (statutory limitations), 357 (torture), 247 (use of nuclear weapons), 398 (woman)

generation, **133** (love)

Geneva Convention for the Amelioration of the Condition of the Wounded and Sick in Armed Forces in the Field (1949), 18 (armistice)

Geneva Convention Relative to the Protection of Civilian Persons in Time of War (1949), 162 (hospital), 295 (rape)

Geneva Convention Relative to the Treatment of Prisoners of War (1949), 340 (food rations), 285 (prisoner of war), 309 (repatriation)

Geneva conventions, Protocol I (1977), 52 (civilian), 60 (compensation), 83 (culture), 114, 153 (environment), 78 (grave breaches), 183 (international law), 179 (journalist), 193 (limitation), 205 (medical unit), 295 (rape)

Geneva conventions, Protocol II (1977), 234 (fundamental guarantees), 340 (starvation), 352 (territory)

Geneva Protocol (1925), 284 (Auschwitz), 46 (Chemical Weapons Convention), 152 (herbicide), 312 (restriction)

Genghis Khan (1167?-1227), 331 (soldier)

genocide, **134** (crime), **135** (definition)

George, David Lloyd (1863-1945), 66 (Treaty of Versailles)

German atrocities, 23 (declaration), 204 (Lidice)

German Empire, 107 (World War I)

German Nazi, 216 (aggression), 147 (air raids), 154 (Amsterdam), 135 (Auschwitz), 178 (Babii Yar), 61 (concentration camp), 239 (conventional bombing), 130 (D-day), 246 (defeat), 70 (Eichmann, Adolf), 343 (exile), 124 (fight), 334 (final solution), 257 (final-solution order), 63 (gas chamber), 133 (generation), 10 (Guernica), 260 (*Guernica*), 64 (Hitler's gas ovens), 254 (Höss [Hoss], Rudolf), 177 (issue), 350 (knowledge), 190 (lifesaving), 203 (martyr), 204 (massacre), 4 (Mauthausen), 220 (nation), 6 (national socialism), 224 (naval battle), 7, 129 (Nuremberg Tribunal), 252 (offer), 62 (one way out of Auschwitz), 11 (Oradour), 258 (Paris order), 272 (pilot), 274 (plan), 284 (prisoner of war), 307 (relocation), 311 (responsibility), 312 (restriction), 192 (Schindler's Jews), 196 (Soviet losses), 348 (tank), 76 (war of aggression), 136 (Warsaw ghetto), 393 (will), 403 (World War II)

German Nazi atrocities, 23 (declaration), 204 (Lidice)

German Nazi leader, 76 (war of aggression)

Germany, 216 (aggression), 147 (air raids), 154 (Amsterdam), 125 (antiwar novel), 135 (Auschwitz), 178 (Babii Yar), 42 (battle), 89 (Battle of France), 336 (Beethoven, Ludwig van), 32 (Black Death), 291 (blockade), 28, 69, 92, 270, 362 (Clausewitz, Karl von), 61 (concentration camp), 239 (conventional bombing), 73 (court), 79 (culpability), 169 (culture of peace), 130 (D-day), 246 (defeat), 93 (destruction), 70 (Eichmann, Adolf), 117 (evacuation), 124 (fight), 334

(final solution), 257 (final-solution order), 63 (gas chamber), 133 (generation), 23 (German Nazi atrocities), 10 (Guernica), 260 (*Guernica*), 11 (Hamburg), 64 (Hitler's gas ovens), 254 (Höss [Hoss], Rudolf), 177 (issue), 350 (knowledge), 56 (Latin America), 190 (lifesaving), 194, 212 (loss), 203 (martyr), 204 (massacre), 4 (Mauthausen), 217, 219 (music), 220 (nation), 6 (national socialism), 224 (naval battle), 7, 129 (Nuremberg Tribunal), 252 (offer), 62 (one way out of Auschwitz), 258 (Paris order), 272 (pilot), 274 (plan), 284 (prisoner of war), 292 (queen), 307 (relocation), 308 (reparation), 311 (responsibility), 312 (restriction), 188 (Richter, Johann Paul Friedrich), 240 (sacrifice), 322 (satire), 192 (Schindler's Jews), 9 (scrap of paper), 221 (Schweitzer, Albert), 328 (Siege of Leningrad), 333 (solidarity), 196 (Soviet losses), 77 (statutory limitations), 343 (step), 41 (Suez), 338, (surrender), 348 (tank), 305 (Thirty Years' War), 66 (Treaty of Versailles), 136 (Warsaw ghetto), 255 (Waterloo), 55, 225, 304, 345, 397 (Weber, Georg), 393 (will), 44, 107 (World War I), 403 (World War II)

Ghana, 96, 281, 354, 491 (Annan, Kofi)

ghetto, 287 (Budapest), **350** (Warsaw)

Gibbon, Edward (1737-1794), 159 (horror), 199 (madness), 33 (sack of Rome)

Gies, Miep (Santrouschitz, Hermine) (1909-2010), 154 (hero)

gift, **137** (rock)

glory, **138** (disregard)

God, **139** (peace)

Goebbels, Josef (Goebbels, Paul Josef) (1897-1945), 274 (plan)

gold, **140** (Croesus), **141** (cure)

Golden Rule, **142** (Jesus Christ)

goodness, **145** (sower), **144** (spread)

*Good Soldier Schweik, The*, 322 (satire)

Gorbachev, Mikhail (Gorbachev, Mikhail Sergeyevich) (b. 1931), 171 (independence)

Gospel of Buddha, 34 (blame), 66 (conqueror), 112 (enemy), 184 (leader), 244 (peacemaker)

government, **146** (money)

Goya, Francisco (Goya y Lucientes, Francisco José de) (1746-1828), 260 (etching)

Granell, Eugenio F. (Granell, Eugenio Fernandez) (1912-2001), 10 (Guernica), 260 (Guernica)

gratitude, **147** (British airmen)

Great Britain, 17 (arbitration), 73 (court), 99 (disarmament treaty), 147 (gratitude), 262 (patriotism), 279 (peace treaty), 272 (pilot), 394 (Queen Anne), 9 (scrap of paper), 338 (spoils), 41 (Suez), 328 (war deaths)

greatness, **148** (child's heart)

Great Patriotic War of the Soviet Union (1941-1945), 178 (Babii Yar), 287 (Budapest), 403 (deaths), 95 (diary), 116 (espionage), 133 (generation), 23 (German Nazi atrocities), 64 (Hitler's gas ovens), 196 (loss), 274 (plan), 284 (prisoner of war), 307 (relocation), 308 (reparation), 328 (Siege of Leningrad), 338 (spoils), 348 (tank), 191 (Wallenberg, Raoul), 391 (widow)

Greco-Persian Wars (ca. 546-ca. 448 B.C.), 90 (Battle of Thermopylae), 222 (nature), 256 (oracle)

Greece, 43 (Aphrodite), 90 (Battle of Thermopylae), 35 (blessing), 400 (citizen of the world), 53, 54 (civil war), 81 (cultural heritage), 45 (decision), 88 (defeat), 87 (foreign field), 23 (German Nazi atrocities), 394 (Helen of Troy), 1, 222 (Herodotus), 228 (Hesiod), 373 (Hippocratic Oath), 395 (historian), 155 (history), 64 (Hitler's gas ovens), 396 (Lysistrata), 230 (Marathon), 59, 120 (Menander), 214 (mourning), 253 (Olympic Games), 360 (Olympic Truce), 256 (oracle), 113 (Pericles), 14, 342 (Plato), 8, 57, 122, 126, 158, 377 (Plutarch), 286 (profit), 376 (Pyrrhic victory), 171 (Pyrrhus), 313 (retaliation), 363, 407 (Socrates), 140 (Solon), 341 (state), 344 (strength), 345 (superiority), 358 (Trojan Horse), 194 (truce), 408 (youth)

Greek Civil War (1944-1945 and 1946-1949), 54 (homelessness)

Greek fable, 286 (profit)

Greek War of Independence (1821-1832), 81 (cultural heritage)

Greenland, 224 (naval battle)

Gudzenko, Semyon Petrovich (1922-1953), 133 (generation)

Gulf War (1990-1991), 349 (American wars), 370 (Security Council), 19 (uranium 238)

Gumkowski, Janusz (Gumkowski, Janusz Stanislaw) (1905-1984), 61 (concentration camp)

Gutman, Roy (Gutman, Roy William) (b. 1944), 135 (Bosnia and Herzegovina)

Gypsy, 64 (Hitler's gas ovens)

Hale, Nathan (1755-1776), 262 (patriotism)

Hammarskjöld [Hammarskjold], Dag (Hammarskjöld, Dag Hjalmar Agne Carl) (1905-1961), 367 (death)

happiness, **149** (peace)

Harald III Hardruler (Harald the Tyrant) (1015-1066), 384 (Viking)

Harold II Godwinsson (ca. 1022-1066), 384 (Viking)

Harrington, Lyn (Harrington, Evelyn Davis) (b. 1911), 54 (civil war)

harvest, **150** (reaping)

Hasek [Hasek], Jaroslav (Hasek, Jaroslav Matej Frantisek) (1883-1923), 322 (satire)

hatred, **151** (wrong)

Helen of Troy (flourished ca. 1200 B.C.), 43 (cause), 394 (comic opera), 358 (trick)

Hemingway, Ernest (Hemingway, Ernest Miller) (1899-1961), 37 (*Farewell to Arms, A*), 406 (wound)

Henry VI (1421-1471), 397 (Orleans)

Henry, Patrick (1736-1799), 186 (liberty)

Herbert, A. P. (Herbert, Alan Patrick) (1890-1971), 146 (government), 394 (Helen of Troy)

herbicide, 46 (Chemical Weapons Convention), **152** (illegality), **153** (Vietnam)

hero, **154** (helper)

Herodotus (ca. 484-ca. 425 B.C.), 90 (defense), 256 (oracle), 1 (pyramid)

Hesiod (flourished ca. 800 B.C.), 228 (neighbor)

*Hesiod: The Poems and Fragments*, 228 (neighbor)

Heydrich, Reinhard (Heydrich, Reinhard Tristan Eugen) (1904-1942), 204 (assassination), 64 (final solution)

Himmler, Heinrich (1900-1945), 136 (extermination), 257, 334 (final solution)

Hiroshima, 163 (A-bomb poet), 199 (Battle of Châlons [Chalons]), 11 (Hamburg), 249 (nuclear arsenal), 248 (poison gas)

history, **155** (repetition)

*History*, 90 (defense), 256 (oracle), 1 (pyramid)

*History of China, The*, 138 (glory)

*History of the Decline and Fall of the Roman Empire, The*, 199 (Battle of Châlons [Chalons]), 159 (First Crusade), 33 (sack of Rome)

*History of the Peloponnesian War, The*, 35 (Hermocrates), 155 (history)

Hitler, Adolf (1889-1945), 6 (aggression), 334 (final solution), 257 (final-solution order), 64 (gas ovens), 177 (issue), 204 (massacre), 272 (pilot), 274 (plan), 403 (plot), 393 (will), 136 (wish)

Holland, 22 (assassination), 336 (bed-in), 95 (diary), 73 (escape), 23 (German Nazi atrocities), 154 (helper), 64 (Hitler's gas ovens), 135 (international criminal tribunal), 260 (painting), 225 (Spanish Armada), 41 (Suez)

Holocaust, 178 (Babii Yar), 154 (Dutch helpers), 192 (flawed hero), 63 (gas chamber), 64 (Hitler's gas ovens), 191 (Hungarian Jews), 190 (Japanese diplomat), 4 (missing hero), 287 (protection), 284 (Zyklon B pesticide)

home, **157** (Jew), **156** (old age)

Homer (flourished ca. eighth century B.C.), 395 (Amazon), 358 (Trojan Horse)

horror, **158** (Gaul), **159** (Jerusalem), **160** (Vilnius)

hospital, **162** (attack), **161** (Crimean War)

Höss [Hoss], Rudolf (Höss, Rudolf Franz Ferdinand) (1900-1947), 61 (concentration camp), 257 (final-solution order), 254 (opinion)

human being, **163** (return)

human rights, **168** (civil and political rights), **165** (common standard of achievement), **166** (European court), **167** (foundation of peace), **169** (right to peace), **164** (unalienable rights)

Hundred Years' War (1337-1453), 397 (Joan of Arc)

Hungary, 192 (Auschwitz), 76 (crime), 64 (Hitler's gas ovens), 191 (lifesaving), 41 (Suez), 379 (victory), 4 (Wallenberg, Raoul)

Iceland, 48 (airlift to Biafra), 14, 25 (Laxness, Halldór), 336 (Lennon, John, and Ono, Yoko), 384 (Magnusson, Magnus), 224 (naval battle), 105 (peace bomb), 247 (use of nuclear weapons)

*Iliad*, 395 (poem), 358 (Troy)

inaugural address, 187, 227 (Kennedy, John F.), 297 (Lincoln, Abraham)

independence, **171** (choice), **170** (India)

India, 122 (Alexander III), 34 (blame), 66 (conqueror), 112 (enemy),

236 (Gandhi, Mahatma), 144 (goodness), 149 (happiness), 170 (independence), 184 (leader), 197 (love), 201 (march), 208 (mercy), 85, 269 (Mother Teresa), 220 (Nehru, Jawaharlal), 233 (noncooperation), 263 (peaceful struggle), 264 (peacemaker), 277 (power), 288 (provocation), 293 (race), 306 (religion), 319 (risk), 3 (Taj Mahal), 247 (use of nuclear weapons), 387 (walk)

Indian fable, 293 (race)

*Indian Wisdom; or, Examples of the Religious, Philosophical, and Ethical Doctrines of the Hindus*, 277 (power), 288 (provocation), 293 (race), 319 (risk)

*Ingenious Gentleman Don Quixote of la Mancha, The*, 317 (ridicule)

inhumanity, **172** (mourning)

initiative, **173** (step)

International Physicians for the Prevention of Nuclear War (IPPNW), 373 (victim)

intervention, **174** (American continents)

invasion, **175** (D-day)

invention, **176** (war)

IPPNW (International Physicians for the Prevention of Nuclear War), 373 (victim)

Iran, 395 (Amazon), 72 (Baha'ullah), 90 (Battle of Thermopylae), 222 (Cyrus), 88 (defeat), 1 (Greco-Persian Wars), 230 (Marathon), 260 (mosaic), 256 (oracle), 345 (superiority)

Iraq, 260 (mosaic), 370 (occupation), 19 (uranium 238)

Ireland, 48 (airlift to Biafra), 85 (death), 123 (fight), 395 (Goldsmith, Oliver), 71, 294 (Nobel Peace Prize), 394 (Queen Anne), 225 (Spanish Armada),

Isaiah (flourished from about 738 to at least 701 B.C.), 298 (refugee)

Israel, 101 (dispute resolution), 70 (Eichmann, Adolf), 131 (future), 4 (Lapid, Tommy), 72 (mediator), 363 (peaceful leader), 200 (Qur'an), 192 (Schindler, Oskar), 327 (settlement), 351 (temper), 247 (use of nuclear weapons)

issue, **177** (fractionation)

Italy, 189 (affairs of peace), 7 (aggression), 22 (assassination), 403 (Axis), 199 (Battle of Châlons [Chalons]), 32 (Black Death), 35 (blessing), 57 (Caesar, Julius), 8 (Cato the Elder), 395 (Colombus, Christopher), 76 (crime), 246 (defeat), 198 (empire), 23 (German Nazi atrocities), 158 (horror), 166 (human rights), 74 (International Criminal Court), 2 (Leonardo da Vinci), 220 (nation), 260 (painting), 363 (peaceful leader), 203 (pope), 287 (protection), 376 (Pyrrhic victory), 171 (Pyrrhus), 110, 253 (Rome), 33 (sack of Rome), 88 (Sicily), 42 (Solferino), 225 (Spanish Netherlands), 41 (Suez), 377 (victory), 406 (volunteer), 37 (World War I)

Japan, 7 (aggression), 71 (constitution), 239 (conventional bombing), 73 (court), 246, 382 (defeat), 116 (espionage), 11 (Hiroshima), 163 (human being), 190 (lifesaving), 199 (loss), 201 (march), 242 (men or women), 243 (Nagasaki reunion), 248 (no first use), 404 (Nozaki, Isao), 249 (nuclear arsenal), 271 (photography), 237 (radioactivity), 314 (return), 39 (River Kwai), 240 (sacrifice), 336 (song), 338 (spoils), 77 (statutory limitations), 347 (surprise attack), 241 (unnecessary atomic bombing), 247 (use of nuclear weapons), 403 (World War II)

Japanese parliament, 71 (Diet)

Jesus Christ, 106 (birth), 170 (Gandhi, Mahatma), 142 (Golden Rule), 22, 225 (Jesuits), 330 (Livingstone,

David), 198 (love), 203 (master), 266 (peacemakers), 280 (prevention), 282 (prince), 236 (principle), 50 (realist), 17 (statue), 359 (truce)

Jew, **178** (Babii Yar), 292 (Belgium), 32 (Black Death), 135 (Bosnia and Herzegovina), 4, 287 (Budapest), 395 (Colombus, Christopher), 154 (Dutch heroism), 70 (Eichmann, Adolf), 257 (extermination), 334 (final solution), 65 (Hitler's gas ovens), 157 (home), 159 (Jerusalem), 350 (media), 62 (one way out of Auschwitz), 143 (Paul, Saint), 192 (Schindler, Oskar), 327 (settlement), 190 (Sugihara, Chiune), 374 (Talmud), 191 (Wallenberg, Raoul), 136 (Warsaw ghetto), 403 (World War II), 284 (Zyklon B pesticide)

Joan of Arc, Saint (1412-1431), 397 (inspiration)

journalist, 179 (civilian)

Junack, Gerhard, 224 (World War II soldier)

*Kalevala*, 390 (sword)

Karadzic, Radovan (b. 1945), 135 (genocide)

Kashlev, Yuri (Kashlev, Yuri Borisovich) (b. 1934), 86 (death), 250 (number)

Kazakhstan, 307 (relocation)

Kellogg, Frank Billings (1856-1937), 7 (aggression)

Kennedy, John F. (Kennedy, John Fitzgerald) (1917-1963) 367 (alternative), 20 (arms race), 21 (art), 58 (Cuban missile crisis), 187 (liberty), 227 (negotiation), 238 (nuclear age), 268 (peacemaker), 291 (quarantine), 333 (solidarity), 335 (solution), 346 (superpower), 387 (walk)

Khrushchev, Nikita (Khrushchev, Nikita Sergeyevich) (1894-1971), 58 (Cuban missile crisis)

Kieran, John (Kieran, John Francis) (1892-1981), 230 (Marathon), 253 (Olympic Games)

killing, **180** (government)

King, Martin Luther (1929-1968), 50 (Christianity), 198 (love), 263 (peaceful struggle)

Kipling, Rudyard (Kipling, Joseph Rudyard) (1865-1936), 128 (force)

Kolbe, Maximilian (1894-1941), 85 (death), 203 (martyr)

Koran, 24 (attack), 151 (hatred), 200 (mankind), 327 (peace), 302, 303, 304 (religion)

Korea, 349 (American wars), 273 (helicopter pilot), 205 (medical unit), 211 (military establishment), 332 (old soldiers)

Korean War (1950-1953), 349 (American wars), 273 (helicopter pilot), 205 (medical unit), 211 (military establishment), 332 (old soldiers)

Kumar, Satish (b. 1936), 387 (walk)

Kutuzov, Mikhail Illarionovich (Golenishchev-Kutuzov, Mikhail Illarionovich) (1745-1813), 55 (cold)

Kuwait, 370 (occupation), 19 (uranium 238)

landmine, **181** (peace)

Lao-tzu or Lao-tze ("Master Lao") (Lao Tan) [Laozi] (from 604 to at least 517 B.C.), 173 (initiative), 375 (victory)

Latin America, 17 (arbitration), 56 (Humboldt, Alexander, baron von), 174 (intervention), 177 (issue)

Latvia, 334 (final solution), 64 (Hitler's gas ovens)

law, **182** (cave men), **183** (Protocol I, 1977)

*Laws*, 15 (anarchy), 53 (civil war), 342 (statesman)

Laxness, Halldór (1902-1998), 14 (amusement), 25 (attack)

Layton, Robert (b. 1930), 218 (music)

leader, **186** (gratitude), **184** (law and equity), **185** (Washington, George)

League of Nations, 98 (disarmament), 236 (extermination of war)

Lebanon, 333 (solidarity)

Leonardo da Vinci (1452-1519), 2 (*Mona Lisa*)

Leonidas I (d. 480 B.C.), 88 (defeat), 90 (defense)

liberty, **187** (price)

Libya, 395 (Libyan Hercules)

lie, **188** (war)

Lie, Trygve (Lie, Trygve Halvdan) (1896-1968), 7 (aggression), 76 (crime), 311 (responsibility)

life, **189** (Egypt)

*Life of Nelson, The*, 119 (Battle of Trafalgar)

lifesaving, **191** (day), **192** (Schindler's Jews), **190** (transit visa)

limitation, **193** (methods or means of warfare)

Lincoln, Abraham (1809-1865), 22 (assassination), 27 (ballot), 329 (emancipation), 86 (Gettysburg Address), 210 (might), 213 (mother), 297 (reconstruction)

Li Po (Li Tai Po) [Li Bo] (701-762), 331 (soldier)

Lithuania, 64 (Hitler's gas ovens), 160 (horror), 171 (independence), 190 (lifesaving), 100 (Niemen)

Lönnrot [Lonnrot], Elias (1802-1884), 390 (sword)

loss, **196** (Soviet Union), **194** (Thirty Years' War), **195** (World War I), **403** (World War II)

Louvre, 2 (*Mona Lisa*)

love, **198** (durable power), **197** (liberation)

Lu Hsun (Lu Hsün) or Lusin (Chou Shu-jen) [Lu Xun] (1881-1936), 91 (defense)

Luxembourg, 51 (city), 23 (German Nazi atrocities)

MacArthur, Douglas (1880-1964), 332 (old soldiers), 314 (return)

MacBride, Séan (1904-1988), 294 (radio)

Macedonia, 395 (Amazon), 198 (empire), 122 (famine), 260 (mosaic), 85, 269 (Mother Teresa)

madness, **199** (king)

Magnusson, Magnus (1929-2007), 384 (Viking)

*Mahabharata* (The great poem of the Bharatas), 149 (happiness), 277 (power)

mankind, **200** (individual)

Mao Tse-tung [Mao Zedong] (1893-1976), 201 (march), 316 (revolution)

march, **201** (Red Army)

Marius, Gaius (155-86 B.C.), 57 (commander)

marriage, **202** (field of battle)

Marshall, George C. (Marshall, George Catlett) (1880-1959), 239 (conventional bombing)

martyr, **203** (Auschwitz)

massacre, **204** (Czechoslovakia in 1942)

Mayor, Federico (Mayor Zaragoza, Federico) (b. 1934), 26 (culture of dialogue and peace), 169 (human rights)

medical unit, **205** (Geneva conventions, Protocol I)

memory, **206** (repetition)

Menander (ca. 343 or 342-291 or 290 B.C.), 59 (comparison), 120 (expansionism)

Mencius or Meng-tzu ("Master Meng") [Mengzi] (372-289 B.C.), 148 (greatness), 223 (nature), 326 (settlement)

Menelaus (flourished ca. 1200 B.C.), 394 (Helen of Troy), 358 (trick)

mercenary, **297** (recruitment)

mercy, **208** (Buddha)

message, **209** (attack)

Metternich (Prince Metternich-Winneburg, Clemens Wenzel Lothar) (1773-1859), 68 (balance of power)

Mexico, 141 (gold), 260 (painting)

might, **210** (right)

military establishment, **211** (influence)

Miller, William Ian (b. 1946), 65 (conciliation)

Miltiades (d. ca. 488 B.C.), 230, 345 (Marathon)

Milton, John (1608-1674), 100 (conqueror), 379 (victory)

*Milton's Sonnets*, 379 (victory)

Miyazaki, Kakuji, 242 (World War II Nagasaki victim)

Mohammed (Muhammad) (ca. 570-632), 24 (attack), 303, 327 (enemy), 151 (hatred), 304 (Islam), 200 (mankind), 302 (Paradise)

Mongolia, 388 (desert), 331 (soldier)

Monroe, James (1758-1831), 174 (intervention)

Montaigne, Michel de (Montaigne, Michel Eyquem de) (1533-1592), 88 (defeat)

monument, **212** (Somme)

*Morals*, 400 (world)

Morocco, 145 (goodness), 372 (value)

Moses (thirteenth century B.C.), 12 (alien), 374 (lifesaving)

mother, **213** (sacrifice)

Mo Ti, Motse or Mo-Tzu ("Master Mo") [Mozu] (470?-391? B.C.), 216 (murder), 265 (peacemaker)

Motieka, Kazimieras (b. 1929), 171 (independence)

mourning, **214** (Athenian)

murder, **215** (commandment), **216** (unrighteousness)

music, **217** (Beethoven's Ninth Symphony), **219** (child), **218** (title)

Myers, Norman (b. 1934), 49 (child), 249 (nuclear arsenal), 369 (United Nations)

Nagasaki, 199 (Battle of Châlons [Chalons]), 242 (men or women), 248 (poison gas)

Nansen, Fridtjof (1861-1930), 98 (disarmament), 267 (peacemaker)

Napoleon I (Bonaparte, Napoleon) (1769-1821), 29 (battlefield), 55 (cold), 66 (Congress of Vienna), 68, 69 (conqueror), 100 (disaster), 160 (horror), 198 (love), 219 (music), 255 (opponent), 389 (pacifist), 36 (Russia in 1812)

Napoleon III (Bonaparte, Charles Louis Napoleon) (1808-1873), 42 (Solferino)

Napoleonic Wars (1800-1815), 219 (music)

nation, **220** (Germany and Italy)

nationalism, **221** (understanding)

NATO (North Atlantic Treaty Organization), 350 (television)

nature, **222** (burial), **223** (tendency)

naval battle, **224** (*Bismarck*)

navy, **226** (D-day), **225** (Spanish Armada)

Nazi, 216 (aggression), 147 (air raids), 154 (Amsterdam), 23 (atrocities), 135 (Auschwitz), 178 (Babii Yar), 61 (concentration camp), 239 (conventional bombing), 130 (D-day), 246 (defeat), 70 (Eichmann, Adolf), 343 (exile), 124 (fight), 334 (final solution), 257 (final-solution order), 63 (gas chamber), 133 (generation), 10 (Guernica), 260 (*Guernica*), 64 (Hitler's gas ovens), 254 (Höss [Hoss], Rudolf), 177 (issue), 350 (knowledge), 190 (lifesaving), 204 (massacre), 220 (nation), 6 (national socialism), 224 (naval battle), 7 (Nuremberg Tribunal), 252 (offer), 62 (one way out of Auschwitz), 11 (Oradour), 258 (Paris order), 272 (pilot), 274 (plan), 284 (prisoner of war), 307 (relocation), 311 (responsibility), 312 (restriction), 192 (Schindler's Jews), 196 (Soviet losses), 348 (tank), 76 (war of aggression), 136 (Warsaw ghetto), 393 (will), 403 (World War II)

Nazi Germany, 216 (aggression), 147 (air raids), 154 (Amsterdam), 23 (atrocities), 135, (Auschwitz), 178 (Babii Yar), 61 (concentration camp), 239 (conventional bombing), 130 (D-day), 246 (defeat), 70 (Eichmann, Adolf), 116 (espionage), 117 (evacuation), 343 (exile), 124 (fight), 334 (final solution), 257 (final-solution order), 63 (gas chamber), 133 (generation), 10 (Guernica), 260 (*Guernica*), 64 (Hitler's gas ovens), 177 (issue), 350 (knowledge), 190 (lifesaving), 203 (martyr), 204 (massacre), 220 (nation), 6 (national socialism), 224 (naval battle), 7, 129 (Nuremberg Tribunal), 252 (offer), 62 (one way out of Auschwitz), 254 (opinion), 11 (Oradour), 258 (Paris order), 272 (pilot), 274 (plan), 284 (prisoner of war), 307 (relocation), 311 (responsibility), 312 (restriction), 192 (Schindler's Jews), 196 (Soviet losses), 348 (tank), 76 (war of aggression), 136 (Warsaw ghetto), 393 (will), 403 (World War II)

negotiation, **227** (fear)

Nehru, Jawaharlal (1889-1964), 220 (nation)

neighbor, **228** (blessing)

Nelson, Horatio (1758-1805), 119 (exhortation)

Neoptolemus (flourished ca. 1200 B.C.), 408 (youth)

Nepal, 34 (blame), 66 (conqueror), 112 (enemy), 144 (goodness), 184 (leader), 208 (mercy), 264 (peacemaker), 306 (religion)

Netherlands, The, 22 (assassination), 336 (bed-in), 95 (diary), 73 (escape), 23 (German Nazi atrocities), 154 (helper), 64 (Hitler's gas ovens), 135 (international criminal tribunal), 260 (painting), 258 (Rotterdam), 225 (Spanish Armada), 41 (Suez)

neutrality, **229** (right)

news, **230** (Marathon), **231** (Nile)

Ney, Michel (1769-1815), 55 (Russia)

Nigeria, 48 (child)

Nigerian Civil War (1967-1970), 48 (child)

Nightingale, Florence (1820-1910), 161 (hospital), 251 (nurse)

Nirvâna: A Story of Buddhist Philosophy, 144 (goodness)

Nobel, Alfred (Nobel, Alfred Bernhard) (1833-1896), 232 (Nobel prizes)

Nobel Peace Prize, 38 (Amnesty International), 96, 281, 354, 401 (Annan, Kofi, and the United Nations), 327 (Arafat, Yasser; Peres, Shimon; Rabin, Yitzhak), 343 (Brandt, Willy), 7 (Briand, Aristide, and Stresemann, Gustav), 75 (Bunche, Ralph J.), 305 (Ducommun, Élie, and Gobat, Charles Albert), 42 (Dunant, Jean Henri, and Passy, Frédéric), 171 (Gorbachev, Mikhail), 104, 367 (Hammarskjöld [Hammarskjold], Dag), 181 (International Campaign to Ban Landmines (ICBL) and Williams, Jody), 373 (International Physicians for the Prevention of Nuclear War (IPPNW)), 50, 198, 263 (King, Martin Luther), 294 (MacBride, Séan), 239 (Marshall, George C.), 269 (Mother Teresa), 98, 267 (Nansen, Fridtjof), 244 (Pauling, Linus; Rotblat, Joseph, and The Pugwash Conferences on Science and World Affairs), 276 (Pearson, Lester B.), 84, 235, 280, 320 (Quakers), 283 (Sakharov, Andrei), 71 (Sato, Eisaku), 221 (Schweitzer, Albert), 385 (Tenzin Gyatso), **232** (theme), 129 (Tutu, Desmond), 310 (Walesa, Lech), 206, 374 (Wiesel, Elie)

Nobel Prize in Chemistry, 244 (Pauling, Linus)

Nobel Prize in Literature, 186 (Churchill, Winston S.), 37, 406 (Hemingway, Ernest), 128 (Kipling, Rudyard), 14, 25 (Laxness, Halldór), 16 (Steinbeck, John)

Nobel Prize in Physics, 80, 405 (Einstein, Albert)

noncooperation, **233** (nonviolence)

noninternational armed conflict, **234** (survivor)

nonparticipation, **235** (Quakers)

nonviolence, **236** (Christ's principles)

Normandy, 226 (fleet), 130 (freedom), 384 (Normans), 275 (plan), 175 (prayer)

North Africa, 8 (Carthage), 350 (destruction), 126 (flight), 33 (sack of Rome)

North America, 13 (NATO), 347 (surprise attack)

North Atlantic Treaty Organization (NATO), 13 (attack), 350 (television)

Norway, 343 (Brandt, Willy), 356 (Brock-Utne, Birgit), 23 (German Nazi atrocities), 181 (landmine), 7, 71, 75, 76, 311 (Lie, Trygve), 98 (Nansen, Fridtjof), 232 (Nobel Peace Prize), 267 (peacemaker), 327 (settlement), 247 (use of nuclear weapons), 384 (Viking)

nuclear accident, **237** (thousands of years)

nuclear age, **238** (little wars)

nuclear weapon, **245** (cobalt bomb), **239** (conventional bombing), **247** (crime against mankind), **246** (defense), **244** (hydrogen bomb), **242** (men or women), **248** (no first use), **249** (nuclear arsenal), **243** (pupils), **240** (sacrifice), **241** (unnecessary atomic bombing)

Numa Pompilius (ruled 715-672 (or 673) B.C.), 363 (peaceful leader)

number, **250** (wars)

nurse, **251** (Nightingale, Florence)

Odysseus (flourished ca. 1200 B.C.), 408 (Neoptolemus), 358 (trick)

offer, **252** (blood)

Offices, The, 189 (affairs of peace)

Olympic Games, **253** (sacred month), 360 (truce)

On War, 28 (battle), 69 (conqueror), 92 (definition), 270 (people's war), 362 (type)

opinion, **254** (heart)

opponent, **255** (Waterloo)

oracle, **256** (empire)

order, **257** (final solution), **258** (Paris)

organization, **259** (catastrophe)

Otway, Thomas (1652-1685), 43 (cause)

Pacific Ocean, 239 (island campaign)

painting, **261** (Churchill), 2 (Mona Lisa), **260** (Picasso's Guernica)

Pakistan, 247 (use of nuclear weapons), 387 (walk)

Palestine, 159 (First Crusade), 157 (home), 75 (mediator), 327 (settlement), 374 (Talmud)

Panama, 395 (Colombus, Christopher), 229 (neutrality)

Paradise Lost, 100 (conqueror)

Parallel Lives, 8 (Cato the Elder), 57 (commander), 113 (enemy), 122 (famine), 126 (flight), 158 (horror), 214 (mourning), 376 (Pyrrhic victory), 377 (victory)

Paris of Troy (flourished ca. 1200 B.C.), 408 (Achilles), 394 (Helen of Troy)

Pascal, Blaise (1623-1662), 127 (folly)

Passy, Frédéric (1822-1912), 232 (Nobel Peace Prize), 42 (prevention)

patriotism, **262** (life)

Paul, Saint (ca. 3-ca. 64), 143 (good)

Pauling, Linus (Pauling, Linus Carl (1901-1994), 244 (hydrogen bomb)

peaceful struggle, **263** (love and nonviolence)

peacemaker, **266** (blessing), **264** (embankment), **267** (opponent), **265** (prevention), **268** (process)

Pearson, Lester B. (Pearson, Lester Bowles) (1897-1972), 276 (poverty)

Peloponnesian War (431-404 B.C.), 35 (blessing), 155 (history), 396 (play)

Peninsular War (1808-1814), 260 (Goya)

Penn, William (1644-1718), 235 (nonparticipation)

Penrose, Roland (Penrose, Roland Algernon) (1900-1984), 260 (Guernica)

Pensées, 127 (folly)

Pensées sur la réligion, 127 (folly)

Penthesilea (d. ca. 1200 B.C.), 395 (Troy)

people, **269** (sameness)

people's war, **270** (condensation)

Peres, Shimon (b. 1923), 327 (settlement)

Pericles (ca. 490-429 B.C.), 113 (enemy), 214 (mourning)

Persia, 395 (Amazon), 72 (Baha'ullah), 90 (Battle of Thermopylae), 222 (Cyrus), 88 (defeat), 1 (Greco-Persian Wars), 230 (Marathon), 260 (mosaic), 256 (oracle), 345 (superiority)

Persian Gulf War (1990-1991), 349
(American wars), 370 (Security
Council), 19 (uranium 238)
Pharnaces II (ca. 97-47 B.C.), 377
(victory)
Philip II (1527-1598), 225 (Spanish
Armada)
Philippines, 314 (return), 403 (World War
II)
photography, **271** (Iwo Jima)
Picasso, Pablo (Picasso, Pablo Ruiz y)
(1881-1973), 10, 260 (*Guernica*)
Pike, Douglas (Pike, Douglas Henry)
(1908-1974), 272 (pilot)
pilot, **272** (Battle of Britain), **273** (Korean
War)
Pitt, Barrie (Pitt, Barrie William Edward)
(1918-2006), 224 (naval battle)
plan, **274** (four months), **275**
(Normandy)
Plato (428 or 427-348 or 347 B.C.),
14 (anarchy), 53 (civil war), 342
(statesman)
Plutarch, 8 (Cato the Elder), 57
(Caesar, Julius), 113 (enemy), 122
(famine), 126 (flight), 158 (horror),
214 (mourning), 376 (Pyrrhic
victory), 377 (victory), 400 (world)
*Plutarch's Morals*, 400 (world)
Poland, 135, 190, 191, 192, 254
(Auschwitz), 224 (*Bismarck*), 61
(concentration camp), 257 (final-
solution order), 154 (Frank, Anne),
63 (gas chamber), 284 (German
Nazi), 23 (German Nazi atrocities),
64 (Hitler's gas ovens), 203 (martyr),
62 (one way out of Auschwitz), 310
(resistance), 321 (sacrifice), 136, 350
(Warsaw ghetto), 70 (Wiesenthal,
Simon), 403 (World War II)
Pole, 64 (Hitler's gas ovens)
Pompey (Pompeius Magnus, Gnaeus)
(106-48 B.C.), 57 (commander)
Ponsonby, Arthur (Ponsonby, Arthur
Augustus William Harry) (1871-1946),
79 (culpability)
Portugal, 48 (airlift to Biafra), 56
(colonialism), 137 (gift)

poverty, **277** (tension)
power, **278** (corruption), **277**
(indiscretion)
power of observation, 128 (force)
preference, **279** (peace)
prevention, **280** (Quakers), **281**
(security)
Priam (flourished ca. 1200 B.C.), 395
(Amazon), 408 (death), 358 (Trojan
Horse)
prince, **282** (peace)
*Principal Fragments, The*, 59
(comparison), 120 (expansionism)
prisoner, **283** (liberation)
prisoner of war, **284** (experiment), **285**
(humane treatment)
profit, **286** (fortification)
protection, **287** (Wallenberg, Raoul)
Protocol Additional to the Geneva
Conventions of 12 August 1949,
and Relating to the Protection of
Victims of International Armed
Conflicts (Protocol I) (1977), 52
(civilian), 60 (compensation), 83
(culture), 114, 153 (environment),
78 (grave breaches), 183
(international law), 179 (journalist),
193 (limitation), 205 (medical unit),
295 (rape)
Protocol Additional to the Geneva
Conventions of 12 August 1949,
and Relating to the Protection of
Victims of Non-International Armed
Conflicts (Protocol II) (1977), 234
(fundamental guarantees), 340
(starvation), 352 (territory)
Protocol for the Prohibition of the Use
in War of Asphyxiating, Poisonous or
Other Gases, and of Bacteriological
Methods of Warfare (Geneva
Protocol of 1925), 152 (herbicide),
312 (restriction)
Protocol I (1977), 52 (civilian), 60
(compensation), 83 (culture),
114, 153 (environment), 78 (grave
breaches), 183 (international law),
179 (journalist), 193 (limitation), 205
(medical unit), 295 (rape)

Protocol II (1977), 234 (fundamental guarantees), 340 (starvation), 352 (territory)

provocation, **288** (injury)

Prussia, 28, 69, 92, 270, 362 (Clausewitz, Karl von)

purchase, **289** (Louisiana)

purge, **290** (Red Army)

Pyrrhus (ca. 318-272 B.C.), 376 (Pyrrhic victory), 171 (victory)

Quaker, 332 (slavery)

quarantine, **291** (Cuba)

queen, **292** (Belgium)

Qur'an, 24 (attack), 151 (hatred), 200 (mankind), 327 (peace), 302, 303, 304 (religion)

Rabin, Yitzhak (1922-1995), 327 (settlement)

race, **293** (human race)

radio, **294** (United Nations)

rape, **295** (protection), **296** (war crime)

reconstruction, **297** (charity)

refugee, **299** (bread)

regional organization, **300** (African Union)

relations, **301** (territorial acquisition)

religion, **303** (enemy), **304** (fire and sword), **306** (founder), **302** (Paradise), **305** (Thirty Years' War)

relocation, **397** (Soviet Union)

Remarque, Erich Maria (1898-1970), 125 (antiwar novel), 93 (destruction)

reparation, **308** (loss)

repatriation, **309** (prisoner of war)

resistance, **310** (dialogue)

responsibility, **311** (individual)

restriction, **312** (gas)

retaliation, **313** (evil)

return, **314** (Philippines)

revolution, **316** (dinner party), **315** (revolt)

Rhodes, Richard (Rhodes, Richard Lee) (b. 1937), 239 (nuclear weapon)

Ribbentrop, Joachim von (1893-1946), 116 (espionage), 311 (responsibility)

ridicule, **317** (Don Quixote)

Rieff, David (Rieff, David Sontag) (b. 1952), 350 (television)

right, **318** (right to peace)

risk, **320** (participant), **319** (victory)

Roman Empire, 198 (love)

Romania, 76 (crime)

Rome, 22 (assassination), 8 (Cato the Elder), 110 (fall), 253 (grandeur), 74 (International Criminal Court), 376 (recruit), 33 (sack), 377 (victory)

Roosevelt, Franklin D. (Roosevelt, Franklin Delano) (1882-1945), 23 (German Nazi atrocities), 308 (reparation), 338 (spoils), 347 (surprise attack)

Rosen, Steven (Rosen, Steven Jack) (b. 1942), 383 (victory)

Rouget de Lisle (Rouget de Lisle, Claude-Joseph) (1760-1836), 380 (victory)

Russia, 178 (Babii Yar), 42 (battle), 29 (battlefield), 55 (cold), 161, 251 (Crimean War), 95 (diary), 334 (final solution), 284 (German Nazi), 64 (Hitler's gas ovens), 160 (horror), 36, 100 (invasion of 1812), 157 (Jew), 330, 250 (Kashlev, Yuri), 58 (Khrushchev, Nikita), 181 (landmine), 218 (music), 273 (nurse), 389 (pacifist), 283 (prisoner), 290 (purge), 321 (sacrifice), 328 (Siege of Leningrad), 338 (spoils), 41 (Suez), 348 (tank), 387 (walk), 391 (widow)

Russian, 64 (Hitler's gas ovens)

Russian Empire, 58 (Khrushchev, Nikita)

Russian Federation, 46 (Chemical Weapons Convention)

Sacred Books of China: The Texts of Tâoism, The, 375 (victory)

sacrifice, **321** (Russia)

Sankichi, Toge (Mitsuyoshi, Toge) (1917-1953), 163 (human being)

Sâo Tomé [Sao Tome], 48 (airlift to Biafra)

Sardinia, 42 (Solferino)

satire, **322** (good soldier)

Sato, Eisaku (1901-1975), 71 (constitution)

Saudi Arabia, 304 (religion)

Schiller, Friedrich von (Schiller, Johann Christoph Friedrich von) (1759-1805), 217 (Ode to Joy)

Schweitzer, Albert (1875-1965), 221 (nationalism)

Scotland, 172 (Burns, Robert), 315 (Carlyle, Thomas), 330 (Livingstone, David), 384 (Magnusson, Magnus), 225 (Spanish Armada), 202 (Stevenson, Robert Louis)

sculpture, **323** (Chinese terra-cotta soldiers)

Second Roman Civil War (49-45 B.C.), 126 (flight)

Security Council of the United Nations, 103 (dispute resolution), 370 (Kuwait), 281 (prevention), 13, 324 (self-defense), 353 (terrorism)

Security Council resolution, 370 (Kuwait), 353 (terrorism)

Sehn, Jan (1909-1965), 61 (concentration camp), 257 (final-solution order), 63 (gas chamber), 62 (one way out of Auschwitz)

self-defense, **324** (right)

self-determination, **325** (all peoples)

Senegal, 40 (national anthem), 82 (M'Bow, Amadou-Mahtar)

Senghor, Léopold Sédar (1906-2001), 40 (brotherhood)

Senn, Alfred Erich (b. 1932), 171 (independence)

Sermon on the Mount, 142 (Golden Rule)

settlement, **326** (benevolence), **327** (inclination toward peace)

Shakespeare, William (1564-1616), 336 (Lennon, John)

Shaw, John (1931-2004), 328 (Siege of Leningrad)

Shih-huang-ti (Shi Huangdi) (259-210 B.C.), 388 (Great Wall), 323 (sculpture)

Shirer, William L. (Shirer, William Lawrence) (1904-1993), 170 (independence), 197 (love), 204 (massacre)

siege, **328** (Leningrad)

slavery, **329** (emancipation), **330** (murder)

Snyder, Louis L. (Snyder, Louis Leo) (1907-1993), 70 (conscience), 334 (final solution), 64 (Hitler's gas ovens)

Socrates (ca. 470-399 B.C.), 400 (citizen of the world), 313 (retaliation), 363 (tyrant), 407 (wrong)

soldier, **332** (death), **331** (return)

solidarity, **333** (free men)

Solomon (ruled ca. 961-922 B.C.), 101 (dispute resolution), 363 (peaceful leader), 351 (temper)

solution, **334** (final solution), **335** (man)

song, **336** (chance)

Sophocles (ca. 496-406 B.C.), 408 (youth)

South Africa, 129 (forgiveness), 66 (Treaty of Versailles), 247 (use of nuclear weapons)

South America, 17 (arbitration), 56 (exploration), 174 (intervention), 177 (issue)

South Vietnam, 153 (dioxin), 152 (herbicide)

Soviet Union, 178 (Babii Yar), 46 (Biological Weapons Convention), 291 (blockade), 287 (Budapest), 373 (Chazov, Yevgeny), 58, 371 (Cuban missile crisis), 95 (diary), 99 (disarmament treaty), 116 (espionage), 334 (final solution), 63 (gas chamber), 133 (generation), 23 (German Nazi atrocities), 64 (Hitler's gas ovens), 171 (independence), 177 (issue), 250 (Kashlev, Yuri), 196 (loss), 237 (nuclear accident), 274 (plan), 283 (prisoner), 284 (prisoner of war), 290 (purge), 307 (relocation), 308 (reparation), 258 (Sevastopol), 328 (Siege of Leningrad), 338 (spoils), 346 (superpower), 348 (tank), 244 (test ban), 247 (use of nuclear weapons), 387 (walk), 191 (Wallenberg, Raoul), 391 (widow), 403 (World War II)

space, **337** (moon)

Spain, 225 (Armada), 30, 219, 246, 292 (Casals, Pablo), 182 (cave men), 317 (Cervantes Saavedra, Miguel de), 395 (Colombus, Christopher), 119 (exhortation), 141 (gold), 10 (Guernica), 260 (*Guernica*), 22 (Holland), 97 (judgment), 26, 169 (Mayor, Federico), 41 (Suez)

Spanish Civil War (1936-1939), 10 (Guernica), 260 (*Guernica*)

Sparta, 90 (Battle of Thermopylae), 43 (cause), 54 (civil war), 88 (defeat), 394 (Helen of Troy), 35, 155, 396 (Peloponnesian War), 358 (Trojan War), 194 (truce)

spoils, **338** (treachery)

sport, **339** (peace)

Stalin, Joseph (Dzhugashvili, Joseph Vissarionovich) (1879-1953), 116 (espionage), 23 (German Nazi atrocities), 290 (purge), 308 (reparation), 338 (spoils)

starvation, **340** (civilian)

state, **341** (hour)

statesman, **342** (external warfare)

Steinbeck, John (Steinbeck, John Ernst) (1902-1968), 16 (animal)

step, **343** (smallness)

Stimson, Henry L. (Stimson, Henry Lewis) (1867-1950), 241 (unnecessary atomic bombing)

Strachey, Lytton (Strachey, Giles Lytton) (1880-1932), 161 (hospital), 251 (nurse)

strength, **344** (fish)

Suid, Lawrence H. (Suid, Lawrence Howard) (b. 1938), 125 (antiwar film), 130 (freedom)

Sun Tzu (Sun-tzu) (personal name Sun Wu) [Sunzi; Sun Zi] (flourished ca. 500 B.C.), 31 (benefit)

superiority, 345 (Marathon)

superpower, 346 (danger)

surprise attack, **347** (infamy)

Sweden, 191 (lifesaving), 186 (Liljestrand, Göran), 232 (Nobel, Alfred), 292 (peace appeal), 287 (protection), 367 (servant of

peace), 152 (SIPRI), 339 (sport), 305 (Thirty Years' War), 394 (Troy), 247 (use of nuclear weapons), 379 (victory), 4 (Wallenberg, Raoul)

Switzerland, 37 (book), 42 (care), 305 (Ducommun, Élie), 192 (escape), 78, 83, 114, 153, 179, 183, 193, 205 (Geneva conventions, Protocol I), 234, 340, 352 (Geneva conventions, Protocol II), 18, 162, 285, 295, 309 (Geneva convention of 1949), 135, (Geneva conventions of 1949), 46, 152, 312 (Geneva Protocol of 1925), 232 (Nobel Peace Prize), 287 (protection), 11 (Red Cross)

Sylla (Sulla), Lucius Cornelius (138-78 B.C.), 57 (commander)

Talmud, 374 (lifesaving)

tank, **348** (Kursk)

*Tao-te Ching* (*Way and Its Power, The*), 173 (initiative), 375 (victory)

telegram, **349** (heartbreak)

television, **350** (Sarajevo)

temper, **351** (control)

Tenzin Gyatso (b. 1935), the Fourteenth Dalai Lama of Tibet, 385 (violence)

Teresa, Mother (Bojaxhiu, Agnes Gonxha) (1910-1997), 85 (death), 269 (people)

territory, **352** (civilian)

terrorism, **354** (humanity), **353** (prevention)

Thailand, 306 (Buddhadasa Bhikkhu), 39 (River Kwai)

Thant, U (1909-1974), 104 (diversity)

Third Punic War (149-146 B.C.), 8 (agitation)

Thirty Years' War (1618-1648), 305 (religion)

Thomey, Tedd (b. 1920), 271 (photography), 349 (telegram)

thought, **355** (mankind)

*Thoughts*, 127 (folly)

*Thoughts on Religion*, 127 (folly)

Thucydides (ca. 460-ca. 400 B.C.), 35 (Hermocrates), 155 (history)

Tibet, 385 (Tenzin Gyatso), 386 (virtue)

time, **356** (war)

*Times* of London, 10 (Guernica)

Tolstoy, Leo (Tolstoy, Lev (Lyev) Nikolayevich), Count Tolstoy (1828-1910), 36 (*War and Peace*)

torture, **357** (order)

Treaty of Peace with Germany (Treaty of Versailles) (1919), 73 (court)

Treaty of Versailles (1919), 44 (cause), 73 (court), 66 (opinion)

trick, **358** (Trojan Horse)

Trojan War (ca. 1200 B.C.), 395 (Amazon), 43 (cause), 394 (Helen of Troy), 408 (Neoptolemus), 358 (Trojan Horse)

truce, **359** (God), **360** (Olympic Truce)

Truman, Harry S. (1884-1972), 239 (conventional bombing), 242 (Nagasaki), 382 (victory)

truth, **361** (casualty)

Tunisia, 8 (Carthage), 350 (destruction), 33 (sack of Rome)

Turkey, 81 (Acropolis), 395 (Amazon), 134 (genocide), 161 (hospital), 88 (Mycale), 256 (oracle), 286 (profit), 41 (Suez), 143 (Tarsus), 358 (Trojan Horse), 43 (Trojan War), 394, 408 (Troy), 377 (victory)

Tutu, Desmond (Tutu, Desmond Mpilo) (b. 1931), 129 (forgiveness)

type, **362** (two kinds)

tyrant, **363** (warmonger)

Ukraine, 178 (Babii Yar), 32 (biological warfare), 161 (Crimean War), 181 (landmine), 251, 273 (nurse), 258 (Sevastopol), 135 (Wiesenthal, Simon)

Ulysses (flourished ca. 1200 B.C.), 408 (Neoptolemus), 358 (trick)

UNESCO (United Nations Educational, Scientific and Cultural Organization), 26 (culture of dialogue and peace), 169 (culture of peace), 98 (disarmament), 141 (mind), 108 (minds of men), 232 (publication), 294 (radio), 82 (return of cultural property), 355 (thought)

union, **364** (division)

United Kingdom, 278 (Acton (Lord Acton)), 17 (arbitration), 95, 290 (Bethell, Nicholas), 287 (Bierman, John), 138, 342 (Boulger, Demetrius Charles), 100 (Brett-James, Antony), 341 (Byron, George Gordon), 315 (Carlyle, Thomas), 46 (Chemical Weapons Convention), 45 (Churchill, Winston S.), 323 (Cotterell, Arthur), 73 (court), 203 (Craig, Mary), 161 (Crimean War), 194, 322 (Davies, Christie), 175 (D-day), 89 (de Gaulle, Charles), 99 (disarmament treaty), 9 (engagement), 117 (evacuation), 37 (*Farewell to Arms, A*), 124 (fight), 334 (final solution), 116, 258 (Foot, M. R. D.), 87 (foreign field), 36 (Freeborn, Richard), 255 (general), 23 (German Nazi atrocities), 146 (government), 147 (gratitude), 153 (Griffiths, Philip Jones), 155 (history), 157 (home), 217 (Hopkins, Antony), 330 (Horne, C. Silvester), 170 (independence), 128 (Kipling, Rudyard), 218 (Layton, Robert), 186 (leader), 384 (Magnusson, Magnus), 355 (Mill, John Stuart), 212 (monument), 49, 249, 369 (Myers, Norman), 224 (naval battle), 226 (navy), 119 (Nelson, Horatio), 48 (Nigerian Civil War), 235 (nonparticipation), 244 (nuclear research), 76 (Nuremberg Tribunal), 261 (nurse), 370 (*Observer*), 252 (offer), 261 (painting), 260 (Penrose, Roland), 272 (pilot), 275 (plan), 79 (Ponsonby, Arthur), 280 (prevention), 84, 320, 332 (Quakers), 298 (recruitment), 308 (reparation), 39 (River Kwai), 240 (sacrifice), 336 (song), 338 (spoils), 77 (statutory limitations), 202 (Stevenson, Robert Louis), 41 (Suez), 66 (Treaty of Versailles), 108 (UNESCO), 19 (uranium 238), 247 (use of nuclear weapons), 378, 381 (victory), 387 (walk), 328 (war deaths), 160

(Wilson, Robert), 403 (World War II), 56 (Zweig, Stefan)

United Nations, 300 (African Union), 169 (anniversary), **365** (armed force), 337 (celestial bodies), 109 (child), 75, 76 (crime), 19 (depleted uranium penetrator), 94 (development), 96 (diplomacy), 99 (disarmament treaty), 103 (dispute resolution), 104 (diversity), 97 (enforced disappearance), 115 (environment), 152 (environmental modification), **366** (force), 46 (Geneva Protocol of 1925), 64, 134, 135 (genocide), 23 (German Nazi atrocities), 165, 167, 168, 398 (human rights), 315 (International Criminal Court), 20, 238, **367** (Kennedy, John F.), 332 (Korean War), **370** (Kuwait), 181 (landmine), 98 (League of Nations), 189 (life), **368** (malaria), 207 (mercenary), **309** (military spending), 108 (minds of men), 401 (Nobel Peace Prize), 13 (North Atlantic Treaty), 7, 76, 311 (Nuremberg Tribunal), 359, 360 (Olympic Ideal), 268 (peacemaker), 281 (prevention), 283 (prisoner), 296 (rape), 301 (relations), 82 (return of cultural property), 318 (right to peace), 324, 342 (self-defense), 325 (self-determination), 77 (statutory limitations), 276 (Suez crisis), 350 (television), 353, 354 (terrorism), 357 (torture), 247 (use of nuclear weapons), 398 (woman), **371** (world war)

United Nations Educational, Scientific and Cultural Organization (UNESCO), 26 (culture of dialogue and peace), 169 (culture of peace), 98 (disarmament), 141 (mind), 232 (publication), 294 (radio), 82 (return of cultural property), 355 (thought)

United Nations General Assembly resolution, 371 (anniversary), 337 (celestial bodies), 99

(disarmament treaty), 97 (enforced disappearance), 115 (environment), 152 (environmental modification), 134, 135, 296, 350 (genocide), 165, 167, 168, 300 (human rights), 74 (International Criminal Court), 207 (mercenary), 359, 360 (Olympic Ideal), 64 (Prevention and Punishment of the Crime of Genocide), 283 (prisoner), 301 (relations), 82 (return of cultural property), 109 (rights of the child), 318 (right to peace), 77 (statutory limitations), 357 (torture), 247 (use of nuclear weapons), 398 (woman)

United Nations International Criminal Tribunal for the Former Yugoslavia, 135 (the war crimes tribunal)

United Nations Security Council resolution, 370 (Kuwait), 353 (terrorism)

United States, 7 (aggression), 20 (arms race), 22 (assassination), 246 (atom-bomb drills), 27 (ballot), 259, 402 (Boulding, Kenneth E.), 75 (Bunche, Ralph J.), 46 (Chemical Weapons Convention), 1, 245, 359, 388 (Cole, Fay-Cooper, and Warren, Harris Gaylord), 2, 182 (Craven, Thomas), 58, 371 (Cuban missile crisis), 175 (D-day), 153 (dioxin), 99 (disarmament treaty), 405 (Einstein, Albert), 329 (emancipation), 37 (*Farewell to Arms, A*), 125 (film), 334 (final solution), 185 (first in peace), 279 (Franklin, Benjamin), 130 (freedom), 134 (genocide), 23 (German Nazi atrocities), 86 (Gettysburg Address), 135 (Gutman, Roy), 406 (Hemingway, Ernest), 152 (herbicide), 64 (Hitler's gas ovens), 3 (Hoag, John D.), 191 (Holocaust museum), 107 (Houston, Herbert S.), 163 (human being), 164 (human rights), 244 (hydrogen bomb), 174 (intervention), 177 (issue), 71 (Kellogg-Briand Pact), 21, 227, 238, 335, 367 (Kennedy,

John F.), 230, 253, 345 (Kieran, John), 50, 198, 263 (King, Martin Luther), 181 (landmine), 190 (Levine, Hillel), 187 (liberty), 210 (Lincoln, Abraham), 205 (medical unit), 242 (men or women), 211 (military establishment), 65 (Miller, William Ian), 213 (mother), 243 (Nagasaki reunion), 175, 226 (navy), 111 (Niagara), 248 (no first use), 235 (nonparticipation), 13 (North Atlantic Treaty), 237 (nuclear accident), 239 (nuclear weapon), 360 (Olympic Truce), 47 (orphan), 268 (peacemaker), 271 (photography), 273 (pilot), 275 (plan), 280 (prevention), 289 (purchase), 84, 320 (Quakers), 291 (quarantine), 308 (reparation), 297 (reconstruction), 124 (rescue), 314 (return), 39 (River Kwai), 383 (Rosen, Steven), 240 (sacrifice), 171 (Senn, Alfred Erich), 327 (settlement), 170, 197, 204 (Shirer, William L.), 70 (Snyder, Louis L.), 332 (soldier), 333 (solidarity), 336 (song), 338 (spoils), 77 (statutory limitations), 16 (Steinbeck, John), 346 (superpower), 347 (surprise attack), 349 (telegram), 350 (television), 353, 354 (terrorism), 44, 66, 73 (Treaty of Versailles), 330 (*Uncle Tom's Cabin*), 364 (union), 94, 103, 167, 324, 365, 366 (United Nations), 241 (unnecessary atomic bombing), 19 (uranium 238), 247 (use of nuclear weapons), 381, 382 (victory), 387 (walk), 328 (war deaths), 206, 374 (Wiesel, Elie), 212 (Winter, Jay), 358 (Woodford, Susan), 195 (World War I), 403 (World War II)
value, **372** (child)
Venezuela, 395 (Colombus, Christopher)
victim, **373** (nuclear war), **374** (victor)
victory, **381** (cause), **376** (conquest), **380** (death), **382** (loss), **379** (peace), **378** (prevention), **376** (Pyrrhic victory), **375** (undesirableness), **383** (wealth)
Vienna Declaration and Programme of Action (1993), 325 (self-determination)
Vietnam, 349 (American wars), 153 (dioxin), 152 (herbicide), 336 (moratorium), 320 (number)
Vietnam War (1955-1975), 349 (American wars), 153 (dioxin), 152 (herbicide), 320 (risk)
Viking, **384** (conquest)
violence, **385** (out-of-dateness)
virtue, **386** (honor)
Voltaire (pseudonym of Arouet, François Marie) (1694-1778), 75 (crime)
Walesa, Lech (b. 1943), 310 (resistance), 385 (violence)
walk, **387** (love of peace)
wall, **388** (China)
Wallenberg, Raoul (Wallenberg, Raoul Gustav) (1912-1947?), 4 (achievement), 191 (lifesaving), 287 (protection), 379 (victory)
war, 7, 76 (aggression), 8 (agitation), 10 (air raid), 17 (arbitration), 19 (arms), 27 (attitude), 36, 37 (book), 39 (bridge), 41 (canal), 42 (care), 43, 44 (cause), 45 (chance), 47, 48 (child), 52 (civilian), 53 (civil war), 55 (cold), 59 (comparison), 64 (concentration camp), 71 (constitution), 75 (crime), 79 (culpability), 80 (cultural exchange), 81, 82 (cultural heritage), 84 (custom), 175 (D-day), 90 (defense), 92 (definition), 93 (destruction), 95 (diary), 96 (diplomacy), 97 (disappearance), 104 (diversity), 108 (education), 70 (Eichmann, Adolf), 111 (end), 114 (environment), 116 (espionage), 117 (evacuation), 124 (fight), 125 (film), 57 (Gaul), 134 (genocide), 86 (Gettysburg Address), 138 (glory), 146 (government), 147 (gratitude), 152, 153 (herbicide), 155 (history),

160 (horror), 161, 162 (hospital), 61 (ideology), 171 (independence), 74 (International Criminal Court), 174 (intervention), 176 (invention), 177 (issue), 178 (Jew), 181 (landmine), 183 (law), 185, 186 (leader), 188 (lie), 189 (life), 190, 191, 192 (lifesaving), 193 (limitation), 194, 195 (loss), 199 (madness), 201 (march), 203 (martyr), 204 (massacre), 205 (medical unit), 206 (memory), 208 (mercy), 209 (message), 211 (military establishment), 212 (monument), 213 (mother), 214 (mourning), 216 (murder), 219 (music), 220 (nation), 221 (nationalism), 222 (nature), 224 (naval battle), 225, 226 (navy), 229 (neutrality), 230, 231 (news), 235 (nonparticipation), 236 (nonviolence), 238 (nuclear age), 239, 240, 241, 242, 243, 244, 245, 246, 247, 248, 249 (nuclear weapon), 250 (number), 251 (nurse), 252 (offer), 253 (Olympic Games), 256 (oracle), 257, 258 (order), 259 (organization), 260, 261 (painting), 263 (peaceful struggle), 264, 265, 268 (peacemaker), 270 (people's war), 271 (photography), 272, 273 (pilot), 274, 275 (plan), 276 (poverty), 279 (preference), 280, 281 (prevention), 284, 285, (prisoner of war), 286 (profit), 168 (propaganda), 287 (protection), 290 (purge), 292 (queen), 294 (radio), 295, 296 (rape), 298 (recruitment), 300 (regional organization), 201 (relations), 304, 395 (religion), 307 (relocation), 308 (reparation), 309 (repatriation), 310 (resistance), 311 (responsibility), 312 (restriction), 314 (return), 317 (ridicule), 318 (right), 319, 320 (risk), 321 (sacrifice), 322 (satire), 9 (scrap of paper), 323 (sculpture), 324 (self-defense), 327 (settlement), 328 (siege), 331 (soldier), 333 (solidarity), 334, 335 (solution), 336 (song), 87 (sonnet), 337 (space), 338 (spoils), 339 (sport), 340 (starvation), 341 (state), 342 (statesman), 77 (statutory limitations), 31 (Sun Tzu), 345 (superiority), 346 (superpower), 347 (surprise attack), 348 (tank), 349 (telegram), 350 (television), 352 (territory), 353, 354 (terrorism), 356 (time), 357 (torture), 358 (trick), 359, 360 (truce), 361 (truth), 362 (type), 365, 366, 367, 370, 371 (United Nations), 372 (value), 373, 374 (victim), 375, 376, 377, 378, 379, 382, 383 (victory), 387 (walk), 388, 390 (weapon), 391 (widow), 392 (wife), 393 (will), 394, 395, 396, 397, 398 (woman), 401 (world), 402 (World War I), 403 (World War II), 404 (World War III), 405 (World War IV), 406 (wound), 408 (youth)

Warr, Bertram (1917-1943), 391 (widow)

Warren, Harris Gaylord (1906-1988), 1 (achievement), 245 (cobalt bomb), 195 (loss), 359 (truce), 388 (wall)

warrior, **389** (pacifist)

Warsaw ghetto, 136 (starvation)

Warsaw Ghetto Revolt (1943), 350 (sympathy)

Warsaw Ghetto Uprising (1943), 350 (sympathy)

Waterloo, 42 (battle), 255 (opponent)

*Way and Its Power, The*, 173 (initiative), 375 (victory)

weapon, **390** (sword)

Weber, Georg (1808-1888), 397 (Joan of Arc), 304 (religion), 55 (Russia in 1812), 225 (Spanish Armada), 345 (superiority)

Weinberg, Gerhard L. (Weinberg, Gerhard Ludwig) (b. 1928), 39 (bridge), 403 (World War II)

Wellington, Arthur Wellesley, duke of (1769-1852), 255 (opponent)

Westing, Arthur H. (Westing, Arthur Herbert) (b. 1928), 152 (herbicide)

WHO (World Health Organization), 368 (malaria)

widow, **391** (soldier)

Wiesel, Elie (Wiesel, Eliezer) (b. 1928), 206 (memory), 374 (victim)

Wiesenthal, Simon (1908-2005), 70 (conscience), 135 (genocide)

wife, **392** (return)

will, **393** (peace)

Wilson, Robert (Wilson, Robert Thomas) (1777-1849), 160 (horror)

Winter, Jay (Winter, Jay Murray) (b. 1945), 212 (monument), 47 (World War I orphans)

woman, **394** (cause of war), **397** (courage), **398** (participation), **396** (peacemaking), **395** (right breast), **399** (women's rights)

wonders of the world, 1 (Great Pyramid)

Woodford, Susan (b. 1938), 358 (Trojan Horse)

*Works and Days*, 228 (neighbor)

*Works of Lord Byron, The*, 341 (state)

*Works of William Cowper, Esq., Comprising His Poems, Correspondence, and Translations, The*, 110 (empire)

world, **400** (citizen), **401** (fair chance)

World Health Organization (WHO), 368 (malaria)

world opinion, 10 (Guernica)

World War I (1914-1918), 209 (attack), 30 (beginning), 44 (cause), 48 (classmate), 107 (cost), 73 (court), 79 (culpability), 104 (democracy), 93 (destruction), 111 (end), 244 (explosive), 125 (film), 87 (foreign field), 133 (generation), 322 (Hasek [Hasek], Jaroslav), 37 (Hemingway, Ernest), 195 (loss), 212 (monument), 219 (music), 221 (nationalism), 47, 392 (orphan), 272 (pilot), 150 (poem), **402** (prevention), 298 (recruitment), 66 (Treaty of Versailles), 361 (truth), 406 (wound)

World War II (1939-1945), 11 (air raids), 229 (American republics), 178 (Babii Yar), 224 (Battle of the Atlantic), 154 (Bergen-Belsen), 45 (chance), 48 (classmate), 61 (concentration camp), 239 (conventional bombing), 175, 226 (D-day), **403** (deaths), 104 (democracy), 135 (deportation), 95 (diary), 70 (Eichmann, Adolf), 116 (espionage), 117 (evacuation), 244 (explosive), 121 (family), 246 (fascism), 124 (fight), 334 (final solution), 257 (final-solution order), 133 (generation), 23 (German Nazi atrocities), 273 (helicopter), 64 (Hitler's gas ovens), 4 (Holocaust), 292 (intervention), 404 (Japanese victim), 71 (Japan's constitution), 350 (knowledge), 186 (leader), 190, 191, 192 (lifesaving), 204 (massacre), 242 (men or women), 211 (military establishment), 243 (Nagasaki reunion), 402 (name), 220 (nation), 221 (nationalism), 249 (nuclear arsenal), 248 (nuclear weapon), 7 (Nuremberg Tribunal), 62 (one way out of Auschwitz), 271 (photography), 147, 272 (pilot), 274 (plan), 284 (prisoner of war), 287 (protection), 290 (purge), 89 (radio), 307 (relocation), 308 (reparation), 314 (return), 39 (River Kwai), 240 (sacrifice), 203 (saint of Auschwitz), 328 (Siege of Leningrad), 196 (Soviet losses), 338 (spoils), 16 (Steinbeck, John), 348 (tank), 349 (telegram), 371 (United Nations), 241 (unnecessary atomic bombing), 382 (victory), 136 (Warsaw ghetto), 391 (widow)

World War III, 104 (diversity), 320 (risk), **404** (understanding), 371 (United Nations), 405 (weapon)

World War IV, **405** (rock)
wound, **406** (knee)
wrong, **407** (suffering)
Xerxes I (ca. 519-465 B.C.), 90 (Battle of
    Thermopylae)
Yevtushenko, Yevgeny (Yevtushenko,
    Yevgeny Aleksandrovich) (b. 1933),
    178 (Babii Yar)
youth, **408** (war)

Yugoslavia, 134 (ethnic cleansing), 23
    (German Nazi atrocities), 64 (Hitler's
    gas ovens), 135 (international
    criminal tribunal), 403 (World War II)
Zanuck, Darryl F. (Zanuck, Darryl
    Francis) (1902-1979), 130 (freedom)
Zupljanin, Stojan (b. 1951), 135 (genocide)
Zweig, Stefan (1881-1942), 56
    (colonialism)

# AUTHOR

A citizen of a country without armed forces (Iceland) the author of this book, Jon Thormodsson, was born in 1943, during the height of World War II. In 1971 Jon married Lilja Gudmundsdóttir, a registered nurse. They have one son, Thormódur Árni Jónsson, an economist who participated in the 2008, 2012 and 2016 Olympic Games in judo (heavyweight).

After Jon was graduated with a degree in law from the University of Iceland in 1971, he went on to Harvard Law School where he received a Master of Laws degree (LL.M.) in 1972, concentrating on international law.

Thormodsson was appointed to the Icelandic foreign service in 1972, where he served until 1979. In Paris he was first secretary to the Embassy of Iceland as well as deputy representative of Iceland to the United Nations Educational, Scientific and Cultural Organization (UNESCO) and to the Organisation for Economic Co-operation and Development (OECD). He was later appointed first secretary to the Embassy of Iceland in Moscow. In 1979 Jon joined the Ministry of Commerce in Iceland where, for example, as deputy secretary-general he negotiated with the European Union (EU).

Among his writings are the 1966 booklet *Outline of Icelandic Shorthand*, the 1977 article "United Nations Educational, Scientific and Cultural Organization" and the 1995 collection of poetry, photographs and information entitled *The Fairest Church in Iceland*.

Jon Thormodsson actually began writing his book *Peace and War: Niagara of Quotations* in 1979 and worked on it for 33 years, 3 hours per day. As a Harvard Law School alumnus, he has had privileged access to all Harvard libraries during frequent research trips. In the ten-storey Widener Library he climbed all the stairs, never used the elevator and never got tired because, if he was about to, he just thought of Auschwitz.

----------

*Peace and War: A Few Quotations* is an abbreviation of *Peace and War: Niagara of Quotations*.